The 7 Keys to a Dream Job

The 7 Keys to a Dream Job

A Career *Nirvana* Playbook!

Dilip G. Saraf

Career Transitions Unlimited
Only for those who dare to practice what we preach....®

www.7Keys.org

iUniverse, Inc.
New York Lincoln Shanghai

The 7 Keys to a Dream Job
A Career *Nirvana* Playbook!

iUniverse, Inc.

For information address:
iUniverse, Inc.
2021 Pine Lake Road, Suite 100
Lincoln, NE 68512
www.iuniverse.com

ISBN: 0-595-31017-6 (pbk)
ISBN: 0-595-66245-5 (cloth)

Printed in the United States of America

This book is dedicated to my wife Mary Lou. Without her inspiration, support, and love, it may never have been written!

erefortut

"God is a comedian playing to an audience too afraid to laugh."
—Voltaire (1694–1778)

Contents

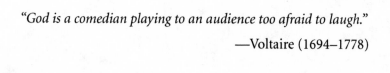

"God is a comedian playing to an audience too afraid to laugh."

—Voltaire (1694–1778)

Contents

Prefatory Matters

"In a time of drastic change it is the learners who inherit the future. The learned usually find themselves equipped to live in a world that no longer exists."

—Eric Hoffer (1902–1983)

Preface

With so many products on how to get a dream job, manage a career, or achieve work-life balance, why one more? The answer to this lies in what this book uniquely offers.

For one, the job market has transformed itself with forces invisible until now. Although this transformation is most noticeable in high-tech, its fallout is already visible in allied industries, because high-tech is the industries' bellwether. In the past few years, the job market has shifted *structurally* to a point where very few have really understood what that shift means to a jobseeker and how to deal with it *systemically*! Navigating through the new landscape now requires new rules. This is where the opportunity lies now: writing your own rules as it is presented throughout the book! Job seekers' salvation will come from not just using or adapting those rules, but *understanding* how to create or generate them, which this book shows. This book will transform its reader, too, from being adaptive to generative in this emergent scene. The reader who internalizes this concept will have an edge, not just in high-tech but outside it as well! Additionally, the book goes beyond just helping its audience success-fully manage career transitions; it shows how to leverage that learning into managing *life's* transitions as its natural extension.

The book covers both high-tech *and* other jobs—traditional manufacturing and service.

In contrast, material currently on the market appears pulled together in a piecemeal manner. There is a plethora of books and CDs on résumés, just as there are on cover letters. None of them, though, have the basic reason *why* a certain résumé design is good or a certain sample cover letter more com-pelling; they are a mere compilation of exemplars from which their audience is expected to copy whatever suits them! This is why most find these samples unusable. Rarely will a résumé or letter exemplar match a particular need, rendering it of mere passing interest. Many examples tend to be "sellsy," presented in a language and tone difficult to adopt for most. Instead, if a concept is clearly presented in a book for a contemporaneous situation with concrete examples, it can be more compelling for its audience to embrace. Even more useful are the cases where "Before" and "After" samples are presented immediately following the principles delineated, as is done throughout this book. In many cases even the outcomes, when known, are presented to show the readers how, following these principles, can transform a campaign. Learning such a communication and messaging skill and then making it a habit are basic to ongoing success, not only in career management, but also in life's journey!

To all those interested in better managing their careers, not just finding a job and getting employed again, this book presents a framework and a process that are unique and compelling. It presents a step-by-step process that is not just conceptual, but proven in one of the toughest job markets. This job market was in a region, the Silicon Valley, where double-digit unemployment drove many to change careers, geographies, and their lives. Additionally, for those seeking jobs and getting back in the workforce, this book also provides the whole picture: from the early positioning (how?) to résumé writing (what?), to writing cogent cover letters (why?) that are congruent with that résumé. It provides a single thread of logic that is undeniably universal and timeless in its appeal. Additionally, nothing worthwhile currently appears available for job seekers on how to deal with jobs that are not posted. Most available advice on such opportunities deals with how to network and find out more to pursue these jobs. But in a tough market that is not enough. You need a more compelling approach that differentiates you from others who also have good networks. Taking this a step further, in a turbulent economy, many companies struggle to stay ahead of their competitors. If someone from the outside, an insightful jobseeker, points out an opportunity for a company, it is easy for the company to see the logic of the argument and create a new job. This insightful jobseeker can now claim this job, often without competition. This is the *generative* transformation that this book provides its readers. And when the reader experiences this transformation, the logic of this approach becomes undeniably compelling!

In short, the book goes well beyond what is available in the market today and is presented in an integrated and coherent way throughout; something that others lack! Its aim is to encourage the reader to take some risks and venture out on a mission to accomplish something that they would not normally think possible, and guide them through that journey!

Although what is presented here may appear foreign to those who feel comfortable with the familiar, it actually presents a different and better view of how to do even the familiar. The material presented here additionally allows embracing a self-paced approach anyone can adopt.

The book approaches a job search more from a standpoint of career management as a process than as an episode with which one must deal, although it fills that need well. It is important to recognize that, with time, uncertainties related to jobs are going to grow. Being out of work is going to be more and more prevalent. Not long ago, changing jobs became the norm. This trend is now going to result in having to change careers as we manage our professional life. In view of this trend, the content presented here is holistic and comprehensive, and yet it is concise, actionable, practical, fresh, and timeless.

Readers may recognize and identify what is presented in this book with their own tribulations while undergoing career transitions. Writing what is here resulted from working closely with those who faced these travails but were not willing to acknowledge them, as they felt that these were of their own making. Those who feel as if they are alone in this journey, reading this book will give them a different perspective and nourish them with hope!

This material, at a broader level, will also change how we look at life's transitions; what is presented here can be leveraged to manage *them* as well.

The content design is interactive, with examples and exercises to immerse the audience in the ideas presented, translating them first into meaningful actions and then into final outcomes. The examples are both contemporaneous and timeless because of the approach they represent. In addition to highlighting what works and why, this book also presents its converse; it explains why certain hackneyed approaches do not work, and it is time to retire them for good!

This book also goes beyond helping its reader how to find their dream job; it shows them how to manage their career once they get situated in their dream job.

* Reinventing Job Search!

This book resulted from working with those laid off during the economic tsunami that hit the Silicon Valley in early 2001, and from helping them find jobs and new careers. For nearly three years, led by the dotcom meltdown, the job market in the Valley transformed as a result of many factors. One of these factors, coincidentally, was off-shoring, which ganged up with the slowing economy, to accelerate the layoffs. Ill-fated mergers and acquisitions added to the malaise. As a result, high-tech industry lost many jobs. The ripple effects of these layoffs affected nearly every economic segment, and finding jobs presented a challenge for which few were prepared. The Silicon Valley unemployment picture, although bleak, was not isolated to this region.

This challenge presented new opportunities for those who were in the career management business. Many career management firms in the Valley flourished despite the gloom that surrounded them. The shifted job market and the structural forces shaping it required these firms to do their own reinvention. The career management firms had to invent new approaches to help their clients find jobs despite mounting unemployment for them to be effective, and continue to get new business. This book documents many of those innovations in career transitions with examples and reasons!

I was fortunate to be offered an opportunity to work as a consultant at one of the premier career transition firms that had just landed a major contract with Hewlett-Packard. During my tenure as a consultant at the firm's Career Center for nearly three years, I worked with HP employees at all levels: from individual contributors to general managers. Also during this period HP trimmed nearly 30,000 employees, with about a third of that number coming from the Silicon Valley. As the economy tanked, that opportunity exploded to other companies and industries in the Valley, further opening up the range of clients, now from union hands to CEOs! In addition, my own private practice provided opportunities to help, not just those out of work, but also those who were already working and looking for a change, those who had retired and were now looking, and many other categories of job seekers, 14 in all.

This book deals with how each of the 14 categories of jobseekers identified in Key-2: Starting At the Start, can find their dream job. These categories represent over 2000 individuals that I encountered, at *all* levels. And yet, the book treats each person approaching their career transition challenge as a unique case and provides strategies and tactics that they can use effectively. For those resigned to their fate by arguing about the "unemployment factor," it presents a fresh perspective and a new reason to jump back into action, yet again, even using familiar methods with a new twist. It empowers them to also rededicate their cause of career transition in a *very* different way! Yes, in this economy there are fewer jobs, and yet there are more opportunities. Many of these opportunities are not even visible to most, even to the employers themselves! This book shows how to identify these opportunities and leverage them into jobs, where no one else is competing. Between these two ends, the book clearly shows how to target a job that one chooses, stretch their wings and get it. To those, who always wanted to be entrepreneurs and yet wanted the security of employment, it provides a new vista to realize their dreams, too.

Much of the material presented here is based on sound principles and theory. With each approach presented and each case outlined, there are *original* examples with disguised details. What also makes this learning compelling is how these examples are presented. Not only are there many worthwhile and successful examples of bold and venturesome approaches shown with their "Before" and "After" counterparts, as mentioned earlier, to clearly demonstrate the transforming messages shown, but also the reader is tutored in how to develop such messages themselves. What is presented here emerged while working with clients willing to embrace new approaches to their careers and who were willing to shed the traditional approaches to career management. What catalyzed the learning in the process were also experiences from years of my own organizational and business consulting, and during the three times that I made major career transitions on my own. The impetus was not so much what I did right during those troubled times. It was, rather, what I did wrong and what I learned from it! The experiences mentioned in this book crystallized that learning. Valorous clients piloted the approaches suggested here; their success was evidence of how they dealt with their entire job-search campaign and the way they landed offers that even they could not believe, even during the Valley's worst job drought! Others who wanted to extend universality of these approaches, then, vetted them in their own ways.

In the spirit in which those who helped develop this content by subjecting themselves to risk, some moments of doubt, an occasional embarrassment, and even a defeat or two, I dedicate what is presented here with my deepest gratitude. For those who recognize the disguised messages they helped create, thank you for all your entrepreneurial spirit and adventure, and for keeping the basic spirit of the Valley an enduring legacy!

How to Use This Book

This book covers ground for everything in a job search and career alignment, from how to get out of denial and start a dynamite job-search campaign, to how to negotiate an offer. It is organized so that the content is sequential and progressive, consistent with a typical job-search process. The book is also organized for its reader to quickly look up something that just crops up, say negotiating salary. Each section on its own can provide sufficient material to fully reveal what is needed to deal with a spot situation effectively. Progressive design of the content merely means that to gain full benefit from a well-run job-search campaign, the reader needs to start from the beginning, follow the material, do the suggested exercises, and use the tools. Throughout, the book is filled with success stories of those who were in a quandary about what they were looking for, yet by keeping their aims high and holding a belief in their cause, they succeeded beyond their expectations.

Coaching is available as an individualized service from the staff at Career Transitions Unlimited. For those who feel that they could benefit from this service as the next step, they are encouraged to get in touch with the professionals and explore further. Our Website www.7Keys.org is kept up-to-date with new and fresh material. The site is also posted with fresh content from ongoing client learning.

Organization

Throughout the book, there are areas one might need to visit more than once. Sections marked with a * are where the reader may find new insights in a moment of exasperation or frustration!

Sections that are good reminders and are worth visiting just to regroup or get a jump-start are marked with a ♠. Because of the holistic nature of the content and a systemic treatment of the topic, sections marked with a ♠ may have broader context and applicability beyond where they appear.

Acknowledgements

This book was over 60 years in the making! There are many who influenced its rationale and prepared me to feel worthy of it. The person who showed me the most in this new area of endeavor, adventure, and learning was Mary Miller of the Lee Hecht Harrison/Hewlett-Packard Career Center. Her willingness to try new things and go outside the boundaries of conventional wisdom came from her own sense of how the market in the Valley had shifted. Much of what is presented here stemmed from these experiments. Most of the clients there came from Hewlett-Packard initially, and then from the merged HP/Compaq organization. In addition, my own private practice provided avenues for learning, experimenting, and validating what worked with one group.

Many colleagues at the Career Center encouraged me to develop the material and some critiqued it with constructive inputs. In addition, Linda Moudakas of the Cisco Career Transition Center helped me experiment with new ideas, providing me invaluable opportunities to learn. Many clients, who participated in this venture helped me validate ideas and provided the litmus test for trying these concepts out in the real job market—one of the toughest in remembered history.

Once the concepts became crystallized and their applications practicable, many friends and *their* friends located throughout the country, used them in their own way to apply and expand what was already vetted in the Valley. This opportunity provided further validation of the universality of the content, and for that, I am grateful to those trusting and venturesome souls.

I also would like to thank our son, Raj, who provided many evenings of deep philosophical insights that remain the building block of much of the material that is here. Raj has the incredible ability to take a complex philosophical concept and reduce it in simple human terms that are practicable in everyday life. My loving wife Mary Lou, did an excellent job of polishing the final copy.

Fremont, CA

Key-1: Getting With the Program

"Significant problems of today cannot be solved by applying the same level of thinking as when we created them."

—Albert Einstein (1879–1955)

Introduction

This Key provides the groundwork for those entering a transition. Transition is a challenging period that underscores preparedness more than finesse in accomplishing what one sets out to achieve. This Key has three main topics to help make a transition productive and fun:

- Managing Transitions
- Getting Organized
- Understanding Yourself

This Key also provides tools to cope with hurdles faced during a transition; tools that provide some sense of control during the process.

Managing Transitions

Managing a personal transition comprises understanding the forces that drive it. How best to deal with these forces common to all transitions can make these transitions meaningful and provide some degree of control to those facing them. It is this control that makes the transition a positive experience. The following discussion presents the anatomy of a transition so that it is not a mystery.

Forces that are manageable drive personal transitions. Although no one can control the events that prompt a transition, understanding how to manage a career transition, or for that matter, any transition, is critical to create a positive outcome. The following discussion demystifies the various factors that manifest during a transition.

1

♠ What is a Transition?

A transition is a journey through which we travel to get to the destination, navigating through both time and emotional space.

During transitions our life is changing; not ending!

Career transition can cause major trauma, especially if it involves finding employment in a tanking economy. Navigating through such a transition can present a challenge that many are not prepared for. We can approach a transition one of two ways. One is to go and retreat in utter defeat and find someone to blame, sue, or go begging after! The other is to take stock, find strength, and summon our innermost resources to discover what we are made of, develop new insights, and go on to conquer something to surprise even ourselves!

It is to this latter group this book will be most helpful! This book is written for and is expected to be most helpful for those who deal with their career transition using the latter approach.

Regardless of the support we have around us, both emotionally and otherwise, we can control how we are affected by these transitions. The difference in the way we deal with these transitions and how they affect us is a matter of our preparedness, attitude, and our emotional constitution. We cannot control what happens to us in specific situations, but we can control how *we* deal with them! We can become victims or martyrs as easily as we can victors and masters based on choices only we can make. It is also a matter of what tools we have in our arsenal to deal with such situations that give us control over how we can do things differently and achieve the right outcomes. This book provides many such tools.

Transitional Nirvana

Before we discuss Transitional Nirvana, let us first discuss Nirvana. After all, the same word also appears in the subtitle of this book.

Nirvana is a Sanskrit word that has to do with a state of bliss, and a state of existence where one is free from cycles of pain and suffering. In some Eastern philosophies, our existence consists of cycles of pain and pleasure. Unless we find ways of breaking this cycle we are stuck in it. Attaining Nirvana means breaking that cycle and finding bliss in our existence. Career Nirvana is a state of that bliss as it relates to our work life and it is achievable by practicing some of what is presented here.

Adapting or even adopting what is presented here is a way to become free from career-related cycles. This is *not* a religious practice; rather it is a practice based on inner spiritual need and drive!

♠ Emotional Price

Emotional price is the non-physical energy expended in making a transition. Interestingly, though, the expenditure of the non-physical energy translates into physically depleting a body. Why? The physical, mental, and emotional resources are intertwined in our being, more than most realize.

When people are emotionally charged-up they are able to do amazing physical feats. When they are physically alert, their mental acuity is high, and when they are mentally sharp, their eyes twinkle. So, all these manifestations of existence are one and the same, except that what causes us to mobilize each is different. When one is challenged, as when going through a major transition, it is important to keep the three energy centers in harmony. The need for emotional energy is high when undergoing transitions so it is important to keep a reservoir of the other two.

As is depicted in Figure-1, equilibrium between the physical, mental, and emotional energy centers is critical to overall health and harmony at any time, especially during a transition. This is why during a transition maintaining a regimen that allows this balance is critical.

Another way to look at the emotional price paid during a personal transition can be expressed by a simple relationship:

Emotional Price = Resistance to change + Resilience

Thus the emotional toll is high when our own resistance to change is high, ergo fighting the change is bad. Lowering our own resistance to change can go

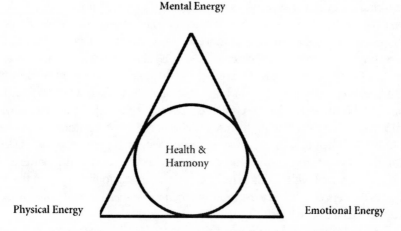

Figure 1: The Energy-Balance Trilogy

a long way in stretching out the emotional reservoir to deal with the transition. And how to do that? One way is to accept the inevitable and then positively look at how to adapt to the changing circumstances quickly. The concept of the Change Curve, Figure-2, describes how change happens and how to manage a transition through this change. Using some of the recommendations, it is easy to make this change speedily. Secondly, the emotional toll is inversely related to resilience. The higher the resilience—the ability to bounce back from a trauma—the lower the emotional toll a transition is going to exact. Detailed discussion on resilience is deferred to the next section but it is important to know here that there are exercises to become more resilient. They appear immediately following the discussion of the two additional factors that come into play during a successful transition presented below.

♠ How We Manifest to Others

There is a triad of factors integral to a successful transition. These three factors influence how others perceive you. Becoming aware of each will allow for an effective transition. There are three factors:

- Managing your resilience
- Managing your chemicals
- Managing your fear

Each of these is now discussed in the following sections with specific tools to help provide a better outcome during a transition.

Managing Your Resilience

Resilience is a quality that allows you to bounce back from an impactful episode of a personal nature (trauma). Resilience lets you regroup and re-engage inner resources in a meaningful way to mobilize actions to move forward. One way to look at the power of being resilient is to look at its opposite: stiffness or rigidity! The classic metaphor of the mighty oak falling down in a gale-force wind and the supple willow plant bending in its path and yielding to its power, has much to convey in the way resilience can work. Those who are not able to yield to the powerful forces, temporary as they might be, can end up surrendering rather than finding themselves challenged by recognizing the power of these forces and then developing strategies to deal with them to rise to the challenge. Fighting these forces takes enormous inner resources, and then, when their power abates, there is no reserve left with which to move forward. Yielding to the forces on the other hand, gives the person a chance to regroup and then move ahead as their power wanes; it always does after a certain time!

To further understand resilience, knowing its components is a good start.

♠ Components of Personal Resilience

The following components are critical to assessing one's resilience in a transition:

- Knowing the situation and having a healthy perspective on it
- Having a deep understanding of yourself and confidence in your value
- Having a good support system: personal, professional, and social
- Ability to take action despite uncertainty and clarity

➢ **Knowing the situation and having a perspective on it:** Being open to different possibilities of how you can go through the transition can be a great resource in developing a healthy perspective. It is normal to not only take such setbacks personally, but also to *personalize* them. The difference between the two is, when you take something personally, you are holding yourself accountable for what happened to you and taking action to move ahead with it. This is healthy. However, when you personalize an adverse situation, you are trying to look at what you might have done differently to avoid it. The latter is a matter of mere speculation. For example, if you have just been laid off, and you believe that if you had done something differently you could have prevented it, you are personalizing the outcome.

➢ **Having a deep understanding of yourself and confidence in your value:** This is the hard part. This is so because we identify our worth with how others value us. Our job is one measure of this value. When that is threatened it is easy to doubt our own value. Losing a job is a temporary setback. What Socrates said nearly 2500 years back is still relevant today:
"Remember that there is nothing stable in human affairs; therefore avoid undue elation in prosperity, or undue depression in adversity."

If this is the first time that you have lost your job and have to deal with such a transition, consider it a wake-up call. If you have done this before, it is time to learn new ways to deal with what you knew from before. If you have never held a job—as a fresh graduate might—then it is time to find out what your value is. Having a deep belief in your own value, worth, and ability to engage productively are key to developing confidence about yourself.

➢ **Having a good support system:** Having a good support system or network is also key to successfully navigating through rough periods in one's life. Such a support system provides emotional, financial, mental, and physical resources. Most underestimate the size of their overall social and support network. The support system consists of personal, social, professional, and other connections. These connections are important in opening up additional resources. For example, if you know someone who works at one company, that person can be tapped to getting more information on the hiring manager or the job of interest.

A detailed discussion on networking is presented in Key-4. A graphic depiction of the Networking Universe is shown in Figure-4 in that Key.

➢ **Exercising the ability to take action despite uncertainty and clarity:** In tough times it is easy to get paralyzed by overwhelming possibilities of actions and not knowing what actions are appropriate and when. Making a methodical plan and then discussing such a plan with someone within the support system can be a good way to move into action. They can also act as your checkpoint for progress. Once you start moving with a plan, you will feel less stressed and more in control, even though you are seeing little or no "action" initially. Remember, there is an inevitable delay between taking the right action and seeing its impact; much like a wall-mounted thermostat taking time to actually change the room temperature.

Going With the Flow

Resilience can also be termed as "going with the flow!" The following story illustrates how this quality can help through life's ups and downs:

> A very old Chinese Taoist story describes a farmer in a poor country village. He was considered very well to do, because he owned a horse, which he used for plowing and for transportation.
>
> One day his horse ran away. All his neighbors exclaimed how terrible this was, but the farmer merely said, "Maybe yes, maybe no." A few days later the horse returned and brought two wild horses with it. The neighbors all rejoiced at this good fortune, but the farmer just said, "Maybe yes, maybe no."
>
> The next day the farmer's son tried to ride one of the wild horses; the horse threw him and broke his leg. The neighbors all offered their sympathy for his misfortune, the farmer again said, "Maybe yes, maybe no." The next week conscription officers came to the village to take young men for the army. They rejected the farmer's son because of his broken leg. When the neighbors told how lucky he was, the farmer replied, "Maybe yes, maybe no…."

The moral of the story, of course, is that the meaning of any event in our lives depends upon how we perceive it. Things do happen and we must learn to take them in stride.

Resilience Exercise

The following prescriptive exercise is designed to assess your resilience.

Managing your Resilience: Exercise

To evaluate your own resilience respond to the following items. Circle the response closest to what you believe to be your own measure of it. Then add up the score at the end.

Situational Perspective:	High 10-9-8-	Mid 7-6-5-4	Low 3-2-1
I have a sense of why I am in transition			
Knowing what I know, the inevitability of why I am transitioning now was			
There are less competent people still working and enjoying their jobs, and the extent to which I can disregard it is			
Self-Understanding: Despite my current situation my confidence in my abilities to be usefully employed is			
In spite of difficult economic conditions my ability to reinvent myself to be productively engaged is			
If I am unable to find something that fits my skills, my ability to re-deploy myself is			
Support System: The degree of support I can derive from my own support system is			
My ability to grow the current circle of contacts quickly, is			

Taking Action:
My confidence in my ability to plan
and move ahead with action is

If the plan needs adjustment based
on the outcomes, my ability to
revise it is

Total Score

If your score is 60 or higher, you can be considered resilient (be honest)! Practice behaviors that move you to a higher score.

*Managing Your Chemicals

This is the second factor that needs managing during transitions. It has to do with how others react to you. We, as chemical-generating organisms, are able to generate, among others, two hormones, and, in turn, *induce* the same in others. These two hormones dictate how others respond to us. Since job search is a social activity involving others, this is important.

The two chemicals contrast each other by their very nature and how they affect physiologically and psychologically: one is epinephrine, more commonly known as adrenaline, responsible for helping us generate instinctive responses, and the other is beta-endorphin considered many times more powerful than even morphine, a highly analgesic drug or a painkiller. Adrenaline helps generate fear, whereas beta-endorphin helps us become euphoric and joyful.

We are able to *induce* in those with whom we interact *their* adrenaline and beta-endorphin, creating an interesting dynamic. For example if we are tense and self-absorbed with our own pain, we induce in those who come near us *their* adrenaline. Adrenaline release has one major affect on those who are experiencing its release: flight or fight! People are uncomfortable if you heap on them too much self-pity and your pain in your interactions with them. Nature blessed us with this gift to react properly in the presence of fear. When one is confronted with a life-threatening situation, the release of their adrenaline causes them to instinctively fight or flight to save themselves from the imminent danger. So, if you cause others to release their adrenaline in your interaction with them, they simply walk away, rather than offering help! When people are suffering personal problems, as can happen from a job loss, their natural tendency is to indulge in self-pity, and tell everyone their woes. So, when meeting someone in a social setting when you are in such a state, rather than launching into a tale of woes as soon as shaking hands, try practicing an alternate behavior.

The preferred way is to start a pleasant conversation—talking about *them*. If you connect with the person, they will sense your body language and perhaps ask questions that may lead to a conversation where you bring up your needs. Even if the other person does not "get it," keep that interaction pleasant. If you, on the other hand, come on too strong with your woes, they may shun you from then on. You have caused them to release *their* adrenalin. In fact, in many interactions people will not generally remember what was said (facts) but how it was said (emotions) or the affect (how that made them feel).

On the other hand when you come across to others as *genuinely* optimistic, positive and outwardly focused, their own reaction to your demeanor results in their body releasing the other hormone, beta-endorphin. This release causes others to experience joy and warmth around you. And, who does not want to be in that state? Putting others in this state can be a learned behavior!

Managing Your Chemicals: Exercise

The following exercise is designed to help you evaluate your response in different situations and how others may respond to you.

Managing Your Chemicals: Exercise

This exercise will explore your natural tendency to "induce" the good (endorphin) or the bad (adrenaline) chemical in your interaction with others. Respond with honesty to make this work for you. An adrenaline inducing interaction is likely to result in people walking away from you!

Behavior	(Endorphin Good	Adrenaline) Bad
In my social interaction with others I am more apt to start with my woes.		X
In my social interaction with others I begin first by asking about others and then sensing how I should hold my end of the conversation.	X	
If others tell me how great things are for them when I know I am struggling, I feel uneasy.		X
In a social group, when I know that I am in a bad space, I withdraw rather than using it to energize me.		X

Behavior	(Endorphin Good	Adrenaline) Bad
When I want someone to help me in my job situation I do not waste time with pleasantries; I get right to it.		X
When I face defeat, as a rejection in a job opportunity, I withdraw from social activities and mope.		X
When I am turned down for a job and I realize that someone I know might be able to pursue it, I keep that information to myself.		X
Even when I know I am flubbing an interview I have the ability to smile and keep my cool.	X	
As I get more and more into my job-search campaign and fail to produce a positive outcome, I feel down.		X
I try to find faults with others and tell them so.		X
I generally believe that life sucks.		X
When a series of things go bad during an early part of a day, I assume that the rest of the day will follow suit.		X
No matter how down I am I have the ability to make someone happy.	X	

If you have many X's circled on the right side of the column, clearly, you need to work on your attitude. Marking your own X on the "Good" side conveys that you have a healthy and positive attitude in the way you are approaching your job search.

Managing Your Fear

The third and the final factor discussed here, that helps in transitional success, is the ability to operate without fear. How? When there is uncertainty, especially job related, there is angst, which can create fear. This emotion deeply affects those who let it run their lives. Fear creates its own adrenaline! This again creates others to see you as someone they want to avoid. Fear is something not kept inside ourselves as most think, it is something that is apparent to anyone who sees us; we wear it even without our knowing it. It is much like a strong perfume we wear that we can no longer smell! Fear impedes one's thinking and power to reason.

Fear surrounding job uncertainty can be managed since it is not instinctive fear. *Instinctive* fear is a gift that we are given to save our lives. It is an internally driven response induced when we know that our life—not our *existence*—is threatened as when someone confronts us with a gun in their hands, or a wild beast we may encounter at a camp unexpectedly. This instinctive fear puts our body in an automatic mode and impels us to react to it by flight or fight. Even under those life-threatening situations, the outcome is far more desirable when you are able to think rationally, and then act rather than react in panic. The only challenge is getting your mind into the thinking mode. Our response to *existential* fear can be managed to provide us the ability to create the best outcome.

During life's transitions certain approaches we choose to adopt can help us. Recent studies have shown that those with an open mind, positive outlook, and without fear are more likely to come out ahead faster in these transitions, than those who retreat, sulk, blame others for their woes, and move in fear. Fear and negativity around a situation can affect our mind by occluding it. An occluded mind is limited in its capacity to perform. Whereas someone who is fully engaged with emotional, mental, and physical resources can deliver so much more! This is why the first requirement in a transition is ridding of the fear factor! This is particularly true of job or career transitions.

Reminder: To successfully leverage one's internal resources and to mobilize untapped potential, becoming aware of the fear factor and overcoming the deepest fears are critical for a speedy transition to success.

Managing any transition *process* can be a rewarding experience, even though the episode prompting it itself can be emotionally traumatic.

Dealing with Sleeplessness

During intense transitions it is normal to experience anxiety. Intense transitions can be those prompted by a job loss, an impending termination or layoff, or anything that creates uncertainty, which leads to fear as we just discussed. Sometimes, this fear then drives certainty—the inevitable actually happens—which culminates in dread! During such episodes it is normal to experience sleepless nights, or awaken in the middle of the night in sweat, and then lying awake with eyes wide open, wondering about what is next and finding meaning behind what is going on. In the quiet of the night, all negative thoughts multiply unchecked and create a paralyzing emotion from within. As situation deteriorates due to a declining economy, personal setbacks, and other factors, it creates further anxiety that impairs normal thinking. This is now a vicious cycle and it permeates our daily existence. Its effect is to slowly attack our own self-confidence and an ability to master our own destiny in an insidious and pernicious way. This fear that causes sleepless nights also vitiates our daily performance in all that we do to get out of the very situation that creates these nightmares. The best way to deal with this quandary is to recognize that such angst is common to most who have to face similar challenging transitions. Holding positive thoughts and painting pictures of blissful outcomes from these transitions can be good tools to combat these negative forces. Of course, thoughtful and visionary planning, diligent execution, and course correction, as learning is derived from ongoing efforts, must fortify such positive imagery.

Focusing on planned actions and holding the belief that the universe provides us its lessons through these travails and that our life is not complete without these lessons is an affirmation that, too, can help us. Such lessons make us strong and are proving grounds for our own inner strength of character. Accepting defeat in the face of adversity and retreating do not complete the intended lesson; they merely defer it. Additionally, one's self-confidence and esteem take a beating in this early admission of defeat. Maintaining a regimen, a plan, and diligent execution of the plan are important for success and early positive conclusion of such transitions. Remember *"Only the brave make the dangerous tenable."*—John Fitzgerald Kennedy.

Managing Your Fear: Exercise

This exercise is designed to assess your ability to control fear in situations that are not life threatening. Existence-threatening situations—loss of status, job, and money—do not warrant a response that is steeped in fear or one that is fear induced. In such situations it is normal to be in a state of quandary. But this is *different* from feeling fear!

This exercise measures your propensity to operate under fear in stressful situations at a job interview, social interactions with others, especially with those whom you consider to be in positions of power, and where the outcome of the situation can affect your future.

Managing your Fear: Exercise

Factor/Score (write your response number for each item listed below):	Fear Factor		
	High 10-9-8-7	Middle 6-5-4	Low 3-2-1

1. When I am called upon to prove my abilities, as in an interview or a test, I become afraid

2. When I am in interactions with others where my abilities can be challenged, I become paralyzed with fear and my fear of failure or exposure is

3. For an interview or a presentation, no amount of preparation can rid the feeling that, if I fail, terrible things can happen to my future

4. No matter how hard I try, I cannot seem to shake the feeling that somehow, what I know and do not know will get exposed, and I will be humiliated

5. I am so anxious to make a good impression on those who matter to me, that I often leave feeling as though I have, in the end, done poorly, because of my high degree of apprehension

6. No matter how well I do in an important interaction (as an interview), I leave feeling that given another chance I would do even better

7. In important meetings, I feel as though the other person is in control and I am solicitous to them

8. For an upcoming job interview, I keep reflecting on the past situations where I flubbed them, and keep thinking that it could happen again

9. In an important social or business interaction, my palms are sweaty before a handshake

10. I often fear losing most of my possessions if I stay out of work too long and the degree to which this bothers me is

Overall score:

Fear Rating:	70 and up	High degree of fear
	50–70	Somewhat fearful
	30–50	Healthy fear level
	30 and below	Almost fearless

Practice behaviors and thoughts that move you to the lower scores.

♠ A Transformational Strategy

To move ahead successfully during a transition, at a personal level, being positive and optimistic greatly help. Here success is not necessarily landing a job immediately, but rather, being able to manage the transition process with some adventure, fun, and personal control over it. Studies have shown that, over time, if you are positive and calm in taking on a challenge in the face of a series of defeats, you will end up on top, largely by being open to the adventure, being optimistic, and holding the belief that you are in control, no matter how many setbacks you repeatedly encounter. The only possible caution here might be that of avoiding *repeated* setbacks by using certain approaches and methods that cause them, then finding a pattern and learning from that pattern are critical to moving ahead positively. Behaviors that generate new avenues of hope must replace patterns of defeat. This is why identifying these patterns is critical before they take hold.

One of the worst feelings during the process of a job search—especially if you are out of work and looking—is the frequent bouts of hopelessness and feeling out of control. This sense will be exacerbated in a tough economy. As disappointments mount to what appear as seemingly perfect jobs, with each setback, rejection, or lack of response, your self-esteem plummets. As your confidence retreats, you start becoming a victim and loose your sense of control. You may even give up hope if the same cycles repeat!

Studies have shown that those who maintain their perspective in such situations are better able to engage the full arsenal of their resources: wit, energy, intellect, memory recall, and composure. In one study, when simple puzzles were given to a group of adults, researchers found that those who were comfortable within their own selves, fully relaxed, and ready to take on the challenge for fun, were consistently able to find clever ways to beat the odds and get the right answer. Those who were apprehensive, unsure, and afraid invariably ended giving up in frustration or taking too long by sequentially dealing with each element of the puzzle. Those who remained calm and were fully engaged with all their resources were able to marshal their intuition and insights and were readily able to find some key or clue that gave them the edge to succeed more quickly. The research also found that those who approached their life positively overall, were far more likely to be able to deal with any adversity as a victor than as a victim! Similarly, in a job search, a positive outlook goes a long way in making you more desirable to others, and helping you reach your goal.

Staying positive and celebrating even minor successes and building on what works in a given situation can create a virtuous cycle. Success releases its own endorphins inside your body, which can help you far more than anything ingested externally in moving ahead to success!

Impediments to Transition

A job loss is often a cause for many changes in one's personal life. When everything is "normal" in a life, issues remain in the background and life sails "comfortably."

A sudden job loss can change that. In some cases its suddenness is immaterial. In a family situation, where two spouses share deeply ingrained but differing views around jobs steeped in their cultural upbringing, there is a potential for problems. These problems surface when even one spouse suffers a job loss. If the couple has not communicated individual views around jobs and what their job means to them personally, the changed circumstances can precipitate a surprise. Overcoming this difference and reconciling the two views after the job loss can take a surprisingly large effort and can affect their marriage or relationship. Marriages or unions that involve spouses or partners from different cultures are particularly prone to this surprise. One client's wife was from one of countries in the Pacific Rim. She held the belief—but never communicated that to him—that his worth was tied to his job and how much money he brought home from it and that she was to manage the family finances. When his income stopped, she continued *her* lifestyle because she believed that his losing the job—even in a bad economy—was his fault and that she should not have to suffer for it. They could not agree to a scaled-down lifestyle after the job loss, and his top priority became saving his marriage.

A job loss can send shock waves in one's personal life. Understanding priorities and then deciding how to move on in a job search can take more time and effort than may be anticipated. Not addressing more important issues before embarking on a job search can be a frustrating experience because of the constant impediments they pose for an effective job-search campaign.

If the situation during your "normal life" does not warrant an audit of how each spouse feels about changed circumstances such as a job loss, it may be prudent to explore these views and communicate them to each other so that when setbacks do occur, there is little or no discord. This simple measure of prevention will allow one to then move ahead during a transition with full focus.

A Philosophical Insight

During transitions people find their lives becoming intense. Everything hits them hard and they start seeing things in a different light than they did when everything was going well for them. A transition is a period of learning and growing. It, too, is a period of finding new meaning in the way our lives impact other lives. Some even see a major transition as a near-death experience with an epiphany!

One rule worth reflecting on during such transitions is the rule of universal giving. In essence, this rule states that if you want something you have to learn to give it in your own way to one who does not have it. In times of our own needs it is difficult to be giving to others. The following true story is probably an object lesson of this universal rule:

A Universal WGACA Story

WGACA stands for what goes around comes around. Often in our lives we encounter instances where we do not treat others in the spirit of the Golden Rule: treat others as you would want others to treat you! This is often perpetrated by our own selfishness, the values we adopt, and the choices we make in our own daily lives. During life's transitions you will encounter situations where lack of simple human courtesies may incense you. You may never hear from an interviewer who gave you all the indications that you would be offered the job. You may never get a call back from repeated messages you left in response to something you had sent for a job opportunity. You may never hear from your "friends" because now you are in need.

The following story is a true tale of how a simple act of doing the right thing selflessly can result in something good at a later time. When times are tough and things do not seem to be going your way, it is easy to transfer that to others. Don't! As this story illustrates, you have the power to break that cycle and do the right thing!

> His name was Fleming, and he was a poor Scottish farmer.
> One day, while trying to make a living for his family, he heard

cry for help coming from a nearby bog. He dropped his tools and ran to the bog. There, mired to his waist in black muck, was a terrified boy, screaming and struggling to free himself. Farmer Fleming saved the lad from what could have been a slow and terrifying death.

The next day, a fancy carriage pulled up to the Scotsman's sparse surroundings. An elegantly dressed nobleman stepped out and introduced himself as the father of the boy who had been saved. "I want to repay you," said the nobleman. "You saved my son's life."

"No," replied the farmer, waving off the offer. "I can't accept payment for what I did." At that moment, the farmer's own son came to the door of the family hovel.

"Is that your son?" the nobleman asked.

"Yes," the farmer replied proudly.

"I'll make you a deal. Let me take him and give him a good education. If the lad is anything like his father, he'll grow to become a man you can be proud of." And that he did. In time, Farmer Fleming's son graduated from St. Mary's Hospital Medical School in London, and went on to become known worldwide as the noted Sir Alexander Fleming, the discoverer of Penicillin.

Years afterward, the nobleman's son was stricken with pneumonia. What saved him? It was the very Penicillin that Fleming had invented. What was the name of the nobleman? It was none other than Lord Randolph Churchill, whose son, Sir Winston Churchill, went on to achieve greatness in his own right. Someone once said What goes around comes around. Work like you don't need the money. Interview like you do not need the job; love like you've never been hurt; and dance like nobody's watching.

The moral here is to learn to give, even when you are lacking in some key resources. Give in your own way and accept nothing in return! If the boomerang effect does not follow immediately, it will in its own way, and *you* will know when it happens.

WGACA Exercise:
Looking at my own current situation I have the following (can be more than one) to give to others who can benefit from it:

#1)
Describe it:

I plan to give it by:

#2)
Describe it:

I plan to give it by:

My own personal thought on WGACA is (this is optional):

♠ The Change Curve

The change curve is a nearly universal representation of any change that involves human affairs. A typical change curve is shown below:

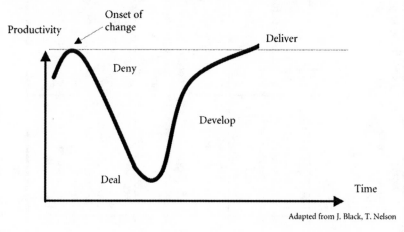

Adapted from J. Black, T. Nelson

Figure-2 The Change Curve

The nature of the change curve suggests that when we are going through a transition, we go from being productive and feeling good about ourselves *before* the onset of change, through becoming aware of it, and then going through a transition process following that change. This dynamic even applies when the change is positive. For example, when someone gets promoted or wins a jackpot, they need to adjust to their new state by going through a simi-lar regressive transition.

Becoming aware of how change takes place using the representation of the curve helps those undergoing the change to manage it. The idea behind the change curve is to get past the stages that take away from being productive and from a state of good mental and emotional balance to another state of equal or better balance. This typically happens through a series of learning and coping experiences. The faster you transition through the curve and the shallower the curve, the easier it is dealing with change in a positive way and getting to the "other side."

There are specific interventions to accelerate the passage through the change curve to the next state in a four-state continuum. These four states are labeled in Figure-2 and described in Table-1, which also describes the inter-ventions for a job transition. The idea is to get to the next state on the curve quickly and to come out reenergized and ready to take on the new challenge by letting go of the past (the death of the past) and embrace the new (rebirth).

From State	Symptoms	To State	Intervention	Tools	Comments
Denial (Inability to face reality and to prepare to act in a constructive way)	Not accepting loss; denying reality. Anger; blame; regret	Deal	Support group; counseling, family members.	Discard past reminders; make plan. Use Tool-1 and Tool-2	Just talking about the loss can help!
Deal (Accepting what happened and finding ways to move ahead.)	Unproductive activities; frustration; feeling lost or even overwhelmed	Develop	Create structure, prepare a plan, engage in activities, and follow the plan.	Get organized. Daily schedule; measure progress and activities. Reward yourself. Use Tool-3, Tool-4 and Tool-5	Use help from others to create accountability for yourself!
Develop (Defining specific actions to move forward and creating accountabilities.)	Feeling encouraged by progress; can see forward movement	Deliver	Coaching; support groups; increased emphasis on metrics Increased networks.	Expanding original plan to greater details based on what works. Use Tool-6, and Tool-7	Focus on your strengths that allow success in specific endeavors. Finalize résumé(s) and Marketing Plan
Deliver (Delivering outcomes that are measurable, culminating in a goal previously envisaged.)	Feel good about the changed state and about accomplishments	Ready for next Performance Level	Doing postmortem, Learning from the transition and realizing what works for you.	Keep daily activity log; measure activity/progress. Reward yourself with something promised earlier. Use Tool-8	Once you have mastered this concept, future transitions are easier. Keep weekly track with Tool-8.

Table-1: Understanding the Change Curve—Accelerating Change

Understanding the change process and how it can be managed is key to staying positive and hopeful during any transition. Table-1 can help those in a job transition and who can use it to move through the change with minimum disruption and feeling good about the future!

As one can glean from this table, a transition *can* last for an extended period of time, depending on circumstances. This is apparent from looking in the Tools column, in which the tools shown here are available throughout the book, starting with the next section. The best approach to accelerating change is to go through the book and spot these tools (see Index) and come back to develop a better understanding of how to manage the change and create the most effective outcome.

*Tools to Accelerate Transition

The following tools (see Index for all tools) can help you better deal and prepare for the transition. They are designed to help you emotionally accept the change and to take you through your change process:

➢ Change State (Tool-1)

➢ Transition Statement (Tool-2)

➢ Positioning Statement (Tool-3)

➢ My Truth! (Tool-4)

Each one is described below and can be used to accelerate the transition:

Transition Statement

A transition statement is an answer to the question others may ask. Why are you looking for a change? This change could be a new job or something else. This statement is your honest response to others to help them help you. It also clarifies why you are seeking the change. An effective transition statement is brief, non-defensive, positive, and blameless. The following examples are illustrative:

"Recent merger of Electronic Industries and Dynamic Enterprises resulted in consolidating their separate operations. My position was eliminated as a result, and now I am out looking for a new one."

"Recent economic downturn forced my company to move its operations overseas, leaving only administrative and management jobs in the US. I am now looking for a design and drafting position nearby."

"After my marriage I decided to take time to start a family and raise kids till they were of school age. All three of my children are in school now and I decided to enter the workforce as an interior decorator and I am looking for opportunities nearby where I live."

"I recently immigrated to the US on a green card. I was an architect in Europe for a number of years and am now looking for similar work here."

A transition statement should be both written and fit for oral delivery. The language and how it is presented are, of course, different. A written statement presented orally can sound stuffy.

Most transition statements are presented when meeting someone. The following samples can help someone who is struggling with the two versions:

Written

After HP merged with Compaq the two organizations were restructured to eliminate duplicate positions. Recent off-shoring trends have further affected the workforce at the new company and, as a result, I am no longer employed at HP. I am now looking for opportunities in the IT support areas in a company that is interested in making its infrastructure more effective.

Spoken

You probably already know about the big merger between HP and Compaq. This has resulted in ongoing reduction of the workforce. As this was going on, off-shoring further impacted those who were in the IT and software areas there. I recently left HP and am looking to leverage what I learned there into an opportunity of making overall IT more effective in a company that recognizes it, and am excited about the possibilities that are now out there!

Laid off vs. "Fired"

While composing a Transition Statement some may wonder how to do it if they were "fired" instead of being laid off. The difference between the two categories for being unemployed is that being "fired" is also called Termination for Cause. This implies that the company had a reason to terminate and let someone go because it believed the person did something to deserve being fired. Being fired is different from being laid-off. The latter is the circumstance resulting from economic conditions and the former a case of some untoward incident that compromised one's being employed at the company. This may also include "performance" issues. Some companies routinely let go the "bottom-ranked" 5–10 percent performers. See Key-2: The Under-Performer Syndrome.

Sometimes these terminations occur for political reasons. The best approach is to first state the reason for looking to make the transition. "*I recently left General Electronics as a result of some changes*" can work in a Transitioning Statement, primarily because the transitioning statement is forward looking. If, however, when asked face-to-face and pressed for details, the best approach is to present the facts in a positive way without having to lie. Also not engaging in an elaborate explanation is wise, otherwise the explanation alone may raise some eyebrows. Many understand how political some organizations are and getting fired is not uncommon. Some companies "fire" a particular employee to protect their ability to claim unemployment insurance; if they resign, they are ineligible for it. In this Key, My Truth! described later can also be used to write down the lesson from this episode for future learning, if there was any!

Tool-1: Change State

Change-Transition Exercise
In my own case of transition, I am currently in state (From Fig. 2):

Reason why I am in this state:

Things I am going to practice to go to the next state:

I will know I am there because:

Things I am going to do beyond the next state:

Tool-2: Transition Statement

Now write your own transition statement in the space below:

Your Transition Statement

Written:

Spoken:

Positioning Statement

Similar to the transition statement, a Positioning Statement tells what you do. It is a short pithy statement of how you create *value* in what you do. It can also be called an elevator speech. A positioning statement has a format of "I am a...." sentence.

Here are some examples of Positioning Statements:

I am an electronic circuit designer with over 10 years designing complex analog, digital, and hybrid circuits. I have designed both board-level and chip-level circuits in a variety of applications and have led many creative teams that have delivered pioneering circuits and devices in a wide range of applications over the years.

I am an administrator with over five years in an office of a major law firm. I can manage a large office and lead all administrative, minor accounting, and organizing functions to make it a smoothly functioning support group for the overall business it serves.

I am a marketing communications specialist with over 12 years in an industrial-controls manufacturing company. My specialty is new products and I develop novel marketing campaigns to make them highly visible and desirable in the marketplace as they become ready.

I am a lawyer with over 13 years in a large high-tech corporation. My specialty is contract law and I can handle general law affairs of a large organization with a staff of 15 or more, supporting the legal matters in today's environment.

I am a nurse with over 20 years in a world-renowned hospital. My specialty is pediatric cardiology, and I have worked with some of the most famous names in this field.

One word of caution: these Positioning Statements are examples of more formal statements presented better in the written form. An elevator speech is better designed for an oral delivery. Reading a statement designed for a written presentation can make it sound stilted. Please make sure that you have two separate forms of these statements, preferably both written out so that they have the same message but sound appropriate when presented. See Transition Statement.

Tool-3: Positioning Statement

Now, write your own Positioning Statement:

Positioning Statement

Written:

Oral:

"My Truth!"

"My Truth!" is a private and personal statement. Sometimes you do not want to divulge all that surrounds your current situation. Sometimes you are not sure what you want, other than just a job. It is a good idea to be clear about the truth so that you are honest with yourself. The better you are aligned with what you communicate and what your own truth is, the more authentic your campaign and more honest the outcome. Most have the innate ability to spot the misalignment between your words and how you present them.

Also as discussed in Laid-off or "Fired", you may want to use this exercise to capture your learning from the episode that resulted in getting fired and how you want to present it to the outside world.

This statement is confidential and need not be discussed with *anyone* if you choose not to.

During a job-search campaign, there will be moments of reflection, doubts, and apprehension, especially for a campaign that drags out because of the economy. Having an honest "My Truth!" statement will act as a touchstone that one can come back to, to verify the authenticity of your campaign. If your campaign is misaligned with this statement, then there is a reason, and the reason can be found on *that* page.

Yet another reason for this intimate disclosure stems from the principle that if you deeply believe something, put it down, and own it; it has the power and ability to manifest. You can create your own future! Carrying the thought that had been written will now become part of your being, and the universe has the obligation to owe you that gift. Just try it!

Some examples follow:

Since my husband's layoff, things have become tough financially. He is too depressed to start looking and I do not know how long that is going to take. To support my family I need to get back to what I did 15 years ago: doing office work and answering phones. Once he gets going again, I may not need the work.

I am going to have my first baby in about eight months. Once I have a child I may not be able to work for a long time and I want to use this opportunity to work as a legal aid so that I have some experience to show, in the future, if the need arises. I may work for about six months.

My current boss is giving me signals that I am not going to advance further in this organization. I need to find for myself if I can move up in an organization where I am appreciated and rewarded with positions of responsibilities. I must explore to see what is out there, before I decide to take an entirely different route, as going into my own business.

Recent losses in the stock market have financially wiped me out. I need to find some startup that is promising, so that I can see it through its IPO and then cash out on my options. Once I hit the $1 million in cashable stock, I am out of there.

After working in high-tech for six years I have realized that I made the wrong choice. I need a more stable and hassle-free work environment. I am going to pursue teaching at a small college or community institution. I already have the credentials I need to do this.

Tool-4: "My Truth!"

Write down your own statement:

"My Truth!"

♠ Getting Organized

One of the more commonplace topics of concern for those getting ready to launch a job-search campaign is how they should get organized to run their campaign and how this should all come about so that there is efficiency, purpose, and discrete identity to it as a process. Most run their campaigns from homes or home offices. Some have the luxury of doing it from the offices of the outplacement service providers through their employers, at least for a while. No matter how one is organized, it comes down to having a different structure to their activities than they did before entering this period of transition. Those who manage their job searching from home or home office are often troubled to realize that there is no space between the demands on their time for job-searching activity, and their obligations as someone who is running a household. They are physically there, so anyone can interrupt. They feel guilty for not being helpful, so they give in. This habit can interfere with their productive campaign.

The following suggestions can help a productive job search, working from home.

Sanctum Sanctorum

For a productive campaign having an office is helpful. This could be a quiet area in a corner of a large room, dining table (which may be difficult), or a room with a door and a complete set up. The following guidelines can help you create such a space:

1. Set aside some space that no one can intrude at will. Create some rules in your household around how you plan to work in the space you have designated for this purpose and how those who come across it should treat it.

2. If you have a room with a door, make it clear that when the door is closed you are not available.

3. Make a routine for your job-search activities and follow it. This provides the structure. If you are out of work and looking, it is easy to not have structure. If you are working but looking for a change, you need to develop discipline, see Key-2: If You Are (Unhappily) Employed and Looking for a Change.

4. Organize your workspace so that it is set up for efficient job-search activities. Your computer, binders, and all support materials should be easily accessible from where you sit to do most of your work. See Key-5: Having Ready Access to Material.

5. If your space is limited, share the space with others in a time-share mode: if you have a student who needs to do homework on your computer at night, structure your schedule for the early hours of the day or during the school hours.

6. Remove TV and other *video* entertainment set-ups from the space where you plan to work. These distractions can be time intruders and will tempt you to lose your focus on what you should be doing. Keep them in a separate room so that you have to make an effort to go watch TV and where others in the household can catch you doing it!

7. If you need a variety in your workspace, find some alternate arrangements and use them throughout the day or week to keep you going. Often, sitting in the same place of work creates monotony resulting in less productive outcomes. Consider your local library.

Tool-5; Getting Organized

My Needs for Getting Organized

Make a list of your needs to run an effective job-search campaign from home and discuss it with the members of your household:

1)

2)

3)

4)

6)

7)

8)

9)

10)

What do *you* have to do so that, as a family unit, you are going to be able to have your needs met. This is not a "give me all"; it is a give and take! Do not dictate your terms to others since you run the household; do this as a process of negotiation. Discuss what's in it for them. (WIIFM)

Structured Distractions

In major transitions, often our life is turned upside down. This is particularly true in job and career transitions. During a job-search campaign, encountering bouts of intense moments can become routine. When these moments sneak up on you, you must learn to just walk away from the flux before getting overwhelmed. This is no reflection on your ability to handle stressful situations; it is learning to deal with stress without yielding to it. One way to deal with such moments of intensity is to have a temporary escape. Indulging in some fun distractions can be refreshing. Taking up a hobby, or attending a yoga class can be helpful at times that are hard to manage. In your routine, work in some fun so that you continually recharge yourself and get back to where you are needed. In episodes of intense angst, just walk away and immerse yourself in an impromptu fun activity. Make time for it and move scheduled things around so that you can make this happen, just for you. Take time to talk to some family member if they are around and check what they are up to. Here, too, try the endorphin route instead of the adrenaline option (discussed earlier).

Often, those who are unable to engage in a serious job-search find excuses for not being able to commit to their search activities as there are pressing projects around the house that require their attention. Interestingly, some of the "pressing" projects can be on their "list" for years and yet they suddenly become urgent!

One way to deal with this temptation is to tackle a project as a reward for some agreed on accomplishment, as long as the project is time-bound and short. "Completed résumé: go finish project #1. First call in response to a job opportunity: go start project #2, etc." Having a prioritized list of projects as your rewards can be a disciplined way to avoid getting run over by pending projects.

Organized Abandon

Many approach their job search (especially those out of work or looking for a change) as a chore that they have to do to somehow get what they are looking for or get something close to it. Looking for work or change in a tough economy is no picnic. So, they approach their search with resignation and surrender rather than approaching the search with determination and resolve. The end result of such a campaign is a so-so job that either may not last very long, or may end up being a regret. If, however, a search is approached with a certain degree of organization, planning, and energy, with high expectations, there is likely to be a pleasant surprise! You need to provide an environment where you get "lost" in the process of job search. Many creative avenues are presented in this book in later sections, that will allow for targeting exciting jobs that *you* want. Some of these jobs may not even exist (see Key-4: Unconventional Approaches, for example). Organized abandon is a state where you are approaching the process in a creatively structured space and mindset, free to explore what your unfettered mind lets you pursue. The results may surprise you!

Managing Creativity

Much of the material in this book evolved from creative moments that clients encountered during their journey to find something better for themselves: better job, better career, better work-life balance. This is especially noteworthy because the state of the economy and job market in the Valley dictated a less ambitious expectation during their adventures. Many felt that approaching career transition in a state of quandary was not making them productive, although many started in that state. One factor that mobilizes creativity is our own inner power that we all posses but seldom use. One manifestation of that power is our own genius. This is further discussed in Key-2: Résumé Elements. Tapping into this natural gift transforms everything around us, allowing us to approach a given challenge in ways that we do not usually attempt. The mentioned clients were intimidated by the very idea of tapping into *their* genius and their creativity (See the quote at the heading of Key-7) and yet when they understood the concept they quickly owned it. Then they started practicing behaviors that transformed their thinking.

Why do we need to be in a creative space during a career transition? In a creative space we surrender our familiar (algorithmic) routines to pursue more risky (heuristic) adventures. Algorithmic routines in a job-search process would be the familiar approaches we adopt to quickly find what we are looking for. A heuristic adventure, on the other hand, would be where one takes risks, finds a clever way to do something using an approach never before contemplated. What does this mean? In a job-search context this means developing an ability to avoid the obvious and taking a different path to conquer the set goal. With this attitude the goal itself now is loftier! This approach does not require abandoning the familiar. The mix of the familiar and the adventurous will evolve based on what works and the degree of comfort one develops in an approach. In heuristic adventures there is no set path, it must be created! And, for that to happen one needs a creative space.

How does one get into a creative space and shed their normal instinctive self. What we presented in previous sections so far is a start: getting organized, having a disciplined routine, and so on. Additionally, there is yet one factor that dominates our being left out of this creative bliss, and that factor is our own fear and uncertainty that surround a career transition. Fear is normal. But fear makes us behave in an instinctive mode; and this does *not* put us in a creative space allowing our mind to explore possibilities. We discussed fear in more detail in Managing Your Fear, earlier in this Key. In a similar vein fear shuts out creativity and makes us like everyone else; *undifferentiated*. Operating at one's true potential requires absence of fear. Ridding fear allows one to tap into their Essence, which is their pure inner self. And it is this Essence that has the ability to intuitively approach a problem in ways that are not possible with linear, sequential, and logical reasoning. Being creative then follows.

Your Telephone Connection

The next item for a successful and effective organization is how one is connected to the outside world. A dedicated telephone line just for the job search business is critical. This line should have an answering device with a professional and personal greeting in your own voice. More lines for routine incoming calls and for family members to call out are the next priority. *Do not* tie up a phone line on an Internet connection if you plan to use that line for incoming business calls. Have DSL or cable service for a high-speed Internet connection. If you cannot afford such a service, then think of going to a library or a facility that gives you access to one. For more discussion on this topic see Key-5: The Interview, specifically, The Telephone Call.

Your Time

Your time, when you are home, is expected to be a free for all, based on the routine that you practiced *before* your transition. This *must* now change. One way to enforce this change is for you to make your own time schedule, mark it on your calendar, and honor it. This approach is particularly important to those who already have a job and are looking for a change. Another aid to this discipline is dinner time discussions with family members on how they can help you through this transition by respecting your time. If you are out of work and home most of the time running your campaign, post your *daily* schedule on the refrigerator for all to see.

One of the major challenges job seekers—especially the unemployed—face is when they awaken each morning they are overwhelmed by what lies ahead. This feeling can lead to despair and even resignation, resulting in your just turning on the TV upon your waking. Once you get into this mode, pretty soon this little indulgence can result in your TV marathon ending with the *evening news*, punctuated only by occasional eating and restroom breaks!

A good antidote when this happens is to plan your next day *before* going to bed and to draw up a schedule for the entire day, hour-by-hour. This is why planning is so important. Making such a schedule and mentally accepting each item on that schedule can create visual images of what your next day might look like. Now you're going to bed with a purposeful tomorrow. As soon as you're out of bed you know what to do! With constant adjustments to what works, a discipline to start your day can be in place. This discipline may also let you sleep better and force you to wake up at a designated time.

Staying Focused

Just as staying organized is a challenge, which you can deal with by keeping your space and time organized throughout your campaign from the get go, as we just discussed here, staying focused, too, is a challenge for many. In the age of the Internet it is easy to get distracted by things that pop up either on the screen or in your mind during your regular activities, especially as you are doing research on job opportunities, companies, and people on the Web. The way many Websites are presented, it is easy to find reasons to stray from the main research topic at hand and explore something by digressing. As you digress from the main topic to something else, yet another distraction takes your focus away from *that*, and on and on. This is called zigzagging!

One way to avoid zigzagging is to, once again, manage your time on the Internet. Once you keep your time there bounded, and have committed your-self on your calendar to research a certain number of topics, during that time, make sure that you honor that and hold yourself accountable. Keep a notepad to jot down distracting ideas, topics, and things of interest that you encounter as "pop-ups" either on the screen, or in your mind, or otherwise. Consider getting back to them as a reward for having done something well, completing something, or accomplishing a goal. Interestingly, if you make such an ongoing list of things you want to explore later while you are in the middle of a task, many items on that list simply become irrelevant when you revisit them at a later time! Remember, that just because no one has imposed a deadline on your assignment does not mean that you can take forever to accomplish it. To that point, if you are deadline driven, create your own and honor them!

Your Expectations

Managing your own expectations is important in a job-search campaign. Let others in the household know what you expect from them and approach this transition as a team effort where the roles of each team member of the household are clear. When a routine is established and everyone honors each other for their time, space, and commitments, reward them with something specific. Without this discipline you will have many excuses and little progress on your campaign.

Keeping Your Cool

During career transition it is normal to feel as if nothing is in your control. On a less than blessed day, it is not unusual to experience a series of setbacks, frustrations, and mortifying lessons. Such days are especially prone to one making more mistakes in sending messages, résumés, and interacting with others. On such days, it is best to recognize what is happening and manage the day so that there is some control over what is going to happen from then on, at least for that day. It is not a good idea to surrender in defeat and withdraw. Especially on such days, being vigilant helps! This also means deferring critical actions that can wait for the next day or a better day, which may just be around the corner.

Rewarding Yourself

As the campaign gets going and you get in the groove of your routine, you need to reward yourself for staying on track, keeping your commitments, or accomplishing a goal that you set out to conquer. This could be as simple as calling a certain number of people, sending a certain number of résumés, or following up on certain networking contacts. Decide your reward before you complete the task and then go get it.

♠ Understanding Yourself

Career transitions are often marked by reflection and examination. Life's transitions are opportunities presented to us—gifts—that allow these indulgences. When undergoing such transitions, those who use these opportunities for engaging in self-discovery and in better understanding of their own purpose in life, find such episodes refreshingly rewarding—looking back! Although in the moment these episodes are stressful, looking back, most accept these opportunities to be a blessing.

This discussion on understanding yourself is presented here for two reasons: One is to help those who are in a transition understand themselves better so that they become aware of how they handle their situations on a recurring basis, and the second, more important reason is to help them understand and manage some of their repetitive behavior patterns that can be puzzling and even frustrating to them. These patterns deal with their interactions with others. This is important to know in a job search where your social and professional interactions with others determine what happens next. This section is presented not so much to *change* who you are, but, more importantly, to make you aware of how you may come across to others. Once that is known, you may choose to *manage* that behavior to create outcomes that are more in line with your expectations.

Professional Evaluation

Professional evaluation is a service available from career counselors and other service providers that can provide insights into your career planning, especially if you are at a crossroads. Those choosing a particular academic path also go through this as a part of their career planning process in high school and college. Career assessments are tools used by professionals and there are many available. Generally, do not expect to find anything new here from these assessments; just validation of what you already knew about yourself or that you suspected to be part of your experiences. Typically, such assessments provide a structure and a language for formally communicating these messages. One benefit is perhaps, understanding of your talents in a broader perspective of the overall job market, and how the currently available jobs can provide an outlet for such talents. New job categories are created continually and there are literally thousands of them. Having a ready list and some linkage of this list with your own talent is a good resource for your own insights. Another tip, too: most of these assessments are available free from a government Website that is updated frequently (see below).

Career Assessment

Many tools and assessment instruments are available for career targeting and planning. Strong Interest Inventory instruments can provide a solid, dependable, career-planning tool. The Strong Inventory measures participant's interests in a broad range of occupations, work activities, leisure activities, and school subjects. Its validity and reliability far exceed those of any other interest inventory. There is a family of Strong/career planning tools commercially available. These tools should be used to help those making a career decision, including:

- Those considering a career change
- Employees seeking more satisfying work within an organization
- Students exploring career options
- Organizations looking to retain star performers and key staff
- Midlife and older adults planning their retirement

A summary of various Strong-based tools is listed on http://www.cpp.com.

Another Website, managed by the U.S. government, is http://www.onetcenter.org, which provides free career assessments.

Personality Testing

There are many tools available for personality tests. One can get immersed in this pursuit and end up getting confused at the end. A simple and proven test instrument, however, is presented here. It is quick, inexpensive, widely available, well understood, and widely applied, so if you ask someone within your circle what Type they were, more than likely you would get a response. This is the Myers-Briggs Type test.

Myers-Briggs Type Testing

The MBTI® is the most widely used personality-typing instrument presently in use. It is provided in several different languages and has been proven to be statistically valid and reliable. Many corporations, universities, governmental agencies, and the military use it to enhance team performance, communications, and organizational development. Individuals also use it to better understand their behavior and ability to interface with members of their family or teams.

The MBTI® was developed at Stanford University in the early '30s by the mother and daughter combination of Isabel Myers and Katherine Briggs in an effort to operationalize the theories of the renowned psychiatrist Karl Jung (*Uyng*). It was used successfully during World War II in placing civilians in jobs required by the war effort. It has since been revised several times and is constantly being tested for validity and reliability. There is a whole industry based on this theory and how it is practiced. The instrument itself addresses an individual's preference for *four* personality traits.

The first acknowledges the individual's preference for Extraversion or Introversion. This dichotomy indicates how individuals view the world around them and whether they are energized by others and their surroundings or prefer to address the inner world of ideas and concepts. Being Introverted is different from being shy, which is a different quality; there can be shy Extraverts. Remember this is just a preference, not an either or. Everyone has a varying degree of both. In fact, this shading applies to all four traits.

The second dichotomy considers how individuals take in data or information. This can be either through the concrete method of Sensing (looking at data or using analytical means) or the more abstract method of Intuition. Differences between individuals in this area can create significant problems regarding how reality is viewed and, consequently, how individuals view each other.

The third dichotomy is the only one that is affected by the individual's *gender*. It indicates how the individual uses information in making decisions. The more logical and objective method is referred to as the Thinking function and is preferred by 60 percent of males. The more value related and subjective method is referred to as Feeling and is preferred by 60 percent of women. These differences can create significant communication difficulties at home and at work and understanding this decision-making process can greatly enhance the functioning of an organization or family unit.

Finally, the Judging/Perceiving attitudes indicate how an individual organizes and operates in the outside world. This dichotomy is usually the easiest one to spot if you are Type watching. The Judging type will be systematic and decisive, while the Perceiving type will be noncommittal and open-ended. They like to decide at the absolute last minute! Differences in the way we conduct our lives can be quite annoying to those of the opposite attitude and need to be understood.

Each of the four attributes are independent of the others. These are determined by a self-administered test that has been validated over millions of samples and that has been refined and made more reliable over the past 50 plus years.

Why is the Type important in a job-search situation? For one, it dictates your approach to the job search. Job search is an activity that primarily involves dealing with the outside world and people in that world. Psychological Type plays a profound role in determining approaches that are likely to work for a job seeker. There are 16 MBTI® Types based on the four combinations of each type randomly grouped together. These types are shown in Table-2. While details of each type can be found in many sources, this discussion is limited to how each group of attributes influences your job-search approach.

Whether you are an Introvert or Extravert, you have "Extraverted functions," and these are very important during job interviews. For Introverts, these functions are auxiliary, and less important aspect of their conscious personality. Reasons for this include:

- The reason for outward-focused activity in job search.

- The statistical prevalence of Extraverts in our society, resulting is what is come to be known as a "Western Extravert Bias."

- The need for communication and interaction as core job-search tools. While our introverted forms of communication can play some role, these tend to be relegated to second place in the job-search process.

In the table below the letters representing each dichotomy appear in groups of four, and what each letter means is summarized here for ready reference. Taking only one of the four letters, in groups of four, make up the 16 Types listed below:

I/E	Introvert/Extravert	Getting your energy (inwardly or outwardly)
N/S	Intuitive/Sensing	Getting your information (intuition or from sensing)
T/F	Thinking/Feeling	Making decisions (mind or heart)
J/P	Judging/Perceiving	Individual's world-view (black/white or shades of gray)

ISTJ	ISFJ	INFJ	INTJ
ISTP	ISFP	INFP	INTP
ESTP	ESFP	ENFP	ENTP
ESTJ	ESFJ	ENFJ	ENTJ

Table-2: The 16 MBTI Types

Career Transition Styles

How different Types handle their transition process is largely driven by their makeup. Since looking for a job is an Extraverted activity, extraverted styles dominate behaviors. Also, certain jobs require certain personality characteristics to be done well. A mismatch there can result in much grief for both the employer and the employee. Therefore, your ability to understand this match is critical in your acing the interview and managing the selection process.

Job search involves Extraverted activities. Even though one may have a Introverted type personality dominant in their makeup, the Extraverted attributes become auxiliary to that person. For example "Perceiving" is an extraverted (outward-directed) category because it has to do with how you interact with the outside world. One can perceive either by Sensing or by Intuiting. Same holds for Judging, which can be based on Thinking or Feeling. Thus there are four auxiliary characteristics that are present in any person as shown here, along with their "themes":

SP   "Ready, Fire, Aim."
NP   "Look at all the jobs out there; I am overwhelmed."
TJ   "Here's what I can do for you; everything must close."
FJ   "We can be good together; I like you, what's with you?"

The following is a brief description of each of the four styles; see also Table-3 on the next page:

SP Style: This style is driven by perceptions formed by data-driven activity. The focus is on taking in, looking at, and wanting data. S types look at raw data, form opinions, and perceive the outside world based on that intake. Since there are an infinitude of possibilities with the data flowing in, SPs often get overwhelmed and react by rationalizing that even if they hit a few of the targets with their "shot gun" they will land soon. So they engage in wanton activity: sending countless résumés, calling every possible lead, going to every job fair just to name a few possibilities. One antidote for SPs, then, is to plan, strategize, be selective, and take some risks.

NP Style: If SPs are mired in data, NPs are sure of their own insights! Intuitive types abhor structures and they take great pride in their ability to synthesize something from nothing—their own intuition. They see things that often simply may not exist. They will pursue opportunities and wonder why no one is responding to their "insights." This is further exacerbated if they are also language limited or poor communicators. N types are particularly poor at teaming and sharing a view with others; they have a hard time following the "pack." NPs tend to care less about their appearance and social norms, so they are at a disadvantage in social and corporate surroundings. Those pushing the far side of 50 can look older than they really are for this reason. So, if an older NP wants to go looking for a job and get ready for an interview they should care about their appearance and social behaviors.

TJ Style: TJs are thinkers. They are at the core of the corporate world's executive cadre. The need for logical reasoning and closure is so dear to these Types that they find it difficult to deal with the FP types. Their focus makes TJ blind to people who factor in every thing they pursue. TJs are poor at small talk or getting to know the person who is interviewing them; they want to get right to the point. They see people as a means to an end—their ends!

FJ: FJs are excellent relationship builders. Their networks are large and productive. Seeking harmony can be to the detriment of this Type, so they have to learn to manage that. You do not have to like everyone who comes across your path in the job-search campaign. Sometimes functional relationship can get you by. Some times F (harmony) can conflict with J (closure) in a relationship, so FJs have to learn to live with "enforced agreement." One strategy FJs can use to favorably impress their interviewers is to show solid logic and an ability to draw conclusions without much rambling and digression. Since the J aspect drives for closure, being aware of the other person's Type can help.

Table-3: Transition Styles for Four Categories (Note your Type. Look for the two letters in it in the Category column below.)

Category	Transition Style	Behaviors	Antidote	Comments
SP (Sensing/Perceiving)	Bias to action: Just Do It	Respond to raw data; look for more data; little planning; action without closures; ISTPs are more likely to search the Internet than network	Look for patterns; form strategy; form theories, think before acting; review results, learn. Form structure for closing open items; create self accountability	Before getting into action, prepare a plan on how you are going to get the most from each step, a planning step.
NP (Intuitive/Perceiving)	Anything goes with anything	Aversion to traditional structures; desultory habits; lack of follow-through, forgetful. In tough job market "an absent-minded professor" is a liability.	Invoke your SJ style for structure and reality. Recognize that others do not share your "insights"; be patient with those who are more "S" than you	Solving problems that others do not see is a typical NP trait. If you must solve a problem, make sure it is recognized first.
TJ (Thinking/Judging)	Executive outlook	Plan and execute transition; goal-driven; people blindness; no subjective values; controlling. "Black or white" outlook; feelings have no place	Know when to let go; seek out feeling and show sensitivity to people issues; relax; hiring is a people process.	TJs tend to connect well with higher-ups because of ethos. Remember, though, that your hiring manager is the one you have to report to!
FJ (Feeling/Perceiving)	Relationships driven	Easy networking; more tactical, less strategic; can take the feeling aspect too far and create discomfort with those who are ISTJs in the interview chain	Think strategy; logic; manager assertiveness; temper your people connection with being detached in getting too close to others too early	FJs do well in people jobs as customer relations, HR, training, front-desk. Leverage these attributes if you are seeking such opportunities.

Type: Practice Exercises

Exercises based on Types:

You are an NP. What is your normal approach to your different steps of the job search and how would you increase the effectiveness of your campaign if you knew this?

You are an SP. What is your normal approach to your different steps of the job search and how would you increase the effectiveness of your campaign if you knew this?

You are a TJ. What is your normal approach to your different steps of the job search and how would you increase the effectiveness of your campaign if you knew this?

You are an FJ. What is your normal approach to your different steps of the job search and how would you increase the effectiveness of your campaign if you knew this?

Summary Key-1: Getting With the Program

This rather long chapter covers many foundational topics critical to the success of a job-search campaign as well as the career management process. In fact, internalizing what is presented here can be a life skill that can help in any transition, not just a career transition! At its core, it prepares you to understand the most fundamental factors common to any transition. Mastering what is presented here can make the difference between running a mediocre job-search campaign and a well-organized one that is sustainable in any job market and economy.

- Looking for a job, either when you are laid off or in any other situation, is a transition and must be approached with a process that can be managed to provide the outcome you desire. During a transition your life is changing and not ending!

- A transition is a life's journey that can be *planned* for by reaching the right destination. This journey can be made adventuresome with some risk-taking and following proven methods.

- Recognize your own fear factor and work diligently to rid it. When you wear your fear others can see it, while you cannot.

- The emotional price you pay during your transition (any of life's transitions) is proportional to your own resistance to change and inversely to your resilience.

- Resilience is your ability to bounce back in an adverse situation and function at your full potential.

- In your interactions with others you release two chemicals within your own body—endorphins (good) and adrenaline (bad). The same chemicals are induced in those you interact with and it is these chemicals that dictate how you come across to them. You can manage which ones you want to release, both in you and in others.

- Remember What Goes Around Comes Around: WGACA! People may mistreat you during this critical period in your life. They will get their just deserts, but you must manage yours on your own!

- The Change Curve shows how you can transition faster and with minimal pain and suffering. Practice the coping strategies. Five (of eight; see Index) tools that will help you accelerate transition are presented in this Key. The remaining tools appear later.

- Getting organized, physically and mentally are critical to launching and sustaining an effective campaign. Physical organization includes your workspace and arrangements, while mental organization includes your attitude and expectations. Develop a disciplined approach to your work.

- Career assessment and personality testing are some tools available for those who want to better understand their preferences. Myers Briggs® Typing tool is useful in understanding your own social style during your job search and how you use that knowledge to manage your own behavior.

This chapter has six exercises to help accelerate the change process and make the transition easier.

Key-2: Starting At the Start

"We aim above the mark to hit the mark."

—Ralph Waldo Emerson (1803–1882)

Introduction

This Key is about how to get your job-search campaign going. The approach presented here is for *any* job market. A bull market, where everyone is hiring and there are more jobs than available resources, can seduce many to take the easy route and grab what comes their way. Even in such a market, following what is presented here can give you an edge, resulting in a better outcome. In a bear job market, what is presented here can make the difference between getting a mediocre job and a long wait, to getting your dream job much faster.

There are 14 categories of those in career transition looking for a change:

1. Those about to be unemployed

2. Those on notice with limited time to find something within their own organization

3. Just out of work

4. Out of work for a while and looking

5. Employed (unhappily) and looking for a change

6. Employed, doing well, but feel lost

7. Work-Visa holders (H1-B)

8. Re-entering the workforce because of a need

9. Have never worked and feel out of touch, but now must earn a living

10. Worked in another country and now looking here for opportunities

11. Worked as a consultant in the past and now looking for a full-time position

12. Want to do something on your own

13. Fresh graduates

14. Coming out of retirement

For those who fall into the last category, reading this material, especially the first part in this Key, will help through the initial transition and for preparing a plan of action. Reading the rest of the book will help with different ideas to make this plan more actionable.

Presenting these categories does not imply that job seekers are not unique. They are, and each one has specific needs. However, at a *macro* level these needs can be aggregated for each category, and then, once the preliminaries are dealt with, as they are presented here, more specific needs can be identified as they are presented in later chapters to customize each campaign.

Each of the 14 categories spells a characteristic that requires a different approach to a job-search campaign. Why? Mainly because the factors that drive a campaign are comprised of ingredients that have different points of focus. For example, someone just out of work has a good sense of what is happening in the job market more than someone who has never worked. So, the former would have some familiarity with how to do a quick assessment of where the jobs and opportunities are, whereas the latter needs to first have some sense of what they are good at or want to do. A secretary (a now dated term deliberately used to show when this person last knew the job market) and an administrator (Administrative Assistant) in today's workforce are two different entities in many ways. So, someone who wants to go back as a "secretary" needs to learn new skills, understand today's market, and then create materials that position them correctly for their campaign.

Regardless to which category a job seeker belongs, the first step in moving ahead is getting ready!

♠ Getting Ready

The first step after coming to grips with having to look for a job, regardless of why, is to make a plan for moving ahead. Inform as many people of your new status as "actively looking for opportunities," as is possible and as quickly as possible after your "grieving." This applies more for those who have lost their jobs than those who are looking because they are searching for better opportunities (categories 5 and 6). In this latter case discretion is the watchword, as we shall see in the detailed discussion for this group of job seekers. For those out of work and looking, informing others hastens getting out of the denial state. Being positive and keeping good humor takes special energy and disposition in this state, but it can be a learned behavior and it is the best strategy during this transition.

Once this burden of "secrecy and shame" is lifted, it is much easier to solicit help from others to move ahead. Your support group may be instrumental in giving helpful input in a variety of areas, including contacts for financial advisors, career counselors, job leads, and hiring managers. Thank them for their concern and input. When you do use their input—and even if you don't immediately find it useful—thank them in some special way so that they remember it. This etiquette needs to be extended to all those who provide you this support, even your closest friends and relatives, to ensure that the flow of this goodwill continues. See Key-7: Job-Search Etiquette, for more on this topic.

At this point surveying the job market by visiting more popular job boards on the Web can be insightful. The next step is to identify which job families are worth targeting. A job family is a group of jobs that share the same or nearly the same competencies or has many common skill requirements.

Writing different résumés of two or three flavors to address targeting multiple job families is covered in a latter section (See Key-3: Multiple-position Résumés).

Regardless of which category a job seeker belongs to, the following steps are necessary for getting ready to move on with the search:

- **Emotionally accepting** the situation and thinking positively to move ahead,

- **Informing** all those around you that you are now looking for new opportunities,

- **Survival planning** for a realistic period during which your cash flow may be limited and fortifying your financial needs with lines of credit when the going is still good,

- **Compiling a list** of all those who can help you in your search and reconnecting,

- **Searching** for open positions on job boards and then forming a plan of action,

- **Understanding** what is happening to jobs (see Key-3 Leveraging Job Trends),

- **Expanding** your targets by resorting to unconventional approaches (Key-4)),

- **Preparing a résumé** for each category of targets (typically three flavors); Key-3,

- **Physical preparations** to get things organized so that you can show your readiness for the job search. These include getting an interview wardrobe, getting your car ready and reliable, organizing so that if you need someone to take care of the household needs as watching your child, infirm, or looking after a pet while you may be out and about, especially for an interview.

Now, having learned these basics about how to get situated for a successful job search, let us focus on the 14 categories of job seekers and identify what needs to be the specific process and strategy for each one.

If You Are About to be Unemployed

Depending on each individual situation, those about to be laid off face two immediate challenges even before getting organized to move on. They are described in the following two sections.

♠ Dealing with the Loss

If you were just notified of being laid-off, you need to accept the news and must deal with your loss, even though you still may have a job. You may have your job from that point on for anywhere between a few minutes (you may be escorted out immediately upon notification) to several months. In either case you are technically out of work. Legally you are not terminated until you can no longer go back to your place of work, but still you are out of a job. No matter how long you had been anticipating this, or especially if this came as a total surprise, there is a degree of shock for which few are prepared when it actually happens.

Some companies routinely let go a percentage of their "lowest ranking" employees (see "The Under-Performer Syndrome" below). Others announce that businesses that are not meeting financial performance goals, regardless of the talent that is staffing them, will be closed and affected people laid off. Although both categories of out-of-work job seekers now have to deal with finding themselves a new job, their circumstances are different, and how they feel about the new status will be colored by their own frame of mind. This will show in the way they project themselves: the language they use, the attitude they wear, and the confidence with which they move forward. The window that they choose to view the world now lets the world see them through that very window. This is why it is critical to get past this state of mind and start behaving positively as soon as one is able.

Burning Your Bridges

After learning of the impending unemployment, many get emotionally distressed. In such a state it is difficult to be rational and think logically through the best course of action that can protect long-term prospects and success. Many, in a fit of pique, hastily react negatively to what has just happened to them and take actions that create more problems downstream for their own success. Some make assumptions about who might have conspired for their being out of work. Based on these assumptions, they hastily act in a way that compromises their relationships with the very people who might have come to their future aid had they been more diplomatic.

There is a subtle and interesting human dynamic at play here that most do not recognize or use to their advantage: If someone has indeed done you harm and was the cause of your grief, your alienating that person is exactly the wrong move. Getting back at them directly in ill will and humor would be a wrong move. Why? If that person has, indeed, caused your termination in an underhanded way, the guilt that person carries may be a factor in your favor. This may sound counterintuitive, but what is at play here is the psychology of guilt. Now, if the need comes for that person to do something for you, they might go out of their way to be helpful and kind to you, since they no longer see you as a threat. If you still feel revengeful then you must wait for an opportunity to return in kind at a later time. Remember the law of Universal Giving (WGACA story in Key-1). Do not waste your valuable time and energy in the moment on negative people.

Bottom line: never burn your bridges and relationships in which you have invested your lifetime in a moment of irrationality. Most terminations and situations surrounding them are irreversible. Do not compound your misfortune by emotionally reacting to a perceived injustice. Even if the action seems perfectly rational in the moment, defer the impulse until you compose yourself and think of its consequences. When in doubt *avoid* attacking or trashing others.

The "Under-Performer" Syndrome

It is particularly difficult for those who are coming out of organizations that lay off their "low performing" employees. In such organizations even if those that are laid off for other reasons—as can happen if a business is closing because of market conditions, or a reorganization—feel that they, too, are now branded as "low performing!" This self-opinion further compounds the negativity around a job loss.

The best way to overcome this feeling of perceived inadequacy in the face of personal defeat is to be reassured by acknowledging that most performance-measurement systems, even in well-managed organizations, are highly political, arbitrary, inconsistent, and subjective. This is why when positioning for job searching, it is a good idea to state that whatever you do, *you* consider yourself tops—as opposed to stating how you were *ranked*. The other sugges-tion here, too, is not to blame anyone or try to explain why you were not "ranked" at the top or let go ("They didn't know what they were doing").

Those on Notice

Often, larger companies that are downsizing are putting employees on notice and giving them a fixed amount of time to find suitable positions from within. During this period, typically three months, employees on notice can scour the company's internal postings to see what is appropriate for them to pursue. Then they contact the respective hiring manager and present their cre-dentials for a face-to-face interview, holding high hopes that they will be selected to continue their employment. Often these hopes are illusory.

The False-Hopes syndrome

Those who have limited time to find alternate positions within their com-pany hold out the hope for being offered something worthwhile. This belief is further fortified by their belief that their tenure with their company would give them priority and special consideration. As a result, they keep pursuing oppor-tunity after opportunity within their own company during this "grace" period. Familiarity with their own organization leads them to believe that their tenure should be enough for their potential hiring managers to be fully aware of their credentials and value, and that their marketing of themselves should be limited to making a few phone calls. Many keep going back to their office to find something useful to do rather than focusing on their own plan to launch a viable campaign. They fully expect to be hired back and continue their employment uninterrupted!

Nothing could be further from the truth. The hiring managers are looking to fill open positions with the best candidate and not the most available or familiar. Invariably, if hiring managers do not find exceptional candidates, they wait until they are able to open the position for outside applicants. In this case you have lost a golden opportunity to present yourself in a favorable way to the hiring manager who might have looked at your candidacy with greater weight if it were presented more professionally, in a more compelling way, and with a bit of a more studied campaign. The insidious effect of holding out hope that you would be rehired is that once the "grace" period is over, you have to launch a more serious campaign from the start anyway for the outside job market. Often, this gets harder after three months of holding false hopes and rejec-tions. More often than not these interviews are given, if at all, more out of courtesy than anything else.

A word of advice: always enter the "grace" period following the notification as a period where you have a renewed chance to make an impression with the hiring managers *within your own company*. This effort in no way should be underestimated because you are now looking from within your own familiar ground. Always prepare as if this were a competitive and open *outside* position, and, depending on circumstances ("low ranking" for instance) for being on notice as an opportunity with minimum chances of success. Most companies show a success rate of "rehiring" within the grace period of less than 10 percent. This means that 90 percent of the positions were filled with candidates from the open market, even when their skills posted on the job requisition were identical to the ones for candidates who were notified and were given the grace period.

The other indignity faced by those given the grace period is that many times hiring managers set up interviews with anxious candidates and do not show up for them. They rationalize that the interviewees are inside the company and have nothing to do and should understand busy managers being suddenly unavailable. If this happens more than a couple of times, complain to the HR recruiter and decide if you really care to hold out further hopes of being "rehired" by your own company.

Just Out of Work

Surprisingly, this category applies to both, those notified and immediately terminated and those continuing for a period after notification. Each one is briefly discussed below.

Out of Work and Terminated

Some companies do not believe in waiting to terminate immediately upon notification. In fact, some are so hasty in the way they remove employees, that employees get invited to a group meeting. Someone remotely familiar stands up and announces that they are all now no longer employees of the company, and are escorted out with a packet in their hands, giving details of their severance. This abrupt process leaves everyone in shock, especially those who had no clue that this was coming.

Out of Work, Awaiting Termination

Some companies notify their employees of the impending termination and let them continue coming to work for a period of time. Sometimes this period can be as much as three months. This, in essence, is being out of work with an agonizing period of being allowed to go back to place of "work" and finding some common ground with those who are still employed there. The sooner you reconcile to the reality of being out of work and stop going to "work" pretending that everything is normal, the better off you are moving ahead.

Like all major changes, the fear of the unknown is a substantial factor and hurdle in coping with unemployment. When we lose our job, we may experience a "death" similar to someone who is close to us passing away. Some even characterize this loss as a near-death experience when they rely on their jobs so deeply, well beyond their financial needs. The grieving process, as a result, varies from person to person but must be dealt with by first becoming aware of it by getting out of the denial state. To keep going back to work, even when you know you have no job there and staying there merely because you are allowed to, prolong the denial stage. Actively making arrangements for alternate employment is the best antidote for this temptation.

Out of Work for a While and Looking

If you have been out of work for a while and looking, it is easy to start getting discouraged after a few months. As this period of inability to generate action and move ahead approaches the first anniversary of being out of work in a tough market, it is easy to slide into a funk. A feeling of despair, hopelessness, and defeat can often follow this. With these feelings, it gets progressively harder to reenergize the job-search campaign and redirect it or find a new approach to pursue with any conviction.

And yet, that is what is needed to galvanize the job search with action, new energy, and a new direction. It is easy to slide into an approach to the job search that incrementally leads to feckless efforts by developing hopes that were unrealistic to start with. Metaphorically, it is akin to turning up the gain or volume on a piece of music that is bad to start with; it does not get better that way. Thus when things do not produce results over a period of time, merely increasing the activity such as sending more résumés, will not generally work. And, why does this happen?

♠ Switching from a Sprint to a Marathon

If the original campaign was started with a willy-nilly approach followed by ongoing tweaking over a period of time, then a less than positive outcome should not be a surprise. You need to attack the job-search campaign with earnest from the get go. One way to approach this is to treat it more like a marathon than a sprint after giving it a fair chance. Why? Because if the campaign does not result in the desired outcome within a reasonable time, say three months in a tough job market, you need to buckle up for the long and rough ride. This is why a patchwork résumé and a weak campaign are not a good way to start a job search, especially in a tough market or a deteriorating economy. With a willy-nilly approach, continued rejection or inaction result in increasingly frustrating experiences. These defeats cause diffidence in your ongoing efforts, which create more defeats, triggering a vicious cycle. If you are financially limited, the impact of this train of events is further exacerbated. Even with adequate finances, this transition can be challenging at the emotional level alone.

This is why for those whose finances do not provide them the staying power necessary for a marathon campaign, it is all the more critical to have spent the time getting the campaign on the right footing from the get go, especially in a tough job market. Ironically, those with constrained finances try to shorten their campaign by hastening the *front-end process*—cobbling together a résumé, haphazardly sending it out even though it is not presentable, and without a marketing plan, and resorting to a shotgun approach, just to get things going, as if in a panic. Such a start takes forever to result in a meaningful outcome, even when the job market is reasonably good. Launching a job search with fits and starts make the overall campaign that much more stressful and feckless. Some even pay for résumé-blaster services that send out their résumés by the thousands, just to get the word out. This is counterproductive. Most recruiters and employers simply delete such unsolicited blasts. This is why it is critical to take the time to get the campaign properly in order and vet it before launching, especially when one's financial horizon is limited.

The other strategy, too, might be to ramp up a campaign with a deliberate plan so that learning occurs as early inputs provide actionable feedback to improve ongoing messages. Additionally, a properly organized campaign laid on a solid foundation makes it easy to switch from a sprint to a marathon.

How to regroup if one has already started their campaign in a less than desirable way and has now come to realize that it is floundering after several months into it? The first step is to recognize what is happening: it can be called trying to solve a management problem with a technical solution.

♠ Solving a Management Problem with a Technical Approach

When a campaign is weltering in setbacks and defeats and appears stuck without any response, the first step is to recognize that this is happening. The second is to take immediate action to negate its effect and recover from it. It is easy to keep hoping that something would change by working harder or tweaking here and there. The wrong thing to do is to translate defeats and frustrations to anger and anger into irrational behavior, and then into fear. This is a never-ending cycle that spirals into a doomed campaign.

In the management lexicon, there is a principle that is used in solving a problem and taking action. That principle is based on solving a given problem using the proper strategy. To solve a management problem, no amount of technical expertise can come to its rescue; management skills and not technical talent must solve it. A technical approach in this case is akin to incremental changes to an already doomed campaign. The management approach is to change the fundamental nature of the campaign and then march ahead.

There is a famous quote of Einstein's that captures the spirit of what is presented in this paragraph: *"Significant problems of today cannot be solved by applying the same level of thinking as when we created them."* This quote also appears at the heading of Key-1: Getting with the Program. The significant problem in this context is that all the past actions have been to no avail. The first thing to do, then, is to start from the beginning and adopt a radically different approach. The best place to start this is to review the whole campaign, its lessons, and extract as much learning from it as is objectively possible to fold it into the next generation of *different* actions. Do not engage in actions that merely increase the speed with which you do the wrong things; things that you learned from your doomed efforts.

The first step in reenergizing the campaign, then, is to identify what jobs are realistically within your reach. For this, starting fresh and compiling a list of jobs that appear within your past experience, talents, and objective are beginnings. It is also a good idea to look at the trends to see what has happened to the jobs in a particular job family, so that you can extrapolate what the outlook is over the next few months or years. (See Key-3: Presenting Yourself; Leveraging Job Trends.)

Once the correct job is identified, the next step is to ensure that the résumé is positioned for that job and provides a competitive advantage in the market. After this is done the remaining actions are similar to the sequence listed in the previous section except that there are some additional factors. The following steps are recommended to *reenergize* a tired campaign.

- **Emotionally accepting** that things need to change and then thinking positively to move ahead with renewed energy, despite past rejections,
- **Identifying patterns** that frustrate moving on to next steps in the job search and replacing them with behaviors that create meaningful action,
- **Reconnecting** with all those around you and communicating to them that you are still looking for new opportunities,
- **Revisiting the list** of all those who can help you in your search and reconnecting with positive and optimistic perspectives. Communicate to them what is now different,

- **Searching** for open positions on job boards and then forming a dynamic plan of action; constantly making adjustments to the message and tactics based on a plan,

- **Developing** an understanding of what is happening to the job market (trends); changing the message in the résumés and cover letters to reflect this understanding *individually,*

- **Positively and creatively** listing the preceding period (out of work) on the résumé as when you were engaged as a consultant, volunteer, or part-time employee,

- **Expanding your targets** by resorting to transformational approaches with even more commitment (see Key-4: Unconventional Approaches),

- **Preparing your résumé** for each category of targets and then fortifying each transmittal with a well-researched and highly targeted cover letter (see Key-3 and Key-4),

- Increasing overall reliance on **networking** and spending more efforts on network-related activities and responses than in the past,

- Being more open to **consulting,** part-time, and ad-hoc assignments to generate engagements even though they may be short-lived and ill paid,

- Being more open to **flexible assignments** where a job requires a broader skill-set not normally contemplated and perhaps at a salary below what was considered "normal,"

- **Developing an alternate trade** or ability to generate work that pays, while simultaneously looking for a job within your career,

- **Seeking professional help** by getting in touch with reputable professionals in the career management field, screening them for a match and then making a small investment in their services.

One approach to overcome the feeling of inaction and to move from a sprint to a marathon is to first map out a portfolio of skills that are in ready demand for a trade job. These skills can generate some relief in your ability to generate quick income by engaging in activities that harness them while continuing to look for jobs within your career. By being able to generate income while continuing to look within the main career, one is able to do more selective targeting and allow more time to land a job in a difficult economy. This is particularly fruitful when one or more of the skills stem from natural gifts or trades.

In one instance, one client, a software program manager, was skilled at remodeling kitchens and redoing residential electrical wiring. So, starting with his own neighbors and friends, he first moonlighted with small jobs—his regular "job" was to look for his career job—earning some income in the process. Soon, he was able to generate enough action to allow him to sustain his regular lifestyle and continue to look for work with confidence and a positive attitude. He was able to manage the trade work on the weekends and other times so that the interference from this activity was minimal in his efforts to find a job during weekdays. He soon landed at a job that engaged him well. See section under Résumé "Dos and Don'ts" item #5 in Key-3: Presenting Yourself.

Another approach to looking at the entire campaign to evaluate what might be done differently is to revisit "My Truth!" discussed in Key-1. Going back to the statement used in Tool-4 in that Key can help shed some light on whether you are running an authentic campaign.

If You are (Unhappily) Employed and Looking for Change

This discussion is presented for the following categories of changes:

➢ Change within the same company

➢ Going outside, but within the same industry

➢ Going outside, but to a different industry

In a tough economy, companies decide their future quarter-by-quarter. With the continuing trend of outsourcing and off-shoring, there is increasing pressure on those who form the core workforce of any company. This is why more and more are working extra hours just to stay off the "radar" in a tough economy.

Surveys conducted in tough times indicate that as many as 80 percent of the employees are unhappy enough to consider leaving their current job. This is despite their not knowing where they might be headed. Many feel under appreciated, overworked, and stuck in dead-end jobs.

This working environment forces many already employed to pursue other opportunities but they are scared to overtly do this. Yet another reason is that they are being worked so hard that they are exhausted from that alone, unable to pursue anything else for want of time and energy.

Whatever the reason, whatever the motivation, and whatever the situation, in uncertain times more people want to change than when times are good. This is perverse!

For those considering a change in tough times or even otherwise the following checklist can provide guidance:

- ✓ **Chose the company first, job second:** Decide first where you want to be working and then chose opportunities that are available, rather than getting a "better position" at a company that may turn out to be a "sweat shop." Being selective about where you work has far more impact on your own well being, long-term, than any salary increase. The added stress of a worse environment is never worth the extra money. Besides, never leave a job out of spite to get at the current employer and land in a situation where you may be worse off. Only you end up being punished by this move.

- ✓ **Explore intra-company transfer:** If you have tenure with the current employer and are unhappy, try to relocate within the same organization if possible. This change may revitalize you without starting over in an uncertain situation, particularly in a down economy! For tenured employees, this also protects their vesting.

- ✓ **Research appropriate opportunities:** After making a list of companies to work for, look for what opportunities appear appropriate to be making the move and taking the risk. Do not assume that your looking around will remain secret beyond a certain period. This may merely accelerate your departure from the company and you may prematurely end up being out of work, just because of the way you handled the job change.

- ✓ **Move up and not sideways or down:** Once the target job is identified—try moving ahead and not down on your career path when seeking a change—make your résumé to position yourself for that opportunity and others like it.

- ✓ **Find people you know in target companies** to present you to the potential hiring managers. Sometimes finding a contingent recruiter might be a good idea. Even in tough times, some companies do retained searches. If your position is one of those that are in demand at the time you are seeking a change, contact reputable retained search firms and position yourself from that vantage point. See Key-4 for discussion on Working with Third Parties to understand how contingent and retained recruiters work.

- ✓ **Research companies** that interest you and then send a well-crafted letter to someone high up to make your case, *without* your résumé! Ask for the recipient to meet with you to discuss this further. See how this can be done by reading Key-4: Marketing the Product—You!

✓ **Go in the stealth mode:** When the interest of the target employer gets heated up and you start being away from your current employer, handle your absence, phone calls, and messages with discretion. If the word leaks out that you are looking, all of a sudden you may be out of work. This may compromise your ongoing efforts to land the new job—employers are typically more interested in pursuing those who have jobs, and not those who don't.

✓ **Make yourself visible:** This may be paradoxical to "going in the stealth mode" from above. It is not. Here the reference is to becoming professionally more visible in the industry forums. Find out where your prospect companies are participating. See if your own organization will sponsor you to participate, attend, or otherwise let you in on the action. Present papers, volunteer, or take some role at these gatherings. If you make a mark, you may get naturally closer to someone from the target company who may seek you out. Let them chase you if you can arrange that!

✓ **Prepare a plan and stick to it.** This plan must include actions, timetables, and enough details to force you to maintain a certain level of active work on the job-seeking front. The reason for this approach is that it is easy to fall into the trap of getting consumed by your current job. See Key-1: Getting Organized.

✓ **Be assertive *and* patient:** Once discussions begin, conclude them with great finesse and alacrity. Stay firm, make your points and wait. If you play it cool and show patience, you will surprise yourself on how well this all works. In your discussions and throughout the process, do not betray your unhappiness with the current employer, find some plausible reason why you are seeking a change and stick with it. Do not bring into discussions your current employer in a disparaging manner.

✓ **Seek advice of a professional career counselor** to help you through the transition in getting your résumé ready, polishing up on the interviewing skills and all other job-search related matters. At times, you may feel torn in your loyalties (see below).

✓ **Take some time off** if you cannot get away from your demanding boss to organize the initial part of your campaign. Having to work hard and long hours can be an excuse for not getting started and focused on a campaign. Talk to your family about allowing you some time to be "home" on vacation and help and support you in the organization of a campaign.

Some, who are looking for a change while holding a job, still feel as though they are betraying trust by looking around. In today's mercenary climate, you should look after your own welfare, giving full measure of your job commitment to the current employer, nothing more. Never fall in love with a *company*; it cannot love you back!

Within the Same Company

There are many benefits to staying in the same company when times are tough. For one, established seniority in that company is protected and there are benefits to be derived from that long term. If a particular place within a company is problematic, then one way to find some comfort is to seek a change where things might be different.

Regardless of the reason, it is a good idea to keep an open eye for a deteriorating situation. We have our own radars that allow us to detect this in advance. This is why waiting for things to improve once something takes its course in such situations is not a good move if you are already thinking of a change. Waiting for the right thing to happen merely creates increased competition.

Make your résumé as if you are going to look for a job outside the company. Start making discreet enquiries about opportunities within the company, especially if the company is a large one with many operations spread out geographically. Explore to see if the company is expanding in any area that interests you, even though the general economy is shrinking. Be the first to be in line for such opportunities. It might even be worth your while to propose such ventures to the right managers.

There is yet one more reason for leveraging your tenure in your own company that is subtler than is apparent to some. This is further presented in more detail in this Key: Employed, Doing Well, but Feel Lost.

The following list summarizes your actions for an intra-company opportunity:

1. If you are disillusioned within your operations, trust your instincts and move on to finding something without waiting for things to get better; they usually don't! If the outside climate is also deteriorating—as the economy—do not postpone for things to get better. Find an opportunity *within* the existing climate.

2. Decide what you want to do if you stayed in the same company and then look for those areas within the company that afford such positions.

Explore to see if such a position would be a résumé builder or a résumé killer. A résumé builder makes your profile look good as you advance your own career.

3. Make a résumé as if you were looking outside and start checking out what is available so that you have a better sense of the market. Do not hesitate to approach your competitors discreetly, or even through a recruiter.

4. Contact search firms and recruiters for advice and retain one to see if they can place you within the boundaries of your requirements. This can be done in parallel if you are able to keep this process in a stealth mode. This is often hard and the timing of this in the process can be critical.

5. Become visible inside your company so other managers can see you in situations outside your own work environment. Present papers, particpate in shows, attend company events where other mangers are likely to congregate and discuss emerging opportunities.

6. Start reading company's plans carefully and suggest opportunities to your management with constructive ideas. You might be tapped when the management decides to pursue one of these in the near future.

7. Maintain good relationships with your immediate chain of command and let them know that you are looking around for the right opportunity and that it is not a reflection of how you are being treated. Here, make sure that this message is not presented in a disingenuous manner.

8. Keep doing your job well and do not complain, even as things start getting worse.

9. If you are under severe stress in your current job and are looking for a change, set yourself a timeline. Start ratcheting-up your outside search. Staying in the same situation under stress can be detrimental to your health.

10. Develop close relationships with a few you can trust. You need support during this time of change. Be *very* careful whom you tell what you are up to, especially within your own company. This can create more problems and you might be eased out if you go about telling everyone what you are up to!

Outside, but Same Industry

Once you decide to go outside a company where you are working, you need to do things a bit differently than if you were to stay and explore alternate venues within the same company. Having a job at a good company and being in a good standing there certainly helps. The idea is to leverage this into a job in another organization when the going is good. This is why the sooner your "radar" detects something is going in the wrong direction for you either at a personal level or for the entire company or its operations where you are vested, the sooner you need to make your move to protect your position of leverage. The following summary of actions can be used as a guide to start your search process.

➤ Once you have decided to leave your employer make sure that you have good relationships with key people upon your departure. Your references are going to come from your current employer. So, if you need to do any relationship mending to protect this, start doing this early and do this somewhat naturally. Taking someone to lunch or remembering their birthday and taking part in it socially may be a good start.

➤ Make your résumé after ensuring that every claim in it is fully supportable and make sure that it shows your contributions to the key areas where there is general interest outside your company. If you have developed proprietary knowledge that has gone on to become a major factor in your company's success then make sure that it is mentioned specifically. If you were a major player in such a cause, then the industry mavens through your publications, awards, and visibility in the specific community probably already know your name. Never keep quiet about your major contributions and accomplishments. Trumpet them. If you do not blow your own horn someone will use it for a spittoon!

➤ Start aggressively attending industry events for your company. If you are not asked, see if you can wangle your way into such events by doing something on your own as writing a paper or developing a showcase on your own imitative. You will then be more likely to be asked to be a presenter at such events.

➤ When you do attend such events, socialize and find out about companies that you plan to target as your potential employers and find out the key players and get to know them at these events. These are golden opportunities for such connections.

➤ Contact a search firm and let them know what you bring to the party and see if someone there can represent you to the competitor of your company in a way that is ethical and moral. If you have an established name within your industry it makes the job of someone who is representing you much easier and compelling. See in Key-3: A Search Firm or Recruiter and in Key-4: Working with Third Parties

> Talk to the customers, suppliers, and channels of the target company where you want to explore and find out something from them that you can leverage into your cover letter or campaign. Since you are already in the field it is much easier to have access to such information.

> Find out what the target company is pursuing in new initiatives and make a presentation to its management through a cover letter or a message so that it gets an audience. See the letter shown in Key-4: Sample Letters (Unconventional Approaches), specifically the one to Enterprise Computers by Charles Smith, as an example.

> Research the target company's past endeavors where they were not successful and find out why. If the new initiative has a similar flavor remind them in a subtle way that you know why it failed in the past on similar ventures and that you can help them this time. If presented appropriately this can be a key to your success at the target company.

> Ask for an informational interview with a key manager at the target company if your research shows that it is doing something that needs your experience and expertise.

> Do your campaign in a stealth mode, so that you protect your position where you are currently enjoying a good reputation. In tough economic times if the word gets out that you were looking you might not be there long.

♠ Outside, but Different Industry

Going outside the industry is not as difficult as most think. Why? There are many common and transferable skills that can be leveraged into other industries. In fact, many job competencies are industry transparent. Common examples are accounting, finance, human resources, logistics, security, IT (some aspects), program management, and most administrative functions, just to name a few. In addition there are many process-based skills that are even more amenable to cross-industry jobs. For example product development process, customer order entry process, to name a few.

There is also another benefit in doing a cross-industry foray. When one sector of the industry is down and suffering, another one that uses similar skills can be on the upswing. For example when high-tech and IT industry were in a slump starting 2001, many other industries did not feel their ravages. High-tech and IT producers had cut their spending significantly, yet the biotech, healthcare, and service industries continued their momentum because they had the money to fund their growth curve. So, if you were an IT specialist, migrating to any one of these industries could have been to your advantage. You just need to learn some of the transferable skills, as we shall discuss presently.

Transitioning from High-tech to Biotech

With the ongoing outsourcing and off-shoring in the high-tech industry, there is growing interest from those leaving it for entry into biotech. Biotech is perceived as having the same entrepreneurial spirit that the high-tech has had and there is some kindred connection that compels those who are tired of the cyclical nature of the high-tech industry to seriously consider it as a viable and attractive alternative. Much of the biotech industry that makes devices and produces items for human benefit shares its armamentarium with the high-tech world, and that factor alone has much to do for the lure of migration from high-tech to biotech.

There are seven areas in what is generally regarded as "Biotech" industry. They are listed below with brief descriptions of the areas they each cover. More information is available from www.bio.org a Washington D.C. organization that acts as a clearinghouse of all that is biotech. Biological Industries Association (BIO) is an industry group for the entire biotech activity.

1. Pharmaceuticals: drug discovery, disease cures, drug delivery

2. Medical devices: biomedical devices including pace makers to lab instruments

3. Diagnostic equipment: MRI, screening and diagnostic equipment

4. Bioinformatics: an amalgam of biology and IT (integrates computer science, statistics to generate molecular maps of genomes)

5. Life Sciences: cancer research and other health-care matters

6. Healthcare: hospitals, clinics

7. Agra Business: genetically altered foods, wine, cheese

Each area has needs for functions that are common to any business such as IT, HR, training, sales, and marketing. In addition the opportunities for specific functions exists as in project management, software, quality assurance (QA), product development.

Those coming from the high-tech world find two compelling selling features in what they bring to migrate to biotech:

- High-tech brings a more disciplined approach to many biotech jobs stemming from the way many of the processes are done in high-tech,

- Many jobs across the two industries are transferable with some training,

A brief discussion on each of the items is presented here.

During the past decade the high-tech industry has been mutated into a commodities producer. With the pervasive Internet, wireless technology, electronic games, and automotive applications, most high-tech output is directed towards consumer markets. This has forced the industry to adopt practices, processes, and disciplines that routinely allow it to spit out a highly complex consumer products in a matter of months, nine to18 months is typical for high-tech. Biotech, on the other hand, takes much longer to take its products to market. Many of these are driven by regulatory requirements, as the FDA approval, adherence to GMP (Good Manufacturing Practices) and other factors. The fact still remains that biotech still could use some discipline in its processes that high-tech pioneered during the past two decades.

The opportunities in biotech, thus, are for those who can see the connection between such processes in the two industries and are able to exploit that connection to their advantage.

The second factor of transferable skills is applicable not just to biotech but also to any other industry. This is because of many functions inside an organization require skills that are industry transparent as we just discussed earlier. Many academic institutions now offer training in many of these areas so that those looking to make a transfer can seriously consider such opportunities with certifications from such institutions if they are required for a job.

As a community, biotech tends to be a bit parochial on how it takes in "outsiders." In many jobs a PhD is expected, particularly if you're in the mainstream function as drug discovery and clinical trials. But, there are many opportunities that can be captured with same or similar training as one has going into high-tech.

♠ Transitioning from High-tech to Other Industry

The same argument offered in the biotech context applies to the other sectors. As service sector becomes more and more a part of the overall economy, job opportunities will become more and more aligned with the manufacturing and white-collar jobs from other sectors. There will be fewer boundaries in job opportunities between different sectors with time. During the past decade, many high-tech executives migrated to other industries for no other reason than to disseminate the disciplined approach and management rigor of the high-tech to other industries. One high-tech executive migrated to a little known construction material supply company and succeeded in making it a highly visible, profitable industry leader that went on to win the Malcolm Baldrige Quality Award for overall excellence in the early Nineties. The following job categories is a partial list of common areas between the high-tech and other industries:

- General management
- Program management
- Customer support
- Logistics
- Sales
- Marketing
- IT
- Human Resources
- Operations

The key to success in making a switch from high-tech to any other industry is to find the points of leverage in the skill sets and transferable skills so that one can present a compelling value statement when making a cross-industry transfer.

For further discussion on making cross-industry transfer see "Playing Golf with Tiger Woods" in Key-3: Presenting Yourself.

Employed, Doing well, but Feel Lost

There is a significant population of those in the workforce doing well and that has gathered certain momentum in their careers. They have had challenging career assignments, their track record is sovereign, their ambitions high, and yet they feel, looking around and ahead, that they need to do something out of the ordinary to change their career path and pursue other avenues to career growth. Typically, these professionals are in their mid 30s and early 40s. Their vision for themselves is that of a CEO or as someone heading a major business making an impact on the world around them. They also see themselves as being far more capable than those running their own business, starting with their own boss. And, rightfully so!

Typically, these professionals have gone through a variety of early assignments and have done well in them varying from, for example in a high-tech company, product development, consultative sales, product management, to leading major projects. They may even get assigned as a lead to some major account and will continue to do well even in that assignment. Since they were not career sales professionals, they look forward to getting out of this assignment to move on to advance their careers. The problem: they are doing so well selling and managing customers that the company does not see them as anything else! They are too valuable in their current role. If they continue to stay where they are assigned they may stagnate there or leave the company just to find themselves another career path. This, too, gets difficult as their résumé now has sales as their most recent assignment. This dilemma is not faced only by those who end up in sales through a variety of tracks; it is just a case in point and the most common.

Some feel that to break the cycle of getting stuck in an area where they sought an assignment to slake their professional curiosity about it and to round out their careers that they have to preemptively take their career path in their own hands. One such way, as they see it, is to get an advanced degree—an MBA if they already do not have one—and repackage themselves as whomever they choose to become and pursue opportunities outside of their company, once they get that degree. They are even willing to pay their way for the degree, often in thousands or hundred thousand-dollar range.

One reason why pursuing an MBA, or any other degree, is not necessarily a solution to the situation is that, unless you are clear of the path that you wish to pursue *after* the degree, the same cycle can repeat and you are back to where you started, just a few more years older than you were the first time. Pursuing a degree is often an escape rather than a means to advance your career in *some* cases.

There is yet another thought that we presented in a previous section—If You Are (Unhappily) Employed and Looking for Change—and the same is repeated here with even more emphasis. Why? Because of what we already said: you are doing well and have gathered career momentum. Leveraging that momentum in your own company has benefits that are subtler than are apparent to some. When you are looking for an outside opportunity, the scope of what you can pursue is limited by what you have already done. Your accomplishments will be on your résumé, and outsiders will judge your value by your track record more than anything else. Within your own company, however, the story is a bit different. Many, who worked with you, have known you as well as your potential and your ambitions. They will also know you for your drive. These factors cannot be articulated on a résumé or gleaned through your employment intake process. Even sophisticated and rigorous selection assessments lasting a few days, sometimes used as a part of employee intake process, cannot identify these qualities. It is much easier to leverage that personal capital within your own company than with an outside employer. This does not mean that you cannot venture out and get a major jump in your position going out. No! This merely suggests that for all those looking within their own companies underestimate the advantage they have, because of the momentum they have created in their careers.

The following suggestions are offered to those who are at career crossroads and wondering if they should stay in their company or venture out:

> ➤ Let your boss know that although you are doing well in the current assignment you need to establish a timetable to seek another career move within the same company and seek an opportunity to advance your career. Openly discuss the possibilities and explore what can be mapped out. In large organizations this is not only possible, but also very likely. After having an initial discussion with your boss and seeing no action, send a written message (email or memo) so that there is a reason for your boss not to ignore your request.

> ➤ Find a mentor within your own organization. Bosses can be parochial in their visions and may not be able to see the bigger picture for you or the company. Find a mentor in another organization of the company, not your own. With a stellar record this should not be a major challenge.

> ➤ Find and cultivate a mentor outside your own company. This is someone you admire, know, or have worked with in your own career path.

> ➤ Define what you want to do as a next step and find companies that offer those opportunities. More than likely you may find this difficult. Another avenue is deciding which company that you find attractive to advance yourself—based on your research—and decide what you could offer this company. Write a letter with a point of view (POV) to someone in a high position and seek an interview. See in Key-4 Marketing the Product-You! Sample Letters: Unconventional Approaches, specifically the one to New Computers by Charles Smith, as an example.

> ➤ With your good track record, you should be able to do the same (point # 4, above) in your current company. If this succeeds, you may get to head a brand-new operation that you envisaged.

For those who fall in this category of professionals, career transitions can be challenging yet fun and adventuresome pursuits. They often find it particularly difficult to seek out someone who can provide objective input. Doing trial and error can be frustrating, expensive, and off the mark and hence should be avoided. You can also lose valuable time in the process. The best answer will invariably come from listening to your own inner voice and following some of the recommendations made here. Seeking the help of a competent career counselor, too, can help. The other consideration is making a move when the going is good. In uncertain times, things can change rapidly and some advantage can be lost if a new boss suddenly appears on the scene, or the company's fortunes change through no fault of yours.

Work-Visa Holders (H1-B)

There are many in the U.S. who are here working (or were) on a work visa. Especially those who are on H1-B status, face particularly challenging times when they lose their jobs under the threat of becoming "out of status." Typically within 30–90 days after losing their jobs, immigrants can come out of status depending on how their termination is structured. In some cases the time clock starts the date after the last paycheck. So, one of the actions you can take as a visa holder is to check to see if you have any latitude in the way you are terminated and how your final paycheck is cut.

After losing a job it is bad enough to be looking for another job when one has financial constraints, losing immigrant status puts a different complexion on the challenge. This is because immigrants do not have financial resources typically available to those already established in this country. If the visa deadline puts you "out of status," it portends deportation. This is a hard deadline that is not negotiable. Borrowing from others and liquidating any assets can overcome financial limitations. Immigration status, now, becomes your driving factor in the job-search campaign.

In addition to pursuing a suitable job, those in this category have to recognize that employers are not willing to readily hire H-1B holders because the conditions are so much in their favor in a job-parched market. It costs them money to sponsor a visa, and there is legal help needed to accomplish this, which some companies are not willing to foot if they can avoid it.

One avenue to delay deportation deadline is to contract some agencies that will, for a fee, keep you as their employee and contract you out where there are jobs. Thus, you are on their "payroll" until something more substantial becomes available. Any implications of this arrangement and the costs associated with this contract have to be carefully considered, especially since this involves immigration and legal matters. Be careful of promises that sound too good to be true, especially if they entail having to front money—thousands of dollars—to accommodate your case!

A Fresh Graduate

To those fresh out of collage with a newly minted degree, a tough job market can be disappointing or even frustrating. It is easy to be insulated for the four years in college and not have a good understanding of the challenges of landing a job in a tough economy, when fewer and fewer companies do college hiring. The other factor that enters the job-search process for the fresh graduates is that sudden market changes obsolete much of what is learned in college, leaving them ill-prepared for what lies ahead. So what is the strategy?

There are jobs even for entry-level graduates. Yes, in a tough economy! The following steps summarize the process:

- **Scour job boards** that list entry-level or near-entry level jobs

- **Differentiated positioning** is a good strategy, which allows you to create a unique message. For example, if you have interned during summers going back to your high school days, then see if you can leverage that experience for the position being posted. See the résumé sample in Key-3: "Before/After" Résumé samples. This example (Karlo Mennig) shows how a fresh graduate can transform a résumé to land a job.

- **Create your résumé** to showcase the past experience and present it as if it were from an experienced applicant. Do not list graduation year or your GPA—even though you might have a straight 4.0. Too much emphasis of grades shows how smart you were in school, not how useful you might be in an organization. (Once again, see Karlo's résumé in Key-3.)

- **Have good references** that can speak to your character, work ethic, and commitment to deliver what is expected of you. If you have such references that are well placed, then you have differentiated yourself in the marketplace and outwitted those who cannot marshal such references.

- **Practice interviewing skills** and telephone skills: once again, this can be a major differentiator.

- **Above all, be open, flexible, and eager** to do what needs to be done. Show enthusiasm.

- **Join professional associations** and attend their periodic meetings to network and socialize with prominent professionals. Also volunteer in these organizations for special events or office positions so that you get exposure to what is going on professionally.

- **Attend trade shows** and conferences in your area that are more professionally oriented within your own field of interest. Look for what is hot and who is on the forefront. Try to make connections with those who run these events and let them help you look.

- **Carry your business card** stating your name and other data with a clever tagline that is memorable. For example, instead of saying Jim Smith, Software Engineer, say Jim Smith, *Software Wiz*! Free business cards are available from some on-line Websites.

Re-entering the Workforce Because of a Need

After being out of work for a while (several years) reentering the workforce can be daunting, especially in a tough economy. In a period of employment draught this feeling can quickly escalate to despair. For a trade position, certifications or licenses are critical. If the skills are rusty, consider being an apprentice to someone in the trade by looking at ads in the local papers or community billboards. Also consider visiting super stores as Home Depot, Lowe's and other major chains, which sell home-improvement materials for job leads. Those who are buying materials are likely in need of some handyperson help.

When entering the workforce as an office worker or a professional, checking how current your skills are is critical. If you are looking to enter or reenter the workforce as an office support person—an administrator, a receptionist, or a legal secretary—look for the open positions and their job descriptions posted on job boards. Usually the descriptions will spell out certifications and other professional requirements for the open positions. Search on the Web to find out how to obtain these credentials with the least amount of effort and investment. Investigate and pursue only those that have enough clout, that mentioning the source of your credentials can give you the leverage you need in a job interview.

The next step is to start networking. If you are established in a community, your social connections can be of help here. Be open and forthcoming to those you know and solicit their help and support in getting names and contacts that can help you further your cause. Join local support groups that churches and other religious organizations sponsor. Attend networking events that are organized around job search. Call local outplacement organizations and businesses that support these activities and go to their meetings. Start looking for ads and postings and start applying to see what kind of responses you get for your campaign. Start the campaign on a small footing with a few responses initially. That way, if you need to change your message or approach, you are not entirely shut out of the entire job market. In a tough economy, community organizations and libraries hold clinics for the unemployed to help them with leads, résumé writing, and connections with local employers. Attend such events, and even volunteer, to expand your circle of connections.

When you have been out of the workforce for a long time, getting back into the mindset of working can be cultural shock. Start socializing with those who are working to get a sense of their life and compare it to yours. This will get you mentally ready to fine-tune your overall attitude to looking for a job. There are many who hire you for your attitude and then train you for skills. The other way does not work for them. Southwest Airlines is one of those employers that has championed this approach to hiring its crew, especially flight attendants.

Yet another consideration for reentering the workforce is evaluating if a flexible or variable work schedule may be of interest to you. Airlines, libraries, and hospitals allow this possibility.

Job sharing is a fairly recent alternative that can allow sharing of your job with someone that potential employer may find compatible with its culture. Typically, partners for such an arrangement have to be initiated from your end, and the discussion needs to take place early in the process.

The following checklist is compiled to summarize how to reenter the workforce after a long hiatus:

- ✓ **Decide which profession** to pursue and what that profession now looks like in today's market
- ✓ **Identify what credentials** are needed to qualify yourself for a job in the profession and get the credentials
- ✓ **Make a résumé** that differentiates you from everyone else
- ✓ **Start networking** by attending social community and job-related events
- ✓ **Write unsolicited letters** to higher-ups in organizations you are interested in working and ask them for an informational interview
- ✓ **Contact local outplacement companies** for information on support groups and for help on how to get ready to reenter the job market. Brush up on interviewing and business etiquettes
- ✓ **Get your image polished** with some accessories that make you look professional
- ✓ **Get a business card** with a clever tagline
- ✓ **Create and execute a marketing plan** (See Key-4: Your Marketing Plan)
- ✓ **Showcase your value,** and not your need
- ✓ **Seek professional advice** from a reputable coach or professional counselor. Make this small investment.
- ✓ **Become a volunteer:** Participate and lead activities at local community events that are organized to help those looking for work, as mentioned in the beginning part of this section. This way you will not only become visible, but also get valuable leads for jobs.
- ✓ **Network** by attending organized weekly networking events and volunteer there

Never Worked

This perhaps is the most challenging of all categories for job seekers. The motivations are obvious: the most compelling can stem from the economic need. An ill-provided widow, someone who lost their savings for medical or other reasons, including circumstances beyond their control, and a variety of other everyday reasons, all require that we seriously consider entering the job market to make ends meet or even to keep us engaged and purposeful. The first key question is always what career or job to pursue so that the objective for entering the job market is met.

There are various ways to identify what job or industry to choose from to launch your career. This is perhaps the most challenging task. With so many choices, which path to take, and what if that path turns out to be not a good choice? All these questions always create a perplexing panoply of challenges one faces.

Here are some suggestions:

1. **Look from within yourself** to find out if something that someone does, you wish you could do. Talk to that person even if you do not know them; they might find it flattering.

2. **Look at the economic climate** and find out what the current job trends are. Find out emerging jobs that are going to create more opportunities in the next five-ten years than just going after jobs that you are familiar with by association. Some job families are now dying rapidly as off-shoring trend continues, particularly in the high-tech area, and in the service industry.

3. **Look for action:** Since you are out of work for a prolonged period or have never worked, your objective is to get *any* reasonable job so that you have recent work history. See where paying jobs are, even though they may be faddish, trendy, or temporary. Some income, with work experience and the fact that you are employable can be leveraged into better, more stable jobs soon after the first wave of stints plays out. If you hold the dated belief that once you get a job you should stick to it, get over it.

4. **Take tests** that determine which professions you might be good at. Caution: these tests are not that precise and often take much effort, time, money, and energy. If you find a good counselor ask if there is something that they recommend. See in Key-1: Personality Testing.

5. **Arrange for an informational interview** with someone you know who works in the area that interests you. By having a first-hand discussion

with this person, or better yet, meeting them in their own office setting to see how they do what they do, might provide insights that are otherwise hard to come by. See in Key-7: Informational Interviews.

6. **Job versatility:** If there is no particular preference, try to find a job that has many allied skills that are transportable to other jobs. For example, if you become a customer service representative at a service company and learn skills to do that job, it is easy to transfer to a manufacturing or product oriented company to work as their customer support person, or at a professional office as the front-desk person.

7. **Job satisfaction:** Look for what gives you the freedom and job satisfaction to offset the extra salary you would not be making. Merely going after money can create problems later on when you discover that you cannot stand the job after you get used to the money. Remember that you do not have the seasoning of a veteran career person in the job. Because of this, you must work yourself into the chosen job and make your value known. This is why selecting the right opportunity is critical. Do not blindly go after big money.

8. **Large vs. small:** In economic uncertainty, target large organizations, where there is ample opportunity to move around or look for growth. Smaller businesses are vulnerable to uncertainties and have limited growth opportunities. Smaller organizations also have less patience to train someone. If conditions are favorable, local, city, state, and federal government jobs are also worth considering. They often have examinations or tests that one must pass to qualify.

9. **Explore volunteering** locally. Many well-connected citizens volunteer their time at such agencies, making it easy for you to socialize and network for leads, connection, and opportunities. If you are feeling desolate and that is what is prompting you to look for a job more than your financial status, this may just be the right avenue to break onto the scene!

10. **Contact your local chamber of commerce.** Usually they have information on community events, jobs lead, and opportunities.

11. **No résumé?** Since you never worked before the likelihood of a presentable résumé is slim. Instead approach opportunities with letters, as shown in Key-4: Sample Letters: Unconventional Approaches.

12. **Send letters** (without résumé) to hiring managers and top company officials with ideas you have about how to make their businesses better.

These ideas do not need to be anything esoteric or highly researched. If you, as a consumer or customer, envision an opportunity inside a company because of the experience you've had with it has been disappointing, leverage that into a suggestion with specifics so that you can get attention of someone who can see you about it in person. You can present that suggestion as an employment opportunity. See in Key-4: Sample Letters: Unconventional Approaches, specifically the one to Mayfair Mall from Pam Smith, as an example.

Getting into the job market after a long break or for the first time at an advanced age can be a mortifying experience. One way to get back your confidence is to start behaving like a professional by changing your routines and then starting to execute the steps in the above list. Getting a professional wardrobe, a stylish haircut, a manicure to boost one's image can go a long way in reestablishing one's image in the professional world.

Worked in Another Country but Looking Here

If you have worked in another country and have come to the US on a Work Permit or a Visa, then looking for a job at a level you can perform is a good start. There are various challenges that immigrants find disheartening, especially in a tough job market.

The following is a checklist of items to be aware of so that your job-search efforts are productive:

- ✓ **Job-board postings:** Visit some well-known job boards and find out what jobs are available that come close to the one you held back home. Although you may have done some of the work that is spelled out in the job posting and familiar with the skills or even have all the skills listed, the way of doing things in this country may not be the same as they are done back home.

- ✓ **Get certified:** Getting certified formally brings your skills at parity with others who will compete with you for a particular job. For example, if someone who has done accounting in India is now looking for the same work in the US, the accounting practices differ in the two countries, although the basic principles are the same. Getting a certificate in accounting would bring your accounting skills at parity with those competing with you. Your basic aptitude for numbers is already validated by your previous education, training, and past experience. You can also get a jumpstart by volunteering with some organization to do its accounting work.

✓ **Identify coursework:** Some jobs require being skilled at certain subject matters. For example in software there are now courses being offered in Java, Microsoft, Sun, and Oracle, SAP, to mention a few. Find out from the job openings which of these are in high demand. More importantly, find out which ones are going to stay. Then call the agencies that offer these courses and enroll to get certified. Also spending some time getting more skilled after taking the coursework can go a long way in making you more valuable in the job market.

✓ **Make your résumé:** Prepare a résumé that makes a compelling message around your skills. Show how you bring value as a result of your experience abroad and leverage that into your new pursuit. For example applying to a company with a German parent and stating your ability to speak fluent German can be an advantage. Use professional résumé writing resources to make yours culturally transparent; often the language in a résumé can betray one's recent migration to this country.

✓ **"Tribalize":** This may sound odd, but if you just migrated from another country, you have some connections here that go back to your roots (tribe). Leverage them in your pursuits for jobs.

✓ **English and etiquette:** Many immigrants struggle with English as it is spoken in the US. Even though they may be coming from a country where English is commonly used as a business language, their understanding of colloquial English is lacking. This can create barriers in the interview—especially the telephone interviews—where the interviewer may have a hard time understanding you. Enroll into any program that is offered by many universities, educational organizations and communities on English as a Second Language (ESL). When at home, listen to local TV or radio stations that broadcast English programs in preference to the ones that broadcast in your own language. Speak English at home, even if you have to force yourself to do that. This way you will become natural at understanding local dialects, colloquial dialog and English as it is spoken in this country. Also read books on business and social etiquette.

Understanding social norms is important for being considered integrated in the culture. Reading nationally syndicated newspaper columns on etiquette and advice can give a good understanding of the topical issues and cultural norms quickly. See Key-7 for Job Search Etiquettes.

Worked as a Consultant, Looking for Full-time Work

There are some who have worked as independent consultants for a long time in the past and have not had a traditional job. They were retained by a variety of "clients" over the years and during that time did successful consulting stints in one or more related areas of expertise. They have now reached a stage in their lives where they want a secure job and a steady income. In a tough economy this becomes a normal practice, just as its converse happens when the economy gets hot and there is suddenly a demand for a particular consulting skill.

The challenge in finding a desirable job here is twofold: The first is the difficulty in finding a job of any respectable flavor even within your own area of expertise because your résumé does not show the expected entries of employment chronology; the second, of course, is that having done well-paying stints in the past of various durations, it is difficult to reconcile to a lower compensation.

One way to overcome the first hurdle is to write the résumé as if you were "employed" during your consulting tenure by an employer, even if that happens to be your own company. Your company name can appear as the employer and the engagements you've had in the past can show as experiences during the time. This part of the Professional Experience section of your résumé now looks similar to the one who held a traditional job. If you have had different employers with whom you worked as a consultant, then list them chronologically as if they were your employers who engaged you in a full-time job. The idea here is to make your résumé look like a familiar presentation of your chronology so that no red flags are in the way of your getting the interview. During the interview you need to present your experience as one might if they had a job in a conventional sense.

The second hurdle—compensation—is easier. You need to accept the market rate for the going jobs in your category. The best way to assess the current rates is to visit one or more Websites that post salary and rate information as salary.com. Although this may be disappointing for someone who generated high income for a number of years, you have to reconcile to the current market conditions now.

Going on Your Own

As the job market gets tougher, those wanting go on their own increase in the numbers. Why? For one, there are fewer jobs to begin with. Secondly, those who are in their 40s and 50s and beyond, assume that entering the job market as a full-time employee may be a long process and then they may have to surrender to this possibility anyway. So, they preempt that possibility with a decision to go on their own—mostly as a consultant. There are several ways to venture on your own. The following checklist can serve as a summary of these opportunities:

- ✓ Independent consulting
- ✓ Becoming an independent agent: real estate or insurance
- ✓ Writing a book
- ✓ Buying a franchise
- ✓ Developing a franchise
- ✓ Owning your own business
- ✓ Buying a business
- ✓ Going as a partner in a joint venture

In each of the categories, follow your own instincts as to what will be most rewarding. Do not follow a path based on making money alone, by imitating someone else's success with their venture. They succeeded in what they did probably because they loved what they did. The prime criterion should be your love for the venture, and not the money. Initially, all ventures require much effort to get going. In a tough economy it takes even more and requires longer to get going. Under these circumstances the only thing that sustains those in it is their love for what they started, and their belief that they'd make it work. If one starts a business because of the lure of money and it fails to materialize, there is nothing to sustain the hope that given some more time and more energy the venture would succeed.

Do all the necessary market research before embarking on making the final decision and committing funds to a venture. Seek professional—lawyer, accountant—advice.

Let us briefly review each of these possibilities and look at the pros and cons.

Independent Consulting

This is perhaps the easiest and most prevalent form of entrepreneurship. As a professional you have already accumulated skills and experience in a specific area. Some companies have internal consultants who have clients with whom they work. It is these who underestimate what it takes to become a consultant and make a go of your consulting business. Why? This is mainly because there is a captive clientele inside the company that is going to use available services. Even if your services are not comprehensive there is a demand for it inside the organization, depending on how your services are structured. There is also a good support group you have available from inside the functional area of your department where you reside. You do not have to go marketing your services and wait for the phone to ring. So, if you are a reasonably successful consultant inside an organization, you are probably optimistic about starting your own consulting business.

One of the hardest areas and a surprise to those just starting out in their consulting business, is how hard it is to find clients. Marketing takes a major effort. Unless you have a highly differentiated value proposition and the demand is high for what you offer, there is no easy way to get clients. It takes several years to establish your practice and reputation. Even with these draw-backs consulting offers some benefits:

- More freedom and flexibility in your work life
- Small financial investment and low commensurate risk
- High income potential
- No one to be accountable to but yourself
- Learn new skills constantly to stay competitive
- Collaborate with other professionals to expand your skill set

On the negative side:

- Your previous income level may not be immediately realizable
- You will do most of the work yourself; no colleagues or support
- You may put your personal finances at risk
- You may miss some job opportunities if you are going into a tough economic period
- You may not be able to work with all clients and may be out of work in an instant
- Your cash flow may be erratic and business cyclical

One avenue to mitigate these risks and challenges is to first engage as an employee of a successful consulting organization that specializes in your area. This makes it easy to understand many aspects of this industry. As you develop your clientele you can decide if at a later time you can start your own business and use the client references to get yourself business based on your reputation and work.

Another avenue is the contracting route. Here you engage with a contract agency, which places you in their client organization. If you are working more as a consultant, then you can build on that experience and decide if you are ready to do this on your own at an appropriate time.

There are many good books on the business of consulting. The consulting methodology is something with which the practitioners of this trade have to become familiar. The consultative process is more of a science than an art. And yet, there is much to be learned by doing things your own way. These books are a good place to start reading up on this topic and learning about the trade secrets of being a consultant.

Independent Real Estate or Insurance Agent

When jobs are scarce, becoming a real estate or insurance agent appeals to many as people's desire for buying and selling homes and securing insurance remains nearly constant. In both cases and other similar ventures, explore to see what the ratio of these professionals is for every 1000 people in the community you wish to serve. Although housing is expensive in many communities, there may be a long wait before you are able to generate income by becoming an agent. No matter what those who are trying to lure you in this profession promise, consider yourself out of much action for at least twice the amount of time they think you need to generate cash flow. There are also no guarantees; you have to hustle! If you cannot visualize doing this work you probably will regret going after this line of profession. Your chances of success are greater if you can find someone who is willing take you under their wings and show you the ropes.

Writing a Book

Many dream of writing a book and publishing what they have learned over the years so that others can benefit from it. Sometimes it is not even what you have learned so much as having something deeply personal to share with others. Publishing a book brings instant credibility to your authority, regardless of how well the book does. Good sales just make you more known.

It is often publishing the book that is more challenging than authoring it. There are many excellent books on this topic. In summary, with desktop publishing, there is a segment of the printing and publishing industry based on print-on-demand (POD) technology that makes it easy to publish as few as 10 or a 100 copies of a professional-looking book for a cost of as little as $10 per copy with some set-up costs. This way you do not have to stock a large quantity of books; they can be printed as needed. Many companies offer graphic design and layout, some offer editing, photography, and printing and binding. They also offer assistance with copyright, registration with book wholesalers, the formalities with the Library of Congress, and sales and distribution through traditional and online booksellers. Some will even coordinate publicity and signings.

As a marketing tool, books can be invaluable. A professional-looking book can establish an aura of authority that can boost sales and credibility for the author in promoting their work. Being published, having a book in print and available for sale, can boost self-confidence and credibility. A small-business owner can become an author for under $1,000.

The following are summary tips:

- Identify a topic that you can write about and explore what the market is if you wrote a book about it.

- It is much easier to write a book about what you know and stream it into the pages of your manuscript than to research all sorts of topics and write about what that research means in your book. Such topics tend to be time limited by the nature of the information. This book is an example of the streaming effect. What appears on the pages is how I felt about the topic and very little is researched or interpreted. What is presented here is a result of my direct experience with my clients in the current (three years) market.

- Writing a book can be a task that requires painstaking effort, especially the first time. Start with an outline and discipline yourself to write a few pages each day. The book will be done before you know it. Once about 50 or so pages are done in the text form, the remainder of the book goes much faster. Often, writing the first draft is the easy part; getting it through the rigorous editing and production process can be a time-consuming endeavor.

- Try self-publishing the book. It is much easier. Desktop publishing has made book writing and publishing much easier.

- Create your own Website and post the book and promote from there. Sell it on eBay.

- Once the book becomes popular, a traditional publisher may publish and promote it.

Buying a Franchise

Buying a franchise can be the easiest way to enter into your own business with a proven model of success developed by the franchiser. Starting a new business is risky. The franchiser has taken much of that risk out and has made running that particular business more or less formulaic. This does not mean that there are no risks; there are risks but the magnitude of those risks are greatly diminished and the uncertainty of the product or service success is already established in the general market. This does not always and necessarily mean that the specific demographics in which your franchise will be operating is a proven concept yet. You have to vet that aspect of it. And, that could be your biggest risk.

Generally, there are two types of franchises:

Business Format Franchise is when a franchiser licenses the rights to sell a product or service and provides proprietary methods for operating a business, including logos, systems, and training. Fast food, mailing outlets, convenience stores, and gas stations fall into this category of franchising.

Product or Trade Name Franchise is where a franchiser sells the rights to use a trademark or brand name as part of existing business. Beverage distribution or brand-product outlets as dealerships fall into this format.

While you take out the risk of testing if a particular format or service sells in a particular market, you pay for that risk mitigation through entry fees. Most franchises are priced so that the start-up costs exceed the cost of setting up a similar business. Since the set up is formulaic, though, it is a proven approach to success, all other things being equal.

Developing a Franchise

Many dream of this idea that involves creating a new business model, testing it, and then developing a replicating process so that you can develop a franchise from this replication concept. Each franchise is identical and is typically run by entrepreneurs. The franchiser can benefit from the initial hard work by both getting initial franchising fees from each franchisee and then annuity payments as each franchise continues to flourish. You own the name and the model so it is hard to copy. The following checklist suggests what to look for in order to develop your business.

- ✓ **Know what you are getting into:** Start small, prove the concept at the pilot level and then develop a more robust business model that is replicable.

- ✓ **Talk to franchise consultants:** This will ensure that you have expert input that your concept is new and that it is scalable.

- ✓ **Reach out to thought leaders:** The people who understand, support, and can stand behind your venture with some clout are good to find. Hook up with incubator programs and alliances that allow you to leverage resources and time. These leaders are now your potential board. Hook up with the local chamber of commerce and venture capital firms.

✓ **Understand the law:** Different states have laws that vary. You may need legal help in making sure that both you and the franchisee are protected.

✓ **Know your professional limitations:** Hire the best leaders. You may be good at new concept and taking them to the pilot stage. Once you have a scalable model, stakes are different. Make sure that you have a professional management team to run the operations.

Starting a Business

For many, starting your own business can be an exciting venture, especially if the offering is something that is novel, or trendy. This can be a gratifying undertaking and in some respects, much like raising your own child and nurturing it to success. Those starting out in a new business underestimate the effort that goes into making the business a going concern. The investment is usually more than most estimate, the time it takes to break-even is longer than expected, and there are surprises along the way that require contingency planning and resources, not apparent in a conventional planning methodology. Fewer than half of new businesses survive past the first two years of operation and fewer than 20 percent survive the first five! The most notorious of these is the restaurant business. The failure rate for restaurants in the first two years is 90 percent!

Before entering a new business careful study of demand, business model, competition, capital availability and management of its operations are critical to launching it. Evaluate all options before entering into a business venture, especially when the economic conditions are challenging.

Buying a Business

Buying an established business is an attractive option for those who are not good at estimating what it takes to get a business going. To use a metaphor, it is like jumping on a moving train rather than getting in one waiting to leave the station; you don't know if it ever will! Each year hundreds of thousands of businesses in this country are bought and sold (there are over 12 million businesses in the US).

Buying a business offers some flexibility. You can run the business yourself or find someone who can run it for you and compensate that person for doing so. A running business can be evaluated by going through its history, talking to its customers and suppliers and checking out its reputation in the community. Buying a business already established that can be improved upon requires that the buyer has a good understanding of the business and instincts, and what would differentiate the acquired business from what it is. This requires a vision and leadership expertise. Before closing a deal, make sure you have done due diligence and researched all liabilities, as you take the business on as your own.

Partnering (with your Spouse)

Going into a business with a partner can be a fun venture. If you can pool your resources including your capital, management talent and expertise, this can be a profitable and productive venture. This can be done in any of the formats discussed above. Good understanding of partnerships and good relationships with the partner(s) are critical to the success of such an arrangement. A contract is also critical to a successful partnership.

If your spouse already has a business or an idea for a venture, it is tempting to be partners. As long as an agreement of roles, responsibilities, and monitoring of ongoing operations to the satisfaction of both can be worked out, this can be made to work. Keeping the household relationship separate from the business is difficult, but can be made to work with some ground rules set up before starting the arrangement.

♠ Formal Aspects of Entrepreneurship

For legal purposes a business can fall into any one of the following categories:

- S corporation
- C Corporation
- Sole proprietorship
- Limited partnership
- Limited Liability Company (LLC)

Each type offers certain advantages and tax structures. Any further discussion on these areas is outside the scope of this material and the reader is advised to consult several good references on these topics and engage a legal counsel or a Certified Public Accountant (CPA) for further exploration. Table-4: Entity Comparison Charts summarize particulars and entity tax specifics merely as guidelines and *not* as legal representations.

* Entity Comparison Charts

Table-4 shows the five different types of entities that can be formed as businesses and their relative operating obligations. Use these as a starting point to explore how you may want to consider structuring your future business and what the attendant issues are for each choice. There is no free lunch. Consult a professional before deciding on this critical matter so that you are not surprised later. These are legally binding entities and, once you are set up, you are obligated to meet all legal, fiducial, and business requirements.

♠ Coming Out of Retirement

Coming out of retirement can be prompted either by sudden change in financial circumstances or by the need to engage productively, at least part-time, in a purposeful pursuit. Many go into retirement because they feel that retired life is something to be experienced, savored, and bragged about, since much is made of not working after a certain time in one's life. It's an image and an idea many hold and look forward to. Someone once defined retirement as being able to do what you want. So, if you want to go back to work, you can redefine *that* as retirement, without feeling guilty about it.

There are a few who, when they experience retirement in its full manifestation get disillusioned by its emptiness and lack of stimulation, both physically and mentally. If, on the other hand, the need is purely financial and was not foreseen at the onset of retirement, it is a different matter. In either case you need to go through the material in Getting With the Program in Key-1, so that your intent is clear and you can move ahead with purpose. Remember that this, too, is a transition back to work. How this transition is handled depends on how long you have been in retirement.

The following list can be a good reminder for starting your process to get back to work from retirement:

1. Be honest about the reasons for going back to work after testing the fruits of retirement

2. If you are out of work and in retirement for a while (more than two years) potential employers can be apprehensive in a tough job market. You may have a hard time getting interviews unless you are aggressive in your campaign

3. In your résumé try not listing the most recent period as that entailing retirement. See if you can justify that period as doing volunteer work, consulting (even just a little), or starting a new business

4. If you're serious about getting back to work, slowly wean yourself from your retirement activities and social circles that indulge in that lifestyle. You need a fresh mindset.

5. Try volunteering at least part-time to engage yourself in productive activity. A productive mindset is critical to searching for a good job, even part-time.

6. Take some refresher courses that will not only update your skills but will also get you in a social circle with more creative and energetic people. You need to see yourself more as someone willing to learn and venture out than as someone who is tired of new things.

7. Network with established professional associations and renew your memberships that may have lapsed as a result of your retirement. Many offer discounted fees for retirees.

8. Start mentoring younger professionals who come across your path. This will energize your campaign and give the fillip you need to make yourself feel useful.

9. Give talks at the local groups and associations that are attended by those looking for work. You have an advantage because of your unique situation. Leverage that experience in your presentations.

10. Explore tutoring opportunities for the young. This, too, can be an energizing experience and can be a résumé builder. Tutors can make good money.

If you get tired looking for employment after a while and are frustrated you may explore the idea of buying a business or a franchise. This may entail your having to invest money—probably your life savings—to get this realized. Be very cautious when it comes to risking your retirement money on *any* venture, even when it may be completely legitimate. Evaluate risks and go with caution. Never give money to anyone whose credentials are suspect. See Age Advantage, Key-7.

Notes:

Table-4: Entity Comparison Charts

CHARACTERISTICS	S CORPORATION	C CORPORATION	SOLE PROPRIETORSHIP	PARTNERSHIP	LIMITED LIABILITY COMPANY (LLC)
Continuity of Life	Indefinite	Indefinite	Cases on death of proprietor	Ends if 50+ percent of partnership interest is sold/exchanged within a 12 month period	Generally no
Management	Centralized; Board of Directors; Corporate officers	Centralized; Board of Directors; Corporate officers	N/A-one owner	General partnership: not centralized, limited partnership generally centralized	Can be either centralized or not centralized
Liability of owners	Generally limited to assets in corporation	Generally limited to assets in corporation	Unlimited	General partnership unlimited, limited partnership, general partner unlimited, limited partner limited to investments	Limited
Tax Return Form	Form 100S	Form 100	Form 1040 Schedule C	Form 565	Form 568
Taxability of income	Generally	To corporation	Taxable to proprietor	Taxable to partner	Taxable to member
Double taxation of income? (Corporation and Shareholder)	No, unless former C corp. and built-in gains apply	Yes, taxed first at corporate level, and then shareholder	No	No	No
Deductibility of losses	Generally deductible by S/H, liabilities do not increase basis for deducting losses except for S/H loans	Deductible by corporation	Deductible by proprietor	Generally deductible by partner to extent of basis; Liabilities may increase basis for deducting losses	Generally deductible by member to extent of basis; Liabilities may increase basis for deducting losses
Passive losses	May not offset active or portfolio income (limits apply at shareholder level)	May offset active but not portfolio income of closely held corp. but not personal service corporation	May not offset active or portfolio income	Cannot offset active or portfolio income (limits apply at partner level)	Cannot offset active or portfolio income (limits apply at member level)

CHARACTERISTICS	S CORPORATION	C CORPORATION	SOLE PROPRIETORSHIP	PARTNERSHIP	LIMITED LIABILITY COMPANY (LLC)
Tax Year	Generally must use calendar year or make Sec. 444 election	May select any fiscal year if not a personal service corporate	Must use tax year of proprietor	Generally must use fiscal year of majority interest partner/make Sec. 444 election	Generally must use fiscal year of majority interest partner/make Section 444 election
Register with Secretary Of State	Yes	Yes	No	Yes	Yes
Necessary Documentation	Articles of Inc., bylaws, minutes of the board, stock record	Same as S-Corp	Minimal	Partnership agreement	Articles of organization; Operating agreement
Distribution to Owner	Nontaxable to extent of basis in stock	Not deductible by corp., ordinary income S/H	Nontaxable	Nontaxable to extent of basis in partnership	Nontaxable to extent of basis in LLC
Liquidation Distribution	At corporation level treated as sales of property, gain passes though increases shareholder basis, trigger built-in gains tax	At corporation level treated as sales of property, gain to shareholder if full market value exceeds stock basis	Nontaxable	Generally, nontaxable; Cash distribution in excess of basis will trigger gain disproportionate distribution of Section 751 assets may trigger gain	Generally, nontaxable; cash distribution in excess of basis will trigger gain disproportionate distribution of Section 751 assets may trigger gain
Maximum Tax Rate	Taxed at individual shareholder level; If corporate-level tax applies: @1.5 percent.	Generally taxed at 8.84 percent.	Taxed at individual level	Taxed at individual partner level	Taxed at individual member level, at LLC level–annual LLC fee based on total income
Minimum Franchise Tax (even with losses)	$800	$800 1st yr. = $300 2nd yr. = $500	None	General Partnership— $0: L/P—$800	$800
Self-employed Income to Owners	No	No	Yes	General partners; not limited Ps	Yes
Classes of Stock/ownership interest	Limited to 1 class; can own subsidiaries	Unrestricted	N/A	Unrestricted	Unrestricted
Number of Investors	Limited to 75	Unlimited	N/A	Unlimited	Unlimited
Eligible investors	Individual, estate, certain trusts, & 501©(3) charitable organizations.	Unrestricted	N/A	Unrestricted	Unrestricted

Summary: Key-2: Starting At the Start

This chapter starts with defining why all job seekers are the *not* same. Where one starts is important in defining how to move ahead. At the macroscopic level there are the 14 categories of job seekers as identified in this chapter. At the microscopic level each individual job seeker needs their individualized approach to moving ahead. These nuances are presented in subsequent chapters. Each category of job seekers must approach their job search with the prescriptions defined under their category. In this chapter we cover the following:

Identify to which of the 14 categories of job seekers you belong:

1. If you are about to be unemployed

2. Those on notice with limited time to find something within their own organization

3. Just out of work

4. Out of work for a while and looking

5. Employed (unhappily) and looking for a change

6. Employed, doing well but feel lost

7. Work-Visa Holders (H1-B)

8. Re-entering the workforce because of a need

9. Have never worked and feel out of touch but now must earn a living

10. Worked in another country and now looking here for opportunities

11. Worked as a consultant in the past 10–15 years and now looking for a full-time position

12. Want to do something on your own

13. Fresh graduates

14. Coming out of retirement

Regardless of the category (of 14), getting ready involves:

- Emotionally Accepting your new state

- Informing those who matter

- Compiling networking contacts list

- Searching for the right open positions

- Understanding the job market (Including trends)

- Expanding your repertoire of marketing space (guerilla, unconventional)
- Preparing a résumé (must be market aligned, see Key-3: Presenting Yourself)
- If considering going on your own read the implications of different entities in the Entity Comparison Charts

Key-3: Presenting Yourself

"Do not pray for tasks equal to your powers; pray for powers equal to your tasks."

—Phillip Brock (1835–1893)

Your Job-Targeting Campaign

A solid job targeting campaign begins after internalizing the last two Keys. Once the preliminaries are out of the way such as deciding what category (of the 14 described in Key-2) is closest to your starting stage, preparing a message that is ready to go out for a job search is in order. This Key presents how to organize that message in a compelling way, and includes the résumé and everything that goes with it.

The Overall Plan

Once the starting and end points are defined, planning is essential before action. Planning puts together all thoughts, ideas, actions, timelines, and contingencies in one place so that there is coherent and articulate actions plan that is ready to be executed. There is a simple rule to remember for success in any undertaking: *plan the work and then work the plan!* For a smooth transition process and a sense of control this plan is critical. Why? Because without it one will be left with having to do a series of actions that look more reactive than something well organized. There will be many more surprises without a plan than if there were one! Without a broad plan that is strategic, with day-to-day details that provide a reason to get up each morning, pursuing a new job can be frustrating. Yet another reason for a good action plan is that the entire process of the job search for any category of jobseeker is filled with emotions. Because of the emotionally charged nature of the endeavor, executing an action on a job-search campaign *without* a good plan can make an already difficult task, that much more difficult.

The *formal* job-search campaign begins with a résumé. Writing a résumé is not where the process begins as we shall presently see. In a bull job market—low unemployment—most write their résumés immediately following their decision to search for jobs. However, in a bear market, this must change. The message one plans to send should be aligned to a known need—the market. The selling part is covered in the next Key, Marketing the Product—You! So, the material in this Key is devoted to the following aspects of the campaign:

- Understanding the target market
- Writing a résumé
- Connecting a résumé to the target
- Knowing (and breaking) the hiring rules
- Going out with your message
- Résumés showcase
- Cover letters showcase

Understanding the Target Market

To really understand a market, the best way to get acquainted with it is to visit it! By going to popular job boards one can quickly assess what the jobs are and their flavors. The job and position descriptions of an open job allow you to assess what needs to be presented to properly respond, so that it is viewed favorably.

One way to create differentiation, is to not only respond to what is already in the job description, but to go a step further in the way the job itself is going to emerge. This is called job trending. Job trending is sending a message to prospective employers that for *their* long-term success, merely meeting stated job requirements is not enough; future needs also must be addressed! This forward-thinking approach can help capture the imagination of prospect employers in ways your competition may fail to!

We discuss this further in Writing Your Résumé, in this Key.

♠ Leveraging Job Trends

Introduction

The job market, especially in high-tech, started experiencing a structural shift even before the dotcom meltdown began in late 2000. This inexorable shift in jobs continues today and most job families are affected by it, although some more than the others. Some job families may take time before they show signs of change. Here we'll explore what that shift is, and the trend of that shift, and more importantly, what that means to someone who has to manage a career.

The Global Economy

In an ironic twist, the success spawned by the creative minds of the Silicon Valley became the source of their grief. How? As the Internet became more pervasive in the late '90s, global communication became a commodity. It was no longer necessary to wait for expensive and unreliable means of communicating at a functional level, where one exchanges large quantities of information freely and near-synchronously around the globe and around the clock. Factors driving a major shift that started affecting jobs in high-tech and related industries are listed below. Other industries will follow suit, and soon:

➤ A large technology pool of inexpensive and expert talent available overseas, especially India, that speaks English.

➤ A large labor pool of manufacturing talent available in China and the Pacific Rim countries. Both these factors accelerated the off-shoring trend.

➤ Many companies started outsourcing key functions they once took pride in performing themselves. Manufacturing was one, among others. This resulted in consolidation of such functions across the entire industry within a sector, resulting in highly narrow job competencies to keep labor costs down.

➤ A fundamentally shifted mindset that is now examining the way we behave in the corporate world and the economy to create value and build wealth. The operating mantra shifted from local job creation to global value generation.

➤ Major technology players as HP, IBM, and Motorola realized that producing consumer goods as PCs, hand-held digital products, and communication devices was not their core competency that differentiated them in the marketplace. These goods had become commodities with short life cycles; some had even become fashion statements. Original Equipment Manufacturers (OEMs) shifted to outsourcing their products to Original Design Manufacturers (ODMs). ODMs provide both product design and manufacturing resources to a major brand. Global players now merely put their labels and provide logistical and marketing channel resources to get the products in the hands of consumers and end users. They also build alliances with other players in the marketplace to enhance customer experience and capture greater value. The focus is now closer to the customer than it is on the side of production (see next bullet).

➤ Organizations began to realize that the value creation process had shifted from back-end to the front-end activities. Traditional back-end activities had been manufacturing, support, operations, and logistics. Front-end activities, on the other hand are understanding the customer, market knowledge, order entry process, and managing the customer account. More and more organizations realized that outsourcing the back-end activities and tightening the management of the front-end activities would provide a competitive advantage to create a business model that would sustain itself as more and more back-end operations got outsourced.

➤ A shift in emphasis from selling products to services and after-sale activities. Starting in the mid 90s, companies as IBM, GE, and HP recognized that as products became more and more sophisticated, customers needed increasingly more help in understanding how to use these complex products in an environment that produces value beyond what was obvious to them. It was thus not enough to merely make a product sale, but also to create an ongoing revenue stream and profits by providing services and solutions to customer accounts and manage those accounts to make sure that they grow on both fronts: product needs and services.

➤ A shift from constantly having to upgrade technologies for speed and functionality to squeezing out the most value from what is already in place and living with what is sufficient, versus what is the best and the fastest! This single factor was perhaps why the high-tech implosion accelerated, starting late in year 2000.

➤ A shift in organizational managers' thinking in the way employees create value: employees are now expected to create an *ongoing* value stream, and not just carry out their work for a paycheck, regardless of how it impacts the *immediate* bottom line and wealth creation; ongoing wealth creation became the operating principle.

♠ Off-shoring and Outsourcing

The practice of outsourcing and off-shoring has come into sharper focus during the past few years, particularly starting with the incidental dotcom implosion in early 2001. During 2003 about 250,000 jobs, mostly high-tech and knowledge jobs, were "off-shored" to India and other countries as China, Indonesia, and the Philippines. Exactly how many jobs were lost to off-shoring is a matter of debate. Some jobs have even gone to Russia and the Eastern European countries. Unbeknownst to many, off-shoring to India began in the early '80s, with many manual computer tasks being shipped for low-cost processing. Only in the past few years has this trend taken on an exponential proportion, brought into sharper focus by the intense media interest and rampant job losses that go well beyond those lost to off-shoring. See below, the "Hype" phase!

The off-shoring and outsourcing of jobs are two somewhat different practices that an organization can adopt. Outsourcing is where an organization
decides to stay focused on its core competencies and farms out its more routine functions to those who can do them more efficiently, *regardless* of the
geography. Typically these functions include payroll, security, front lobby
administration, mailroom, and other routines. Outsourcing practice has been
a management alternative since the late '80s and it accelerated in the '90s. This
trend is not going to change. More and more companies are going to find ways
of consolidating their routine tasks and finding ways to cut costs to become
more efficient in what they do. This cost advantage is what keeps them competitive; they are not so much strategic practices, as they are survival tactics.

Off-shoring is a different matter: companies have found that some functions, even core functions, can be "off-shored" by keeping a pool of labor
forces overseas that can do many jobs more efficiently, allowing them to
develop an ongoing capability to perform critical tasks competitively. India has
emerged as one country with resources that can support many such initiatives.
Major Fortune-500 companies in the past few years have "off-shored" many
white-collar jobs to India and other countries. This practice is not limited to
call centers and administrative functions; it has now pervaded almost all
knowledge work, which now includes even radiological diagnostics, using
some of the physicians trained to interpret medical tests and MRIs. This trend
will not reverse; it is, in fact, going to accelerate.

Many complain about the low cost of knowledge work in India. By some
estimates there is a 6-10:1 salary advantage for comparable skill between India
and the US. Considering the overhead and other costs, the net saving can easily be 4:1. But this is not the whole story, particularly in software. Not only is
the salary of a comparable software professional less by a significant factor in
India (compared to the US), the efficiency of production is much higher to
boot! How is this possible?

One reason is that, in the US, we focused on cranking out constantly
revised, complex, and functionally cumbersome software during the pioneering phase of the software and the personal computer industry. India, on the
other hand, focused on streamlining software development methodology by
adopting a disciplined approach. This is much analogous to what happened to
the automotive industry in the '70s when the Japanese ate Detroit's lunch by
beating them on the quality of their automobiles at a lower cost. In software
there is a methodology for improving the effectiveness of how it is developed.
In this methodology there are five levels at which this development can take
place and it is called Capability Maturity Model (CMM). In this model, Level
one represents the most rudimentary approach to software development

methodology, and Level five, the most evolved. The ratio of the outputs between the two levels is typically tenfold.

Much of the US software development process, on average, operates at level 2+, according to experts. The level at which India produces software is at level-4 or even level-5. This means that the output difference, *not* accounting for quality issues, is two to five times what is produced here! This is a significant factor to combat. This is why software and IT projects will continue to gravitate to India in the future, despite any political backlash from the migration. The force is economic and compelling for software.

The rate at which the off-shoring trend across a broad skill set, not just software development, is going to accelerate will depend on a variety of factors. When an initiative captures public attention, as off-shoring has, since the early Millennium, it is usually in its early stages of "hype." As a result, many perceptions about the advantage of off-shoring are distorted. Why? Let us take a closer look.

Any major "new" idea or fad evolves before it is adopted as a valid and accepted business practice across a wide range of industries. There are four stages in this evolution:

- Hype
- Disillusionment
- Redeployment
- Integration

The first phase "hype" is when there is much public focus on the issue and there are constant media reports about the initiative, including its political ramifications. Many companies jump on the bandwagon and follow those who are "successful" adopting the new fad. Soon there is a backlash as a result of the hyped activity. The gains are not what they expected, there is political backlash, there are hidden costs, and there are social pressures and so on.

Enter disillusionment, the next stage! During this stage many companies back peddle the initiative and retract their positions. On the off-shoring front, recently Dell and IBM have backed off and pulled some of their functions back into their U.S operations. This trend will continue as will the trend to outsource, as more and more tasks and functions are identified during this shakedown.

Redeployment is where organizations learn the true cost of implementing an initiative and use that learning and other factors to develop their long-term plan on how to stabilize their operations and benefit from the positive aspects of the trend. During this stage, the initiative looses its media interest and pure economic rationality and organizational considerations drive their fate. The off-shoring trend is not yet seen this stage, but is expected to see it within the next year or so. The off-shoring initiative is one of those inevitable economic forces resulting from the global economy spawned by the Internet. The irony here is that those who made the Internet a commercial success have been hit the hardest by its emergence!

The final stage is integration, where the initiative matures and so do peoples' perspective on it. Their long-term benefits tend to become visible. This horizon is a few years away for the off-shoring trend.

The idea presented here validates the concept of the Change Curve of Figure-2 presented in Key-1.

High-tech has suffered the most impact by the off-shoring trend. It is estimated that in the coming years about one in seven jobs in this industry (mostly in the Silicon Valley) is going to be off-shored, mostly to India. In 2003 about 250,000 jobs were lost to India as mentioned before. Even though there were some three million in the US labor pool who had lost their jobs (and nearly 15 million out of work or underemployed!) in the past three years, each one of them thought that *their* job had gone to India. This is called perceptual amplification!

The reality, though, is that as companies find better ways to manage global resources, more and more jobs are going to go overseas. It is estimated that by 2015 about 3 million jobs are going overseas. But by the same token, new jobs are going to be *defined* right here. Typically those jobs are more "upstream" in the value chain. This means getting closer to the customer and developing business models that are more service based. This trend has implications that are worth considering for the future well being and management of one's career.

♠ Career Implications

The factors listed have now resulted in an inescapable shift in the way organizations are considering how to fill open positions. Some are using a conscious effort to take the emerging trends into account; others have to be reminded by those looking for opportunities in these organizations. In a bear market employers are selective. It is no longer enough to be the best at what one once did; what they now need to demonstrate clearly is that skills presented in a résumé will benefit the target organization's *future* needs. Being aware of the emerging trends and the way future job competencies are shaping up will give job applicants an edge in their search. Table-5 in this Key is a partial list of traditional and emerging job competencies for some job families. Using this map of forward-looking competencies, job seekers must now position themselves for a favorable consideration—even an edge—during the hiring process.

♠ Integrating Job Trends in Your Message

Integrating job trends in a message is an advantage that must be exploited in each opportunity. Why? There are three reasons:

- Most posted jobs do not reflect today's reality. They're often constructed by "copy and paste" of the past ones, often dating back a few years!

- Most applicants responding to job openings try to match what is already described in the job posting. Having a message that goes beyond this description, and the one that captures an employer's imagination gives an edge!

- Demonstrating an understanding of how a position can create greater value by integrating broader aspects of a job can create a competitive advantage.

Job trends are an important element of the overall message of a job-search campaign. For example, for a software developer, especially in high-tech, the very nature of the development process has changed dramatically in the US. Much of the work is now parceled out to India and overseas. No matter how great you are at developing software, unless you understand how this trend of off-shoring is going to affect the potential employer, you are not going to have a long-term job there. Even if a company does not have any language in the job opening about off-shoring now, responding to an opportunity with the knowledge of this trend is an advantage. This insight can be presented in the following way in a Career Objective:

Before

Career Objective: A position as a software development lead

After

Career Objective: A hands-on technical lead in software responsible for: collaborating with customers to capture their requirements, organizing teams and setting up projects that include off-shore resources, managing overall projects to ensure that the final solution is delivered to delight the customer, and managing the entire product life-cycle for a profitable revenue stream.

A more detailed discussion on Career Objective is covered in résumé writing, which follows. Letters that reflect these messages are in Sample Letters, at the end of this Key.

Creating a résumé for a job with an employer that supports outsourcing or off-shoring requires specific messages. One cannot present a message without awareness of the needs. For example, if someone is looking to migrate from a traditional manufacturing organization, an OEM, to a company that supports outsourced manufacturing, even to the same OEM, the skill set required in the new position is different from the one expected in the comparable position at the OEM. Why? This is mainly because the focus of value creation in the two organizations is different. The OEM, typically, requires a broad set of skills to achieve the manufacturing capability. Working across a broad cross-functional organization is critical to make this position create value for the OEM. For the outsourced manufacturing organization, however, the focus is the depth of a given function more than the broad knowledge because this is how the outsourced business achieves cost benefits: doing repetitive operations at minimal cost. The résumé and the cover letters must incorporate this awareness in unambiguous messages. One example of the two flavors of résumés, albeit in the contracting domain (vs. job domain), is presented in Key-7 under Contracting.

♠ Differentiating Yourself

Throughout this Key we have and will continue to emphasize that differentiating is a key strategy for a successful job search. Differentiation does not just start during the marketing process; it goes way back with the first piece of a message—the résumé! Even before the résumé is written, how one thinks has much to do with how it all ends up being differentiated.

The concept of differentiation is hammered throughout this book. It is presented in various sections to show different aspects of this theme. For example, knowing the job trends can help in creating a differentiated message in each résumé.

The next section presents how to differentiate with your résumé message.

Notes:

Table-5: Emerging Job Trends in Today's Economy: A Sampling

#	Traditional Job	Traditional Role	Emerging Job	New Role	Drivers	Opportunities in
1	Account Manager	Sell to generate revenues, protect accounts/revenue streams standing	Relationship Manager	Understand customer drivers, value transfer equation, long-term relationships, alliances	Customer loyalty, cost of landing new accounts, cost of defections	Customer intimacy
2	Business Development Manager	Promote business, create new revenues, make profits, and expand	Opportunities Seeker	Explore what is NOT happening and ID avenues to catalyze it	Current value creation not supporting expectations competition, commoditization	Alliances, value loops with suppliers, consolidation
3	Component Engineer	Define and specify components/vendors	Applications Engineering	Define new applications for components, creative single source	Simplicity, reliability, alliances, partnership	Alliance creation in value chain
4	Customer Support	Post-sale customer support	Customer Experience Champion	Understand customer needs, use, issues, and know how to close	Product complexity, customer impatience and expectations	
5	Does not exist	N/A	Account Executive Process Steward	Promote organization-wide process to match large accounts with senior execs to manage discovery, relationship, and growth,	Large accounts are orphans left to the will of the Account Managers; account defections, lack of long-term visibility	Global and strategic accounts
6	Facilities Manager	Construction, utilities, services, space allocation, special facilities, regulatory	Facilities Overseer	Real-Estate Custodian, strategic planning, Hoshin, energy incentives, subcontracts	Cost; globalization, work habits, virtual orgs, regulatory compliance incentives	Subcontracting services
7	IT Specialist	Design and support IT infrastructure with the latest and the greatest	IT Resource	Make available what is installed, increase investment effectiveness	Installed capacity, low availability, utilization, and capital, increased hurdle rates, IT as a business partner	IT effectiveness; welding business ops to IT

#	Traditional Job	Traditional Role	Emerging Job	New Role	Drivers	Opportunities in
8	Maintainability Engineer	Product life-cycle, downstream costs, logistics	Revenue protection engineer	Find creative ways to enhance product's overall appeal in its long-term life	Throwaway designs of the past, environmentalist, back-to-basics	New models of maintenance logistics, self-help diagnostics
9	Marcom Specialist	Develop product/service communications and collaterals	Marcom Generalist	Guerilla approaches to reaching end users, creating product excitement/demand vacuum	Limited budgets, multiple avenues, savvy but time-constrained end user, highly customized real-time collaterals	Customer-intimate campaign capabilities, HP's new INDIGO venture is a case in point. Print-on-Demand collateral
10	OD Specialist	Organizational development, teams, training, leadership development	OE Catalyst	Project Teams, PM Methodology, Career Ladders, reward structures, Operating Protocols, Six Sigma	New Team Paradigms, Structure (PMOs), Alignment, Cycle Times	Organizational effective initiatives
11	Procurement Manager	JIT, quality, multiple sources, vendor ship,	Supply Network Catalyst	Supply chain integration value capture, ecosystem dynamics, transform resources to provide package goods.	Complex ecosystems, dynamic world economy, M&As, cheap labor	Cultural training, values, supply network dynamics value exchanges
12	Project Manager	Lead product/service development, deliver against set objectives	Profit Center, autonomous units, line of business, accountable to customers/supplier	Value-chain network, team leadership, cross-functional cooperation, subcontract management; customer experience	Web capability, team dynamics, life-cycle, Earned Value, Global workforce	New team paradigms; PMO and benchmarking
13	Product Development Engineer	Translate inventions into profitable product suites, platforms and derivatives	ODM Specifier	Liaise between R&D, emerging component technologies, capabilities, and ODMs for differentiated products.	Major players are now brand promoters, not operational participants, technology commoditization	Prototype capabilities in-house and ODM development.
14	Production Planner	Develop detailed work/material flow/logistics, inventory	Production Overseer	Align demand with capacity, shift loads, global cost awareness	Global resources, ODM	Integrated planning.

#	Traditional Job	Traditional Role	Emerging Job	New Role	Drivers	Opportunities in
15	R&D Manager	Lead creative teams to generate new product stream, new platforms, future revenue streams	Innovations Catalyst	Establish a new core competency for innovation. Establish organization-wide process for innovation	Slow inventions, lack of continuity of new platforms, future value and competitive advantage	Leveraging innovations across entire organization not just in R&D.
16	Reliability/ Maintain-ability	Predict performance	Product Experience Engineer	Technology life, value alternatives, availability, value experience	Emerging technologies; value alternatives	New approaches to Product Design; manufacturability.
17	Software Developer	Translate requirements into code, then rework as needed; keep doing version iterations to create complex, hard-to-use s/w	Product Developer	Translate Customer Needs to Requirements, liaison, teaming, validation, customer champion, disciplined development	Process integration, accountability, cost, schedule, customer experience, and globalization.	Extreme programming, Capability Maturity Model (CMM); S/W Reuse Coaching/Mentoring. Off-shoring integration.
18	Software QA	Validate code, document, Configuration Management	Product Assurance/Support	Liaise between customer and developer, strategic testing, life cycle, customer experience	Process integration, Outsourcing, India connection, CMM,	Extreme Programming, Software Reuse
19	Technical Writer	Develop materials to help customers with product use.	Product-use facilitator	Create print, Web and other deliverables with interactive capabilities; up-to-date materials	Web, complex products, Limited training, language barriers, product changes.	Multi-media skills; knowing how users need information managed/delivered.
20	Test Engineer	Design test scenarios to validate new products, assure compliance, support complaints.	Test Champions	Participate early in design process; help create test simulations, test as an ongoing process and then final testing.	Cycle times, test capabilities, Automated testing computerized simulations, test costs and time.	Outsourced testing.
21	Training & Development	ID Needs, develop content, deliver training	Training Management	ID opportunities, find resources, TTT Line managers, monitor how it impacts bottom line	Emphasis away from Level-1 measurements,	Developing training designs to affect the bottom line Level-5 not just Level-1
22	Usability Engineer	Product use; User interface	Customer Experience Engineer	Ease of use, post-purchase experience, clever/creative applications	Consumer disillusionment value expectations, innovation	Speaking customer and user language in final deliverables.

Résumé Writing

Résumé writing is an art. It is also a science. Writing one's own résumé is one of the most challenging undertakings, because on the one hand, it is hard to be objective, and, on the other, it is important to showcase accomplishments in a way that creates clear differentiation in a crowded marketplace. The other difficulty comes from packaging accomplishments and then creating a message around them so that it appeals to the decision maker or hiring manager. Yet another frustration that enters creating a résumé, is that once it is complete and is circulated for critique, it is hard to find anyone who does not have an opinion and a specific comment about it. Having spent much time and energy creating a "self-portrait" during an emotionally charged state, it is hard to ignore all the advice that is offered, and at the same time manage the process to get going on the job-search campaign!

A Storytelling Tool

There are a few myths about a résumé; let's disabuse them at the outset.

First, a résumé is about yesterday, or looking back.

Most write their résumés by capturing their past and starting their résumés with a "Summary" statement. Such a statement, of necessity, is backward looking. Typically those who have been working for a number of years accumulate a variety of skills and their experience is replete with assignments that look like a veritable smorgasbord of projects, tasks, and accomplishments. Such a presentation can show a lack of focus. A résumé should start with a focused message about what you want to be doing *tomorrow*. Starting a résumé with a compelling Career Objective does this well. A Career Objective is not just a job description; rather, it is a compelling statement of how one creates value for *them* (the target employer).

Second, it is all about you!

Most start writing their résumés by looking back at what they have done and then listing chronologically their assignments (not accomplishments). This approach results in an accurate chronology of one's past but fails to present how value is created for a potential employer or how leadership will be marshaled to address the challenges on hand. Even more important is how one has successfully managed a career to progressively deliver increasing value in each job! Metaphorically, it ends up more like a collection of rummage or job assignments pulled together for a flea market, rather than a showcase for an upscale department store that presents a carefully scripted story for a select clientele and a theme. This story and the theme for the résumé have to be derived and assembled by research from a list of target companies.

Third, it should be a compilation of all past experience with data, for an expert reader in mind.

The résumé should list only that which supports your value proposition, which is the Career Objective at the top of the résumé. Any work experience of skills that do not directly support this value proposition should be relegated to the background, de-emphasized so as not to detract from your focus. This detraction may creep in, for example, from being in the workforce long enough to be seen as "too old!" In this case, take your experience back to the time when your job still strongly supported your value proposition and list all your previous experience before this point under *last year* just listed *and prior.* To wit, if a career spans 30 years, direct experience you have which supports the value proposition may span 12 years, and if you are writing the résumé in 2004, the chronology could list job details going back to 1992. All the preceding experience is listed under a single heading as "*1992 and Prior,*" with a line or two for each company and some relevant detail. See attached illustrative sample résumés in this Key in Résumé Showcase.

Also, the writing should be presented so that anyone with some familiarity with the subject matter can understand the content, not *just* experts. Presenting the accomplishments in a *story* format, creating intrigue, and avoiding acronyms, special terms, and gobbledygook can compel the hiring team or the decision maker to read a résumé! Anyone reading it should understand its cogent message. This is a true test of a well-written message. Specific tools, languages, or techniques used (all nouns) in a particular technology or specialized task can be listed as "Skills Used" followed by a string of these nouns, separated by commas (see examples in Résumé Showcase).

A Branding Tool

One way to get attention in any market is to differentiate the product or service. If it is *you* you're selling, it, too, could benefit from the same treatment.

Why not, indeed! Few consider themselves worthy of a brand image! "It is only for the celebrities and the rich" they rationalize. In any economy there is value in differentiating. Differentiating comes from branding and identifying a few unique characteristics that provide value over and above their competitors. The value you create in the job in which you are engaged is not a one-time benefit to the employer, but rather, it is the stream of benefits on an ongoing basis. A brand can be built over time. Clever messaging can also create it; messaging that resonates with the buyer.

How does one do this in a résumé?

One way to brand yourself is to show how different you are from the pack. Showing this uniqueness crisply and compellingly can serve as a branding tool. Our genius can be a means of creating this uniqueness. Here we define genius, not as some transcendent intellectual capacity, but rather as something that creates unique value. We all have our own genius about us in some way. Pulling this out, articulating it in a compelling way and then calling this something that does not create an aura of arrogance are good ways to present the brand that differentiates you. This is discussed in more detail in the Unique Skills section below. Another way to brand is by creation of an image.

Image creation goes beyond the words on your résumé. Image has to do with how you present what you create. That includes how the résumé is presented, how you present yourself, how you dress and speak, among your other attributes, cultivated or otherwise. This will be discussed in more detail in the interviewing skills section. See Key-5: The Interview.

Having laid this foundation for the philosophy of good résumé writing, let's go back to the storytelling aspect and see how such a story can now be presented with the foregoing guidelines, element by element.

♠ Résumé Elements

A good format for telling a story and a format that provides a consistent yet flexible framework for the writer consists of the following elements:

- **Career Objective**
- **Experience Summary**
- **Unique Skills**
- **Technical Skills**
- **Professional Experience**
- **Educational Background**
- **Professional Development**
- **Other Accomplishments**
- **An Optional Headline or Tagline**

Career Objective: This is a forward-looking, focused statement of a value-creation process that, at once, commands attention by its imaginative phrasing and concise presentation. This statement makes a few claims about how you create value for the target employer in a couple of lines with a bolded position title to grab visual attention. A career objective is *not* just a position title. A sample below can show the power of a well-crafted Career Objective:

Before
Career Objective: R&D manager in high-tech or software

After
Career Objective: A **Leadership position in R&D** responsible for: Catalyzing technology visions and then quickly turning them into high-revenue products; uncovering unusual applications of existing technologies and discovering new approaches to unsolved problems to mainstream emerging technologies; creating an environment of innovation *throughout* the organization.

In this example how the applicant immediately differentiates by articulating value creation in the R&D labs *and* outside is much more specific and is worth noting.

A colon following the phrase *responsible for* as is shown in the example above, allows for a list of responsibilities to be presented, separated by semi-colons and commas.

Experience Summary: This is a summary statement that highlights overall experience and supports the *claims* made in the Career Objective. This element is about four to five lines in length. This element is different from Professional Experience, and is in addition to it.

For example, in the case of the R&D manager above, the Career Objective can lead to writing an Experience Summary using the following observations. There are three claims in this Career Objective: first, catalyzing technology visions and then quickly turning them into high-revenue products; second, deploying existing technologies to solve problems; and, third, mainstreaming emerging technologies. Here is a well-presented Experience Summary:

Five years most recently at HP-Labs, leading creative engineers and scientists, translating proprietary and patentable inventions into new product offerings to lead technology markets. Previous four years at various HP divisions working directly with GMs offering innovative solutions to problems using mature technologies that resulted in creating $2B in new business. Two years defining ways to accelerate diffusion of new technologies to lead the marketplace.

The function of Experience Summary is to showcase the relevant past that supports the Career Objective claims. As mentioned, this element is separate from, and in addition to, Professional Experience. Why? This is because the latter is a chronological—and hence sequential—presentation of a career history. Experience Summary, on the other hand allows editorial freedom threading through the entire career and pulling out parts that are relevant to support the claims of value regardless of when these relevant parts occurred. As an example, if a particular claim is supported by one year of the most recent experience doing a particular assignment, by two years five-years back, and by one year eight-years ago doing the same task, then a total of four years doing this task can be claimed in the Experience Summary. Without this element the reader has to mentally do this arithmetic by carefully reading the résumé, something for which most on the hiring side do not have time. Even if they do take the time, they may not get it in the way you would want to present it!

Unique Skills: As we discussed during the branding concept, every one of us has a genius about us. This genius can be defined as a special gift that differentiates us from others in what we do well. Putting this in the résumé, gives it the extra element of differentiation early, up-front and allows you to define your brand as we discussed earlier. Unique skills are a portfolio of five to seven items listed in rank order of importance—to the employer—that are unique to you and that differentiate you from *everyone else*. It is presented typically as a two-word phrase that is intriguing and is followed by a one or two line description of what that phrase means in the context of the target. Crafting the bolded phrases that capture your uniqueness is one of the most creative—and differentiating—elements of writing a résumé. Each phrase, when read, immediately conveys the message of how you create unique value *without* a need to read the descriptor. Intrigue, pith, crispness, and uniqueness are all at the heart of this phrase.

For most, writing this part of the résumé is difficult and frustrating. They invariably end up putting down statements that do not create differentiation and that lack any excitement. One way to overcome this difficulty is to collaborate with someone who can help you dig out your inner passions and gifts and then help you articulate them in a compelling way. This also requires trial and error and command of being able to write concisely.

For example, someone has a genius for understanding complexity and then breaking it down to its elements, so that it can be analyzed for easy understanding. This unique skill could read:

Simplifying Complexity: Quickly analyze complex systems, situations, and environment; reduce them to their most elemental blocks by identifying patterns to show how they interact so that they can be easily understood and tackled.

More examples of these messages are in the résumé showcase, at the end of this Key.

These three headings (Career Objective, Experience Summary, and Unique Skills) for a résumé are at the top ("above-the-fold" in newspaper lexicon) to help the reader, in a *few seconds*, know why your résumé should be read in its entirety. The rest of the résumé is "evidence" presented in Professional Experience, your formal education, and other historical background.

Technical Skills: This element is important for those in software, hardware, systems, and any technical area in which they participate. In the case of a software expert, it lists all major platforms (mainframes, Solaris, McIntosh), operating systems (HP-UX, Linux, NT), languages (C++, Java) and applications (Oracle 11.0) in which one is claiming expertise. This is all listed as a string of nouns, separated by commas; there are no verbs.

Technical skills are not limited to only technology professionals, they are relevant to anyone possessing specialized skill as it may be for a lawyer, advertising executive, or a financial analyst. Each profession has its technical specialties and this element of the résumé is where they are presented, in addition to their mention in each or some of the accomplishment stories listed in Professional Experience.

The remaining parts of the résumé are included below:

Professional Experience: This is the *evidence* to satisfy the reader on the claims made in a résumé. If this part of the write-up is provided with accomplishments in a "what" and "so what" format, it can carry weight.

Why?

When listing accomplishments on the résumé, narrating short stories that capture the "what" and the "so-what" with relevant facts is far more compelling than merely lacing a statement with statistics in a dry, matter-of-fact style, as is done with listings in a telephone directory. Most write this part of their résumés in the traditional Tasks/Responsibilities format with statistics to make their point; there is a better way!

Past work experience written in a Task/Responsibilities or even Task/Accomplishment format can create a limitation in a reader's mind about the scope of the writer's leadership capacity. Sticking to what was at hand and how the writer succeeded in accomplishing the objective is good, but not enough, especially when the market is tough. If, instead, the writer goes and tells a leadership story about how the accomplishments were achieved, then the story can present the writer in a broader and more compelling light than as just someone who may have completed a given assignment successfully. The illustration presented here (in "Before" and "After" format) clarifies this point. Writing past experiences as a story that presents the caliber of one's leadership can create a broader appeal for the résumé than just narrating the same experience in a traditional Task/Accomplishment format. This is especially important if one is going outside their past area of the job search, or making a career change; for example from high-tech to biotech.

Having entries in the Professional Experience section with just factually accurate information also does not make for good reading or create intrigue! Using powerful verbs, crafting a concise story, and then weaving facts to present a case, can vivify an otherwise dull résumé, just as does a well-written narrative. Only a few bullets, strategically placed early in the résumé—page one, and early page two—that capture recent-vintage stories that are well written, can punch up a résumé. Leaving the remaining accomplishment bullets as one-liners, can give the reader a sense of the writer's leadership quality that supplement and complement the earlier, more detailed bulletized text. All Experience does not have to be in this detailed story-telling format. That can be both time *and* space consuming!

Another consideration for how these stories are told and where they are placed on a résumé, are based on how the Unique Skills are presented. The Unique Skills are presented in ranked order (to the employer) of importance. The stories that are narrated in the résumé are based on how these skills are presented, and are tied to these Skills in an unambiguous way!

An example of a well-written story in her Professional Experience for a software data architect follows in a "Before" and "After" format.

Before

Delivered a project with Legacy migration application on time and on budget. This was an enterprise-wide success.

After

Led, single-handedly, a critical initiative involving data source migration for a well-entrenched legacy system application that supported sensitive business performance data. This involved transforming a batch-driven operation (two-three per day), to one involving several thousand real-time transactions, which required having to become an expert in a totally unfamiliar technical area within weeks. Result was a successful launch of an entire major geography ahead of schedule, delighting all involved. This success, which became a model, set the stage for the entire migration project, saving countless resources.

Key Skills: Oracle, Kshell, Perl, XML/SAX parser, and XSLT.

Note: This "After" statement looks nothing like the "Before" version. Why? This "After" statement resulted from having read the original one as written, and then engaging with the client in a discovery dialog for about 15 minutes to extract the details, which the client was eager to give. Upon reading the rewritten version, she could not believe that she had accomplished this feat during these challenging times. When I asked her why she did not write this statement originally, which carries so much power, her response was, "I was going to explain it face-to-face in an interview." Most do not realize that résumés not written compellingly do not always result in an interview! Granted this statement, as it appears, takes more space. With accomplishment statements of this caliber, though, you need only a few; the rest could be more compact or even cryptic one-liners to complete the résumé!

Education: List only formal degrees and leave professional development out of this paragraph.

Other Accomplishments: List special awards, patents, publications, and presentations at major conferences.

Professional Development: Company-sponsored training and education without giving too much detail.

Optional Tagline/Headline: This element is optional because it takes confidence, ability to capture your main gift in a simple, powerful phrase, and good marketing sense to pull it off with impact. When you are hurrying to do your résumé, you'll probably come up with a trite headline that can detract from a résumé.

The placement of the tagline is important because if a résumé is scanned and the tagline is on the top, the scanner may interpret this as a name. Make sure that the tagline is placed appropriately for maximum impact and minimum confusion.

Résumé Editing: Everyone has some input on a résumé! Before you get frustrated with all the inputs that are provided, gratuitously or otherwise, be mindful that there are three types of editing:

- Story Editing
- Copyediting
- Layout Editing

Most do not differentiate between the three. Most are good at the second and the third categories. Story editing, on the other hand requires subject matter expertise, market knowledge, and how to position a résumé with the right *story* to get the message across to the right reader so that it *is* compelling, coherent, and concise. All the elements of a résumé mentioned above have to be integrated and then crafted to present this story. It is one of the most challenging tasks of résumé writing and editing.

Copyediting entails checking errors such as grammar, correct usage, spelling, run-on sentences, and other such copy elements. Good English majors and other professionals, as career counselors, usually provide this service. Some career counselors can also provide aspects of story editing, based on their own depth of a particular subject matter. Layout editing entails making a résumé consistent and pleasing to the eye in terms of its overall look, feel, and presentation. In this day of scanned résumés this is perhaps less important in most cases. However, if a résumé is presented for a visual review, it must be edited for proper layout as well.

Tool-6 Résumé Elements

Practice Exercises:
In the space below write the following elements of your own résumé:

Career Objective: 1):

Career Objective: 2):

Career Objective: 3):

In the space below write your **Unique Skills** and their descriptors:

Set #1 For Résumé flavor #1:

Skill 1:

Skill 2:

Skill 3:

Skill 4:

Skill 5:

Set #2 For Résumé flavor #2:

Skill 1:

Skill 2:

Skill 3:

Skill 4:

Skill 5:

Set #3 For Résumé flavor #3:

Skill 1:

Skill 2:

Skill 3:

Skill 4:

Skill 5:

You may use some Unique Skills as common across different flavors of résumés. The idea is to have a portfolio of these for any particular flavor of a résumé, so that each résumé stands on its own and conveys the message you intend to deliver.

Résumé "Dos and Don'ts"

In the previous section, we discussed the elements of design for a good résumé—what to do to achieve a good outcome. Here we present what not to do, to avoid bad messaging. The following list is presented as a summary of what to do, and what not to in writing a résumé. This is not a complete list, but a good sampling of the most commonly questioned items:

1. **Too focused on job duties**

   A résumé is not a chronological listing of job duties; it is a catalog to showcase achievements that created employer value. Merely listing tasks on an assignment is not as effective as showing what *difference* you made. Focusing on unique accomplishments that created impact is worthy of mention. If you cannot answer to "so what?" after writing down each accomplishment in clear business terms, that accomplishment would not be as compelling as the one that accompanies a compelling business-impact statement.

   Those engaged in more administrative or routine jobs, may find this suggestion academic. Even in these jobs, there are many occasions and opportunities where what you did made a difference. Search! Write down what's worthwhile. The person, who can list more of these on the résumé, will certainly have an edge over those who don't. See an example of such a résumé in: "Before/After" Samples, at the end of this Key.

2. **A general flashy header Summary**

   Many start their résumé with a Summary self-aggrandizing statement of their perceived capabilities (A résumé that opens with, "A highly gifted marketing leader with extensive list of accomplishments that extend over 15 years of a brilliant career is now available for hire!" is likely to see the trash heap without getting a chance to be read beyond this point). Instead, start your résumé with a clear statement of objective. A Career Objective must be specific and imaginative that creates reader-impact and intrigue.

   A vague and feel-good Summary, again, may result in the résumé getting tossed into the trash pile. For example, "A challenging management position that affords me to grow and contribute to the welfare of the company, allowing me to rapidly advance..." is too self-serving, vague, and certainly not compelling as a header. If instead the statement is, "A position in a high-tech company responsible for leading technical teams that rapidly respond to the market by delivering to its customers their articulated and unarticulated business needs…" is a more forceful objective statement.

3. **Too short or too long**
   Forcing a résumé to one page can cause crowded text and not afford the ability to present accomplishments in a compelling way. Those who believe that all résumés get read, and that reading a two-page résumé takes twice as long perpetuate the myth of a single-page résumé. The fact is that if introductory parts of a résumé, such as the Career Objective and Experience and Skills Summaries, are compelling, the reader will be drawn to reading the rest of it to verify if what is claimed at the start of a résumé, is well substantiated in the rest of the résumé. Try to stay within two pages. Some executive résumés can be longer than two pages (see Executive Résumés).

4. **Use of personal pronouns ("I" and "me") and articles ("an" and "the")**
   A résumé written in telegraphic form is more acceptable than one that uses non-functional words sprinkled with personal pronouns. For example,

   ### Before:
   I developed a new product that added $2 million in sales and increased the gross margin of the company's market segment by 12%. (23 words)

   ### After:
   Developed new product increasing sales by $2 million and market-segment gross margin by 12 percent. (15 words)

   Having your name and particulars at the heading of the overall résumé tells a reader who the author is, therefore, personal pronouns are not necessary; save them for your cover letters (see Key-3: Sample Cover Letters)

5. **Documenting the "jobless" period**
   In a tough economy, one can encounter prolonged periods of being out of work. After a few months of a vigorous job-search campaign, it is a good idea to engage in activity that can be a résumé builder as you search for jobs. Volunteering, consulting, or organizing purposeful

groups can be experiences. If the job drought extends beyond your financial capacity, it may force you to take on trade jobs as remodeling or contracting. When documenting this period on your résumé, the following example provides how to creatively package this experience without hurting your prospects. The client in this example was an engineering program manager in high-tech and was out of work for nearly two years. He found that remodeling kitchens and baths kept him financially sustained until he was able to find suitable employment. This is the way his write-up was modified for that period:

Before:
2001–2003: Did odd jobs remodeling kitchens and baths

After:
2001–2003: Consulted with well-off clients and provided them with advice and counsel on improving their net-worth and quality of life.

The entry intrigued a hiring manager and this client was invited for an interview.

6. **Listing personal or irrelevant information**
Include personal interests such as reading, skiing, snowboarding, etc. only if the position you are looking for relates to your interests. For example, if you were applying for a position as a ski instructor, listing cross-country skiing as a hobby would be appropriate.

If you are compelled to writing something of a personal nature, explore to see if you can package that experience as an added value to a cause that made you grow in a way that would benefit the new employer. Also be prepared to discuss and defend it during the interview.

Personal information such as height, weight, religious beliefs ("pray three times daily since the terrorist attacks…"), family history ("father was a mean drunk"; "twice divorced but still pay alimony on time") must be left out.

7. **Using functional format with a good career history**
Connecting a good work history with accomplishment in a chronology makes for a compelling presentation. Unless you are making a major

career change or if you do not have a good work history, stick with a chronological format. If you must, when preparing a functional version, create a hybrid design (see Functional Résumé sample in this Key), which includes a paragraph of easily readable employment chronology with company names, dates, and positions held, while the body of the résumé is in the functional format. If you send the functional résumé, always have the chronological résumé for the interview as well. Present it when appropriate.

8. **Not including a "Headline section" that makes an initial reader impact**
   The "Headline section" of a résumé is the initial textual presentation that includes: the Career Objective, Experience Summary, and the Unique Skills. Some of these statements may be telegraphic and bulleted, but they must be compelling for the hiring manager to get intrigued by what you present.

9. **Finding someone to blame**
   In the Professional Experience write-up, avoid presenting accomplishments that were not taken to conclusion because of a transfer, cancelled project, or changed market conditions. In some cases candidates find some reason or someone to blame for their inability to complete a project with which they were enamored. Statements like "project not completed because the boss was an idiot…" do not belong on a résumé. Instead, focus on those that are worthy of mention and that make you shine. Also focus on your role in the project and how you made that succeed.

   For example, if you delivered a product ready for marketing on time and the market suddenly died, resulting in the product not getting shipped, writing "despite market uncertainties and feature-creep, delivered product on time and on budget" sounds much more presentable—and accurate—than stating "marketing sabotaged a greatly designed product through their incompetence, and this happened often."

10. **Omitting keywords**
    Since most companies scan and store résumés in databases these days, if a résumé does not contain certain key words (nouns), the résumé may not bubble up to have someone see it. A separate section for these words is suggested in addition to all key nouns and phrases sprinkled

throughout a résumé to get a computer's attention. For an electronic résumé, use eight point type at the end of the résumé to list all key words, phrases, and titles, so that a scanner can catch all key words that are in your background, but not necessarily on your résumé. If you are in doubt, borrow from the job posting. The computer scans for nouns; the humans hunt for action verbs ("*Led* a diverse cross-functional team…). Use adjectives sparingly; instead fortify your résumé with attention-getting answers to "so what?" statements in factual business terms.

Don't merely repeat the descriptors from the job posting. Those who can show imagination in the way they position themselves for the job, *in addition* to what is required in the job posting will have an edge!

11. **Salary requirements and references**
   Avoid any entries with these details or statements. Many have the redundant "References available on request" under the heading of References. Salary history is similarly inappropriate. This heading, and the contents under it, not only take valuable space, but also may get in the way of meaningful discussions, particularly the salary information. You may also elect to leave blank the space in an employment application that asks for your salary and salary desired (which may be filled in as "Open"). See Key-6: Negotiating the Offer.

12. **Grammar and typos**
   A résumé should be the reflection of you and should contain absolutely no grammatical or typographical errors. Do not rely on the spell check feature of your word processor; it does not check for misused words (*to* vs. *too*). At least have another pair of eyes peruse your résumé before it goes out or is posted. If you use the grammar check feature, do not rely on it entirely either. Also make sure that the chronology is tenable and accurate.

13. **Lying**
   Avoid *any* statements that are not true, no matter how hard they may be to verify. You may bluff your way to getting hired, but if the truth surfaces later, you may be shown the exit door. Besides, would you want to start a brand-new relationship with a lie?

14. **Graphics and fancy stock**

    Graphics and fancy paper may create good visual impact, but since computers scan many résumés these days, the process may introduce errors and funny characters you did not intend on your résumé. Stick to a clean, black and white text that is easy to read, and make sure that the visual impact is that of an open, friendly presentation with well-laid out and symmetrical margins.

    Fancy stock with embossed logos and watermarks are out, but don't print your résumé on a cheap stock, either. Use a good-quality white 24# stock.

15. **Attachments**

    Do not attach any supporting documents or copies of publications cited in the résumé. *Never* attach originals of any documents. Certain documents are illegal to copy (some immigration papers). If your success in landing a job depends on these papers, take the originals or copies as appropriate, to the interview.

16. **Mismanaged expectations**

    The purpose of a résumé is to get you an interview. If the overall impression from the descriptors in your résumé conveys a certain impression about you to the reader, then the reader has the right to expect something close to it when it comes to the interview. If you are trying to hide your age by shortening your chronology and highlighting a more recent college degree and its vintage, the reader has a right to expect to see someone who fits that image. If, as you walk in for the interview, the interviewer sees, instead, someone who is much older than expected, it may be a barrier hard to overcome throughout the interview. Yes, there is a law against age discrimination, but there is no law forcing an employer to hire whoever shows up for an interview.

17. **Address, phone number**

    When listing your email address, avoid using an address with an *edu* extension (e.g. dsaraf@stanfordalum.edu). If you are a recent graduate, you must try to convey that you are no longer living in the academic world, but are ready to move into the world of commerce and industry. If you are proud of your alma mater, the place for it is in the body of the résumé under "Educational Background."

Additionally, make sure that the number listed on your résumé is not on a line that you use for the Internet. Have a separate line for the job search activities with a call-waiting feature. For more complete discussion on this topic, see in Key-1: Your Telephone Connection.

18. **Version control:**
    In a tough job market, it is likely that the job-search can last several months. During this period, a résumé can get revised to incorporate new insights and messages to enhance marketability. As the revisions are made, what had been already sent remains in the hands of those who were the recipients of earlier versions. It is critical to keep track of each version so that when a caller asks you to explain a résumé entry, you know exactly what they are looking for. If your version and theirs do not match, it can scuttle your prospects for the next step in the process. The best strategy to avoid this is to keep each version controlled with a small (6 point) font at the bottom right corner in the footer of the résumé with a date. As you discuss your résumé, asking the caller to read the small print shows that you are disciplined about this detail. (See Key-5: Having Ready Access to Material)

Electronic Résumés

In the Internet era, very few companies receive paper résumés. There are many formats and approaches to doing eRésumés. Following is a brief description of this topic.

How to Choose the Right eRésumé Format

Sending a résumé electronically, requires formatting it in a way that is readable by other scanners, computers, and compatible with other software programs. It is always a good idea to write the résumé in the MS Word application so that visually it looks presentable. It can then be converted by saving that file in the required particular format.

Transferring Résumés Electronically

The Internet transfers, stores, and retrieves data in electronic files. A file is a collection of information, such as a program, a set of data used, or a user-created document similar to those created in a word processor or text editor. To successfully transfer a résumé from one location to another, both people and computer programs must be familiar with a few compatible file types, distinguished by their "format." By convention, files normally have a two to four-letter extension at the end of their filenames, such as dilipsbio.tf.. These formats exist so that applications can store and retrieve data electronically. File formats also give files different degrees of functional *richness* in terms of the kind of information they contain; how the information is presented, and appears to the visual reader.

Three Flavors of ASCII Résumés

You can create an ASCII (*Ask-yee*), rich, rich text, doc, or a HTML format résumé, depending upon how you intend to transfer your résumé file electronically.

ASCII file formats are the most common type of data files transferred electronically via the Internet, including email. ASCII stands for the American Standard Code for Information Interchange. There are three common ASCII file formats that erésumés files are transferred as:

Plain Text (.txt)—Plain-text document files are exactly that—plain. The benefit is that PCs, Macintoshes, UNIX Workstations, or mainframe terminals can read these files. The phrase electronic résumé usually refers to plain text documents since there is no formatting.

If you are required to transmit your résumé via email, the résumé is stored on your PC and viewed with an email reader as Microsoft Outlook. When you transfer this file to someone else's computer, you may not know what email program they have that opens to view your résumé. In this case, the most common format to use is plain text.

Another common use of plain text files, is when you are asked to copy and paste a text version of your résumé into a window located on job board résumé builders or job application forms online.

A sample plain text résumé appears in Résumé Showcase

Rich Text (.rtf)—Most job seekers are used to creating their résumés in a word processor (MS Word or from the Microsoft Office Suite), which does provide fancy formatting options. This rich text file is compatible across different brands of word processors, while retaining its character as a formatted document during and after the file has been transferred, and only if it is viewed in a compatible word processor. The following guidelines can help when dealing with this format type:

If you are asked to provide your résumé via an email attachment, or an online résumé builder, it allows you the option to upload a word-processed version of your résumé; in both cases, you can transfer/upload your résumé as a rich text file.

If the résumé builder indicates that you can upload "Word files" or ".doc files," you can upload your résumé using the Microsoft Word native file format with the .doc extension.

If you are not sure, do a "*Save as*" in your brand of word processor, and then save the document as an .rtf (Rich Text Format)

Hypertext (.html)—Web pages are also ASCII files. ASCII is not used interchangeably with plain text. When creating a document in HTML, which stands for Hypertext Markup Language, it is "marked up" by using "tags" that will render the desired format when the document is viewed using a Web browser like Microsoft's Internet Explorer. Do not use this format causally, use it only when specifically asked.

For more information on electronic résumés visit www.eresumes.com.

Multiple Résumés

In a tough job market, it is a good idea to present messages in a variety of ways, to be able to apply to jobs that require different skills mix. Positioning this way increases your chances for jobs that may not be readily within your target search criteria. This positioning can be done at all levels, including hands-on jobs as software developer, financial analyst, or IT administrator, among others. As a person's experience gets richer and seniority of their job title shows higher levels of responsibility, multiple positioning is almost a requirement for a successful job search, and creating options for you in ways that are not possible otherwise. One can also carry this too far, creating confusion and stress in your campaign.

So, what is an ideal number of ways in which you can position yourself?

There is no hard and fast rule here. But depending on the previous job level you can easily determine how many ways you can effectively market yourself. For example: someone in software development can position themselves as a software developer, as a software team lead, as a software project manager, or even as a product development or systems development specialist, depending on the level of experience they bring to the campaign. As mentioned earlier, a résumé is about tomorrow, not yesterday. This implies that if you have enough experience to claim a certain position based on your understanding of that job, it is worth considering doing this early in the campaign. How does one determine what the *allied* jobs are?

One way to see different flavors within a core job family, is to research the job openings in a particular area of search. Targeting different job boards and then researching job families that fall within your reach is a good start. How many types of jobs within a family, then, are worth targeting? Although that depends on the job level, three or four types within a job family are typical. More than this number can create confusion, not just in your campaign, but also within your own mind as well, vitiating the overall effectiveness of the process. Too few can limit your target job search and companies.

The following list is a small sampling of how a particular résumé can be flavored for a more effective campaign:

Circuit Designer:

-Product Designer

-System Developer

-Team Lead

-Project Manager

Financial Analyst:

-Business Analyst

-IT Support Specialist

-Business Process Specialist

Marketing Manager

-Business Alliance Specialist

-Business Development Lead

-Channel Development Lead

The actual titles are, of course, determined by the job categories that populate the job board for any particular position type.

Once the "flavors" are determined, the next step is to assess which of the flavors are most credible within your own expertise and background, and which ones will get the most action in the job-search campaign. Once this determination is made, specific résumés can be written to campaign for those jobs. Spinning off résumés for these flavors does not entail complete rewriting of the résumé; rather it entails flavoring the main résumé to reflect the language from the job descriptions for which each flavor is targeted.

The best way to achieve multiple positioning, is by having different résumés so that your career objective clearly states your value proposition in that segment of the job market. Of course, the Career Objective is only one, albeit a headlining, element of the résumé. The remaining elements of the résumé, then, need to be in harmony with that headline, so that the entire message is consistent on how the "product" is packaged! An example of how to have two different Career Objectives is shown here:

I. Career Objective: A position as a **software lead,** responsible for developing product requirements working with customers and then leading teams to deliver those products to meet customer needs.

II. Career Objective: A position as a **project manager** responsible for: working with customers to develop software and system product requirements and then organizing and leading teams to deliver these products on time and within budgets; managing the overall product life-cycle to generate profitable revenues throughout the life of the products.

The remaining sections of the two résumés, which have to be in harmony with the respective Career Objectives for the same person, are shown in the samples presented in the Résumé Showcase, specifically: multiple-position Résumés. Also, job-search résumés and those for targeting contracting jobs have different messages, as discussed earlier. A sample contracting résumé derived from its job-search counterpart is presented in Key-9: Contracting.

Customized Résumés

Customized résumés are individualized résumés created for each *important* job opportunity. Taking the one that generically comes closest to the opportunity being targeted, and then changing the language to reflect the one in the job description for the posted opening, results in a customized résumé. Although this may seem like a good idea, it can create problems in keeping track of multitudinous versions and making sure that each is sent with no errors: each résumé has to be perfect. This can pose a challenge for a person who is not well organized or is not good at spotting errors in written text. Even with another pair of vigilant eyes looking over each customized version, this approach can be problematic.

A preferred approach is having a few flavors (three typical, five maximum) that cover the job families of interest, and then bridging the gap with a compelling cover letter. This is more work, but it is the only way one can ensure that the outgoing presentation has the ability to differentiate the candidate. As presented in Cover Letters, any opportunity to make a mark deserves a cover letter!

Executive Résumés

Executive résumés can have certain variations in their presentations from what is presented in previous sections. One element that can be different is the Career Objective; here replaced with a Summary in its place. Why? Many senior managers and executives, approach their search differently. Often, they are presented through recruiters or search firms handling their case who dictate how they are positioned. These intermediaries know client needs, and have a good sense of how to communicate these needs to the clients. For this approach, a header Summary statement can represent a better alternative to a Career Objective.

The other factor that is different is their length. Many senior executives believe that their accomplishments and track records justify longer résumés. Although this is true, and some experts suggest this approach, the key here is not its length, but how a résumé is presented. Although the material provided in this Key, under Résumé Templates and Samples, as a part of Résumé Showcase, suggests a two-page layout, more pages can be accommodated for a compelling cause.

However, more is not necessarily better. As we said earlier, a résumé is not a chronological listing of assignments, tasks, and responsibilities. It is a carefully compiled script of your value proposition that is dripping with your acts of leadership and creative force that differentiates you from others. If there is a leadership story in an experience narrated on your résumé, and if that story repeats in another assignment, then there is nothing new. A single bullet summarizing the stint is enough the subsequent time around. Each citation of an assignment mentioned in the résumé should cover different aspects of a leadership dimension, and should not be a confirmation of leadership qualities already stated. Also, leaving some intrigue can result in a phone call. This is one reason why a résumé should contain just enough information to create intrigue; it is not a document for full personal disclosure!

Résumés of senior executives should also reflect a highly polished, precise, and impactful language. A sample résumé is shown in Résumé Showcase.

Connecting Your Résumé to the Target: The 4-Ps!

In any job pursuit, marketing yourself is the most important aspect of the overall job-search campaign. Marketing has to do with the classic "4-P" approach, with you as the product! These "Ps" refer to the Product, Placement, Price, and Promotion. These are the 4-Ps of marketing anything!

The "Product" is you. What you have to offer that an *employer* is interested in, is what makes the product compelling! Your Career Objective is the value offered. For the product to be noticed and to have a differentiated value as perceived by the potential employer, it is critical that the Career Objective and everything that supports it are compelling.

The second "P" is the placement. This has to do with both the value packaging, and the appearance of the "package." How a product is placed for delivering value to the intended customer, is at the heart of this "P." This means that you carry the burden of showing to the potential employer, that you not only bring the value stated in the message you sent—your résumé and cover letter—but that you become desirable to the hiring manager as a candidate that no one else can compete with. This includes your "appearance," your ability to clearly and compellingly create a "hire me; I am it" message in everything that you do from the first contact, to the final offer—contact to contract! The appearance here includes how you create the first and subsequent impressions through whatever you send and how you send it—your résumé, cover letter, how it is presented, and how it is sent, especially if you have the opportunity of sending it FedEx, whenever possible.

Price is the third factor. This is a key item in your overall campaign. Price cannot be set at the end, if the original positioning is done incorrectly. Maintaining a consistent message and communicating that throughout the interview and hiring process are important in protecting the price factor—your compensation. Despite adverse market conditions, it is advisable to protect what you want, if you have done a good job of projecting a consistent differentiated value message. If you have successfully delivered a message of differentiated value, it is easier to receive a strong offer. This offer can then be negotiated (see Key-6: Win-win Negotiations). And, yes, even in a tough job market (see in Key-6, Negotiating: Sally's Tale)!

The fourth factor is promotion. This has to do with how you are positioned within your own group of competing candidates. Promotion has more to do with the perception of value than almost any thing else. A compelling statement of value to the hiring manager goes a long way in setting up a differentiated position. For example, if you are a software developer, your focus on your ability to merely do projects on time and write great code, will be a common factor on which all candidates will compete. But if the employer is also doing heavy off-shoring and outsourcing on software projects, your ability to know what it takes to manage large offshore and outsourced software projects, and knowing how to set up, manage, deliver, and support projects in countries as India and China, will go a long way in setting yourself apart from the pack. Candidates that recognize this, especially if it is not already part of the job description, can immediately differentiate themselves as more desirable.

Promoting is a mind game as it is shown in the example below:

♠ Promoting Yourself

Promoting yourself has to do with how you create value for the prospect employers—as perceived by them in their *minds*. Promoting is more of a *mental* process than a physical one! It forms a view buyers hold of the offering, based on how they see the item creating value for them. Promoting and packaging are integrally related in the marketing world. By bringing together creatively different aspects of value you can develop an integral message that communicates greater perceived value by the buyer, which might be unique.

The price for a correctly promoted product may also be driven by the power of how it is cleverly exploited.

A simple everyday example of promotion and its power are offered here: A spring-loaded center punch is used to mark a tiny indent on metal to aid hole drilling. Most hardware stores sell it for $1.99, packaged simply.

The center punch, through its snap action, can also be used for shattering glass of electric widows, when a car goes in the water. Often, when submerged, the car's electric windows become inoperative. The only way of escape for trapped occupants is by shattering the glass, because the water pressure prevents the car doors from being opened. The center punch, packaged differently, with a suitable life-saving message, is also sold in auto stores for $14.99.

This is the power of positioning. It is designed to appeal to your emotional needs!

Positioning and promoting yourself for a job can take the same approach, albeit perhaps, in a less dramatic way! Thus, a promotion has to fill an unmet *or even* unrecognized need for the employer, for it to work in your favor. So, if you are an engineer who has done mostly software development in the past, and are now looking for a job, your résumé must have a message about today's off-shoring trend. Promoting in the résumé, that you can collaborate with customers to understand their needs, and also work with an off-shoring team to execute the design, accomplishes this. Thus, you may change your "package" from a software engineer, to a "software product champion." See an actual example of a letter shown in Key-7, Guerilla Job Search.

Résumé example shown in Key-3, "Before/After" Samples, illustrates how promotion can be exploited to leverage value (from an Office Administrator to an Executive's Right Hand. Also, see testimonial from the same client in that section).

♠ *Playing Golf with Tiger Woods!*

Often, those looking for jobs, find that they're challenged by all the skills they wish they had. They lament the fact that they passed up many opportunities to learn the very skills that are now basic requirements for their dream jobs! The number of new courses, certifications, and job requirements that they must now master, overwhelms them.

There are two types of skills that one needs to understand to make themselves sellable in a job:

- Basic certifications that are discipline driven
- Subject-matter certifications that are technology driven

A few examples in each case will clarify the situation: If you are going into Biotech, you may be required to be certified in Good Manufacturing Practices (GMP) or Good Laboratory Practices (GLP); if you are seeking to pursue a career as a program manager but do not have formal program management training, you may consider being certified by the Program Management Institute in Program Management; if you want to run seminars and meetings you may want to consider becoming a Certified Meeting Planner (CMP) and so on. These certifications are a bit like diplomas that are granted upon completion of basic coursework and demonstrating proficiency in the subject matter that does not change with changing technology.

The second category of certifications is, however, different: they require completing coursework in an ever-changing content that is purely technology driven. Examples of some certifications in this category are: Microsoft Office, Oracle Database, Cisco Network Certification, and so on. Each year these offerings change, making obsolete the previous year's certification as new products are offered. Staying current and expert in these subjects is a full-time job. Unless you plan to move into an area and then plan to stay in it for the long haul, taking one of the certifications just to *qualify* into that job market can be wasteful.

Going back to the first category, you may want to decide to move your focus in one of the areas that promises more opportunities as you grow in that particular area of certification. Program management and Six Sigma are two areas that are likely to offer such avenues in a variety of industries. Similarly, if you want to venture into biotech, getting certifications in GMP and GLP might prove useful.

Sometimes, taking appropriate courses on your own, and reading books specific in the subject areas, can let you get familiar in a specific area of interest. However, if you are planning on leveraging that accomplishment into landing in a job where these areas of knowledge are job requirements, then you are playing golf with Tiger Woods! Why? There are thousands of jobseekers that perhaps did what you just read about to develop familiarity, in their past jobs and are expert at it. And, now you are competing with these experts in the same subject areas to qualify for a job!

A better avenue to get yourself "waved on" through a key-word search is to have the correct descriptions on your résumé for a particular job. Then advance an argument that makes *that* requirement irrelevant in the way you have positioned yourself for that job! Now, you are no longer playing golf with Tiger! An example of how this is done successfully is shown in this Key in the Cover Letters section (Catherine Jenkins letter).

Once you decide to become certified or knowledgeable in any one of the areas, you can then include that on your résumé in the Technical Skills section in one of the following categories:

- **Expert in:** These are areas of skills where you can create new knowledge and solve complex problems.

- **Proficient in:** Proficiency means having an ability to solve everyday problems with ease

- **Familiar with:** These are the areas where you read a book, took a course, or have some familiarity.

Since résumés are scanned for key words, your chances of being picked up based on the key word usage (regardless of where they are located and how) are good, if you follow this guideline without getting caught in a lie.

Optimizing Your Targetability

Once the "4-P" exercise is done, the next step is to bring together the best mix of these four factors to create the most impact in a given market and for a specific opportunity. Not only is getting the best job offer important in a market, but also long-term prospects and quality of work life. It is advisable to not just focus on getting the job that is available, but in addition, making sure that you protect the long-term view of your career prospects in every possible way. This is why marketing by bringing in the right balance of the 4-Ps is important.

Developing a marketing strategy has to do with striking the right balance between various alternatives, without letting one heavily influence the others. Researching companies that suit your own needs is critical before sending out résumés to any open position. Many business publications publish a ranked listing of companies with specific employee focus. For example, *Fortune* publishes an annual list of the top-50 companies to work for. The American Association of Retired Persons (AARP) has a publication that lists companies that value an older workforce. *Working Woman* publishes its annual list of companies that encourage working mothers. Selecting and then targeting companies from these lists can greatly increase your odds of landing where you want to. Besides, as we shall show later (Key-4 in the section on Non-Existent Jobs in Your Dream Company) you can land in these dream companies even when there is no posted job for you!

Once the marketing strategy is clear, actual marketing is an execution of this strategy. This entire material is covered in the next chapter, Key-4: Marketing the Product-You! Making a résumé without this forethought can cause problems marketing.

Looking at Other Industries

As the high-tech bubble burst in early 2001, many began to wonder if they should turn their attention to other industries that are either "more stable" or at the very least, were up as the high-tech was down. Some of the cyclical industries were up during and immediately following the dotcom implosion. Some of these industries were construction, defense, healthcare, service, and biotech. So, the natural inclination of those migrating away from high-tech, was to try getting into one of these growth sectors. But, how? Without relevant experience in that industry or sector, conventional wisdom tells us how hard it is to compete with those already ensconced in those specific areas. We presented some aspects of this in Key-2 in Outside but Different Industry.

When making an industry transition, approaching only one transition at a time from a place that offers superior capability to the potential employer can work. Making more than one transition can be unrealistic. For example, going from product development in high-tech to biotech can work well for this reason, even if your knowledge of biology in product development is marginal. Potential employers are taking a risk when considering a candidate from another industry. Your approach should be to mitigate that risk by showing that the strong skills and expertise you bring, more than compensate for the lack of experience you have in that particular industry. A double transition here may entail also looking for a job as a program manager in biotech, where your knowledge of the industry is critical to the success in that position. It is unlikely that such a double transition can work well.

Similarly, taking the IT development experience from high-tech to biotech can be equally promising, since the skills of the high-tech world in the areas of IT are more demanding in certain areas than they perhaps are in the biotech industry.

Each of these avenues and targets require unconventional strategies as outlined here. Migration can be fun and rewarding. See Key-4 Sample Letters: Unconventional Approaches, Specifically, letter to Genentech (Non-Existent jobs).

One thing to remember in making transition to another industry is that, if the target industry is facing growth, your chances of selling yourself based on the strength of your skill set can play in your favor. This is yet another factor in showcasing your secondary and allied skills that make you a stronger candidate for a particular job in the new industry. For example, coming from high-tech to biotech, your secondary skills as product developer might be cross-functional teaming, along with your knowledge of computer networks and software applications. If the potential employer seeks these skills, by all means, leverage them to land the job you want to pursue.

Switching industries in the manner presented here, can yield rewards even when the general economy is tanking. As long as the target industry to which you are migrating is healthy, and you are bringing a valued set of skills, it is manageable transition. For additional discussion on this topic, see Key-4 on Unconventional Approaches.

Knowing (and Breaking) the Hiring Rules

As the job market tightens up, differentiation is key. In a crowded market, if a job opening is posted and everyone who considers qualified to apply sends a résumé, there is a flood of résumés. Very little can be done to differentiate résumés, except from what is sent by going through each one. As the employer is flooded with résumés, yours may not even be seen, if it lacks the criteria used for screening out the less relevant candidates. Such screening is first done electronically by keyword search. The résumé then is seen and read by a human to take it to the next level of decision-making.

Being part of such a cut-and-dried pre-selection process can be daunting, especially for those who lack the savvy of crafting their résumés. Since writing a résumé specifically for each posted job of interest is time consuming and wasteful, there needs to be a different approach. This different approach uses a changed set of rules and is not based on being part of the crowd seeking to be considered for a particular job opportunity. It is based on defining a new set of hiring rules, different from what are typically set for a job that is posted; you have changed the rules from the outside. How can *you* change the hiring rules? Of course, by breaking them!

The strategy is to approach the search process differently. How? Instead of waiting for a job posting, identify an opportunity within a company *you* are interested in pursuing, even though that company is not hiring at the moment. This takes having to start with a list of companies one is interested in, rather than merely applying for a specific job posted by any company that may be of interest.

The next step is to research the company starting with its financial statements. There are three financial statements available for any company: the income statement, the balance sheet, and the cash flow statement. For public companies, these statements are published either on the company Websites, or in their annual reports to the shareholders. Many subscription services also make these statements available through their Websites. Everyone who is interested in a corporate job must be familiar with how to interpret these financial statements, because they tell the unvarnished story that goes beyond the glitz and glamour a company is putting out to create an image in the public eye. Although perusing these reports cannot pinpoint a specific opportunity within an organization, it can lead you to pursue a certain line of exploration that might point in the right direction. Once you have inferred a message from the financial statements, the next step is to find additional materials to infer what is going on in a company. These additional materials are in the form of CEO statements, analysts' reports, and industry analyses published in a variety of media outlets.

Let's take an example:

If a target company is showing declining profits and its revenue is down in an otherwise good economy—this can be easily gleaned from the three financial statements mentioned earlier—then it's slowing down. If the quarterly or annual message from the CEO mentions that the recent product launches have been late to market, with customers complaining about the quality of the new products and the warranty costs are mounting on those products, then the opportunities are in any one of the following areas: streamlining product development, market research and marketing, customer relationships, product testing and quality, and product design itself. If any of these areas are of interest from a job perspective, then developing a point-of-view (POV) letter, with a specific angle with the company to pursue, then it is certainly going to get some audience. Of course, such a letter needs to be articulate, compelling, topical, and written in a way that shows your insights through research. A letter sent by special courier service as FedEx or Express Mail to an executive of the company *without* a résumé, can generate interest enough to bring about the first round of phone calls, and an interview.

Also see Key-3 in the POV Letters section. Many such sample letters that resulted in follow-ups are shown in Sample Letters: Unconventional Approaches.

All "A" companies on the marketing plan should be considered a target for this approach. See Key 4-Marketing the Product—You!

Going Out With Your Message

As you develop your message of value through your carefully targeted résumés, it is a good idea to explore different ways of sending this message to different targets. A more detailed discussion of how this is done tactically, is in the next Key: Marketing the Product—You! However, that discussion is more a "How-to," whereas this discussion is a "What." Here, we're strategically getting ready for the next step. Unless this part is done carefully, no amount of tactical marketing can make up for shortcomings in this very leveraged area! One reason for this discussion here, is that the target and the channel by which that target is sought to be acquired, dictate the message: its intent, value, and the language!

This is one reason why early message testing is important. Once you have a message in a given market and have positioned yourself to align with that market, it is critical to assess the alignment as the *market sees it, not you*! Why? Simply because what is intended is not what is received! Only by trying your message on some trial targets can you assess the validity of your message and how it comes across on the receiving end. It is not merely enough to seek advise from friends and others who do not share this perspective.

Developing a Targeting Mix in Your Campaign

As the job market gets tough, it is critical that the approaches to getting employers' attention are not based on a monotone approach. Most typical and familiar is the one that employs sending résumés to any company that has a posted job opening. This is, of course, a start, but it is this approach that is used by anyone looking for a job. This approach, thus, offers no differentiation at all to anyone adopting it. For a successful campaign, one needs to use a mix of approaches and decide which ones provides the highest leverage. The more difficult or different an approach, the more likely it is to payoff sooner. Why? Chiefly because, most take the easy route! The following approaches are recommended and are ranked with increasing effectiveness.

➤ Sending résumés in direct response to a posted opening.

➤ Sending a résumé and a researched cover letter in response to a posted opening.

➤ Working through a search firm or a recruiter.

➤ Tapping your network to uncover unposted jobs and then presenting yourself.

➤ Identifying target companies and sending a POV letter.

Let us now take a closer look at each one.

Sending Résumé in Direct Response to a Posted Opening

In a bull job market this approach works well. But, then again, when demand exceeds supply, everyone is pounding on your door to have you come and join them! For those who are less visible, even under those circumstances, responding to an open job with a targeted résumé can work well. If you enclose a cover letter that is reasonably presentable, you are differentiating yourself from those who do not. There is nothing out-of-the ordinary about this approach so we'll not dwell on it.

Résumé and a Researched Letter for a Posted Opening

This approach entails having to research the target company so that a cover letter using this insight grabs the attention of someone reading it and the attached résumé. This cover letter goes well beyond what is commonly approached by responding to the list of competencies and requirements listed in the open position or why you are qualified for this position. A very prosaic cover letter also repeats what is in the résumé. The danger here is that once you repeat or summarize what is already in the attached résumé, you are giving the reader an excuse not to read the attachment!

Typical research about the target company centers on the position itself and delves into why the company is seeking to fill this position. If the position has been opened because someone previously holding it has left, then the research must find out why.

At the outset, this may look difficult. And *that* is the point. The harder a thing appears at the outset, the less likely that many would go ahead and do it. This now becomes a differentiator! In most instances, appearances can be deceiving. Digging just a little deeper and using commonly available company information makes it easy to draw an inference about why a company needs to hire someone in a particular position. Articulating that inference in a cover letter can pay off big dividends in getting that phone call.

Let us take a hypothetical case: a high-tech company has an opening for a director of product development. Your research shows that there was someone in that position until recently (there are ways to dig this out fairly easily). You also discover that the company has been late marketing its new offerings for the past two years and that the launched products are failing in the field. Customers are unhappy and both the revenues and profits are down during the same time period. How do you know all this? By visiting the company Website and then reading the CEO messages which tells where the company is struggling. Looking at the annual financials can tell much about the trends in revenues, profits, and specific areas of expenditures (R&D). Calling the customers many companies mention on their Website can be a gold mine. Synthesizing all this into coherent pieces of information and drawing an inference from them is not as hard as most fear. In this particular case, the information points to lack of leadership in product development. Start with understanding customer needs. Delivering robust products and meeting these needs on time are something the company has not done well, based on all the information that is available.

In this case the cover letter, then, begins with a statement about the research and how you plan to change what the company is striving for. See Key-3: Sample Cover Letters.

♠ A Search Firm or a Recruiter

Working through a search firm or a recruiter has its pros and cons. A more detailed discussion of this topic is also included in Key-4: Working with Third Parties, as a part of marketing. Here, we present a summary of what role search firms can play in developing insights in a target company and how these insights can help in developing a message. How to work with these professionals for marketing is presented in the later section.

Specialty recruiters and search firms have their own client accounts that they service. If a company of interest happens to be a client of a search firm you have contacted, it is likely to share with you information about the client if it believes that there is a benefit to them from this exchange. Working collaboratively with a search firm or a recruiter can help you develop insights into a company's affairs, develop a message, and help you present that message in an effort to get an interview. Even if a recruiter does not have a direct opportunity on which they are working, vetting a prepared résumé or a message before broadcasting it through someone so familiar with the job market is a good idea.

Responding to Unposted Jobs

Most underestimate their own network and even more think that their network cannot help them in ways that will benefit them! This is unfortunate because statistics of how people land their jobs indicate that networking overwhelmingly defeats all other ways of landing *combined*. This is further presented in Key-4: Networking.

A disciplined approach to tapping, developing, and using a network on a regular basis can be a boon to your job-search campaign, particularly for spotting unposted jobs. Layoffs and job changes are now a matter of common occurrence. In view of this prospect, it is a good idea to start thinking of investing time in networking and protecting that investment for ongoing needs you may have as a result of the emerging job-market environment. See Sample Cover Letters for an example of an unposted job (Mark Shields letter: Third-party Introduction: Cold Call) in this Key.

POV Letters

Point of view (POV) letters are well-researched letters sent *without* a résumé. This approach to a job search may be considered unconventional, primarily because it does not involve looking for a posted position in a company and then responding to it. The premise for this approach is based on the fact that every organization has latent opportunities. Even the insiders are unaware of these possibilities, unless someone from the outside points them out to them.

To get a company's attention for an unsolicited position, a point of view letter incorporating insightful research information can work well. How do you get this information? For most public companies this information is publicly available. In addition, these sources post the CEO's quarterly report, analysts' research, industry views, and competitors' perspectives. Leading media publications such as the *Wall Street Journal, Fortune, Forbes,* and *Business Week,* among others, routinely publish articles about companies that are in the forefront of news and in the public eye. Thus, there is currently much available information about a company.

Deciphering this information to infer a compelling message and crisply articulating it can be challenging. However, such an approach can be used at all levels, not just senior executives. Samples shown in Key-4: Sample Letters: Unconventional Approaches, include letters that were sent by individual contributors as well as senior managers.

Formulating a point of view (POV) based on the information available can be achieved following this example: For an IT specialist coming from high-tech and looking to migrate to biotech, with a specific company in mind, one area of focus to create a POV letter, is to research how fast that company is growing and how it is spending the IT budget. The former piece of data can be obtained from public records, the latter, however, needs more effort. By looking at industry-specific data and how the biotech sector is spending its IT budget, one can infer this company's IT budget as well as its focus in developing the infrastructure. Once this information is known, a letter can be drafted to show your insights and how you can help such a company through its growth period and challenges in the IT infrastructure.

A well-drafted and compelling letter sent to the CFO, typically responsible for IT (not the CIO), could be a good investment of time. Such a letter is sent without résumé and via a courier, where the recipient has to sign for its delivery usually produces results. Following up with the one who signed for the letter and then calling the one to whom the letter was originally addressed in a few days, can lead to an interview in many cases.

An example is shown in Key-4: Sample Letters Unconventional Approaches, specifically, Brim Brene letter to Genentech. This letter took three hours of research and one hour to prepare, working with an expert coach. Jobseekers often underestimate the effort it takes to prepare a good letter with a compelling POV. Initially, some clients have reported taking as much as a week to come up with a researched message that then needed to be packaged in an articulate presentation. Even if one such letter goes out each week, it is a good start. With practice and confidence more such messages can be sent out as a campaign matures.

Résumé Showcase

This section presents a résumé template based on the structure and design described above and several examples of disguised résumés.

Résumé Templates and Samples

Use these examples and template for crafting your own résumé.

Note: The résumés in the following showcase have elements with specific examples shown for illustration only. Do not copy these in your messages, especially the Unique Skills. If readers of this book use the same Unique Skills, especially the way they are phrased here, they are not unique any more! Work at it!

All résumés in this Showcase are laid out to conform to the book's format. Final résumé is two full pages (8-1/2"x11").

Anatomy of a Résumé

Value-Driver Writer ← Optional Tagline

Colter E. Berg   P.O. Box # San Ramon, CA 05157   **(000) 555-0000**
email@email.com

Career Objective:
A position as a technical writer for a high tech company with responsibility for...

> This is your Value Statement: process by which you create value for THEM!
>
> This is TOMORROW.

Experience Summary:
Sixteen years with a Fortune 50 company, responsible for product documentation, development of....

> This is a carefully extracted summary of all your past that supports the CLAIMS you make in your value statement.

Unique Skills:

- *Knowledge Assimilation:* Develop and release new product prototypes by reviewing specifications, interviewing developers, and testing prototypes.

- *User Champion:* Represent user's perspective in cross-functional product development teams to influence and guide final product interface design and features.

Professional Experience:

Hewlett-Packard Company
Learning Products/Information Design Engineer,
IT Resource Center, Cupertino, CA,

> Unique skills (5-7) are your geniuses that separate you from the rest. All descriptors are in present-tense verbs. This is TODAY.

Provided Web documentation for worldwide, 24x7 response center support tool and the award-winning customer support site.

Colter E. Berg P.O. Box # San Ramon, CA 05157   **(000) 555-0000** Page 2/3

Reduced repeat Website visits by 60% by developing online help and system administration guides for knowledge database support tool (used raw html coding); completed one month ahead of schedule.

> This is the EVIDENCE of your value-creation past. This is YESTERDAY. Use "What?" and "So What?" format. Leave out who, why, when, etc. and create a short story with intrigue that gets you the phone call. These stories should be telling anecdotes of your leadership quality, creating intrigue.
>
> Stop your chronology at a point where it no longer supports your value statement, typically 10-15 years back.

Technical Marketing Engineer,
Marketing Development Center, Cupertino, CA   *1993–1995*
Technical marketing deliverables and beta-site management for real-time operating system releases.

- Compiled and proactively released product support plans to prepare field and support engineers for upcoming releases. Result: Upcoming releases were 100% complete and supportable.

- Increased customer loyalty by 11% (from 72% to 83%) in six months by producing release documents and datasheets; wrote articles for newsletter and user group publications to inform customers of upcoming features and activities.

Learning Products Engineer,
Technical Publications Center, Palo Alto, CA   1992-1993
Updated, reviewed, and submitted manuals to manufacturing release for real-time operating system, networking, hardware, and subsystem products (representing approximately 60 manuals); migrated manuals from proprietary-tagged to InterLeaf publishing format; managed manufacturing part numbers.

Colter E. Berg   P.O. Box # San Ramon, CA 05157   (000) 555-0000   Page 3/3

Software Production Engineer/Support Engineer,
Software Development Center, Sunnyvale, CA   *1989–1992*
Liaised with operating system release team ensuring timely integration of performance subsystem products and coordination of dependencies. Released product CD's for testing, beta site.

Offline Support Engineer,
Office Product Systems, Cupertino, CA   1987–1989
Developed and delivered worldwide training to field engineers for one of company's first TCP-IP based networking products. Developed self-paced networking product training to reduce need for instructor-led sessions in introductory curricula.

Prior Professional Experience:
Sunbelt Communications, Ltd./The Research Group, San Luis Obispo, CA

Education:
B.S., Business Admin. *(MIS),* California Polytechnic State University, San Luis Obispo, CA

Technical Experience:
Operating Systems: Windows 98, Windows NT, HP-UX (Unix), MPE/iX, RTE
Web: HTML, Cascading Style Sheets, JavaScript, FrontPage, HomeSite, EditPlus
Multimedia: Macromedia Flash, Adobe Photoshop
Publishing:

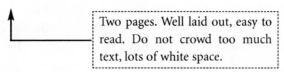

Two pages. Well laid out, easy to read. Do not crowd too much text, lots of white space.

VALUE-DRIVEN WRITER

Colter E. Berg   P.O. Box # San Ramon, CA 05157   **(000) 555-0000**
email@email.com

Career Objective:

Technical writer for a high tech company responsible for identifying user needs and translating them into communication requirements, delivering customer-friendly Web-based or print-form output, assessing ongoing end-user interface effectiveness, and establishing effective procedures.

Experience Summary:

Sixteen years with a Fortune 50 company, responsible for product documentation, development of real-time, Web-based help for customer support site, training courses, manuals, and user aids. Technology areas included a real-time operating system, system performance and networking products, and a knowledge-database support tool. Four years with a start-up market research organization pioneering quality initiatives and then establishing streamlined workflow to sustain robust processes.

Unique Skills:

- *Knowledge Assimilation:* Develop and release new product prototypes by reviewing specifications, interviewing developers, and testing prototypes.

- *User Champion:* Represent user's perspective in cross-functional product development teams to influence and guide final product interface design and features.

- *Web and Print Deliverables*: Develop and maintain online help, system administration, installation guides, frequently asked questions, quick reference cards, and training materials prompted by users.

- *Usability Assessment:* Evolve effective training and user materials through ongoing usability testing and improvements.

- *Product Validation:* Validate and troubleshoot product features to ensure user delight.

- *Multi-Platforms and Tools:* Work in multi-platform environments, learn/create new tools, and then use them effectively to enhance user experience.

Colter E. Berg   P.O. Box # San Ramon, CA 05157   **(000) 555-0000** Page 2/4

Professional Experience:
Hewlett-Packard Company   1987–2001
Learning Products/Information Design Engineer,
IT Resource Center, Cupertino, CA,   1995–2001
Provided Web documentation for worldwide, 24x7 response center support
tool and award-winning customer support site.

- Reduced repeat Website visits 60% by developing online help and system administration guides for knowledge database support tool (raw html coding); completed one month ahead of schedule.

- Streamlined and unified HP-wide presentations by implementing a standard format and style sheets across 7,000+ system-wide global Websites.

- Saved over 50% of visitors' time for complex support Websites by discovering their needs, coordinating across teams, and then implementing latest designs/content.

- Achieved a 75% reduction in incoming audience visits/calls by first developing a page of *frequently asked questions (FAQs)* and then linking content to the real-time release-to-release product features.

- Cut version-search access time by 70% across all document releases by synchronizing the development-and-build version-control process and establishing release protocol.

- Represented user-interface concerns on cross-functional release teams, accelerating customer-friendly sites. Usability index steadily rose from 62 to 97 in less than one year.

- Designed screen mock-ups, reducing deployment from three months to one.

Technical Marketing Engineer, Cupertino, CA   1993–1995
Technical marketing deliverables and beta-site management for Operating System releases.

- Compiled and proactively released product support plans to prepare field and support engineers for upcoming releases, resulting in 100% complete and supportable releases.

Colter E. Berg   P.O. Box # San Ramon, CA 05157   **(000) 555-0000** Page 3/4

- Managed beta-site process—from procurement of sites, tracking resolution of errors, to final user satisfaction survey report—thus ensuring user acceptance.

- Increased customer loyalty by 11% (from 72% to 83%) in six months by producing release documents and datasheets; wrote articles for newsletter and user group publications to inform customers of upcoming features and activities.

Learning Products Engineer,
Technical Publications Center, Palo Alto, CA   1992–1993
Updated, reviewed, and submitted manuals to manufacturing release for real-time operating system, networking, hardware, and subsystem products (representing approximately 60 manuals); migrated manuals from proprietary-tagged to InterLeaf publishing format; managed manufacturing part numbers.

Software Production Engineer/Support Engineer,
Software Development Center, Sunnyvale, CA   1989–1992
Liaised with operating system release team ensuring timely integration of performance subsystem products and coordination of dependencies. Released product CD's for testing, beta sites, and masters for final production. Developed support documentation and training course material.

Offline Support Engineer,
Office Product Systems, Cupertino, CA   1987–1989
Developed and delivered worldwide training to field engineers for one of company's first TCP-IP based networking products. Developed self-paced networking product training to reduce need for instructor-led sessions in introductory curricula.

Prior Professional Experience:
Sunbelt Communications, Ltd./The Research Group, San Luis Obispo, CA
Computer Services Manager: Leader data processing: Coordinated computer installations. Supervised training of data-entry staff for accounting/market-research.

Colter E. Berg   P.O. Box # San Ramon, CA 05157   (000) 555-0000 Page 4/4

Data Processing & Quality Control Supervisor: Managed workflow of data processing for accounting and market research; instituted quality control and processes.
Accounting Assistant: General ledger data entry to preparation of monthly financial statements.

Education:
B.S., Business Administration *(MIS)*, California Polytechnic State Univ., San Luis Obispo, CA

Technical Experience:
Operating Systems: Windows 98, Windows NT, HP-UX (Unix), MPE/iX, RTE
Web: HTML, Cascading Style Sheets, JavaScript, FrontPage, HomeSite, EditPlus, e-Project
Multimedia: Macromedia Flash, Adobe Photoshop
Publishing: Microsoft Word, Microsoft Publisher, Framemaker; InterLeaf
Unix text editors: vedit, emacs
Other: PowerPoint, Excel, Visio, Snag-it.

Software Wiz!

| Gouls Sneha | (000) 555-0000 | email@email.com |

OBJECTIVE

Software Design Engineer responsible for: Web-application development, distributed frameworks and security; working first with customers and then leading cross-functional teams, analyzing problems, developing solutions with a quick concept demonstration, and delivering final products with innovative and cost-effective designs.

EXPERIENCE SUMMARY

Four years in application development driven by customer needs on various distributed frameworks and Web-service infrastructures with expertise in requirements engineering (usecase analysis), architecture definition and analysis, design (design patterns), programming (Java, C++), distributed application programming, enterprise application integration, internet protocols and application security (SSL, X.509, SPKI). Hands-on experience with full software development life cycle.

UNIQUE SKILLS

- **Customer Needs:** Collaborate with customers to translate business needs into requirements.

- **Rapid Prototyping:** Develop prototypes to validate proof-of-concept and get customer approval for design definition using the Extreme Programming Methodology.

- **Leading Teams:** Organize and lead cross-functional teams and drive overall project to successful conclusion. Manage cross-team communication.

- **Product Life cycle:** Plan, develop, release, document, and support total product.

- **Structured Methodology:** Establish structured methodology; reduce overall time-to-market.

- **Novel Solutions:** Identify situations demanding formal problem resolution approach and create a process to eliminate the root cause

- **Creative Architectures:** Develop novel architectures that are easy to implement and modularize. Develop novel ways to conduct full testing with minimum risk and time.

TECHNICAL SKILLS
OS—UNIX, Linux, Windows 95/NT, OS/2.: **Languages**—JAVA, XML, UML, C++, C.
Tools—Sun JDK, IBM Visual Age for Java, Rational Rose 98, Xerces XML parser, Tomcat, Netscape Directory Server (LDAP), Cryptix cryptographic libraries, IBM San Francisco, WebSphere Application **Middleware**—HP E-speak, CORBA, J2EE, Java RMI, EJB, Servlet, JSP, JDBC, SOAP, WSDL, UDDI, **Internet Protocols**—HTTP, TCP/IP, UDP, SMTP. **Databases**—Oracle 8i, DB2, HP OpenView Object
Security—SSL, X.509, SPKI, XML-Encryption, XML-DSig, XKMS, SAML, JCE, JSSE.

PROFESSIONAL EXPERIENCE
Software Engineer, Hewlett-Packard Company, USA   2001–Current
HP OpenView Data Protector Development, an enterprise class network data product.

- Investigated the framework and infrastructure requirements for enabling seamless interoperability and reliable communication between new and legacy components on heterogeneous platforms. Recommended the HP Black-Box Communication model and built a prototype to validate concepts. This concept went on to become the infrastructure backbone of the final product architecture.

- Formulated requirements for OmniWrapper, an external proxy component for Data Protector, and Discovery Service that lead to release of comprehensive requirements, which resulted in a highly reliable product design.

- Used OpenView Object Server to model component object design, which resulted in effective object reusability. This concept drastically reduced time and complexity to generate the front-end GUI.

- Accelerated overall schedule and design robustness by reviewing completed documents

Gouls Sneha   (000) 555-0000   email@email.com   Page 3/4

- Uncovered Data Protector's functional flaws and extensibility of account management by investigating architecture. Recommended improvements for better access control.

Software Consultant, Asquare, Inc., USA   2000–2001
Client Companies: Hewlett-Packard Company, USA, Annuncio Inc., USA
Collaborative Portal Framework development enabling creation of franchised villages or hubs for secure Web services mediation on E-speak technology (HP's Java/XML platform for the creation of dynamic and intelligent Web-services).

- Designed and implemented user/account management for effective credential and preference management, eliminating vulnerability to unauthorized access.

- Designed, implemented and deployed SPKI based security infrastructure for automatic deployment of secure Web-services and to enable single-sign-on and trust mechanisms between clients and service providers. Mitigated risk due to security breach by decentralizing the trust allocation.

- Developed rule builder, rule language (XML), and rule data-structures using ILOG JRules for business rules infrastructure that reduced the time for deployment of personalized e-merchandising campaigns on electronic storefronts. Seamlessly integrated the rule-engine with **transactional** backend datastore for reliable manipulation of business objects using the new business rules.

Software Engineer, IBM Global Services India Pvt. Ltd., Bangalore 1998–1999
Inventory Control/Workflow Management Tool development for document workflow/process control.

- Designed and implemented the server side business logic (EJB) for workflow management to streamline process control. Implemented Web-interface for integration with the backend business.

- Used Object Oriented Configuration Services (OOCS) to implement callbacks to TCP/IP configuration datastore for the TCP/IP Configuration Tools enhancements.

- Designed and implemented the secured printer queue by configuring and enforcing access control to print jobs and clients' print requests (based on RFC 1179).

EDUCATION

MS in Electrical Communication, Indian Institute of Technology, Bombay, India
BS in Physics, Bombay University (First Ranked)

MAJOR ACHIEVEMENTS

Two pending patents on Application Security, one paper in IEEE Transactions.

PRODUCT INTEGRITY CHAMPION

James Bower   (000) 555-0000   email@email.com

Career Objective

A hands-on technical lead responsible for: overall **PCB and system design integrity**, including EMC/EMI, vendor qualification, manufacturability, regulatory and international compliance, component-, subsystem-, and system-level qualification; collaborating with technical development teams and outside partners to achieve time-to-market and cost goals.

Experience Summary

Over fifteen years of progressive engineering experience with strong EMI/EMC capability in all phases of design, mitigation and testing. Extensive experience from PCB to system design, schematic review, placement, critical nets, routing rules and signal integrity including pre-layout, post-layout and static timing analysis (STA). Collaborate with vendors on a variety of issues. Develop new alliances.

Unique Skills

- **Early Collaboration:** Team-up with development engineers to identify early risk in EMC, test failures, manufacturability, and cost; develop strategies to minimize impact.

- **Practical Focus:** Develop quick means to verify design integrity without resorting to expensive testing/analysis to validate a concept before finalizing a major design.

- **Systems Thinking:** Approach all complex designs with systemic thinking to prevent downstream surprises and provide systems perspective to all component development.

- **Rapid Troubleshooting:** Rapidly converge on root causes of system failures and provide quick fixes/design improvements for test completion and customer delight.

- **Meeting Commitments:** Plan to develop best means to achieve final deadlines, despite test and equipment failures, design surprises, and finger pointing. Provide leadership in.

- **Broad Perspective:** Go beyond immediate problems to see what can be done to improve outcomes with minimum resources and time. Devise ingenious solutions.

Professional Experience
EMC Compliance Engineer: Cisco Systems Inc.,
San Jose California   1998–Present
Designing/managing Router line from concept to final EMC compliance.

- During the introduction of the current Router (UBR 10012) EMC/EMI compliance testing revealed a failure in radiation testing. Preliminary analysis and course of action indicated possible board redesign, which would have required several weeks of new work and several months delay in product release. Using various diagnosing and sniffing techniques identified the culprit and was able to continue the testing with a simple design modification of a shielded cable, releasing product on time.

- Identified various deficiencies during testing and protected test and release schedule by devising simple yet permanent fixes to the Router.

Key words: Product management, cross-functional team efforts with NPIE, ME, CE, HWE, analysis, design, mitigation and qualification, technical reports to worldwide standards, NEBS, signal Integrity, IBIS validation, pre- and post-layout and Static Timing Analysis (STA).

EMC Consultant: EMC International
Consulting Salt Lake City, Utah   1995–1998
Engineering consulting in EMI/EMC design, mitigation, compliance, modification/training.
Successfully led entire test program that entailed initial marketing, collaborating with clients, understanding their products, and then devising appropriate tests to certify domestic and international compliance. Units tested were as diverse as commercial, medical, and industrial products, each with their own compliance requirements.

Facility Manager: DNB Engineering Inc., Salt Lake City, Utah 1993–1995

- Managed Chalk Creek EMC facility in Coalville Utah: Site management, marketing, assisting customers with design problems and liaison with home office in California.

- Marketed testing facility, designed tests, delivered final certification and reports to customers and clients with products ranging from commercial, medical, and industrial.

- Increased within less than two years overall business by over 40%.

Senior EMC Engineer: Unisys Corporation,
Salt Lake City, Utah 1993 and Prior
Designed products to meet EMC/ESD specifications in first pass; redesigned established and upgraded products for compliance. Created diagnostic software for test equipment.

- During FCC compliance testing of a new model PC, which was to be released for a major customer, one test failure caused entire PC design to be questioned. Modifications would have entailed time-consuming redesign and getting back in the FCC test queue, which was months. Quickly devised a change while still in test, resulting in full certification and with no loss of delivery date. Product sale (several million dollars) was protected, beating competitors.

Education
MBA/Master of Business Administration, Santa Clara University, Santa Clara, CA
BS/EE Electrical Engineering, University of California, Berkeley, CA

Professional Development: (Certificates)
James Test Lab., CA, High Speed, Signal Integrity and High Bandwidth Models.
NEBS Training Seminar, San Jose, California, Completed two days class by ITS.
University of Missouri-Rolla, CA, Grounding & Shielding Electronic Systems/PCB Design.
University of California, Berkeley California Completed High Speed PCB and System Design.

R&B Enterprises, Washington D.C. Completed Microwave & Electromagnetic hazards course.
Chicago University, Chicago, IL Hazard RF and Electromagnetic radiation.

Software Tools: Visula, Aleegro, Intercomm, Valor, Hyperlynx, and Hotstage software tools.

Awards/achievememts
Several awards for outstanding performance, team work and for going "Above and Beyond" on most projects.

- Two citations from clients on delivery of project on time in demanding circumstances.
- Three published papers on EMC compliance in professional journals, one winning the "Best Paper Award."

BIO-PHARMA SCIENTIST TRAILBLAZER

Sally Smith
Arbor Ct. San Jose, CA 95121
(000) 555-0000   email@email.com

CAREER OBJECTIVE:
A Sr. scientist leading a team of RAs in pharmaceutical/Biotech to oversee chromatography and collaborating/participating with different functional groups to contribute to discovery and pre-clinical and clinical drug development.

PROFESSIONAL SUMMARY:
A scientist with broad background, including analytical, physical-organic, pharmaceutical, and biochemistry, with more than 20 years in a large pharmaceutical and a fast-paced small Biotech company. Proven record in generating high-quality data to successfully support drug R&D activities at various stages, including small-molecule and peptide/protein project.

QUALIFICATIONS SUMMARY:
- Progressive hands-on experience in: GLP/GMP basis laboratory, FDA/ICH guideline, and a senior team member in partnered and internal projects-driven environments to efficiently support discovery, exploratory, pre-clinical and clinical (phase I/II) programs.

- Strong in HPLC with demonstrated problem-solving ability for underline technical issues observed in drug R&D programs, and with the responsibility to oversee functional HPLC lab to ensure quality and training, and R&D chromatographic lab compliance standards.

- Ten years of preformulation study on four small molecules and three peptide/protein to generate physicochemical properties to support formulation development, stability issues and NDA/International filing,

- Eight years of pulmonary dry powder aerosol formulation development and characterization for peptide/protein, including novel excipient identification to support potential commercial viable formulation, and one drug product in phase III trial.

- Three years of peptide/protein drug substance release testing/COA preparation using various qualified/validated analytical methodologies to ensure drug material's integrity. Process impurity/degradant isolation and collaborative identification, CMC documents.

PROFESIONAL SKILLS:
HPLC (RP-, IE-, SEC, -CE); Electrophoresis (native-, IEF-, SDA-PAGE, Western blot), ELISA, total DNA Assay, LAL (endotoxin test), spectrophotometer (UV, fluorescence, IR), Karl Fischer, Buchi spray-drying, Horiba particle sizer, Anderson Cascade Impactor, MDSC, TGA, scintillation counter, GLP/GMP basic training, FDA/ICH guidelines, LIMS and VAX network.

EXPERIENCE:
Scientist I/II: Inhale Therapeutic Systems, San Carlos, CA   1994–2002
Pharmaceutical Research, Physical Analytical Chemistry Group   2000–2002

Chromatography and electrophoresis lead to resolve mass recovery issue, directed proof-of-principle studies, and led contract lab audit to support exploratory/development (phase 0, III).
HPLC functional oversight included facilitating focus/user groups communication to successfully complete customized training courses in areas of technical, workstation software and instrument troubleshoot/maintenance; collaboratively completing HPLC training module revision to ensure user's qualification; working with IS and validation group to ensure R&D workstation validation and participating in software part 11 compliance.

Pharmaceutical Drug Development Department   1996–2000

- Lead scientist in a partner (protein) project team responsible for HPLC method evaluation and transfer, preformulation, solid-state efforts, recommending new formulation approach, working with peers on powder performance and characterization, establishing stability tracking systems, communicating data, issues, and preparing memos/reports. Supervised a RA. A novel excipient was identified and potential viable formulation was tested.

- Lead scientist in internal/partner (peptide) project team: Directed a team's RA on preformulation, formulation screening, stability-indicating HPLC method development, powder characterization, process impurity investigation, and stability studies. Communicated plans, data, and issues to project team. Participated in preparing and reviewing numerous memos, GLP/GMP documents, and formulation development reports. Completed milestone.

Protein Chemistry, Formulation Group   1994–1996

Task leader in an internal (peptide) project team: Hired and supervised a RA for phase-I formulation development and pharmacosintigraphy study; communicated plans, data, issues to project team; prepared and reviewed memos, GLP/GMP documents, and technical reports.

- Primary lead scientist in an internal (protein) project team: responsible for hands-on preformulation, formulation screening, analytical methods, stability studies, and experiment document preparation. Supervised a temp. RA. The formulation is now in phase III trial.

- Primary lead scientist in partner (protein) project team: responsible for protein bioassay, (ELISA) to ensure quality data for formulated powders evaluation, communicated data, issues to project team. Reviewed/authored reports, maintained protein inventory.

Syntex Research, Palo Alto, CA   1981–1994
Chemist II/III

- Analytical Method Development Department, AER   1991–1994

- Analytical Metabolic Chemistry Department, BMR   1991–1991

- Preformulation Department, IPS   1981–1991

California State Water Survey   1981–Prior

Jr. Scientist/Analytical Chemist in Aquatic Chemistry Group/Analytical Chemistry Lab Unit.

Academic Environment

Research Assistant/Teaching Assistant Chemistry Department of University of California.

EDUCATION: M.S. Chemistry, Stanford University; B.Sc. (Chem), Bombay University.

Sally Smith   (000) 555-0000   email@email.com   page 4/4

TRAINING/ACHIEVEMENTS:
Certifications in various software, laboratory, drug development, regulatory, management.
12 patents (some pending), 23 publications, 7 awards, one fellowship, and a committee chair.

EXECUTIVE RÉSUMÉ

David Hemming

Vista Buena Way
San Francisco, CA 94111
(000) 555-0000: email@email.com

Career Objective:
A senior leadership position in a premier and dynamic **wealth management organization** responsible for: pioneering, leading, and delivering novel initiatives to capture new market space and expanding traditional markets, identifying innovative and profitable revenue streams that significantly improve market competitiveness.

Experience Summary:
Over 11 years in a variety of leadership positions at Smith Barney, aggressively driving its wealth management business in California, including pioneering and developing its integrated Private Client Services, Private Banking model, and its West Coast Family Office. Responsible for launching highly aggressive initiatives that defined leadership norms throughout Smith Barney, particularly during the past five years. Operations paved the way for exceptional financial performance despite recent economic downturn.

Unique Skills:

- **Novel Initiatives:** Pioneer aggressive initiatives that create new market space, and then execute to demonstrate viability and consistent results.

- **Market Leadership:** Spot trends in highly dynamic markets and then initiate specific campaigns to attract thought leaders in the client base to leverage additional client influx

- **Staffing Excellence:** Consistently recruit top talent, train, mentor, and demonstrate superior institutional leadership to achieve exceptional performance and productivity.

- **Organizational Innovation:** Continually monitor operational processes and identify opportunities to enhance overall effectiveness and cost efficiencies.

- **Trusted Advisorship:** Cultivate relationships with strategic clients and drive each relationship to where it is looked upon as a trusted advisor.

David Hemming   (000) 555-0000   Page2/4

- **Team Leadership:** Provide needed leadership to both self-starters and team players so that they are effective in their delivery of results.

Professional Experience:
City Corp/Smith Barney   1991–present
Regional Director/Managing Director, San Francisco, CA   1993–present

- Conceived the idea of consulting with philanthropic and charitable institutions to capture new business from them and their wealthy stakeholders. Formed a nucleus group to pilot concept and quickly spring boarded it into a full-fledged business enterprise. Within six years this business grew to over $1 billion in assets in California alone, and has commutatively provided $10 million in revenues with ongoing growth.

- Championed the concept of the West Coast Family Office, targeted for ultra-high net-worth prospects and clients. Aggressively recruited top talent to spearhead effort, garnering $1.2 billion in new client assets within the first six months with accelerating growth.

- Catalyzed the formation of West Coast Corporate Services Group by recruiting coveted talent. Trained and mentored teams internally to achieve exceptional performance. Formation resulted in 12 new corporate relationships and $34 million in cumulative revenues.

- Provided thought leadership to strategic initiatives as an operating committee member since 1997. Significant accomplishments include: major changes to organization's pricing model, compensation schedules, client support services, and partnership initiatives with other key Smith Barney and City Bank business groups as Fixed Income, Equity Capital Markets, Commercial and Corporate Banking, and Private Banking.

- Opened first co-branded financial-services office between CitiCorp's credit and trust services division and Smith Barney's financial advisory business unit resulting in $12 million cumulative revenues since 1998. Provided critical lending feedback and direction as a member of the Smith Barney Credit Committee, resulting in a highly effective credit risk management model. Previous models resulted in losses.

- Built and branded a reputation as one of the most respected wealth management firms in the San Francisco Bay Area through highly effective media and community relations, resulting in attraction, retention, and loyalty of high caliber clients and employees, the competition's envy!

Vice President 1991–1993
Denver, CO
As an Assistant Branch Manager of a 32-broker office, generated $7 million annually. Pioneered several new management and team initiatives.

Boettcher & Company/Kemper Securities Group 1986–1991
Investment Executive, Denver, CO

- Exceeded performance benchmarks and ranked in top ten percent of all executives
- Successfully managed over $30 million in retirement plan distributions for Pepsi Cola Corp., Martin Marietta Corp., and USWest.
- Generated $200,000 in revenues in second full year of production.
- Spearheaded the organization's training effort and managed 10 developing brokers.

Professional and Community Achievements:

- Gordy Taylor Award Winner (Smith Barney Branch Manager of the Year) 1996
- Smith Barney Top Branch Recruiter 2000, 2001, and 2002
- Chairman, Securities Industry Association, Western District 2002–2003
- Chairman, Economic Education Committee, Securities Industry Association, 1999
- Executive Committee Member, Securities Ind. Association, Western District, 1996–2003
- Board Member/Exec. Committee Edgewood Center for Children and Families 2002–

David Hemming   (000) 555-0000   Page4/4

Education:
University of Pennsylvania, Philadelphia, PA, Bachelor of Science, Finance
University of California, Berkeley, CA, Masters in Business Administration

Sample ASCII (eMail) Résumé

Susan Hammer
Berkeley Ave.
Fremont, CA 94555
(000) 555-0000
email@email.com

Objective
A position as a Senior I/T Specialist responsible
for applications development, project management,
and customer-focused implementation, including
off-shoring and outsourcing.

Unique Skills:
*Client Needs: Collaborate with clients to nail
  down requirements and deliver the final product
  on time and budget.

*Leading Teams: Lead teams globally to achieve
  results and deliver them to delight customers and
  provide ongoing support throughout life cycle.

*Rapid Prototyping: Quickly show concepts are
  understood and valid before committing resources.

*Forward Outlook: Think ahead and anticipate cus-
  tomer needs before they become problems that
  drain resources and create dissatisfaction.

TECHNICAL   ABILITIES: C,   C++,   Shell,   HTML,
JavaScript. RDBMS (Oracle, Informix, DB2) MQ
Series Messaging, Visual Basic, UNIX, UnixWare,
AIX, Windows NT, Lotus Notes, Project Management,
Client Consulting

EDUCATION
University of California, Berkeley MSEE
Area of Specialization: Computer Engineering

GMI Engineering & Management Institute, Flint,
Michigan, BSEE
Minor: Computer Science

Project Management coursework toward certifica-
tion, Lucent
Technologies and Stevens Institute of Technology.
PMI Certification pending.

EXPERIENCE
GMC Corporation-Columbus, Ohio
GMC Global Services-Senior I/T Specialist
11/98-present

*Deliver solutions to clients in response to var-
 ied business requirements, utilizing product and
 technology skills.

*Currently design and develop application enhance-
 ments to a MQSeries middleware solution for a
 major insurance company. Languages and environments used are C, C++, SQL, AIX, Windows NT.

*Developed code and procedures for a data conver-
 sion project, utilizing mapping a data conversion
 project, utilizing mapping methodology for a
 pharmaceutical company. Languages used were
 Visual Basic, Data Junction, SQL.

Big Bear Technologies, Bell Labs Innovations-
Kansas City, Kansas Communications Software-
International Custom Development Team Leader
2/97-10/98

*Team leader/project management tasks, which
 include development life cycle estimates, project
 planning, resource planning, team coordination,
 risk assessment, organization, and control.

*Developed customized software for a network fault management product to international customers.

*Performed implementation of network fault management product onsite with international customers (Italy, UK, Spain).

Honors and awards:
*Two papers on coding techniques in SQL for optimum throughput.
*One patent application on a unique method to accelerate CPU throughput.
*Presented paper at the International Conference on IT Effectiveness.

"Before/After" Samples

As we present these samples it is perhaps instructive to see a testimonial a client sent that shows the impact of doing a résumé makeover in the proposed format. Many "Before" samples have messaging, grammatical, and usage problems. They are presented verbatim vis-à-vis their "After" counterparts to show how such a message can be detracting in addition to being weak. The original layouts are preserved. Clients had responded to job openings with these résumés and messages!

An unedited email testimonial is below, together with the sample résumé and cover letter. (Personal details are disguised about the client who emailed the grateful response!)

Hi Dilip,

This is Cheri. I attended your Two-day workshop last week with other people. I know that you thought that we were not "engaging" in your class, but I was actually picking up on things ☺!

I finally sat down yesterday morning and re-configured my résumé and cover letter using your method. Took me about five hours. Did a bit of detective work to find out "who" was the hiring manager and recruiter contact. Sent off my cover email, with résumé about noon yesterday. Six hours later, I got a call from the HR person from the company! I fully believe that it was your "style" of cover letter and résumé that got me the call. I am now trying on suits to interview in!!!! Thought I would share this with you, because I think it was your method of presenting what I "could do" for them that caught their eye. Sure didn't get any calls with my method and I really thought that I had a nice cover letter and résumé before!

I have attached a copy of my résumé, as well as the cover letter that I used so that you can share it with others that come through your way. I used the sample résumé that you shared with me to help me configure mine for this position.

Thanks again, hopefully the next email you get from me is with the new company's letterhead?

Cheers,

Cheri Waxman

(000) 555-0000 home
(000) 555-0000 cell
~Ride safe through life~

Do you Yahoo!?
Protect your identity with Yahoo! Mail AddressGuard

Author's Note: Cheri sent the original email spontaneously. After a few months, as the idea for this book crystallized, I emailed Cheri, asking for her permission to use her testimonial (disguised) in the book. Cheri's grateful email response follows:

Hi Dilip,

It's so nice to hear from you. How neat, I now know someone that has written a book! I will go out and get it when it comes out.

You can use anything from my experience with your service that you want. I don't care how disguised or not it would be. Everything in my life is an open book! No pun intended!

I'm doing fantastic. I told you about the amazing results that changing my resume per your instructions did. Seriously, I had at least three different interviews where they commented on it and asked about it. I ended up getting a position with a Stanford Cardiac Surgeon, managing his office. I'm a "Stanford University" staff member now, who would have guessed I would end up there?

In any case, I love my new position, I love all of the new areas that I have to learn about and I'm very very happy being out of the corporate world!

A big "thank you" goes to you, I don't think I would have gotten all of the interviews had it not been for my revised resume.

You take care, and if you remember, send me an email when your book comes out so that I can go out and pick up a copy!

Cheers, Cheri
(000) 555-0000 home
(000) 555-0000 cell
Ride safe through life

Do you Yahoo?
Get better spam protection with Yahoo! Mail.
http://antispam.yahoo.com/tools

"Before"

Old Santa Cruz
Los Gatos, CA 95033

Phone (000) 555-0000
Fax (000) 555-0000
E-mail:
email@email.com

Office Administrator
Cheri Waxman

Qualifications

Over 15 year's administrative process experience, with emphasis in marketing and manufacturing environments. Proficient on computers, operating both PC and Mac's. I am comfortable using all software and calendaring systems. I have strong organizational and communication skills. I am able to work with minimum supervision and I am a very proactive admin. I am comfortable supporting an executive level person, as well as general group support in a team structure.

Professional experience

Hewlett-Packard Company, Cupertino CA   2000–Present
Executive Admin to Managers of the Partner Marketing Group
Support two senior managers and marketing group of over 50 people with general administrative duties. Calendaring, travel, special mailings, customer meetings and project cost tracking. I am responsible for generation of all purchases orders, check requests, facility needs, supplies and new hire setups. Required to interface with internal & external customers/partners at all levels.

National Semiconductor, Santa Clara CA   1977–2000
Senior Admin to Director of Design & Applications Group, Interface Products Support Director and Senior managers in Design & Applications Group of 50+ people with all administrative needs. Responsible for updating dept. Web site and generation of sample customer product packs. Support 1 Director and 4 managers, calendars, schedules and all generic administrative needs of the 50+ group.

Senior Admin to Director of ASIP Product Development Group and Director of Human Resources, CORE technologies Group
Admin to Director of new product development and HR Director with reporting mangers. Responsible for helping to develop infrastructure of SAP Database and populate the software with divisional information. General HR admin functions including processing of all personal requisitions, offers, new hire/termination processes, while working in a confidential environment. SAP data entry, employee payroll problems and issues.

Other positions held at National include:
Systems Scheduler/Product Definition System (PDS) co-coordinator in charge of developing and controlling all product line build sheets/specs sent out to manufacturing sites and maintained documentation library of above.
Component Scheduler in charge of forecast spreadsheets, pulling corporate data for Product Line Managers and producing monthly financial reports for Marketing Engineers, using FOCUS programs to obtain this data.

Sr. Masking/Diffusion Fabrication Operator trained in all masking operations, diffusion, thin films and final inspect areas. Material handler/expediter for fab area.

Graduated from Cupertino High School, Cupertino CA

Education:

CPS Certified, International Association Of Administrative Professionals, 9/98
Certificate of completion: Management & Supervision, Mission College
Certificate of completion: Purchasing & Material Control, DeAnza College
Certificate of completion: FOCUS Language, Script, XEDIT, Negotiation & Time Mgmnt

"AFTER"

An Executive's Right Hand
Cheri Waxman
\# Old Santa Cruz Way
Los Gatos, CA 95033
(000) 555-0000: **email@email.com**

Career Objective:
An **administrative assistant or office manager** with overall responsibilities for an entire department, its executives, and their teams.

Experience Summary:
Three years at a Fortune 500 high tech as a Partner Marketing Assistant to two senior Directors and their 50+ reporting team members. All administrative and customer service responsibilities in complete support of these teams. Pervious long-term experience at major semiconductor manufacturing facilities with extensive manufacturing and engineering support experience.

Unique Skills:

- **Autonomous Administrator:** Manage all office and administrative functions for large and small groups effectively with little supervision

- **Mastering Priorities:** Set priorities in a very busy office to manage overall executive effectiveness related to calendar and schedules

- **Budget Driver:** Organize internal and external customer events and off-site activities.

- **Hassle-free Habits:** Maintain and generate presentations, reports, update Web site and internal databases for teams and supervisors for a hassle free routine.

- **Anticipate Needs:** Proactively monitor and supply needs of busy executives and offices.

- **Fiduciary Champion:** Ensure and maintain complete confidentiality of sensitive matters related to all company information and direct reports of the executive

Computer Skills Summary:
MS Word, Power Point, Excel, Outlook, Lotus Notes, Rapid, SAP, Best Buy, Flagship.

Cheri Waxman   email@email.com   (000) 555-0000   page 2/4

Professional Experience:
Hewlett-Packard Company, Cupertino CA, Executive Assistant   2000–Present

- Devised a new system for keeping track of schedules in real time, creating a streamlined boss-availability calendar. Also developed a process where staff could access boss's calendar and schedule their own meetings. Similarly reduced time to schedule a meeting facility from typically taking up to two hours to 15 minutes.

- Streamlined a process for small purchase orders (under $1,000) thus eliminating both long delays (from one week+ to one day) and multiple signatures on urgent items.

- Implemented a new customer-call escalation system where incoming calls were screened for urgency and customer ranking before boss got involved. Increased customer satisfaction (from 56 to 78% in six months). Freed up engineers from these calls.

- Automated travel arrangements for routine and frequent destinations, eliminating manual work totaling about two hours daily.

National Semiconductor, Santa Clara CA   **1977–2000**

- Senior Admin to Director of Design & Applications Group, Interface Products

- Support Director and Senior managers in Design/Applications Group (50+) with all administrative needs.

- Identified need for updating department Website, resulting in eliminating call taking and manual handling of customer sample shipments. Sample shipment turnaround was reduced from three days to two hours, increasing customer satisfaction. Freed up two hours of administrator's time daily as a result.

- Posted department calendar on the intranet, eliminating manual queries. Automated meeting facilities scheduling function by identifying, purchasing, installing, and implementing state-of-the-art software. This process became an enterprise-wide model.

- Supported all generic administrative needs and posted communications of section heads to all employees via the intranet. This was previously done word-of-mouth with "drive-by" communication.

Sr. Admin to Product Group Director and Director of Human Resources, CORE technologies Group

- Senior Assistant responsible for developing SAP Database infrastructure, populating it with divisional information and maintaining confidential environment.

- Handled all general HR admin functions including processing of all personal requisitions, offers, new hire/termination processes, while working in a confidential environment.

- Carried out SAP data entry, handled field and employee payroll administration and problems.

- Helped organize large yearly technology offsite meeting (150 attendees) for technologies Director. Within three years reduced costs 20% annually and increased meeting effectiveness.

Other positions held at National:

- Systems Scheduler/Product Definition System (PDS) Coordinator.

- Component Scheduler, forecast spreadsheets, pulling corporate data for product line.

Education:
Graduated from Cupertino High School, Cupertino CA
CPS Certified, International Association of Administrative Professionals, 1998
Coursework:
Management & Supervision; Purchasing & Material Control, De Anza College, Cupertino CA
FOCUS Language, Script, XEDIT, Negotiation & Time Management, National Semiconductor.

Other Accomplishments:

- Officer of the Santa Clara women executive support staff

- Headed United Way fundraiser events at the county level for the past three years

Cheri Waxman   email@email.com   (000) 555-0000   page 4/4

- President Toastmasters Club in Los Gatos, CA for two years
- Certified Meeting Planner (CMP)

> This résumé and the cover letter got Cheri a response from the potential employer within *six hours* of her submittal on line when the unemployment rate was over 10% locally! See testimonial at the beginning of this section! Her previous résumé (also shown) got *none*!

"BEFORE"

James Bower   (000) 555-0000   email@email.com

Career Objective:
A **technical leadership position** in an entrepreneurial organization responsible for: Identifying customer needs to translate them into product requirements and work hard with cross-functional teams to meet customer-driven initiatives to achieve specific business goals. This would allow me to combine my ethics, and strong technical expertise with my MBA knowledge and skills.

Experience Summary:
Over fifteen years of progressive engineering experience with strong EMI/EMC/SI capability in all phases of design, mitigation, and testing with nearly two years of diversified management. Extensive experience with PCB and system design including schematic review, placement, route reviews, and signal integrity.

Professional Experience:
EMC Compliance Engineer: 1998–Present
Cisco Systems Inc., San Jose, California

- Design networking product from concept to final qualification to meet the EMC compliance requirements worldwide standards including NEBS certification.

- Responsible for Signal Integrity of the design. This includes IBIS validation, pre-layout, post-layout and Static Timing Analysis (STA).

- Led and mentor test engineers to provide quality testing and quality technical reports.

- Manage overall product from design, testing, verification, mitigation and qualification to provide better quality product and meet customer needs way before the FCS date.

- Cross-functional team collaboration with NPIE, ME, CE, and HWE to deliver high quality product with cost control.

- Received several Team Achievement Awards.

EMC Consultant: **1995–1998**
EMC International Consulting, Phoenix, AZ
Engineering consulting in EMI/EMC design, mitigation, modification, and training for local companies.

Facility Manager: 1993–1995
DCX Engineering Inc., SLC, Utah
Managed Chalk Creek EMC facility in Coalville Utah. These duties consisted of site management, marketing, assisting customers with design problems and liaison with home office in California.

Senior EMC Engineer: 1993–1979
Unisys Corporation, Ann Arbor, MI
Designed and redesigned product development so they met EMC and ESD specifications. Created and updated the diagnostic software and other programs for test equipment. Maintained close liaison with design, manufacturing, product safety, production control, and purchasing.
Recognized as employee of the month for completing a product on an extremely tight schedule.
Received special commendation work on a PC product line on time release required "personal sacrifice."
Voluntarily wrote and updated software for automated test equipment in addition to regular duties. Created interactive software for testing that eliminated frustrations and reduced hours required by 40%.

Education:
MBA/Master of Business Administration, Pepperdine University, Malibu, CA
BSEE Santa Clara University, Santa Clara, CA, graduate coursework

Certificates of Completion:
- **MegaTest Lab.,** San Jose, California, completed three classes of High Speed, Signal Integrity and High Bandwidth Models.
- **NEBS Training Seminar,** San Jose, California, completed two days class by ITS.
- **University of Wisconsin,** Oshkosh, WI, Grounding & Shielding Electronic Systems Design.

- **University of California**, Berkeley, California, completed High Speed PCB and System Design.

- **R&B Enterprises**, Washington D.C., completed Microwave and Electromagnetic hazards course.

- **George Washington University**, Washington D.C., completed hazard RF and Electromagnetic radiation course.

- **Jim Smith Consulting**, San Jose, California, Grounding and Shielding.

Professional Development:
Leadership and team building skills, project management, communicating for results,
Visula, Alegro, Intercomm, Valor, Hyperlynx, Hotstage and FLOEMC software tools.

AFTER	PRODUCT INTEGRITY CHAMPION

James Bower   (000) 555-0000   email@email.com

Career Objective

A hands-on technical lead responsible for: overall **PCB and system design integrity**, including EMC/EMI, vendor qualification, manufacturability, regulatory and international compliance, component-, subsystem-, and system-level qualification; collaborating with technical development teams and outside partners to achieve time-to-market and cost goals.

Experience Summary

Over fifteen years of progressive engineering experience with strong EMI/EMC capability in all phases of design, mitigation, and testing. Extensive experience from PCB to system design, schematic review, placement, critical nets, routing rules, and signal integrity including pre-layout, post-layout and static timing analysis (STA). Collaborate with vendors on a variety of issues. Develop new alliances.

Unique Skills

- **Early Collaboration**: Team-up with development engineers to identify early risk in EMC, test failures, manufacturability, and cost; develop strategies to minimize impact.

- **Practical Focus**: Develop quick means to verify design integrity without resorting to expensive testing/analysis to validate a concept before finalizing a major design.

- **Systems Thinking**: Approach all complex designs with systemic thinking to prevent downstream surprises and provide systems perspective to all component development.

- **Rapid Troubleshooting**: Rapidly converge on root causes of system failures and provide quick fixes/design improvements for tests completion and customers delight.

- **Meeting Commitments**: Plan to develop best means to achieve final deadlines, despite test and equipment failures, design surprises, and finger pointing. Provide leadership in.

James Bower   (000) 555-0000   email@email.com   Page 2/4

- **Broad Perspective:** Go beyond immediate problems to see what can be done to improve outcomes with minimum resources and time. Devise ingenious solutions.

Professional Experience
EMC Compliance Engineer:
Cisco Systems Inc., San Jose California   1998–Present
Designing/managing Router line from concept to final EMC compliance.

- During the introduction of the current Router (UBR 10012) EMC/EMI compliance testing revealed a failure in radiation testing. Preliminary analysis and course of action indicated possible board redesign, which would have required several weeks or new work and several months delay in product release. Using various diagnosing and sniffing techniques identified culprit and was able to continue testing with a simple shielded-cable modification, releasing product on time.

- Identified various deficiencies during testing and protected test and release schedule by devising simple yet permanent fixes to the Router.

Key words: Product management, cross-functional team efforts with NPIE, ME, CE, HWE, analysis, design, mitigation and qualification, technical reports to worldwide standards, NEBS, signal Integrity, IBIS validation, pre- & post-layout and Static Timing Analysis (STA).

EMC Consultant: EMC International
Consulting Salt Lake City, Utah   1995–1998
Engineering consulting in EMI/EMC design, mitigation, compliance, modification/training.

Successfully led entire test program that entailed initial marketing, collaborating with clients, understanding their products, and then devising appropriate tests to certify domestic and international compliance. Units tested were as diverse as commercial, medical, and industrial products, each with their own compliance requirements.

Facility Manager: DNB Engineering Inc., Salt Lake City, Utah   1993–1995

- Managed Chalk Creek EMC facility in Coalville Utah: Site management, marketing, assisting customers with design problems and liaison with home office in California.

- Marketed testing facility, designed tests, delivered final certification and reports to customers and clients with products ranging from commercial, medical, to industrial.

- Increased within less than two years overall business by over 40%.

Senior EMC Engineer: Unisys Corporation, Salt Lake City, Utah 1993 and Prior
Designed products to meet EMC/ESD specifications in first pass; redesigned established and upgraded products for compliance. Created diagnostic software for test equipment.

- During FCC compliance testing of a new model PC, which was to be released for a major customer, one test failure caused entire PC design to be questioned. Modifications would have entailed time-consuming redesign and getting back in the FCC test queue, which was months. Quickly devised a change while still in test, resulting in full certification and with no loss of delivery date. Product sale (several million dollars) was protected, beating competitors.

Education:
MBA/Master of Business Administration, Santa Clara University, Santa Clara, CA
BS/EE Electrical Engineering, University of California, Berkeley, CA

Professional Development: (Certificates)
James Test Lab., CA, High Speed, Signal Integrity and High Bandwidth Models.
NEBS Training Seminar, San Jose, California, Completed two days class by ITS.
University of Missouri-Rolla, CA, Grounding & Shielding Electronic Systems/PCB Design.
University of California, Berkeley California Completed High Speed PCB and System Design.
R&B Enterprises, Washington D.C. Completed Microwave & Electromagnetic hazards course.
Chicago University, Chicago, IL Hazard RF and Electromagnetic radiation.

Software Tools: Visula, Aleegro, Intercomm, Valor, Hyperlynx and Hotstage software tools.

Awards/achievememts:
Several awards for outstanding performance, team work and for going "Above and Beyond" on most projects.

- Two citations from clients on delivery of project on time in demanding circumstances.

- Three published papers on EMC compliance in professional journals, one winning the "Best Paper Award."

"BEFORE"

Donald Samari	(000) 555-0000	email@email.com

Career Objective:
A position to improve customer relationships in a company so that I can grow with the company.

Experience Summary:
Marketing consultant with a diverse and extensive knowledge of product structuring from both an IT and marketing perspective. In-depth relationship in both IT and business resulting in being an effective conduit between these key areas. Demonstrated successes in building, nurturing, and repairing customer relations to significantly enhance business outcomes.

Skills:
Highly motivated marketing professional with in depth knowledge of product structuring.
Excellent track record of building and maintaining customer relationships
Proven track record of uniquely applying knowledge of product identification theories.

Professional Experience: Hewlett-Packard Company
Marketing Consultant, Product Data Management Organization   1999–2003
   Consult, communicate and interpret HP's Marketing policies throughout all global businesses.
   Analyzed and defined an opportunity in HP's Serial Number Policy that better utilizes system capabilities.
   Defined and proposed a new format that better serves HP's current needs. Executed the clean up of HP product family numbers translating into higher compliance.

Business Implementation Manager,   1998–1999
   Marketing Policies & Commerce Services
   Create, organize, lead, and facilitate all project management functions within the release of software application releases.

   Led team that implemented the release of CPA resulting in an improved customer experience by consolidating HP's customer's discount relationships into a single reporting tool.

Created a global cross-functional team utilizing the best people to meet deadlines and create the most robust tool available.

Product ID Specialist & IT Support Engineer, 1996–1998
Enterprise Business
Consult, interpret and administer all of HP Product ID policies including UPC and product numbers.

Identified a hidden flaw in a software application that drove HP's entire product line ($65B).
Defined and scoped problems and presented them to management for funding; many rejected causing company trouble.
Led the team and executed projects ahead of schedule and under budget
No interruption in the shipment of products.
Repaired and created winning customer relations.
Led the team to replicate the product identification process within Agilent ahead of schedule with no interruption in product shipments.

Marketing Associate, 1992–1996
North American Distribution Organization
Managed all account responsibilities for multiple $30M+ accounts

Created and led a program that increased peer collaboration and a synergetic work environment while building morale.
Reconciled over $1M of outstanding debt; reducing debt by 75%.
Led the team that shipped HP's first products under a new consignment relationship.
Executed first shipment of HP's consumer based PCs ahead of schedule.

Telemarketing Representative, 1990–1992
Direct Marketing Division
Managed sales orders for end-user customers

Created and repaired relationships by displaying empathy and compassion when dealing with hostile or irate customers.
Increased customer loyalty through action and commitment.

Inventory Coordinator,   1989–1990
Direct Marketing Division
Responsible for maintaining accurate inventory counts and forecasting future needs

Created a process to locate high-priced inventory.
Created training curriculum.

Material Handler,   1987–1989
Direct Marketing Division
Responsible for the accurate completion of orders and executing training of new employees

Created a training program with documentation thereby having a consistent training methodology that did not previously exit.
Executed training of all new employees.
Leader of the Pull Quality Forum; resulting in 30% fewer errors within 3 months

"AFTER"   PRODUCT-ROADMAP IMPRESARIO

Donald Samari	(000) 555-0000	email@email.com

Career Objective: A **marketing position** responsible for customer advocacy initiatives and relationships. Lead projects for product identification and how that affects overall customer buying habits and experiences. Develop strategies to simplify complex product offerings.

Experience Summary: Over 10 years defining corporate marketing initiatives that resulted in disciplined processes, project/program management and supporting a global customer base. In-depth relationship in both IT and business resulting in being an effective conduit between these key areas. Demonstrated successes in building, nurturing, and repairing customer relationships to develop loyalty.

Unique Skills:

- **Understanding Customers:** Insights into what motivates customers to do repeat business and develop loyal relationships and how to leverage those for generating sales.

- **Market Advocacy:** Ensure customer is represented in all marketing efforts and bring first-hand input of their experiences into marketing campaigns.

- **Issue Escalation:** Work with upset customers and prevent issue escalation by providing intervention and empowerment, without giving up too much and win their loyalty.

- **Product Identification:** Design easy-to-understand product hierarchy to develop a better product roadmap resulting in increased sales without excessive intervention.

- **Loyalty Measures:** Develop and implement unique and highly effective metrics for capturing customer loyalty; develop initiatives to increase loyalty on an ongoing basis.

Professional Experience:

Hewlett-Packard Company   1987–2003

Marketing Consultant, Product Data Management Organization   1999–2003

Consult, communicate and interpret HP's Marketing policies throughout all global businesses.

- The then existing product numbering system created much confusion in channels and sales teams when configuring new offerings for sale, resulting in delayed sales frustrated channel partners. Championed a new initiative comprising key customers, sales, channel partners and product teams. Result was new and universal product numbering string that readily allowed traceability and history. This resulted in smoother sales, increased revenues and satisfied customers and channel partners across *all* of HP ($40B+).

- Recognized need to streamline entire product family numbers to create better internal compliance for bookkeeping. Devised a new method for a higher-level compliance.

Business Implementation Manager, Marketing Policies & Svcs.   1998–1999

Led all project management functions within software application releases

- Led the team that surveyed customers to better understand their specific requirements prior to launching projects, resulting in a release the was well received.

- Collaborated with the sales account teams and channel partners to devise a method to create a parts "tree" for complex configured systems and custom architected solutions that eliminated ordering confusion and pricing ambiguity. Within less than a year the new system allowed easy ordering of customer solutions and capturing revenues that were identifiable to divisions.

- Led team that implemented release of CPA resulting in an improved experience by consolidating HP's customer's discount relationships into a single reporting tool.

- Created a global cross-functional team to meet marketing deadlines and create robust tools.

Donald Samari   (000) 555-0000   email@email.com   **Page 3/4**

Product Identification Specialist, Enterprise Business Solutions   1996–1998
Consult, interpret and administer all of HP Product ID policies including UPC.

- Key customer relationships were adversarial and uncooperative resulting in delays and lost sales. Identified root-cause and then initiated a partnership with customers promoting respect and teamwork.

- Identified a hidden flaw in a application that drove HP's entire product line ($65B).

- Defined and scoped problems and presented them to management for funding.

- Led project ahead of schedule and under budget with no interruption in service.

- Led the team to replicate the product ID for Agilent ($8B) ahead of schedule.

Marketing Associate, North American Distribution Organization 1992–1996
Managed all account responsibilities for multiple $30M+ accounts

- The NA Distribution organization suffered from rich and valuable sources of collective knowledge. Each one held what they knew close to themselves, creating a morale problem. Recognized the issues and created a team that developed a program rewarding individuals for sharing what they knew. Result: key knowledge transferred quickly, translating into faster and better customer service while increasing morale.

- Restored relationships with customers through direct action and commitment.

- Reconciled over $1M of outstanding debt; reducing debt by 75%.

- Led the team that shipped HP's first products under a new consignment relationship.

- Executed first shipment of HP's consumer based PCs ahead of schedule.

Donald Samari   (000) 555-0000   email@email.com   **Page 4/4**

Telemarketing Representative, Direct Marketing Division   1990–1992
Managed sales orders for end-user customers

- Created and repaired relationships by displaying empathy and compassion when dealing with hostile or irate customers.

- Increased customer loyalty through action and commitment.

Inventory Coordinator, Direct Marketing Division   1989–1990

- Responsible for maintaining accurate inventory counts and forecasting future needs.

- Created a process to locate high-priced inventory; resulting in a 90% loss reduction.

- Create training curriculum, which reduced the complexity of inventory reconciliation.

> Donald got two interview calls within three weeks of sending this résumé to posted jobs. With his prior version he got only one telephone interview in four months of campaigning!

"BEFORE"

Susan Sallumani   (000) 555-0000   email@email.com

Objective
A challenging and rewarding position in Software Quality Assurance or Services so I can stay in this country.

Highlights of Qualifications
Strong QA experience in NonStop fault-tolerant application testing, windows-based application testing and POSIX testing.
Extensive experience in NonStop Himalaya systems, Windows/Windows NT, POSIX, UNIX (Solaris), C/C++, SQL, QA Partner (Windows-based QA automation tool), client/server.
Expertise in test plan preparation, test case design, test implementation, and test automation.
Excellent in coordinating with Development, Release Management, Product Management, Technical Documentation, and Support groups to constantly improve product quality and customer satisfaction.
Good written and verbal communication skills.

Professional Experience

Hewlett Packard, NonStop Enterprise Division, Cupertino, CA   1995–Present
(Formerly Compaq Computers Incorporated, formerly Tandem Computers Inc.)

2000–present: Lead QA Software Designer

Lead QA engineer for verification and acceptance of new function and sustaining updates of the NonStop kernel application Measure.
Designed and developed tests for feature validation, NonStop fault-tolerance, and stress resiliency.
Reproduced CPU halts, process traps, and other product failures reported by customers and created tests to verify the fixes for these problems.
Led large QA project of advanced Measure support of POSIX compliant Open System Services (OSS) delivered in 2002. Analyzed product requirements, created test plan and designed tests, wrote test design specifications, coded tests, and integrated test development efforts of other programmers. Extensive testing was conducted for AF_UNIX sockets, AF_INET sockets,

FIFOs, pipes, name servers, and POSIX File System and File Manager operation.

Wrote test drivers and tools using C in UNIX Solaris environment.

Analyzed product requirements and designed tests by writing test design specifications for POSIX compliant Open System Services (OSS) support delivered in 2001. Responsible for test execution, evaluation, and status reporting for all QA activities during QA life cycle.

Took full responsibility for QA of a major release that introduced new system networking capability delivered in 2000. Conducted NonStop Client/Server testing.

Used a new development process step, product testability inspection of requirements and external design, to shorten test design phase and insure completeness of testing plan.

Mentored less experienced team members, assisted team on technical issues.

1997–2000: Lead QA Software Designer

Lead QA engineer for testing of a C++ Windows-based GUI application, Measure GUI. Analyzed product requirements, created test plan, designed tests, and wrote test specifications.

Developed an extensive automated test suite for the product using QA Partner, C/C++, and SQL.

Took full responsibility for executing testing tasks and reporting testing status. The project size and effort was estimated using modified delphi-wideband estimation techniques.

- The test suite was delivered on time and within 5% of the original estimated effort.

- The test suite uncovered more than a hundred product defects and was instrumental in producing five sustaining update releases of this product.

1995–1997: QA Software Designer

- Studied code of a NonStop kernel performance instrumentation product, discovered and analyzed the code coverage of the existing QA test suite for the product.

- Proposed new tests to exercise and verify the code not exercised by the existing QA test suite.

- Automated tests using C/C++, SQL, and Tandem Nonstop script language TACL

InfoWorld, San Mateo, CA, Software Engineer   1994/1995
Designed and implemented a Windows application, Drainer, in C and SDK to test life time of notebook batteries.
Developed standalone and client/server database applications using Paradox for Windows, Oracle, Informix, C, C++ and MS-Test to do database comparison testing.
Wrote benchmarks in C, C++, MS-Test, Visual Basic to test PC performance, storage devices and PC utility.
Designed and developed a test suite to test OS/2 multitasking system performance.

Education

- Bachelors of Science, Computer Science, Harbin Institute of Technology, China.

- Masters of Science, Computer Science, Memphis State University, USA.

- SEI training in Requirements Management, Project Estimating and Tracking,.

- Intensive classes of C++, OOP, Windows Programming, QA Partner, Oracle 7, UNX.

"AFTER"

BOOTSTRAP SOFTWARE QA CHAMPION

Susan Sallumani	(000) 555-0000	email@email.com

CAREER OBJECTIVE: Software QA Engineer with responsibilities for: collaborating with development teams and customers to finalize product functionality and translating into QA test requirements; organizing and leading QA teams, developing test strategies to achieve a high-confidence final product release; streamlining development using CMM and other processes.

EXPERIENCE SUMMARY: Over **nine years in software,** including database application development and QA functions as follows: five years as a software lead responsible for a team of up to five with specific mission to release a fully tested business-critical applications that run *all* stock transactions, critical banking exchanges, and commercial transactions worldwide.

UNIQUE SIKLLS:

- **QA Test Planning:** Develop test strategies and plans to validate software designs.

- **Leading Teams:** Lead cross-functional teams to analyze and define project requirements then organize QA team to meet these needs though outstanding communications skills.

- **Identifying Customer Needs:** Creating goal and test specifications that meet or exceed customer needs and translating these needs into specific software requirements.

- **Documentation:** Wrote user documentation, installation guides, trouble shooting reference guides, and training tools based on product features.

- **System Configuration:** Installed, upgraded, and configured distributed software.

- **Streamlining Development:** Using CMM, bring entire software development/release process under a disciplined and repeatable environment, including off-shoring projects.

Susan Sallumani   (000) 555-0000   email@email.com   Page 2/4

TECHNICAL SKILLS:
Operating Systems: HP-UX, Windows NT, Solaris, AIX and MS-DOS
Languages: XML, C, HTML, Java Scripts, PERL, Shell Scripts and SQL
Networks: HTTP, SMTP, FTP, TCP/IP, DNS, and RPC
Databases: Oracle
Window Systems: X-Windows and MS-Windows
Middle Ware: Message Broker
Application Servers: Apache
Coursework: C++, OOP, Windows OS, QA Partner, Oracle 7, UNIX API Programming, Java.

PROFESSIONAL EXPERIENCE:
Hewlett Packard, NonStop Enterprise Division, Cupertino, CA   **1995–Present**
Lead QA Software Designer   **2000–present**
QA Lead for new functionality and updates of the NonStop kernel application Measure.

- Led project to test and validated a complex product with over 100,000 lines of code by pioneering a new approach to testing that involved collaborating with a development team on the one hand and the customer on the other. Devised a strategy that brought key members of a cross-functional team to initially identify key aspects of the original requirements and the external specifications together, which were then ranked for test risk. Developed tests for the ranked list of functionality from this and created a comprehensive test plan, a first. The resulting release was on time and was received by customer with no major complaints: another first!

- Designed and developed tests for feature validation, NonStop fault-tolerance, and stress resiliency.

- Reproduced CPU halts, process traps, and other product failures reported by customers and created tests to verify the fixes for these problems.

- Led large QA project of advanced Measure support of POSIX compliant Open System Services (OSS) delivered in 2002. Analyzed product requirements, created test plans and designed tests, wrote test design specifications, coded tests, and integrated test development efforts of other programmers. Extensive testing was conducted for AF_UNIX sockets, AF_INET sockets, FIFOs, pipes, name servers, and POSIX File System and File Manager.

- Wrote test drivers and tools using C in UNIX Solaris environment.

- Analyzed product requirements and designed tests by writing test design specifications for POSIX compliant Open System Services (OSS) support delivered in 2001. Responsible for test execution, evaluation, and status reporting for all QA activities during QA life cycle.

- Took full responsibility for QA of a major release that introduced new system networking capability delivered in 2000. Conducted NonStop Client/Server testing.

- Used a new development process step, product testability inspection of requirements and external design to shorten test phase and insure completeness of testing plan.

Lead QA Software Designer   1997–2000

- Lead QA engineer for testing of a C++ Windows-based GUI application, Measure GUI. Analyzed product requirements, created test plan, designed tests, and wrote test specifications.

- Developed an extensive automated test suite using QA Partner, C/C++, and SQL.

- Took full responsibility for executing testing tasks and reporting testing status.

- The project was scoped using modified Delphi-wideband estimation techniques.

- The test suite was delivered on time and *within* 5% of the original estimated effort.

- The test suite uncovered more than a hundred product defects and was instrumental in producing five sustaining update releases of this product, creating a loyal customer base.

QA Software Designer   1995–1997
Provide QA to a variety of projects individually and through team efforts.

- Studied code of a NonStop kernel performance instrumentation product, discovered and analyzed the code coverage of the existing QA test suite for the product.

- Proposed new tests to exercise/verify code not exercised by existing QA test suite.

EDUCATION:
Bachelors of Science, Computer Science, Harbin Institute of Technology, China.
Masters of Science, Computer Science, Memphis State University, USA.
SEI training in Requirements Management, Project Estimating/Tracking, Inspections.

AWARDS:
Three certificates of recognition for "Special Efforts" on critical projects, resulting in customer loyalty and beating out competition. Two papers published (coauthor) in a Software QA Journal.

FRESH GRADUATE: "BEFORE"

KARLO MENNIG
Adriana Avenue
Cupertino, CA 95014
Phone: (000) 555-0000: E-mail: email@email.com

Education:
BSCS, University of California, Berkeley, 2001, 4.0 GPA

Work Experience:
Hewlett-Packard, Research Labs, Palo Alto, CA
R&D Software Engineer   June–August 2001

- Served as the top Linux expert in the NetServer Division, resulting in a highly focused and forward-looking business outlook for Linux services.

- Performed research and collaborated with internal and external partners to change the direction of support for Linux for NetServer platforms.

- Integrated IA-64 Linux operating system pre-releases with NetServer platforms.

- Made recommendations to other internal groups regarding the utility of Linux and its suitable applications for their projects, resulting in an improved development platform for next-generation products.

- Qualified as an ANSI Certified HP Server Engineer.

Other Experience: Worked as a summer intern for over eight summers in different companies engaged in electronic design work.
Foreign Languages: Speak German

PROFESSIONAL DEVELOPMENT:
Coursework and experience in a variety of computer and science-related topics include:

Machine structures	Data structures
Computer networks	Operating systems
Efficient algorithms	Intractable problems
Compilers and programming languages	Computer graphics

Database systems   Fractals, chaos, and complexity
User interfaces   Human-computer interaction

References: Available upon request.

Hobbies: Computer programming, circuit design. Skiing.

With this résumé, Karlo was unable to get any response to over 400 submittals he had made during a two-month period in mid 2001, at the onset of Silicon Valley's worst job draught. The example of the résumé shown below resulted in two job offers within five weeks.

FRESH GRADUATE: "AFTER"   DELIVERING BULLETPROOF SOFTWARE

KARLO MENNIG
Adriana Avenue
Cupertino, CA 95014
Phone: (000) 555-0000: E-mail: email@email.com

PROFESSIONAL OBJECTIVE
A position as a **software design engineer** responsible for the design, development, testing, and documentation of technology products, including identifying and defining product features as well as implementing designs to deliver functional products.

EXPERIENCE SUMMARY
Eight years in a variety of companies and industries, including a Fortune 50 high-tech leader as well as a start-up. Responsibilities include coding solutions, developing product specifications, identifying user requirements, system administration, and delivering industry-defining results while also beating deadlines. Versed in project management methodology for rapid cycle times.

UNIQUE SKILLS
- **Identify** user needs and then translate them into product specifications.
- **Develop** and implement efficient algorithms.
- **Communicate** exceptionally well via both written and verbal means.
- **Write bulletproof** code to implement new features or version-one products.
- **Troubleshoot** mission-critical bugs, and then incorporate enhancements.
- **Collaborate** with others as part of a team as well as with internal and external partners.

PROFESSIONAL EXPERIENCE
Hewlett-Packard Corporation, R&D Software Engineer   2001
- Served as the top Linux expert in the NetServer Division, resulting in a highly focused and forward-looking business outlook for Linux services. Developed plans for new offerings.
- Performed research and collaborated with internal and external partners to change the direction of support for Linux for NetServer platforms.

| KARLO MENNIG | (000) 555-0000 | Page 2/4 |

- Integrated IA-64 Linux operating system pre-releases with NetServer platforms.
- Made recommendations to other groups for utility of Linux and its suitable applications for their projects, resulting in an improved development platform for next-generation products.

Elusive Entertainment, Software Design Engineer (Consultant)   2001–present

- Wrote an optimized 3-D collision detection module for complex object interaction.
- Mentored and supported other engineers, delegated responsibility, and met deadlines.
- Identified key goals and characteristics of the "Urban Jungle" project.

Minerva Networks, Software Engineer (Internship)   2000

- Developed alpha-blending and text anti-aliasing engines for most successful DVD authoring.
- Used MFC and ActiveX controls to embed video from the company's presentation product into Web pages to drastically expand the customer base for the product.
- Planned and wrote foundation library for spline-based object representation and manipulation for an MPEG-4 authoring tool. Assisted in defining goals and characteristics of the tool.
- Implemented automatic generation of HTML menus, incorporating JavaScript, to remotely control the playback of video server content through set-top boxes.

Compression Technologies, Contract Programmer (Consultant)   1998–present

- Coded a Java port of the Cinepak Pro video compression codec.
- Developed applications to order products online and monitor demo product downloads.
- Consulted with company members to identify appropriate budget, needs, and timeframes.

KARLO MENNIG	(000) 555-0000	Page 3/4

Pinnacle Systems, Software Developer (Internship)   1997

- Developed a windows-based program to run diagnostic tests on video products using C++.
- Defined and implemented an extensible, general plug-in model for the diagnostic tests.

Micro Computer Products, Software Engineer   1996–1997

- Coded "Story Tools," a digital video application that captures, edits, and publishes content.
- Managed source code control system for a project with an approved budget of over $1.2M.
- Administered/maintained many servers and workstations running various operating systems.

Sun Microsystems, Web Programmer (Consultant)   1995–1996

- Identified goals, guidelines, and appropriate tools for the Disneyland project.
- Wrote and tested professional HTML code for the Disneyland Website.

NASA Ames Research Center, Computer Engineer (Consultant)   1994–1995

- Managed NASA's Quest UNIX server and provided support to users of the system.
- Served as a student instructor for Internet classes with over 30 students each.
- Designed HTML and graphics for NASA's K-12 Initiative Web servers.

COMPUTER SKILLS
Comprehensive knowledge of C, C++, Java, Scheme, Pascal, HTML, and Perl languages; experience with MIPS, OpenGL, and Matlab. Experienced with UNIX (Solaris, SunOS, Linux, SCO), Windows (9X and NT), MacOS. Server/network administration/support Windows/Unix.

| KARLO MENNIG | (000) 555-0000 | Page 4/4 |

EDUCATION
B.S.E.E. and Computer Science, University of California at Berkeley, Berkeley, CA

PROFESSIONAL DEVELOPMENT:
Coursework and experience in a variety of computer and science-related topics include:

Machine structures   Data structures
Computer networks   Operating systems
Efficient algorithms   Intractable problems
Compilers and languages   Computer graphics
Database systems   Fractals, chaos, and complexity

Multiple-Position Résumés

These résumés on the following pages show examples of how someone, who has been engaged in a variety or jobs that represent different competencies, can position variously to address different job opportunities. In a crowded job market, having three flavors of résumés is typical but five may be too many!

Some guidelines: Multiple résumés are a tempting alternative to open up a wider audience and market for your job-search campaign. As one matures in their careers, they tend to get exposed to richer experiences even though they have stayed in the "same job!" This also suggests a career management strategy: keep asking for challenging assignments throughout your career so that you become more marketable, if you were to leave your job. Some companies offer flexible job titles or even multiple titles for the same position. Use them creatively in making your respective résumés, so that you can leverage that experience to springboard into a new job!

FLAVOR-ONE

ACE SOLUTION ARCHITECT

| Kristoff Whilhelm | (000) 555-0000 | email@email.com |

Career Objective: A Solution Architect responsible for: developing solutions using PA-RISC and Intel Based systems and their integration with storage, imaging printing, and network design to create unique business solutions; collaborating with customers to translate their needs into highly effective business and technology solutions.

Unique Skills:

- **Understanding Customers:** Collaborate with to understand customers' business needs and then translate those needs into viable requirements. Provide simple yet elegant solutions.

- **Chalk Talking:** Quickly demonstrate understanding of customer needs by diagramming and validating requirements before resources are committed, thus accelerating time to market.

- **Simplifying Complexity:** Reduce highly complex ideas to their most basic, easy-to-understand parts, then present them in a way that is understood across a broad constituency.

- **Leading Teams:** Organize and lead global teams to effectively deliver final solutions.

- **Life Cycle:** Map out product life from start to ensure competitive advantage and value.

- **Technology Knowledge:** Using emerging and mature technology synthesize low-risk and high-value solutions of problems in business, scientific, and commercial domains.

Technical Experience: Hardware: PA-RISC, Intel based systems, high-availability, scalability
OS: HP-UX, Windows 98, NT, 2000, XP, Linux "United Linux kernel" and Red Hat

| Kristoff Whilhelm | (000) 555-0000 | email@email.com |

Professional Experience:
Hewlett-Packard Corporation, Cupertino, CA   1996–2003
Project Manager   2000–2003
Clearly define goals and objectives with customers to successfully compete and win against alternative solutions both tactically and strategically, collaborating with global sales teams.

- Managed a critical initiative involving the creation of a data source that supported multiple business units. This involved creating a model of over 90 GB, which would run on a daily basis, improving upon the legacy batch program in place. Result: a successful launch of the America's geography *ahead* of schedule, delighting all involved. This success set the stage for the entire migration project becoming a model saving countless resources. The original $10M project was paid for within 24 months.

- In highly competitive multi-vendor offerings, and a down economy, played a lead role in securing HP as supplier of choice. Collaborated with key client teams and identified solution needs. Architected two configurations, which resulted in an effective solution that saved $420K in hardware alone. The outcome was a loyal customer and increased future business and market share.

- When a key customer had chosen HP systems for future and worldwide product rollout, customer also selected an independent software supplier, claiming certain functionality. Suspecting false representation, initiated independent testing to ascertain claim. Using special test methods quickly identified that claims were untenable resulting in having to recommend an alternate platform that *was* compatible to honor customer preference. Alternate solutions resulted in 18% cost reduction and 20% faster delivery in addition.

- Using customer knowledge and technology roadmap approach successfully created sales of over $205M and delivered a portfolio of systems to strategic and other accounts. This resulted in an average of 123% of quota over preceding 30 months, in declining market.

Kristoff Whilhelm   (000) 555-0000   email@email.com

- Achieved approximately 212% of server quota for HP-UX in 2002, one of the top 10 in North America. Expected ongoing service revenues of over $400M over two years.

- Leveraged cross-functional divisions (inside sales, marketing, and executive management) to close business.

- Appointed Western Region strategic specialist for Supply Chain Management and Collaboration application providers include SAP and i2.

Product Engineer/Enterprise Account Services (EAS)   1998–2000

Provided technical response to customer inquires for HP's largest enterprise accounts.

- Championed a new quote process reducing turn-around time from 12 hours to four.

- Pioneered a short- and long-term account plan. Designed and delivered effective training, and informational documentation to create accountability and for performance management.

- Transitioned EAS from pilot to production status within 18 months, an HP record.

- Led major customer satisfaction thrust by implementing novel customer-friendly approaches. Awarded "Designated Technology Contact" for entire EAS.

Presales Customer Representative   1996–1998

- Provided solutions for corporate and end-user customers on a wide product mix that included 28 product lines encompassing over 323 individual products, live with customer.

- Appointed to support HP Gold Accounts "Care One Program" due to customer care and commitment. Recognized by management, peers and customers for providing excellent customer satisfaction. Appointed to Product Coach position within nine months of joining the Direct Marketing Organization through own initiative.

- Assisted in training of new personnel and development and design of training tools.

Kristoff Whilhelm   (000) 555-0000   email@email.com

Various sales and administrative positions in retail industry   **1994–Prior**

- Consistently achieved highest sales and profits. Approach was showcased for new hires.
- Streamlined various administrative processes, reducing costs and improving customer experience in every operation for over six years

Education: B.S. Business Administration, University of Phoenix (Candidate 2003)

Technical Skills: Multimedia: Adobe PhotoShop, Acrobat Professional Edition Web: HTML, FrontPage, Publishing: Microsoft Word, Other: Microsoft Project, PowerPoint, Excel

FLAVOR-TWO

HANDS-ON TECHNICAL PROJECTS MANAGER

Kristoff Whilhelm   (000) 555-0000   email@email.com

Career Objective:
A **hands-on technical project manager** responsible for: collaborating with customers to translate their articulated and unarticulated needs into requirements, organizing cross-functional teams, leading overall projects to ensure that final Enterprise IT solution delights the customer; managing the entire life cycle of the project to generate a profitable revenue stream.

Technical Experience:
Hardware: PA-RISC, Intel based systems, high-availability, scalability Unix editors: VI, emacs
Operating Systems: HP-UX, Windows 98, NT, 2000, XP, Linux "United Linux kernel"/Red Hat
Multimedia: Adobe PhotoShop, Acrobat Professional Edition
Web: HTML, FrontPage: Publishing: MS Word: Microsoft Project, PowerPoint, Excel, Visio

Unique Skills:

- **Understanding Technology:** Collaborate with customers to understand their business needs and then translate those needs into viable product requirements. Provide simple yet elegant technology solutions.

- **Customer Intimate:** Intimate knowledge of customers, their business and their customers to articulate what solutions help customers and delight *their* customers.

- **Rapid Validation:** Quickly demonstrate understanding of customer needs by diagramming and validating customer requirements before resource commitment, accelerating deliveries.

- **Simplifying Complexity:** Reduce highly complex ideas and solutions to their most basic, easy-to-understand components and then present them in a way that is understood across a broad constituency.

- **Leading Teams:** Organize and lead global teams to effectively deliver final solutions.

- **Life Cycle:** Map out product life from start to end-of-life to ensure competitive advantage and customer value, without compromising revenues or profits.

Professional Experience:

Hewlett-Packard Corporation, Cupertino, CA	**1996–2003**
Project Manager	2000–2003

Work with key accounts, capture requirements, and deliver innovative solutions through A/C teams. Clearly define goals to compete and win against alternatives tactically and strategically.

- Through effective planning delivered a project 20% faster than originally scheduled while reducing the expected worldwide project cost by approximately 18%.

- Designed re-usable building blocks for customers, which allowed one customer to save $420K in hardware on a single project that was hardware budgeted at $2.5M.
  Using customer knowledge and technology roadmap approach successfully created sales of over $205 M and delivered a portfolio of systems to strategic and other accounts. This approach resulted in an Average of 123% of quota over preceding 30 months, in a declining market. Achieved 212% of server quota for HP-UX in 2002, one of the top 10 in North America. Expected ongoing service revenues of over $400M over two years.

- Appointed western region strategic specialist for supply chain management and Collaboration application providers include SAP and i2.

- Led the technical sale of 11 SuperDome computer systems. SuperDome systems generate the highest percentage of profit for the PA-RISC platform. Averaged 123% of quota over last 30 months, generating approximately $205M in revenue in a declining market, by overcoming customers' technical objections on new and existing product lines. Achieved approximately 212% of server quota for in 2002, one of the top 10 in North America.

Kristoff Whilhelm   (000) 555-0000   email@email.com   3/4

Product Engineer/Enterprise Account Services (EAS)   1998–2000
Provided technical response to customer inquires for HP's largest enterprise accounts.

- Led presales and technical support for HP PA-RISC servers, workstations and Intel servers, workstations, Imaging/Printing, networking and software, which resulted in follow-up with the customer. Researched and provided assistance with questions pertaining to solution recommendations, design add-ons, system upgrades, high availability comparison, application and cabling, performance, and environmental issues.

- Acted as a primary liaison with the account team during the configuration quote process. Reduced the average turn-around time from 12 business hours to 4.

- Created short and long-term account plans, effective training, and informational documentation for department personnel.

- Awarded "Designated Technology Contact" for EAS department for both hardware and software issues by providing high level of customer satisfaction and technical expertise.

Presales Customer Representative   1996–1998
Provided solutions for corporate and end user customers on a wide product mix that included 28 product lines encompassing over 323 individual products, live with customer.

- Product knowledge included Netserver, Information Storage, Kayak, Vectra, mobile computing, Imaging/Printing, and Networking.

- Appointed to support HP Gold Accounts "Care One Program" due to customer care and commitment. Recognized for providing excellent customer satisfaction.

- Appointed to Product Coach position within nine months of joining the Direct Marketing Organization through own initiative.

Kristoff Whilhelm   (000) 555-0000   email@email.com   4/4

- Assisted in training of new personnel and development and design of training tools.

  Retail Accounts   1994–1996

  Financial Industries   1994–1996

  Securities and patrol industries   1992–1994

Various Retail and Customer Services Organizations   **1992 and Prior**

Education: Bachelor of Science in Business Administration, University of Phoenix

Technical Skills: Multimedia: Adobe PhotoShop, Acrobat Professional Edition; Web: HTML, FrontPage; Publishing: Microsoft Word: Other: Microsoft Project, PowerPoint, Excel.

FLAVOR-ONE

SOFTWARE PROJECTS ACE

| Tess Alexy | (000) 555-0000 | email@email.com |

Career Objective:
A **Software Engineer** responsible for: implementing critical business computer systems utilizing proven project lifecycle methods; taking a design from concept to production including analysis, design requirements, external/internal specifications, coding, testing, and release.

Experience Summary:
A software engineer with 10 years experience in quickly assimilating complex technical environments in a diverse spectrum of industries including retail, manufacturing, aerospace, and the military. Strengths include applying creative solutions to business requirements to produce fast-time-to-market software deliverables with verifiable quality. Selected by management to lead most challenging technical assignments for complex and critical product rollouts.

Unique Skills:

- **Customer Needs:** Collaborate with internal customers across functional organizations to translate their business needs into product requirements.

- **Rapid Prototyping:** Develop prototypes to validate proof-of-concept and to expedite customer approval for design definition.

- **Leading Teams:** Organize and lead cross-functional teams to drive the overall project to successful conclusion.

- **Product Life Cycle:** Plan, develop, release, document, and support total product to meet or exceed customer expectations.

- **Structured Methodology:** Follow established structured methodology to streamline software development and reduce overall time-to-market for software deliverables.

Technical Skills:
HP NSK Guardian, HP NSK OSS, HP-UX. C, C++, MS Visual C++, Java, HTML, TAL, pTAL, COBOL85, FORTRAN, PASCAL. ServerNet Cluster, ServerNet Fox, Remote Server Call, TCP/IP. SQL, Oracle, ENSCRIBE,

ENFORM, MS DBAccess. SilkTest, MS Word, MS Excel, MS PowerPoint, MS FrontPage, MS Project.

Professional Experience:
Software Engineer, Hewlett-Packard, Inc, Cupertino, CA.   **2000–Present**
Led critical, highly visible, large revenue-generating projects as software QA engineer in NonStop Enterprise Division.

- Designed testware for customer products with fluid specifications amidst declining resources and shortened product release cycles. Strong skills in performing risk assessment to maintain product functionality.

- Implemented an alternate strategy that cut estimated development time for new testware by 70% for the **Object Code Accelerator (OCA)** product as part of a new generation of HP Nonstop Servers based on **Intel's 64-bit Itanium processor.** Realized a savings of approximately six months effort by embedding rules-based processing into the test harness. Accomplished early corrections to the OCA design before its port to the test platform during the testware design phase based upon careful review of OCA External Specifications.

- Successfully completed quality assurance testing of the **Native Object File Tool (NOFT)** in time for inclusion in the initial release of the new **Dynamic Link Libraries (DLLs)** Project for HP Nonstop Servers. Oversaw the design, test, and actual execution of NOFT testware needed as part of a larger rollout of the DLLs Project which was critical for expanding the division's market share in the growing Web enterprise market.

- Selected by management to perform the technical lead role on a 6-person QA team responsible for performing regression testing on the **ServerNet Fiber Optic Transmission (Fox)** legacy product. Oversaw the team's testing of FOX's ability to interoperate with the newest high-speed interconnection technology known as **ServerNet Clusters (Starburst)** which serves as the division's flagship product.

Programmer Analyst, Ross Stores Incorporated, Newark, CA.   1996–2000
Served as the main technical contact for issues involving the **Distribution Center Information System (DCIS)**, an interactive, real-time software

application supporting most aspects of the distribution center's operations. This system handled incoming shipments, allocated merchandise nation-wide, and identified carriers for outgoing shipments.

- Produced approximately $250,000 in yearly savings after leading inter-departmental review of a competitive vendor bid for computerized price-tag generation. Selected by IT director to provide in-depth techni-cal knowledge of how the business computer system can interface with the vendor's system. Led meetings presenting risk/benefit analysis on vendor selection to the heads of the IT, warehouse, and purchasing departments.

- Quickly resolved an average of production 10 outages per day in this high-transaction volume enterprise environment that consists of a UNIX client interface using an Oracle DBMS and communicating to a host HP Nonstop SQL database using **Remote Server Call (RSC)** and **TCP/IP** as the communication protocol.

- Selected by management as the primary technical analyst in the IT department with providing uniform and standard training to technical staff on all aspects of the Distribution Center Information System.

Senior Consultant, United States   1991–1996
Worked for various recruitment firms servicing Fortune 500 companies throughout the US including: Safeway, Motorola, Boeing Aerospace, Elder-Beerman, NASDAQ, Pacific Bell, and the US Air Force.

Training/Education:
Microsoft University   1995
Certificates in MS Visual C++ Programming/MFC Library

Computer Learning Center, San Francisco, CA.   1988
Certificate in Computer Programming, Distinction and Honors

California State University, Hayward, CA.   1986
Bachelor of Science, Computer Science

FLAVOR-TWO

Tess Alexy	(000) 555-0000:	email@email.com

Career Objective:
A **Software Quality Assurance Engineer** responsible for creating test plans for new, critical, revenue-generating software products and tools; designing test-ware and setting up environments for test execution necessary for product validation and its final release.

Experience Summary:
A software engineer with 10 years assimilating complex technical environments in a diverse spectrum of industries, including retail, manufacturing, aerospace, and the military. Strengths include applying creative solutions to business requirements to produce fast-time-to-market software deliverables with verifiable quality. Selected by management to lead most challenging assignments for complex and critical product rollouts.

Unique Skills:

- **Product Requirements:** Collaborate with customers across functions to understand their needs. Validate these needs through final testing.

- **Early Collaboration:** Team up with development personnel to get an early insight on issues and use that knowledge to develop a robust test suite and build test strategies.

- **Leading Teams:** Organize and lead cross-functional teams to drive the overall projects.

- **Release Process:** Plan, develop, release, document, and support total product to meet or exceed customer expectations. Manage product life-cycle.

- **Structured Methodology:** Follow established structured methodology to streamline software development and reduce overall time-to-market for software deliverables.

- **Configuration Integrity:** Ensure configuration control documentation and all other release formalities are in place prior to final shipment.

Technical Skills:
HP NSK Guardian, HP NSK OSS, HP-UX. C, C++, MS Visual C++, Java, HTML, TAL, pTAL, COBOL85, FORTRAN, PASCAL. ServerNet Cluster,

ServerNet Fox, Remote Server Call, TCP/IP. SQL, Oracle, ENSCRIBE, ENFORM, MS DBAccess. MS Word, PowerPoint, Excel.

Professional Experience:
Software Engineer, Hewlett-Packard, Inc, Cupertino, CA.   2000–Present

- Rotated among critical, highly visible, large revenue-generating projects as quality assurance software engineer in the NonStop Enterprise Division. Designed testware for customer products with fluid specifications amidst declining resources and shorten product release cycles.

- Implemented an alternate strategy that cut estimated development time for new testware by 70% for the **Object Code Accelerator (OCA)** product as part of a new generation of HP Nonstop Servers based on **Intel's 64-bit Itanium processor.** Realized a savings of approximately six months effort by embedding rules-based processing into the test harness. Accomplished early corrections to the OCA design before its port to the test platform during design phase based upon careful review of OCA External Specifications.

- Successfully completed quality assurance testing of the **Native Object File Tool (NOFT)** in time for inclusion in the initial release of the new **Dynamic Link Libraries (DLLs)** Project for HP Nonstop Servers. Oversaw the design, test, and actual execution of NOFT testware needed as part of a larger rollout of the DLLs Project which was critical for expanding the division's market share in the growing Web enterprise market.

- Selected by management to perform the technical lead role on a six-person QA team responsible for performing regression testing on the **ServerNet Fiber Optic Transmission (Fox)** legacy product. Oversaw the team's testing of FOX's ability to interoperate with the newest high-speed interconnection technology known as **ServerNet Clusters (Starburst)** which serves as the division's flagship product.

Programmer Analyst, Ross Stores Incorporated, Newark, CA.   1996–2000
Served as the main technical contact for issues involving the **Distribution Center Information System (DCIS)**, an interactive, real-time software application for distribution center's operations.

- Produced approximately $250,000 in yearly savings after leading inter-departmental review of a competitive vendor bid for computerized price-tag generation. Selected by IT director to provide in-depth technical knowledge of how the business computer system can interface with the vendor's system. Led meetings presenting risk/benefit analysis on vendor selection to the heads of the IT, warehouse, and purchasing departments.

- Quickly resolved an average of production 10 outages per day in this high-transaction volume enterprise environment that consists of a UNIX client interface using an Oracle DBMS and communicating to a host HP Nonstop SQL database using **Remote Server Call (RSC) and TCP/IP** as the communication protocol.

- Selected by management as the primary technical analyst in the IT department with providing uniform and standard training to technical staff on all aspects of the Distribution Center Information System.

Senior Consultant, United States   1991–1996
Worked for various recruitment firms servicing Fortune 500 companies throughout the US including: Safeway, Motorola, Boeing Aerospace, Elder-Beerman, NASDAQ, Pacific Bell, and the US Air Force.

Training/Education:
Microsoft University   1995
Certificates in MS Visual C++ Programming/MFC Library

Computer Learning Center, San Francisco, CA.   1988
Certificate in Computer Programming, Distinction and Honors

California State University, Hayward, CA.   1986
Bachelor of Science, Computer Science

Functional Résumé Sample

So far, we have presented the most commonly used format: the chronological résumé. Functional résumés present an alternative design and a message that could be useful when making a career change, or when positioning for a job that is out of the normal trajectory in a career path. Functional résumés also are written when you have multiple points of engagements in your history that span different job assignments that are diverse. Functional résumés are written without its main body having any reference to a sequential chronology. The focus is highlighting the functional achievements, not how you progressed in your career arc.

Functional résumé format is not commonly used in job searches. Why? Those who are familiar with reading résumés are used to reading in a chronological format (all our previous examples are in this format). So, anyone sending a functional résumé is seen with suspicion—as if there is something to hide either in the chronology or the job progression. Since a functional résumé does not have chronology, hiring managers are most concerned about this aspect of your background. One way to overcome this concern is to provide a summary chronology at the end (this is the hybrid version, and a sample follows). But even then, there is some lingering doubt about the verity of a functional résumé that is hard to overcome. One reason for this apprehension is, perhaps, that a chronological résumé can be molded in to its functional counterpart like a chameleon in the hands of an expert résumé writer, and this concerns some.

One antidote is to *first* prepare a chronological résumé and then translate that into its functional counterpart. Another one is to use a hybrid format previously mentioned (the shown functional sample is a hybrid). An example of such a pair is presented. Yet another defense, is to take the chorological résumé with you, and present that during the discussion of your accomplishments, so that the interviewer can judge on the merit of your past how suitable you are for that particular position.

The following two examples show the author's résumé in chronological and functional (hybrid) format.

Dilip G. Saraf

My Home Street   Fremont, CA 94555   (000) 555-0000
email@email.com

Career Objective:

Senior Consultant, practice office of a global career management organization responsible for: building on current business and taking it to new levels of performance and possibilities; adding an increasing book of business using imaginative, innovative, and novel concepts and then sustaining it to showcase new approaches on how to profit in a turbulent economy.

Experience Summary:

A well-rounded hands-on organizational, management, and business executive with over 14 years consulting in wide ranging assignments and industries, including three years at a major career outplacement center of a global leader. Major emphasis on business development and capturing sales in imaginative ways. Consulting experience includes selling and then working with CEOs and top executives to successfully transform organizations.

Unique Skills:

- **Business Development:** Identify unarticulated needs/latent opportunities and then move clients to partner and realize unprecedented value propositions. Mobilize teams to embrace the new and lead initiatives to execute and demonstrate results.

- **Client Loyalty:** Provide relentless leadership developing practices and behaviors that engender client loyalty. Establish routines making loyalty a watchword.

- **Business Performance:** Establish stretch standards to deliver outstanding results and then continually improve operations to showcase best-in-class performance.

- **Team Building:** Inspire to embrace new learning to create ongoing value; lead initiatives to improve value creation/delivery for sustaining competitive advantage.

- **Community Leadership:** Champion community causes to create presence in meaningful endeavors and participate to promote franchise.

Professional Experience:
Consultant   **2001–Present**

- Senior Consultant, Lee Hecht Harrison. Worked in a variety of assignments with the jobless from client organizations helping them reinvent themselves. Outstanding record of landed clients, especially those using unconventional approaches, including CEOs. Initiated, designed, and delivered over ten innovative and high-demand roundtables. Invited as a guest speaker to organizations. Authored several articles on career issues and published a major book on the topic.

- Business consulting with several private clients in business development, reinvention, organizational effectiveness, strategy, and business performance.

- Marketing consultant to several private clients (up to CEOs) helping them define their business vision, reinvention, coaching, and innovative marketing.

Personnel Decisions International, San Francisco, CA   **94–98; 99–2001**
Senior Consultant

- Transformed a product offering into a high-value consultative solution that resulted in $650K in annual individual billings.

- Redesigned a money-losing workshop and transformed it into a profitable, highly-rated leadership development experience for a Fortune 100 high-tech client.

- Consulted with the Managing Director and his executive team in a financial institution to identify new market opportunities and then coached the team to capture the opportunities.

- Individually coached executives on how to meet or exceed business objectives and increase leadership effectiveness.

- Working with senior executives within an industrial products group of a Fortune 100 company, developed a process of structured discovery to capture customer insights, using these insights transformed client's business into a value-added partnerships.

Dilip G. Saraf   email@email.com   (000) 555-0000   Page 3/4

Louis Allen Associates, Los Altos, CA   98–99
Director

- Redesigned and marketed a unique leadership development program for managers.
- Established distribution channels for ongoing profitability.
- Worked with international consortia to deliver products.
- Customized leadership workshops for clients to address specific business needs.
- Delivered training to client executives and then coached them 1:1 to enhance effectiveness.

Total Quality Consulting, Inc. Los Altos, CA   89–94
CEO (founder)

- Designed and implemented a streamlined product development process at a major biotech company, accelerating time-to-market by half.
- Developed a client-specific project management methodology; then delivered a customized solution for organization-wide implementation.
- Created a process for effective cross-functional product teams.
- Conceived and implemented a product-platform concept for a biotech client, resulting in fewer product lines and sharper focus.

Varian Associates, Palo Alto, CA   87–89
Chief Engineer, Microwave Communications Division

- Transformed entire department through restaffing and retraining to be the leader in design innovation, delivering a series of groundbreaking products in a crowded market to lead the pack
- Transformed the overall product development process that increased throughput by 60%. Increased design reliability, and overall design quality of newly released high-tech products.
- Increased overall design productivity by 50% in two years by aggressively implementing design automation, standardization, and steadily eliminating rework efforts.

- Developed a structured process for identifying customer requirements and then translating them into viable products.

Kaiser Electronics, San Jose, CA, Projects Director   **87 and Prior**
SRI International, Menlo Park, CA, Senior Research Engineer

Client Roster (Consulting):

•Hewlett-Packard •Boeing •Motorola •Agilent Technologies •Goodyear and others

Other Achievements:

- Authored/published a major book on job search.
- Led a customer-loyalty CEO Roundtable for the *Chief Executive* magazine.
- Two patents in biomedicine.
- Pioneered a workshop on quality for designers and engineers to enhance product design integrity.
- Two publications in Harvard Business Review.
- Listed in Who's Who.
- Member of the board of a non-profit for 10 years.

Education:
B. Tech (Hon.), IIT Bombay, India; MSEE Stanford University, Stanford, CA

FUNCTIONAL VERSION

RE-INVENTION CATALYST

| Dilip G. Saraf | (000) 555-0000: | email@email.com |

Career Objective:
A **consulting position** in a global career transition organization responsible for: Developing new business opportunities; delivering services; collaborating with clients to implement workforce-reduction initiatives and then engaging with individual career transitions; developing change management strategies to achieve efficiencies at organizations following workforce reduction.

Experience Summary:
An organizational, management, and business consultant with over 14 years in: executive and employee career rehabilitation, career counseling and coaching, executive assessment and development, strategic organizational assessment and transformation, designing and implementing internal change to create market alignment, and leadership- and people-effectiveness initiatives. Twenty years in high-tech as an individual contributor, collaborator, and a technology line manager.

Unique Skills

- **Career Reinvention:** Help and coach senior executives and others in career reinvention.

- **Executive Assessment/Coaching:** Design and conduct assessments for development and leadership effectiveness. Collaborate on coaching plans and deliver coaching services.

- **Organizational Effectiveness and Change:** Develop organization-wide initiatives for large-scale change. Collaborate across broad range of leadership to deliver measurable results.

- **Strategic Initiatives:** Consult with top executives to develop business strategies and implement them for competitive positioning and long-term results. Set execution plans.

- **Customer Loyalty:** Develop/implement novel initiatives to increase loyalty/market share.

- **Business Development:** Identify new value-capture opportunities, develop marketing plans, and then create revenue streams. Implement cross-and up selling initiatives.

Professional Accomplishments:

Career Reinvention

Worked with laid-off executives and others to help them seek new career paths and opportunities using an experiential coaching methodology. Evolved and developed an approach to successfully redefine career paths especially for those with technology backgrounds by helping them repackage their value propositions. Worked with hundreds of individuals to help them identify their passions and then created a process for defining new career paths.

Executive Assessment/Coaching

Conducted, as a lead assessor, executive assessments for selection, promotion, and development. Using a one-on-one coaching process, helped managers and executives with specific development plans for achievement of business objectives and individual career goals. Helped executives in a broad range of industries through career transitions.

Strategy and Management Consulting

Worked collaboratively with the Managing Director of a financial services business and identified four strategic areas for penetrating new markets. Developed mission statements for each business team and identified critical factors for team success. Coached team leaders.

Organizational Effectiveness and Change

Implemented a structured process for measuring value received by clients' customers and then identified specific areas to increase delivered value without adding cost. Developed a change plan to implement customer-driven initiatives, achieving ongoing improvement in overall customer satisfaction (from 71% to 87% in one year), market share (up 9%) and profitability (up 23%) for a $40M/year division of a Fortune 100 company.

Customer Loyalty

Implemented a process of face-to-face, structured discovery with clients' customers. From this discovery synthesized and then selectively implemented changes that resulted in both increased revenues and customer loyalty for clients. This process helped a client transform a consumer commodity business into a value-added partnership in the automotive industry. Collaborated with senior client executives to implement a customer-loyalty initiative that more than doubled revenues within two years. Helped a Fortune-100 client increase revenues from $16M to $40M within two years using loyalty-based strategies.

Business Development

Transformed a product offering into a high-value consultative solution that resulted in $650K in annual individual billings. Collaboratively redesigned a money-losing workshop and transformed it into a profitable, highly-rated leadership development experience for a Fortune 100 high-tech client. Repackaged and repositioned a service offering with declining revenues into a successful international product line and then established distribution channels for ongoing profitability. Worked with consortia globally to deliver products and services overseas.

Significant Achievements:

- Authored and published a major book on job search and career reinvention.
- Founded and successfully ran a management consulting business.
- Led a customer-loyalty CEO roundtable for the *Chief Executive* magazine.
- Two publications in the *Harvard Business Review;* two patents in ultrasound and biomedicine.
- Taught graduate courses at the University of Santa Clara, CA; listed in *Who's Who.*
- Member of the Board of a non-profit human services agency.

Client Roster:

- •Hewlett-Packard •Boeing •Motorola •Agilent •Rockwell International •AlliedSignal •Becton Dickinson •Sun Microsystems •Goodyear •Piper Jaffrey •Goodyear •Ingersoll Rand

Employer Chronology:

- Independent business consultant (May 2001–current)
- Personnel Decisions Int'l, San Francisco, CA (1994–1998; 1999–2001); Sr. Consultant.
- Louis Allen Associates, Los Altos, CA (1998–1999); Director, Business Development
- Total Quality Consulting, Inc., Los Altos Hills, CA (1989–1994); Managing Director
- Varian Associates, Palo Alto, CA (1987–1989); Chief Engineer
- Kaiser Electronics, San Jose, CA (1978–1987); Projects Director
- SRI International, Menlo Park, CA (1970–1978); Sr. Research Engineer

Education:

- B. Tech (Hons) IIT, Bombay, India; MSEE Stanford University, Stanford, CA.

♠ Cover Letters

Cover letters are an element of the job-search campaign in importance at par with the résumé! Why? Simply because a cover letter can enhance the overall message well beyond what a résumé by itself can! As mentioned in the résumé section, a résumé should be tailored to each *category* of jobs. It is not uncommon in a tough market to have up to five different résumés for the same person, depending on the market one is trying to capture (please see résumé examples in this Key). A well-written cover letter complements the résumé message and does not repeat it. If the résumé is not about you—as we emphasized in that section—a cover letter is even less so! It is even *more* about them than the résumé. One concession in cover letters: you can use personal pronouns (I, me, mine) that we railed against using in the résumé. Use this concession to your advantage in the way your letter creates a "I know you" message with the target company.

There are various formats and styles of cover letters. The least effective is the one in which you open it with the job description or job reference, and then start repeating what is in the job posting to show why you are a good match. The other equally prosaic approach, is to summarize what is already in the résumé and then urge the decision maker to call you for an interview. Neither of these shortcuts to writing a cover letter adds any value to the message already in the résumé. In fact, it may detract from it. Why? Because of the time constraints, if the cover letter offers a good summary of the résumé, the hiring manager may not even feel the need to read the résumé.

Some compensate for this by making a custom résumé for each job to which they are responding. Taking this approach is even more dangerous because of the sheer volume of jobs to which one needs to respond to in a tough market. Sending customized résumés poses a further problem of keeping track of what has gone out and a possibility of inadvertently sending résumés with errors because of *your* time constraints.

A résumé is not something that should be changed casually. It is time consuming to craft a résumé and then proof it so that it is flawless. Every time!

As presented in the marketing part of the campaign, each category of target companies needs to be treated differently in the way a résumé is sent. Use cover letters in *all* cases where it is possible. All things being equal, this element provides the added factor to differentiate. It can also be a detractor if not done correctly. The following is a list of dos and don'ts in cover letters:

Dos:

- Be concise, compelling, and cogent: about ¾ page
- Present your case so that the letter naturally leads to your résumé
- Make most of the letter about *them*, not about you
- Send it to someone who can be contacted to follow-up
- Send it, wherever possible, in an impactful way, e.g. FedEx

Don'ts:

- Don't repeat what is in your résumé
- If you are proposing an idea, be concise and intriguing; give just enough
- Make more than one major point of argument in the body of the letter
- Avoid "but"; use "and" instead (e.g. I do not have 15 years in sales, but I bring rich field experience. Instead say: I bring sales experience in major geographic theaters of the world and know cultural preferences of markets where most growth is expected)
- Do not send a mediocre letter using an impactful method (FedEx)

In addition to a compelling cover letter what is even more important is how the entire package—the résumé and the cover letter—is sent. If a posting requires sending the résumé using a Website, then exploring if the response allows a cover letter with it can be worthwhile. Some Websites allow posting a résumé with a cover letter; they present a disadvantage if that is the only way you can transmit your response. If the target company is a "Gold" or "A" company, a priority target in your campaign (See Key-4, Target Segmentation), then the extra efforts to make sure that both the résumé and a compelling cover letter go in a differentiated way is critical. Merely relying on the Website to get your message in the most impactful way is chancy. Why? Mainly, because, the response will be piled up with all other responses, and will only be viewed, if the key word filters that the target company uses lets yours through for it to be seen. For priority targets—Gold and Silver—extra effort is justified to ensure that the cover letter is compelling, allowing you to stand out from the crowd and that it is delivered (courier), especially if the manner in which the response is typically requested does not easily allow for one. Taking the extra effort to find out who the recipient is and then sending a courier pack with a great cover letter and stellar résumé can win the day. Very few will take this route and *that* is your differentiator.

In addition to making an impact, the courier method allows for easy tracking. Once the package is delivered, you know who signed for it. Calling that person, then, in a few days allows you to find out to whom the package was delivered, and then from there, you can start your follow-up process. Another point that might help you further differentiate in the process: send the response to both the hiring manager and the recruiter for a priority target company. And, once again, make sure that each recipient knows that the other also got the same package. That simple expedient will ensure that if the hiring manager is interested, the recruiter is more than likely to get a "pull" call to bring you in for an interview. It is that effective.

Sample Cover Letters

Following examples show how résumés can be sent with these cover letters:

Asim Kedaur   email@email.com;   (000) 555-0000

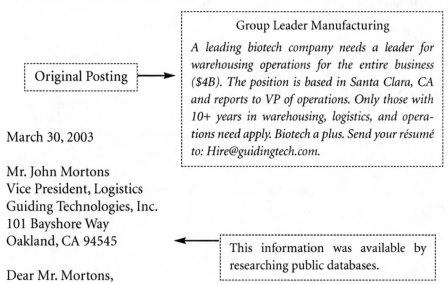

Group Leader Manufacturing

A leading biotech company needs a leader for warehousing operations for the entire business ($4B). The position is based in Santa Clara, CA and reports to VP of operations. Only those with 10+ years in warehousing, logistics, and operations need apply. Biotech a plus. Send your résumé to: Hire@guidingtech.com.

Original Posting

March 30, 2003

Mr. John Mortons
Vice President, Logistics
Guiding Technologies, Inc.
101 Bayshore Way
Oakland, CA 94545

This information was available by researching public databases.

Dear Mr. Mortons,

I am pleased to respond to the open position of Group Leader, Manufacturing (Job # 21058). My résumé is attached.

In addition to meeting or exceeding all of your job requirements, my specific strengths, which will create immediate value for Guiding Technologies are:

Leading initiatives to reduce Guidant's relatively low inventory turnover, to a number, more in line with today's business norms for this industry, or a more acceptable number. I have a proven track record of doing this aggressively in a complex environment, and in a variety of settings, with impressive outcomes.

Looking at the overall logistical flow *systemically,* and then collaborating with other functions, suppliers and alliances to reduce the overall investment, exposure and increase material and cash flow velocity significantly.

Looking at the logistical locations, international tax and tariffs, and then making recommendations for overall improvements in the way they impact the bottom-line. With 30 percent business overseas, this affords an attractive opportunity for globalization of logistics.

I am excited about exploring this opportunity further with you, and am looking forward to hearing from you. If I do not hear from you within about a week, I plan to call you.

Cordially,
Asim Kedaur

Enclosure: Résumé

> Most of the data was inferred from publicly available sources and finances.

All comments are removed to present a clean version of this letter on the next page.

Asim Kedaur   email@email.com   (000) 555-0000

March 30, 2003

Mr. John Mortons
Vice President, Logistics
Guiding Technologies, Inc.
101 Bayshore Way
Oakland, CA 94545

Dear Mr. Mortons,

I am pleased to respond to the open position of Group Leader, Manufacturing (Job # 21058). My résumé is attached.

In addition to meeting or exceeding all of your job requirements, my specific strengths, which will create immediate value for Guiding Technologies are:

Leading initiatives to reduce Guiding's relatively low inventory turnover, to a number, more in line with today's business norms for this industry, or a more acceptable number. I have a proven track record of doing this aggressively in a complex environment, and in a variety of settings with impressive outcomes.

Looking at the overall logistical flow *systemically,* and then collaborating with other functions, suppliers and alliances to reduce the overall investment, exposure and increase material and cash flow velocity significantly.

Looking at the logistical locations, international tax and tariffs, and then making recommendations for overall improvements in the way they impact the bottom-line. With 30 percent business overseas, this affords an attractive opportunity for globalization of logistics.

I am excited about exploring this opportunity further with you, and looking forward to hearing form you. If I do not hear from you within about a week, I plan to call you.

Cordially,

Asim Kedaur

Enclosure: Résumé

Ben Smith
Prospect Street
Fremont, CA 94002
email@email.com: (000) 555-0000

May 28, 2003

Mr. James Dregmist
Chief Technology Officer
Community Hospitals, Inc.
1 City Plaza, Suite 2600
Oakland, CA 94612

Dear Mr. Dregmist,

I am responding to your posting for Manager, IT Project Portfolio Administration.

In addition to meeting or exceeding the job requirements, I bring the following perspectives:

➢ In-depth understanding of strategic IT initiatives, and how to execute these across an enterprise, with culture steeped in siloed thinking. Your current EPIC initiative, for example, would require, a deep understanding of each of the functional areas that it touches, and how to get all these silos to understand, what it takes to embrace change and maintain their identity. I am familiar with this change barrier.

➢ Immediate knowledge of IT industry and emerging trends, enabling me to provide ongoing input to ensure that the *most* effective solutions are planned for implementation. This outlook will provide a flexible, effective, and forward-looking infrastructure so critical to a large organization's long-term and strategic success.

➢ Skilled in project management and cross-functional teams to allow me to manage effectively a broad portfolio of critical projects, and maintain performance, schedule, and budget integrity.

➢ Excellent understanding of leadership needs to oversee, lead, and deliver major initiatives involving large-scale change. Creating a seamless experience in the minds of those who touch an organization, and those who support it, are critical to maintaining the overall vision for the change. I have a good understanding of how to leverage that, and achieve exceptional results under very challenging circumstances.

I look forward to speaking with you to explore this further. I plan to call you in a week.

Cordially,

Ben Smith

Encl: Résumé

Each of the items above came from researching the target organization using publicly available information. This research took about six hours. The recipient called the candidate the following week for a phone interview, followed by a face-to-face.

Mich Apps
Terrace Ct.
Belmont, CA 95434
(000) 555-0000: email@email.com

August 15, 2003

Ms. Joan Sanders
Recruitment Manager
McAfee Enterprises
3001 Stevens Creek Blvd
Cupertino, CA 95014

Dear Ms. Sanders,

I am responding to your job opening for Software Engineer and I am listing below a brief summary of accomplishments during my five years at Hewlett-Packard and NEC:

I designed and developed several complex software applications with minimal supervision. For example, one business-critical Web application project assigned to me with aggressive deadlines and minimal definition, was delivered ahead of schedule. When QA tests were conducted, this application was found to have *no* errors, and was then integrated with the corporate Website seamlessly. All my development work is delivered error-free.

Working closely with QA, I collaboratively helped them define test strategies and helped minimize test time and test risks. I have an excellent record of promptly correcting any uncovered defects, regardless of who wrote the original code, prior to my involvement on the project.

During the critical integration phase, I have on many occasions, volunteered to help facilitate the process and provided innovative solutions to deliver the product on time.

I enjoy working in teams, large and small, and work to deliver final products on aggressive timelines. I have also *led* teams to deliver critical products when the occasion required it.

I am excited about exploring this further and looking forward to discussing with you in person. I'll call you in a week to follow-up.

Cordially,

Mich Apps
Encl: Résumé

JOB AD

Senior Designer Needed!! Reply to: email@email.com Date: 2003-10-01, 3:27PM

Senior designer needed for extremely busy residential resale property staging business. Looking for a very organized, self-starter with a good design eye, to quickly set up homes and other properties being marketed for sale. Must have a trained eye for accessories and furniture. Must be able to manage a team. Lifting and some physical work required. Must have a car, van preferred. Can be full or part time, some weekends. Must have professional interior design experience. Window merchandizing experience excellent. This is interior design emergency ward work! Very fair compensation and room for advancement. Please do not call, if you are not experienced! Call Carolyn @ (000) 555-0000

RESPONSE

Asmita Page
Lost Leaf Ave.
Los Altos Hills, CA 94022
(000) 555-0000: email@email.com

TRANSFORMATIONAL DESIGNER:

October 1, 2003
CAROL DeSOTO
email@email.com
Bus. (000) 555-0000

Dear Carolyn,

I happened to see your ad on Craig's List and am anxious to find out more!
My background combines staging, interior design, real estate, marketing, and creative services management. Following is what you're looking for and why I can help your business:

Residential Real-estate Staging Business:
I currently work with several peninsula realtors and contractors, preparing their listings for market. This includes meeting with sellers, renting furniture, and re-designing using existing furnishings, shopping for accessories, paint color and finish selection/coordination, hosting broker tours, and open houses to monitor property feedback.

Very Organized:
As a freelancer, I manage multiple projects in a time-driven environment. Earlier this year, my staging experience included work for Jo Ann James Design Group in Menlo Park, CA. I worked on her projects in Atherton, Woodside, San Mateo, and Menlo Park. Listings ranged from $2.5–$20 million.

Self-Starter:
While managing creative services and advertising at Hewlett-Packard, I was named a "Top Marketing Leader Worldwide." In parallel with that successful career, I completed my interior design certification from UC Santa Cruz ext., and remodeled a Los Altos 1930s Spanish style home. I'm an "accredited staging professional" and my Bachelor's Degree is in Design and Advertising.
Carol DeSoto

October 1, 2003
Page 2

Keen Design Eye:
I was a *Sunset* Magazine renovation design contest winner. My interiors were featured in *Palo Alto Design & Garden* and the Los Altos town newspaper. Contractors and realtors hire me for my design advice.

Quick Set Ups:
Staging is my life. I spend weekends looking at open houses so I can learn better, faster, easier, newer ways to approach designing property to sell.

Manage Teams:
The HP corporate leadership management-training program was completed and my local direct reports ranged up to 27 employees. Others were geographically dispersed throughout the country. They were given opportunities to learn and grow and enjoyed my collaborative style.

Physical Labor:
I keep in shape by regularly participating in Jazzercise and a community services dance performing group.

Transportation:
My driver's license is current and my vehicle is regularly maintained.

Professional Experience
Former Madison Avenue designer, Lynn Hollyn, hired me as a freelancer. I also worked for her as an intern. Currently, I work with clients on interior design consulting and direction.

Window Merchandizing:
While attending college, I designed visual displays for merchandising for a retail hardware and house wares outlet.

Flexibility
I can work as much or as little as you like. My freelance schedule is flexible. My passion is seeing the transformation of property and sales results.

So, just call me. That way we can both learn more! Best of luck in finding a good fit.

Regards,

Asmita Page

June 30, 2003   **By email**

Dear Mr. James Hillburn,

I am pleased to respond to the position of IT Analyst. In addition to meeting or exceeding all your requirements, I bring to following additional value to the position:

I am intimately familiar with gap analysis that drives change in how IT applications are deployed in business-critical situations. At HP, I conducted such gap analyses for a team of senior business managers on how a new application could successfully replace one that was a part of the Legacy system, and was business critical. This had a user base of over 10,000 globally in the finance and marketing domains. My analysis not only showed a clear implementation strategy, but this work, and the subsequent implementation of it, went on to become a company-wide showcase of how to lead such critical initiatives for successful outcomes.

One of the key challenges in successful execution beyond the gap analysis is management of change. One reason for my success stems from my ability to collaborate with key stakeholders, who are affected by the change, and then communicating with them in ways that shows them clear benefit in their day-to-day work. Shifting from resistance to excitement with those most affected, is at the heart of the change process.

Additionally, I understand that Cisco is currently in the process of migrating its business systems to a different platform. I have delivered on multiple migration projects, where I overcame various challenges, both technical and organizational, to a successful finish.

Additionally, I bring a value-add to this job with my past experience, specifically in the following areas:

➢ Dual Business and IT role, and how to *weld* IT to business to make it successful

➢ Integration of data from various technical platforms as SAP, Legacy as well as business domains as finance, customer, product, and transactions

➢ Design new systems/modify existing ones to quickly adapt to changing business models

I am interested in exploring this opportunity further. I look forward to hearing from you. I can be reached at phone (000) 555-0000 or email email@email.com

Best Regards,

Anshima Mapp

Encl: Résumé

Sumi Jarvis: (000) 555-0000
Century Wy.
Cupertino, CA 95014   email@email.com

July 5, 2003

Maura Fox
Manager, Embedded & Personal Systems Div.
Electronic Systems, Inc.
Pruneridge Ave
Cupertino, CA, 95014

Dear Maura,

Thank you for taking the time to chat with me about the open position for Manufacturing Development Engineer. I am enclosing my résumé for your review. I am also summarizing below critical parts of my background for this position:

I bring a unique combination of skills that embody both a deep understanding of basic PC technology as well as the manufacturing processes, and how these processes are a result of successful alliances of diverse supply-chain partners. My experience at Dyno Systems includes taking advanced products through a rapid manufacturing, and delivering a series of successful net-servers in a demanding environment. My skills include:

> **Technology Roadmaps:** Develop and communicate technology roadmaps to cement alliances and future product success in a competitive setting.

> **Alliance Development:** Forge strategic alliances with key providers and maintain ongoing partnerships to ensure high-integrity supply chain.

> **Quality Processes:** Set quality standards in both products and processes by aggressively driving continuous improvement and reliable process technology.

> **Cross-Functional Teams:** Collaborate across global teams and cross-divisional boundaries to ensure leadership of new products and their manufacture.

> **R&D/ODM Interplay:** Lead ongoing product transition from R&D to ODM and manage qualifications at ODM sites.

> **Components/BOMs:** Develop a robust process to manage common component use across, ensuring latest product revisions, compatibility, and lowest costs

I am looking forward to further exploring this position with you and am excited about the possibilities and opportunities this presents.

Please call me when you would like to explore this further.

Cordially,

Sumi Jarvis

Enclosure: Résumé

Pamela Moon
Grant Road
Mountain View, CA 94040
(000) 555-0000, email@email.com

December 2, 2003

Imported Stores, Inc
20332 4th Street
Oakland, CA 94607

Dear Recruiting Manager,

In response to your posting on your Website for an **IS Network Manager**, I am enclosing my résumé. The following table summarizes my candidacy:

Your Needs	I Bring
Ten years supporting IT in corporate environment	Over seven years solid experience that includes corporate IT environment.
Leading teams of software developers, networking specialists, and business analysts	Hands-on experience with some team-lead assignments. Collaborated with business area managers to identify their IT software needs and then implemented projects.
Skilled at network operations and support	Managed a group of engineers and technicians in a complex networking environment. Maintained 24x7 operations at a major B-B division.
Off-shoring skills and familiarity.	This is a new trend and I am confident that I can learn this quickly.
Certified in Cisco systems	Certified in Cisco systems.
Multi OS familiarity	Have worked in business environment with Windows, Unix, Linux, and Mainframe OS
Develop Helpdesk capability and support	Demonstrated Helpdesk experience.

Your Needs	I Bring
Customer centric focus	Have always worked closely with customers and kept high level of satisfaction.
Negotiate SLAs and manage outsourcing and vendor activities	Have developed several SLA and vendor contract agreements.
Develop training, mentor teams, create procedures for ongoing success	Mentored teams/coached new hires. Written policies and procedures.

I hope that you will consider me favorably and call me for an interview.

Sincerely,

Pam Moon

Encl: résumé

> In a tough job market the résumé is not likely to be read because of the presentation. This letter screams "Don't waste time reading résumé; I've summarized right here!" Avoid this format *even* when there's a perfect match!

Pamela Moon
Grant Road
Mountain View, CA 94040
(000) 555-0000, email@email.com

December 2, 2003

Imported Stores, Inc
20332 4th Street
Oakland, CA 94607

Using one element of research from Hoover's, this letter ties the potential need of the business to what Pam brings to make it happen. This letter was a winner!

Dear Recruiting Manager,

In response to your posting on your Website for an **IS Network Manager**, I am enclosing my résumé. Your 23 percent sales growth and the addition of 41 stores over the past year are now behind you. This is, indeed, an impressive achievement in the current economic environment.

As the economy now rebounds, your growth rate for the coming year could be now even more. With this growth rate, however, comes additional challenges particularly in the IT infrastructure and the support necessary to sustain this rate. During my tenure at General Merchandise, I have consistently supported growth stemming from ongoing acquisitions of various businesses, which required having to support a larger client base representing double digit increases. During these times, I provided design, support, and operational procedures to ensure resources and infrastructure did not limit growth.

I have extensive experience in corporate network operations, including several years as a front line network operations manager. Most recently, I conducted contract negotiations for Internet services resulting in a projected $5M annual savings.

I am customer focused and have experience with and developed internal and external SLA agreements, network policies and procedures, security guidelines, and delivered technical training sessions for helpdesk personnel, resulting in increased customer satisfaction. I am proficient in Cisco configurations and have a background in UNIX and Windows system administration.

I look forward to meeting with you to discuss in more detail how my diverse background and qualifications can quickly work for you.

Cordially,

Pam Moon

Encl: résumé

Cheri Waxman
Old Santa Cruz
Los Gatos, CA
(000) 555-0000
email@email.com

Dear Hiring Manager:

I would like to introduce myself, and provide you with my current résumé.

My name is Cheri Waxman, and I have been in the clerical/administrative field for over 15 years. I would like very much to be considered for your administrative position. I currently work at Hewlett-Packard Company, in Cupertino California.

I am looking to find a position in a progressive company, where both my skills and my "can do" attitude will be put to good use. I would like to find a company that is both pro-active and where customer service and the sense of urgency in product delivery are high.

If after reviewing my résumé, you find that there is a match in our requirements, please feel free to contact me at the numbers enclosed. I feel strongly that I could be an asset to your company and would love the opportunity to interview with you.

Thank you in advance for your time and consideration.

Respectfully

Cheri Waxman

This cover letter was sent with the "Before" résumé shown in this Key to no avail! (See testimonial in that section.)

Subject: Good morning Mr. Swan, I would like to be your new admin!

Good morning Mr. Swan,

In response to the opening, Administrative Assistant req # 8140329 for the PPS (Portable Power Supply) Operations Department, I am pleased to submit my résumé, which is attached.

In addition to meeting or *exceeding* all of the requirements for the job, I bring to this position the following additional value:

Complete familiarity with National Semiconductors' policies and procedures, little to no training needed to start right away!

Pro-active approach to all administrative functions and support of the manager and teams associated with the group, intuitive self-motivated and able to multi-task with very little supervision.

"Excellent" event coordination and employee recognition's within our limited budgetary constraints!

I am excited about this opportunity and am looking forward to exploring this further with you in an interview.

Respectfully,

Cheri Waxman

This cover letter, together with the résumé shown in the earlier section for the same person resulted in a phone call _within six hours_ of the résumé submittal by email. The same person had failed to get any responses with her previous approach. See "Before" résumé and the cover letter for the same person in their respective sections.

Charles Waggoner
Filbert Street
Cupertino, CA 95014
(000) 555-0000, email@email.com

November 10, 2003

Mark Shields
Director
Veritas Software   THIRD-PARTY INTRODUCTION: COLD CALL
Dixon Landing Road
Mountain View, CA 95476

Dear Mr. Shields

Diana Kyle suggested that I contact you and forward my résumé. Diana was my manager at HP.

I was at HP for over nine years, including nearly two years at the merged company that acquired Compaq. I came to HP from the Digital-Compaq lineage where I worked on advanced database architectures and innovations for nearly eight years. Throughout this period, my role had remained the same. In summary I bring the following expertise:

➤ Delivering highly creative solutions to long-standing problems in database architectures that resulted in breakthrough products over the years.

➤ Leading the development of unique architectural solutions using Oracle platforms that went on to pioneer new sales in the marketplace. For example, I created the solution for Oracle RAC on HP servers with grid-enabling capabilities for HP UDC, this changed strategic direction for HP in being able to make offerings previously not on their product list.

➤ Brought the emerging HP/Compaq capability to the forefront by developing Tru64 UNIX Cluster File System and Advanced File migration project, which positioned HP favorably in the marketplace vis-à-vis IBM, and others.

➤ Throughout my tenure at HP/Compaq/Digital my accomplishments are centered on developing unique capabilities using multiple vendors and integrating their offerings with pioneering and seamless breakthroughs.

There may be more than one opportunity at Veritas in the area of Database Architecture and storage software management. I would be very interested in exploring these with you so that we can jointly determine where I can add most value to Veritas in the context of its current needs.

I look forward to hearing from you with the next few days. I also plan to call you in about a week to pursue this further.

Cordially,

Charles Waggoner

> Charles was interviewed within a week of this letter and was offered a job within 30 days of this letter.

Catherine Jenkins
View Court
Los Altos, CA 94022
(000) 555-0000, email@email.com

July 21, 2003

Ms. Megan Eiken
Director, Marketing and Sales   "PLAYING GOLF WITH TIGER WOODS."
International Meetings and Events
33 Great America Parkway #22
Santa Clara, CA 95054

Dear Megan,

Thank you for meeting with me today and explaining to me what you are looking for to start a new sales territory in the Silicon Valley. Your company's track record is, indeed, impressive! I think that the Silicon Valley is a good springboard for your statewide growth plans.

As I research your competitors, how they market and sell in this area, the market itself, and the forces that are shaping the current market, I find the following:

➢ Your competitors' main selling strategy is based on opportunistic and transactional selling. They look for companies that are holding or planning to hold major meetings and events, respond to their requirements and then give a low bid to win the deal.

➢ The overall experience the attendees walk away with is marginal at best. Yes, they come to attend the event but what impact did the overall event and the way the logistics was organized leave on the attendees mind? Are they likely to do more business with the client companies as a result of this experience? My view is pessimistic!

➢ With the current state of the economy, especially in the Silicon Valley, I think that there is a greater opportunity to be had if you approach the client companies with a more strategic view of these events. One approach can entail doing some research with their attendees and participants and then helping the clients design the entire event based on the expectations coming from this research. I have some ideas on this.

Since California is your new frontier, wouldn't you like to break new ground in the way this entire offering is presented to your clients here and blow the competition out of the water?

With all your staff that already has their CMPs and direct selling experience, many of whom I hope to be teaming with, I think the critical areas of focus are what I have outlined above: creating a memorable and actionable participant experience, and strategic selling.

I am looking forward to our next meeting to present some of these ideas in more detail.

Cordially,
Catherine

CJ did not have either of the two job requirements: CMP or sales experience. But by sending an earlier letter to pique their curiosity she was able to land an interview. This letter was sent subsequent to that interview, where she was told that there were six candidates ahead of her who met *all* the job requirements. Catherine was invited to the next round of interviews based on this letter and was offered the job two weeks later!

James Portola
Echo Lane
Atherton, CA 94025
(000) 555-0000, email@email.com

October 22, 2003

Mr. Harrison Chrysler   "LEVERAGING JOB TRENDS"
Senior Vice President,
Programs
Allied Defense Systems
11 Lockheed Way
Sunnyvale, CA 94086

Dear Mr. Chrysler,

I am pleased to enclose my résumé for the position of program manager: commercialization business.

With the current trends of off-shoring and early test marketing, commercialization of defense technology provides interesting and rewarding possibilities. These two trends alone can create a short-term competitive advantage to Allied in ways that was unthinkable just a couple of years ago. Once the declassified components of the program to be commercialized are identified, I think it would be prudent to explore if commercialization can be done first here in the US to sanitize the sensitive parts of the program, and then structure the development so that some of the more labor-intensive software can be developed in India. I did just such an off-shoring program at General Electronics, where I was their director of software development and new products.

The other idea of early test marketing is also a promising avenue to take out risks from overall commercialization of already demonstrated technologies. I have successfully test marketed a variety of products and services over the past four years saving countless hours of trial and error and lost time and resources. There are some lessons I learned doing this well and those lessons are transportable to almost any product and industry.

With these two major innovations, your commercialization business can be made profitable early in its life for most projects and products. I am excited about demonstrating that to you. I am confident that my international experience in setting up off-shoring operations and demonstrated track record in taking out risks from product marketing will to be assets to your new venture.

I am looking forward to exploring this opportunity further with you and meeting you face-to-face in the near future.

I plan to call you in about a week to follow up.

Cordially,

James Portola

Enclosure: Résumé

Greg Newton
Sunset Court
Santa Clara, CA 95054
(000) 555-0000, email@email.com

July 14, 2003

Samuel Barton   "LEVERAGING JOB TRENDS"
Manager, Supply Chain
Router Products
Cisco Systems
One Morgride Way
San Jose, CA 95131

Dear Mr. Barton,

I am pleased to enclose my résumé for the position of commodities manager in your group.

With the current thrust Cisco has embarked on to reduce costs, managing product bill of material (BOM) and vendor expenses, can be a boon to the overall initiative. As a commodities manager within your Router Products group, I can think of three novel ways to streamline costs:

Review all emerging product designs and scrub them for minimal new parts and total number of line items that go on to make the overall BOM. As an engineer, I can persuade other design teams to consider alternative approaches to finalizing a design by using common parts proactively. I have done similar work at HP when I was heading its Server Products for enterprise applications. Although it was not within my purview, I initiated routinely reviewing BOMs for emerging products, and found that it was relatively easy to eliminate about 10–15 percent of line items by slightly changing designs and consolidating parts. I called this initiative parts commonalization. As an engineer, I was better able to communicate this to product designers, and got their buy in.

With the current trend of off-shoring, it would even be prudent to create guidelines for preferred parts to Cisco's ODM suppliers and enforce the guidelines to reduce service costs and inventory on an ongoing basis.

With the emerging trend of value loops with alliances, it might be to Cisco's advantage to share the preferred parts list guidelines with them to make sure that up and down the value chain, parts commonality is maintained, not just as an initiative but also more as a habit!

These three ideas can significantly add to your overall parts cost savings immediately and can be then spread across other product and business lines. These are not mere ideas but proven business practices I have successfully implemented at HP over the past six years.

I am looking forward to meeting with you face-to-face and showing some of the non-proprietary evidence I have from the work in this area. I plan to call you in a week to follow-up.

Cordially,
Greg Newton

Summary Key-3: Presenting Yourself

This section deals with starting your job-search campaign. The following steps are suggested in presenting yourself:

1. Carefully research the job market first, in which you want to campaign and find current opportunities and identify the job families that interest you for your search.

2. Select two or three job families that you want to pursue with your experience and those that appear challenging. Even in a tough market do not surrender your expectations to finding something at or below your level; look up and not down.

3. Prepare your résumé starting with a Career Objective looking ahead. Do not start your résumé with a Summary statement, which is always backward looking.

4. Now you are ready to write your résumé for your future and the one that is aligned to what the market is looking for. Remember, your résumé is about tomorrow and it is about "them" not about you!

5. No matter how routine you think your current or previous job, discover what skills differentiated you in the way you did your job and write them as your Unique Skills. This is our genius and we all have it. This is a difficult part of writing your résumé.

6. Look for trends in the job families you have chosen to pursue and incorporate these trends unambiguously in your résumé. Even if the opportunities posted do not use this language *you* must use it to differentiate yourself from others.

7. Write your Professional Experience to highlight your leadership skills and not just your tasks and responsibilities in a factual way. Tell them a story here. The Professional Experience write-up should be anchored to the Unique Skills; this is the evidence part of those skills.

8. Once you have your core résumé, look at the different job families you have targeted and spin off as many résumés (five maximum) with messages that harmonize with these opportunities.

9. Target your résumé to specific market segments using the 4P approach and develop your final messages and packages. This is strategic marketing.

10. When you are pursuing an opportunity that requires a skill you do not have, do not pretend that you do, if you are merely familiar with it.

There are other ways to overcome this limitation. This is called "Beating Tiger Woods by not playing golf with him!"

11. To get noticed in your job search campaign, you must break hiring rules. Prepare a mix of approaches and pilot a few of them to see what works and to vet your résumé. Start small, learn, revise, and ramp up.

12. Cover letters must be sent with résumés after carefully researching the opportunity.

13. The chapter ends with a showcase of résumés and cover letters.

14. There are many examples of "Before" and "After" résumés and cover letters.

15. There are examples of résumés of different flavors for the same person, as well as an example of a functional résumé. Merely changing the Career Objective of different flavor résumés is not enough; the entire résumé must be aligned to this message.

Key-4: Marketing the Product—You!

"Your reach should be greater than your grasp."

—Ralph Waldo Emerson (1803–1882)

The Marketing Campaign

Marketing brings together all previous activities, so that the message you have developed is sent out for others to see. In addition, it also entails identifying targets and opportunities where your message needs to go. Your marketing campaign can take on a variety of shapes and forms, and often, is a mix of different approaches, coming together in a coordinated way.

Introduction

Once the résumé is ready, there is a need to go back to the starting point—the market—and shift gears. Why? In the previous Key we presented *how* to send the résumé and letters, including cover letters, without discussing *where* to send them! We explore that in this Key.

The résumé was based on market *survey*. The survey provided the boundaries of the job-search perimeter, so that you have a good idea of "what" types of jobs—job families—to address in the résumé. Once it is done, it is time to go to the same well in a different vein. This time the intent is to use the marketplace information to actually create a marketing campaign and launch it with the résumé to answer the "where" question. Now in the same marketplace you are changing your mode from *surveying to researching*; you are gathering intelligence.

Sources of Market Intelligence

Gathering market intelligence entails finding rich sources full of information to leverage, so that there is a solid marketing plan. This plan consists of target companies carefully selected and ranked in order of their potential targeting value and desirability in landing your dream job. Looking at job boards and postings that are publicly available, and then merely sending résumés to these open positions, does not create a differentiated advantage. It *cannot!* Your résumé is one of thousands that are received in response to a posted job. In fact, it is best to expend minimal efforts on such opportunities because the yield on them, typically, is so poor.

The effort invested in a marketing campaign, applying for jobs, should be targeted to where the action is. For example, spending an hour per day (in a typical eight-hour day) on the Web, sending responses to jobs *already* identified and posted is excessive. As presented in this key on networking, most of the action is in working within a network and that is where most of the effort should be invested. You can use the information gathered on the Web to prime your network and leverage it into more direct avenues of getting your candidacy known to the target company. This is how you can justify spending up to two hours (25 percent of your time) daily, on this approach, to do your job searching. Any additional time on the Web should be spent doing company research and sleuthing.

Posted Jobs

There are job postings available through a variety of channels as a first source of market intelligence. Some of the more familiar avenues for this fountainhead of openings are:

- Job boards on the Web: there are dozens of these but some familiar ones are Monster.com, Careerbuilder.com, Chiefmonster.com, Hotjobs.com, among others
- Classified advertisements in print media as newspapers, magazines, and trade publications
- Company Websites
- Special Websites hosted by outplacement and other career-focused companies
- Public bulletin boards
- Employment newsletters and other publications
- Other public sources of information

Any of these sources can be a good starting point for researching jobs of interest. In this Key, in Target Segmentation, we shall see how to rank-order a target opportunity universe into three categories, so that how to leverage this information to get what you are after will be decided.

Once the job opportunity is identified, the next step is to formulate a response so that it is consistent with the marketing strategy. As we shall see in

Target Segmentation, the level of effort in formulating a response will be consistent with this segmentation. Gathering this market intelligence from posted jobs, however, is just one avenue to tapping into the job market and responding to it.

Company Sources

Information available from companies of interest can be a veritable source of job knowledge, overt and covert. Overt jobs are the jobs companies are openly seeking to fill. These jobs are on the company Website, job boards, and other sources of public information. Covert jobs, on the other hand, are the openings about which the company does not want just anyone to know. One reason may be that the incumbent may be eased out and it needs someone qualified to replace that person. These covert jobs can be of two categories: one that the company recognizes, and for which it is willing to entertain a candidate for consideration; the other is where the company does not even know or recognize that such a job should exist because its management has not thought about the need. We discuss this latter category in Unconventional Job Search, Key-4, and how to go after it.

Quality of Information and Your Time

Information from job boards and company Websites can be found to be disparate. Why? Organizations post jobs and other information on job boards to disseminate openings. Often these openings get cancelled, filled, modified, or even consolidated depending on the flux of factors that change from company to company and economic realities. It is not uncommon to find a posting from a company on a well-regarded job board, which, when you visit the company Website, may not exist. This can be frustrating. What is even more frustrating, is to find a posting on a company Website, of a recent vintage, and then find out that the location, where the company posted the opening, does not even exist. Why? One reason may be that the task of posting, managing, and removing job openings takes resources. Since the cost of posting an opening on various job boards is trivial, compared to what print media charge, most companies do not bother to diligently keep their posting up-to-date. This is not expected to change any time soon.

One such incident happened to a client, who, after getting frustrated with the integrity of openings posted on job boards, decided to go directly to the company Websites. One such company—a Global Fortune-10—had just posted a job, very much in line with what she was looking for, about a mile from her home! Having been disappointed with such tantalizing opportunities before, she decided to explore more about the job and find the name of the hiring manager, through someone she knew, who worked at another part of the same company. She was crushed when she discovered that the physical location posted for the job did not even exist. They had disbanded that operation, some three years back, and had dispersed it to several different locations in California! It is, therefore, a good idea to check on all opportunities before investing *significant* time in response to them. If you plan to send a mechanized response that takes less than a minute, then it may be worth your while to chance it! But, then do not spend inordinate amounts of time following up on such transmittals; consider them "fire and forget" job-seeking missiles!

Analysts and Industry Experts

Industry and financial analysts can be a source of latent jobs a company may be contemplating. These industry mavens have insight about what direction a company is or should be taking, and are able to influence the company's management on a variety of matters. Typically, these positions are at a higher-level—director and above—so that if you do not have interest in those levels of openings, you do not need to focus on this avenue.

Customers, Suppliers, and Channels

Every company has customers, suppliers, and channels through which it distributes its wares. Those who are in this category of company's stakeholders have inside knowledge of what its needs are in the current and future terms. These needs may not be openly known to others and certainly are not in the public domain. Tapping these constituencies can be a useful source of knowledge and intelligence on how a company is going to fill certain positions.

Industry Press and Publications

Industry and trade publications can be a veritable source of what is going on inside a company. If these sources are suggesting, in their news coverage, a need for a certain position either openly or insinuatingly, then it is worth pursuing these leads. Your approach based on this intelligence will, again, be driven by what segment of your target the company in question falls.

Recruiters and Search Firms

Even in a down economy, companies find it useful to pursue bringing on potential candidates through retained or even contingent recruiters. Search firms mostly work on a retained basis. A retained search is one where a company contracts a particular search firm to fill a position. The company pays the fee regardless of the outcome of the process. A contingent search, on the other hand, is where the recruiter is paid only when a position is filled through *that* recruiter. A search firm will not divulge the client company's name unless the process is well under way. Talking to recruiters and search firms can be a veritable source of knowledge on where the action is and what kind of talent is getting action. In a tough job market, these resources, however, are stretched thin as their business levels are down and their databanks full of candidates looking for work through these channels. Do not expect much cooperation and openness from recruiters in a tough job market!

For more discussion on this topic, see the section on Working With Third Parties in this Key.

♠ Culling your Target List

Your list of targets should be compiled from search criteria that you can assemble based on a number of factors, some obvious, others less so! Some of the more obvious search fields are listed below:

- ✓ Industry
- ✓ Geography
- ✓ Employee count
- ✓ Sales volume
- ✓ *Fortune* ranking
- ✓ Domestic vs. foreign presence
- ✓ Product line
- ✓ Geography/distance to work
- ✓ Company track record
- ✓ Reputation
- ✓ Management
- ✓ Financial performance history
- ✓ Employee treatment/layoff history
- ✓ Minorities/women treatment
- ✓ Growth history
- ✓ Future plans
- ✓ Defense/Non-defense

The lesser known attributes of a company are listed below and should be part of your search equation:

- ✓ How a company treats those over 40 (AARP publishes a company list)
- ✓ How a company treats women in management and promotions

✓ How a company provides for working mothers

✓ How a company supports special causes (e.g. does not invest in countries having poor human rights records)

Of course, as the job market becomes tighter, the search criteria have to be somewhat broader than when the job market is less so. Even though you may be looking for a job in an employers' market, it does not mean that you should surrender your principles for want of a job where you are not likely to be happy. You can always choose your offers based on your final criteria and judgment.

It is better to start with less restrictive criteria and then limit them, which will make the list smaller. If you are focused on getting what you know you want, you will more than likely get it. If you go after any company that has a job opening, you probably will get into one of them of no particular appeal to you. It helps to be choosy even in a bear market!

One way to tap a list of companies from criteria that you develop, is to use one of the more commonly used industry databases. This is discussed in this Key under Some Search Tools. The databases will provide a list of companies that match your criteria. This list could be of any length depending upon your criteria and size of the database (number of companies in it).

♠ Target Segmentation

Once the list is available, the next step is to select from this list those companies matching your finer criteria, suggested from one of the lists above. Then segment the companies into three categories:

> "A" or Gold
> "B" or Silver
> "C" or Bronze

Gold companies or those on the "A" list are your dream companies based on criteria you selected. The same goes for the Silver and the Bronze list.

To have a good list for a robust marketing campaign the following mix is suggested:

Gold	10 companies
Silver	25 companies
Bronze	100 companies

At any given time, in a good campaign, you need to ramp up to have a **mix of 135 companies** that are on your radar screen or in your pipeline of activities. We'll use the radar screen metaphor to talk about the *target* companies and the pipeline metaphor to talk about the *activities* on these companies, such as how many résumés, how many letters, how many follow-up calls, etc. in your campaign that you are shepherding.

The list should be a dynamic one; as you remove those that do not pan out, you toss new ones in the mix so that they come in and out on the radar screen. You need to constantly keep a list of back-up companies, in each category or segment, so that your radar screen has the same number of target companies and the pipeline has the same flux of activities. It is important to keep your activities at a level high enough, to keep you engaged and visible in the marketplace. Managing this mix of activities takes a full time effort—at least 40 hours per week, giving you a reason to get up in the morning if you are out of work and looking! It takes time to ramp up to this level of activity, starting with nothing at the beginning of your campaign. Those looking for a change from their current job can start and work with a smaller number and fewer targets; they perhaps do not need to have any "C" targets.

Opportunistic Targeting

In addition to the targets identified by the segmentation approach, one must also pursue opportunities, as they become available, even when they are not on the radar screen as originally targeted. The 135 targets are identified, as the campaign gets rolling, to give focus, visibility, and priority to those targets that are worthy pursuing. In a tough market, one must also pursue opportunities as they become known and add to the list already in place, even if that goes beyond the 135 targets mentioned in the previous paragraph. That number was the starting point. As more target opportunities become visible, even beyond that pool, they should also be reviewed for their priority: Gold, Silver, and Bronze, and treated accordingly.

The approach described here works in any market. In a difficult job market, this approach provides the discipline and a structure needed to start an aggressive campaign. It forces those seriously looking for jobs to go after selected companies that interest them, rather than reactively applying for anything that appears, and then sending a response.

♠ Some Search Tools

There are several search tools and databases available to cull company lists. These databases and lists are maintained on an ongoing basis to keep them current and user friendly. They offer different information to the client and are usually fee based. The following resources are available for doing on-line search.

Reference USA

Reference USA is a good starting point for a broad search for companies within the US. This tool is available from most public libraries (hence free) and can be accessed from home on the Internet. It lists over 12 million businesses within the US. Once you know what your general boundaries of search are, this tool provides a way to mark these boundaries and find every target within these boundaries. After entering custom search criteria, the database produces a list of companies that meet the criteria. Once this list is printed, names can by highlighted in three colors to identify Gold, Silver, and Bronze target companies.

Hoover's

Hoover's is the next level of research tool where you can get more detailed information on any chosen target from the Reference USA list. For more information visit www.Hoovers.com. This is a subscription service, although a stripped-down version is available for free.

Other Sources

There are a variety of sources available to do search in a specific area. Most of these sources are subscription-based services.

♠ Working with Third Parties

Third parties in a job-search campaign provide an added dimension to a marketing effort. They represent a whole class of professionals who can provide resources, contacts, and help bring the employer and employee together to create a win-win situation. Even in a down economy, third parties can provide value to both sides as discussed here. In this section a brief overview of different types of third parties is provided.

Introduction

Third parties are catalysts who connect employers, who have job opportunities, with those seeking to fill them. They range from highly dispersed organizations with international presence to individuals. Typically, they facilitate connecting the employers with potential employees and vice versa, and include a variety of businesses based on different models. Many job boards and ISPs such as AOL and Yahoo! provide electronic job-search agents that allow job seekers to post specific search criteria for their dream jobs, and have the "agent" notify them of a match. They each play a role in some way to make the connection between the demand and the supply of human resources for organizations. As in every business, economic conditions and the demand and supply equation drive how these providers create and bring value to the process of putting employees on employers' payrolls. What makes this business interesting, from a jobseeker's viewpoint, is that most jobseekers—especially those out of work—get involved with them in an emotional state, and are driven by how they are able to manage these emotions more than any other factor.

This section is an overview of how a third-party can play a role in your placement and how you can leverage that resource to your best advantage. Also knowing their business model can help you make the right choice. This is critical to avoid getting hurt before getting emotionally and financially involved.

The basic economic rule for third-parties existence is how they are able to generate revenues by helping attain your job-search goal. Some actually place you; some get you ready, so that you can do this yourself; yet others provide some service so that you can decide how you want to go about this process yourself. In some cases—outplacement—the cost is borne by the employers, so that individual clients do not bear any cost of the service for a limited time. Some get it from the government, as is the case of the Employment Development Department (EDD), so that there is no cost to participants. There is no free lunch, however! The quality of what is available is not only driven by the cost to you but also by the way the business is conducted.

A brief overview of different resources available from third parties is provided here. There are dozens of books written by those who are engaged in this business. There are many books that list the names of these organizations, and these books are kept up-to-date with revisions. Constant, though, are the fundamentals on which each business model is based and the nature of the business in which each one is engaged.

Search Firms

Search firms are organizations that are retained by employers to find the right candidate for a particular position. The company in which the open position exists, pays the retained firm. This is generally true, although there are contingent search firms that will base their activities on *placing* the right candidate and then invoicing its client organization.

The way a search firm works is that each one has a pool of client organizations that they service. These client organizations place their employment needs in the form of a requisition or job description to these firms. For a retained search, the firm gets paid regardless of its placing a candidate in the client company. Enterprising search firms scour the market for the right candidate, poach its clients' competitors, and pirate talent just to meet its clients' needs. In good times, this is rampant. Search firms are even given the names of particular employees that the client company is interested in poaching from its competitors. In favorable times this is a good business. Search firms handle candidates at all levels, each firm specializing in a certain talent pool.

Generally, search firms also operate on the practice of specializing within an area and assigning specific recruiters to it. Sometimes, a recruiter is assigned to a client company, and sometimes, a recruiter is assigned to a specific job category. If you position yourself as a candidate with a particular specialty, a recruiter may handle your résumé. This recruiter may not even be aware of opportunities that exist within the same search organization for someone with a different flavor (see multiple résumés in Key-3), especially if you have not promoted that flavor with someone else in the same organization. This can result in some missed opportunities.

Generally, search firms (and recruiters) do well for themselves, their clients, and those seeking employment. In tough times (high unemployment), things are interesting and are worth some caution. With talent available from the street, tight operating budgets, and employees available from competitors, client companies are unwilling to use search firms as readily. The positions at which these searches take place in tough times move up substantially, and it is rare to see those below a director or a vice president level being pursued by a search firm for placement. The action, too, happens not so much for the unemployed, but more for those already employed. This is why for those who are out of work and looking, this is not as good an avenue as it may seem. Search firms are in the business more to re-employ those who are already employed than those out of work and looking! This is why looking for work through a search firm is much more productive when you are already working.

Recruiters

Recruiters are mostly contingent third-party employment brokers who help those looking for a job—employed or out of work—and keep track of where hiring is going on. They, too, have their client organizations that pay them after a successful employee intake. If a particular recruiter is unable to place a candidate, they do not get paid. This is the contingent part.

In tough times, there is plenty of talent on the street looking for work. The only reason recruiters are brought into the process by a company is because the process of selection can be costly, using internal resources, especially for a smaller organization. The recruiters do all the work prior to presenting candidates and qualify them. Some companies use internal recruiters—company employees—to do the same. Some companies outsource this function so the recruiters are hourly contract employees. This is why it is critical for a candidate to be clear who has approached them before getting excited about the prospects. It is a good idea to ask a calling recruiter their way of operating and how they are being compensated.

In times when unemployment is high, recruiters do not do well. Companies are unwilling to pay to bring someone on board if they can get comparable talent from the street. This is why protecting your marketing and how you are marketing yourself are so important. Many desperate recruiters, in tough times, will raid job boards for résumés because they can have access to them and call those, whose résumés they find interesting, with an enticing sales pitch. If you have not seen much action on the job front, you could be lured in by such calls, and in an emotional exchange, might hear perhaps what is not even said. After you get in bed with an unscrupulous recruiter, your résumé can go to many employers in the country and even abroad in a very short time. Once a recruiter has a résumé in a company's hands, directly seeking a job there on your own is compromised, even at a later time, because the company now owes this recruiter their fee. This fee becomes a factor even though if that résumé results in filling a different position. Many jobseekers are frustrated by getting blocked from consideration, even for positions in a company for which it sees them as a good fit, because of what a recruiter can do using these tactics. Companies do not want to pay recruiter fees in a tough economy, so as a result, you end up getting sidelined.

This is why it is critical to carefully screen all recruiter calls, when approached after posting a résumé on a public job board. This, too, is why it pays to be selective in posting a résumé only on reputable job boards, and then staying with just the reputable professionals.

Some Tips on Posting Your Résumé on a Job Board

The following tips are offered to make your job-search campaign more effective, if you want to use public job boards to post your résumé:

1. Make some subtle way in which your résumé, posted on a public job board, is uniquely identifiable to *you*. When your résumé lands on someone's desk through a recruiter, it is competing with the one you might send directly. What also matters is which version reaches a company first. One way to make this differentiation, known only to you, is to change, for example, the address from "Street" to "St." on the two versions, so that you can identify your version. The recruiter may block you from employment in that company by demanding the commission, if you are offered a job there. Having this identifier on the résumé can help if it comes to a showdown on whose résumé got the action.

2. Make sure that only you, the recruiters, and companies have access to your résumé. If anyone—another competing candidate—who logs-in,

can access any posted résumé, then you are losing your competitive advantage by someone stealing ideas of differentiation from your résumé. Many career management firms give free access to all clients' résumés, which are posted on their site and are in their database.

3. Periodically revise your posted résumés and purge the older versions.

4. Do not put any information of personal nature as a Social Security number or a complete street address on your résumé; merely the name of your city is enough along with the contact information.

5. Keep track of all versions you have posted and then periodically update and purge as market conditions change.

6. Post résumés only on select job boards, and tag each one discreetly, so that you can identify the source when someone calls you as a result of your postings.

7. Take all your posted résumés off the boards after you have landed a job and started working.

Outplacement Firms

Outplacement firms are third parties engaged by their client organization to facilitate employee termination and their subsequent transition. They help terminated employees manage their transitions so that the client company is perceived as a caring and humane organization in the eyes of those affected by terminations and those who matter to the company. The outplacement service is also seen as a part of a compensation package and is a factor that can make a company a preferred employer. Outplacement firms are also known as career management firms.

Outplacement firms provide a variety of services depending on the agreement with the client organization. The services provided, typically, include the following:

Orientation and Venting: This step helps you deal with your job loss, immediately following your termination. This is where a career counselor from the outplacement firm can provide emotional support and guide you through what services are offered during your transition. It may also provide optional services, you can purchase from them, beyond what is contracted with your ex-employer.

Résumé Workshop: This is a one or two-day workshop in a group setting—typically your company group—that walks you through how to make your résumé and how to market yourself in the particular geography and conditions.

Résumé Service: The service includes some support preparing your résumé, making multiple copies, mailing them to a list of employers, and administrative support, such as computers, copying, faxing, and access to the Internet.

Assessments: This may include a battery of tests and assessments that let you develop some insights about your career preferences. This is usually included in a high-end package as assessments can be expensive. They include Meyer's Briggs Type Indicator, and Strong Inventory, among others.

Career Counseling: These are face-to-face sessions with an experienced counselor. The number of sessions is negotiated as a part of the contract.

Success Teams: These teams meet weekly to discuss their progress searching for jobs. An experienced counselor typically facilitates these sessions.

Roundtables: These are one or two-hour discussion sessions where a trainer presents topical information on a particular subject of general interest to the group.

Special Workshops: These are one-day workshops on topics such as entrepreneurship, consulting, contracting, among others.

Job Consultants: Consultants with specific expertise in job search and connections with employers are available as a part of this service.

Job Fairs: Many firms stage their own job fairs where they invite outside employers who are hiring. This is a good opportunity to participate in a more intimate and non-threatening event for those who are new to this process.

Networking Events: Special events are organized to help those who are shy coming together in a social setting looking for work or sharing their needs with others.

Résumé Bank: Most keep their own databank of résumés of internal clients. Employers and recruiters who pay a certain fee to have this privilege subscribe to this bank.

Job Bank: Employers who have an agreement to post new jobs, post their openings on the job lead link. This link can be part of the Website accessible by clients who are on the service roster at any particular time.

Alumnus List: Past alums of the organization are listed on this page from the Website. This can be a good networking resource.

Company Website: Most have a comprehensive Website to provide research, informational, and support data to its clients. Access to this portal is controlled.

Outplacement services can be expensive and when companies are watching their bottom line in a tight economy, they want to manage these costs. Some employers open up their own outplacement center internally to help those exiting their company. While some employer-run centers are good resources, employees' views on such an arrangement are mixed. One reason is, perhaps, the exiting employees resent having to come back to the company that just let them go. Another reason may also be that having to come back to their place of work—albeit at a different location—and having restrictions on access, facilities, and what they can do, while still at "their" company. Some also find it awkward dealing with their old colleagues. Quality of available services varies.

The typical length of service for outplacement contracts varies from one day to six months or more. In tough times, when companies are cutting costs, they do whatever possible to make sure that their costs are contained while offering outplacement services.

Job-Placement Specialists

Job-placement specialists are professionals who help clients with assessment, coaching, and connecting with employers who have specific openings that are exclusively or non-exclusively known to them. Fees vary.

Career Consultants

Career consultants are specialists who do assessments and help clients interpret these tests in the light of emerging job trends and career choices. They also provide individualized coaching. Fees vary.

Often, career consultants are professional therapists, or those in HR, who have decided to do something on their own. They bring some value to the process as career consultants. Some are focused on the process and are not versed with content. What does this mean? In many cases they will verify to see if a résumé is correctly presented, but may not be able to help in how to repackage it with the knowledge of the job market. Their *content* knowledge is not their forte, their process knowledge is. If you are not clear yourself what you are seeking, the value in such an arrangement could be less than if you sought out someone who understands the job market and has been in such jobs, and who can also be an excellent coach. Before engaging a consultant, check out fees, references, and background.

"Information" Brokers

"Information" Brokers are a somewhat shady bunch of businesses that exploit their clients' fragile emotional state and their desperate situation looking for an opportunity. Often, they represent the ugly underbelly of the employment brokering business. In addition to a variety of more commonly available services of some or marginal value—assessments, emotional support, résumé preparation, etiquette, among others—they claim to have an "inside" track to the "secret jobs" in client companies that no one else knows about. They mostly cater to the immigrant population known to have saved money during good times, whose language skills and cultural knowledge to successfully navigate through a job search are marginal. Their sales pitch is based on appealing to clients' perceived inability to network, market, and develop viable leads. A majority of their clientele is frustrated looking for work, using ineffective methods, and are unable to generate action on their own. They are also running out of funds or options in their current situation. These unscrupulous "information" brokers rope in such clients with a promise to generate action on their search front, for an up-front fee that can be as high as $15,000. Some will even promise action to those who are close to losing their visa status and are willing to pay any amount just to stay in the country.

When dealing with such underhanded operators, the watchword is caution. If something sounds too good to be true, it probably is. Never sign any agreement where there is money involved, without making some inquiries and checking references. Some do not even believe in a written contract; just a "trust me" pitch. Those who get sucked into deals with these unscrupulous brokers, are often too embarrassed to admit that they have been duped.

Contract Agencies

Although many are employers, their main business is derived from hiring contract workers and then filling open positions for "temporary" work in their client organizations. Some temporary engagements can last several years, some even resulting in full-time jobs. They have their own recruitment process. Some organizations specialize in connecting temporary consultants with client companies. They help position opportunity seekers with their clients without any cost to them, and derive their income from the fee as a percentage of the billing for the time of engagement.

Employment Development Department

Most states have EDD as a part of the state agency that administers the unemployment benefits and provides help to those looking for some type of retraining, as market conditions change. These agencies also double as clearing houses for job-related information and provide some basic resources critical to all job seekers. Résumé preparation—typically for low-end and union employees—copying facilities, and seminars for the jobless are some of the services provided at these centers. In tough times EDD offices provide resources to professionals by conducting seminars and inviting guest speakers to motivate job seekers and help them.

Job Fairs

There are various types of job fairs. The main two categories are private and commercial.

Private job fairs are organized and hosted by individual employers interested in hiring. They are also hosted by private third parties such as career management firms, who invite employers to participate in an organized event, as well as by those who may organize them and invite employers to come and screen potential hires. For example, many career transition and outplacement companies, and even in-house career centers, routinely hold job fairs as a part of their service to its clients. For more detailed discussion on job fairs see Key-7.

Job-search "Agents"

Job-search agents are usually electronic hounds that sniff out the job one is looking for and notify of a find without having to constantly look in a certain domain as a job board. Many job boards, ISPs as AOL, Yahoo!, and others have a simple and user friendly interface on their Websites that allow for job seekers to create job alerts by entering their search criteria into a data bank. When a job that meets the criteria is posted on their data bank, the alert or agent creates a notification, automatically going to those who are looking for that match. This can be a time saver for those who are searching many job boards and have different "flavors" of jobs they are looking for in different markets.

Networking

As the job market tightens up, networking becomes the prime source of landing jobs. In the Internet age, many rules of searching for jobs have changed. This was followed by a sea change in hiring rules, following the dot-com implosion in 2001. Even in a slow economy, millions of jobs are visible with questionable integrity on the job boards. This is perhaps because it is more trouble for companies to review what is on these boards on a regular basis and have someone manage them. Newspaper job ads and print media are different. Only paid ads get published and stay in the print until someone decides not to pay for them anymore, a much more controlled and reliable way to trust what is in the printed media. Similarly, from the side of those responding to jobs, it takes a few seconds to keystroke and send a ready résumé to a company for a posted position. Millions, thus, respond to posted jobs, even when they know that the match between the posted requirements and the response is marginal at best.

This mode of posting jobs and how applicants respond to them has spawned a new approach to processing incoming responses. Most résumés and incoming responses are scanned electronically, then sorted and organized by key words. Only those that match a certain threshold are passed on to the next level, where someone visually scans them in an electronic format on a computer screen. The whole process has become increasingly more robotic and impersonal. Many smaller companies have simply given up on using their Website for job postings. They cannot handle the avalanche of responses for even the most esoteric jobs, especially when the unemployment rates are high.

One countermeasure for this impersonal approach to selection process and to leverage information on unposted jobs, is to find someone who has an inside track on an opening. Although people are still hired by a variety of approaches, social networking by far is the most prevalent way by which they land their jobs, because it allows them this inside track on an opportunity. This approach to job search has become a favored mode for employers, since the advent of the Internet over the past decade. This implies that for jobseekers to be productive, they had better start social networking to get what they want. The following list shows how different approaches to job search are ranked based on the *action* they generate in landing a job:

Networking	64%
Search firms/recruiters	12%
Advertisements (Print)	11%
Other (job fairs, etc.)	9%
Internet	4%

These statistics were compiled from a variety of sources and have remained indicative of the emphasis of how jobs are found in this Internet age. The percentage of jobs landed by those using the Internet has steadily declined over the years. Additionally, for those making in excess of $60, 000 annually, the percentage of landings, using the Internet, is considerably smaller than those at the lower end of the salary range.

It is, therefore, safe to conclude that networking beats the Net at least 16:1 for *landing* an opportunity, if not for a job search. The Internet still can be a good source for *searching* posted jobs! It is also a good source for *researching* information about companies and the job market as we presented in Key-3: Presenting Yourself. One should know when to switch from the Net to networking and how to use each one synergistically.

Those who feel lost in the networking maze wonder what a good starting point is for networking activity. The following graphic, Figure-3 (adapted from a model developed by Vivienne Powell, a career counselor) is a good tool to start the process. Networking is often disparaged or even maligned by those who engage in professions where their social skills are not at a premium in the performance of their jobs. Engineers, scientists, and those who engage in highly technical fields as individual contributors share this view, as do shy and timid individuals and Introverts!

Looking at the statistics of what creates action in the job-search arena, networking by far wins hands down. In an economy where jobs are scarce this percentage remains high.

Networking Forums

Those who find themselves suddenly out of work and are not well "networked" find it discouraging to start connecting. They believe that their expertise in the areas of their field and their modicum of connections will get them going. Their next logical action step—after their denial and grieving—is to start their résumé and start sending them out. This can be frustrating. As we just presented, networking is the most productive way to get action in a job search, *even* in a good economy. Those engaged as individual contributors in functions that do not require social connections as a part of their job find it challenging to start socializing with others who can help them. They believe that since they have nothing to give, they have no right asking others for information. This is a misperception!

As a part of getting into gear, looking for opportunities following a job loss, one of the first actions must be to find out where the local networking events are held. For those who are looking for a change while holding a job, this is a bit easier because they live in a working environment, where information and interactions flow. In a job market with fewer jobs, those unemployed can represent a large population. Many enterprising, out-of-work job seekers start their own networking events. Some events grow to become weekly scheduled activities with hundreds attending. Often such groups gather at a restaurant, early in the day, and network, followed by lunch and a guest speaker. Even though several hundred attend such events, the design of the event allows great latitude in the way people come together. As people start to gather, one or two hours before lunch, they start socializing, networking, and exchanging information.

One such successful networking forum, in the heart of Silicon Valley, emerged out of a group of jobseekers coming together to share leads and support each other. This forum, now named C-Six, gathers every Tuesday and boasts an attendance exceeding 200 and a membership ten times that. This number of participants allows for a rich exchange of diverse information in current areas of interest and the information is very fresh. Despite its size, the way it is run provides the intimacy of a small group and a way to exchange leads, information, and needs (www.csix.org). It now has chapters around the Bay Area, in many communities.

One good way to break the fear or even shame of networking is for you to force yourself to go to such events early in the jobless state. Those who are working and are looking for outside opportunities, may find this forum awkward, because of the need to keep the search private and its possible conflict with work schedule. Another apprehension many have, is that they believe that they do not have much information to give to others early in their search. The best approach here, is to state the obvious during your introduction at these events and mention that you are new to this process and do not have any leads to share. Even in that case, if you can share information about your employer, that just let you go, it may be of help to some in the group.

As you progress in your search, your networking becomes more effective. If you are turned down for a job, you can now share that information in your group and share the names of the hiring manager and others in the interview chain, so that others can benefit and, in turn, you can get similar information in return. It is not the lack of information that holds people back from networking; it is their shyness and diffidence. Get over it and network!

The other benefit of networking socially is that it provides the much needed support that is an emotional tonic for those who feel isolated, especially in a jobless state. Even for those who have jobs, and are seeking a change, this support is important.

Virtual Networking

Virtual networking is done in cyberspace, not face-to-face! This is a boon to the shy, the timid, and the Introverted. One example of this cyber forum is www.linkedin.com, with an appropriate tag line, "Your network is bigger than you think." For those who prefer to do their "socializing" on the Internet, this resource can be an option. It is designed to connect people and provide degrees of "separation" similar to a social network.

For example, if you want to connect with someone at the second or third degree of separation, you had better get someone in the second degree, to introduce you to the one you are trying to connect with. The etiquette here is not much different from the one in social networking. This is an emerging concept and its business model is not yet defined, so its success remains to be seen.

Networking Universe

Figure-3 shows how a typical networking universe can be modeled. Even for those who believe that their networks are marginal, might be surprised to discover how extensive it is, if they map out their own network as shown in the diagram. Do not underestimate your networking capital! A brief description for each category, within the universe, is given below.

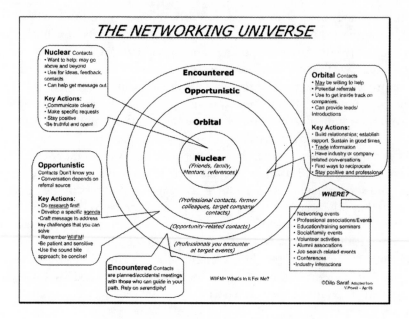

Figure-3: The Networking Universe

Nuclear Contacts: These are your most immediate connections—your social nucleus. Your friends, family, relatives, and even some colleagues fall in this category. "Nuclear" also means that you can take these contacts and "explode" them into a much bigger universe! One criterion by which you can identify contacts in this category is that, if you called them at any time, they will take or return your call.

There is an irony in this most intimate of networking domains. Because those who belong to it are intimate in their connections to each other, assuming that everyone in this domain knows your business and future plans, can be risky. Because of this very closeness, many within this category may be embarrassed to ask you about your business and what specifically you do or are looking for. The best way to overcome this apprehension or even misapprehension is to send them your résumé and marketing plan. It is even better if this is personally presented to them and discussed so that there is no confusion about your goal. If this circle of contacts is large, it is normal to segment this circle so that each segment has the correct version of the résumé (if you have multiple flavors of them) and the appropriate marketing plan and target companies. Do not give more than one message to a group within this circle. It can confuse them; keep it simple (see below: Networking Segmentation).

Orbital Contacts: These are contacts that you have developed over your career. The idea is to get people who have target company information, and bring them to this sub-universe. Those in this category will typically return your calls, when called during normal business hours.

Opportunistic Contacts: These are carefully developed connections and your purpose with them is somewhat selfish. They know it. So, you need to expend special efforts to get their attention to serve your cause. Those in this category may not even return your calls. A client tried one clever approach of opportunistic contacts, to expand his strategic network successfully. He was a mountain-bike enthusiast and a runner. Many companies have groups of employees who jog or bike regularly during their lunch breaks. This client waited outside targeted companies and joined the groups that departed for their recreational activities at lunch. During this outing with the group, he connected with a few joggers and found contact information. He tried this at three target companies and two offered him interviews and the third a job!

Encountered Contacts: These are chance encounters. If you keep your social radar turned on and your antennas up, you will run into many such encounters. For these contacts rely on serendipity.

Networking Segmentation

Similar to the market segmentation we presented in Key-4, a network also needs to be segmented, especially for multiple résumés. If you send every version of a résumé to everyone in your networking contact, confusion can ensue, which may, at best, result in no action, or worse, in confused action. You should make special efforts to segment your network for each version of your campaign and then keep them each separate, and manage that process for most impact. This is why keeping *different* flavors of a résumé should be limited to five.

*Keeping in Touch!

It takes a tremendous effort and time to build a network. This is because most put their focus on this activity only in the time of *their* need. So, if you have not kept in touch with your contacts when times were good, it becomes difficult to reconnect after a long pause. It takes a special effort to overcome this inertia stemming from years of being out of touch and then re-igniting a long-faded relationship. Once the reconnection is made, however, keeping up with the renewed relationship is easier. The Internet makes this possible. Ironically the very source that has made cyber networking easier for staying in touch has also been the reason for having the need for social networking!

One approach to nurturing networked relationships and sustaining them over time is to start your own newsletter. Send this newsletter in times, good and bad, to all those whom you contacted as a result of your job search. Job uncertainties are the wave of the future. Keeping abreast of what is happening in your search, as a part of the newsletter (monthly or so), can be a good way of staying in touch without intruding or imposing. A newsletter could be one or two pages of tidbits or things of interest to the circle of network. These tidbits could typically include family matters, education, finances, humorous anecdotes, and some personal details of general interest. Although a newsletter takes time and effort to pull together, it is a good and effective way to protect your investment and build on it.

If you are out of work and aggressively looking, or if you are working and looking for a change, you must discipline yourself to network two-three times weekly, and make sure that it happens. If you are unable to engage in in-person networking, one of these "events" could be some scheduled time you set aside for yourself on the Internet, and do some serious cyber networking, no *more* than once a week. The remaining interactions must be in person.

Another rule for success in networking is to give more than you take from the network. See Key-7 for networking etiquette.

Cold Calling

Cold calling is a term that is often used in the context of making sales calls to potential buyers. Telemarketing is a cold call, since the caller calls the unsuspecting prospect and explores avenues to make a sale. Cold calling has thus become a dreaded phrase especially for those who are not in the selling business. Even to those who are looking for jobs on their own turf—sales and marketing professionals—cold calls are an anathema. Why? The success rate is very low for telemarketing cold calls (typically about three percent), and in a job search it is probably even less, and it takes an emotional toll on your psyche, because the product is *you*!

However, cold calls can also be *redefined* as a call made after you have been introduced to the called party in some way. When this is already done it is no longer a "cold call" in its classical sense. There are a variety of ways to getting introduced to the person you'd like to call. In the order of increasing impact they are as follows:

- Someone refers you to the person you are trying to contact

- You send an unsolicited letter that piques a person's interest and then call that person to follow-up

- Someone (known) calls the person you want to contact before your call to them

- Someone calls the person while you are on the line, a three-way call, introduces you, and lets you connect, and then you continue on your own

- Someone introduces you to the person you want to contact in a special way, preferably face-to-face

Even if someone refers you to call another person, the best way to get that person's attention is by first sending a letter or email stating who has referred you and why. The letter of introduction should be functional, compelling, and polite, with a reminder that you will be calling this person in a few days to introduce yourself. Now, this is NOT a cold call anymore in its classical sense!

The best antidote for fear and apprehension around a cold call is to send a proxy—a letter, email, a third party call, an introduction—to obviate the awkwardness of a true cold call!

There is another strategy for successful cold calls: once you have sent something ahead to announce your cold calling, make many "cold calls" in a block of time one after another. Making 10–15 calls in one sitting is far more effective than randomly calling. Also, make these calls when you are at your peak alertness and energy. That way those who refuse to take your calls or disregard you in your first encounter with them, will not bring you down as much. Besides, when you are at your best, you are far more likely to make a good impression with the proper tone of your voice and your telephone personality.

Always follow-up a cold call with a thank you note.

A sample letter of introduction was presented at the end of the previous Key. A "cold call" a week or so after such a letter is in order.

*Sending a Differentiated Response

Unless your response to a job opening is differentiated, it is not likely to get a response. This process of differentiation begins at the first contact and continues until the offer is accepted. One way to find a key to keep this differentiation at each step, is to ask yourself this question: what would everyone else do to respond to this opportunity, and how would they respond? Whatever the answer is, do its opposite, so that your message is effective.

In Key-7 is guerilla marketing. We also discuss unconventional approaches to job search (Key-4). The reason for presenting both these sections separately, is because they each present a different perspective to candidates, each allowing them to think outside the box. Part of the challenge is managing a campaign, so that it employs a variety of creative approaches, to produce an effect that is not possible by just any one of its components. You may decide to emphasize one or more of these approaches in your campaign mix, based on your own learning, and your appetite for taking risk and having fun.

In the space below, various creative ways to marketing are listed in the order of increasing differentiation impact. The easiest is ranked first:

- Sending a well-articulated résumé in response to an opening without a cover letter
- Sending the résumé with a cover letter
- Sending the résumé with a *well-researched* cover letter
- Sending a package through a courier service delivered directly to the hiring manager
- Sending a Point-of-View (POV) letter to a high-level executive *without* a résumé
- Sending an attention-getting letter to an executive and then "cold calling"

A good campaign should use these methods to target companies for a response. This is where the Gold, Silver, and Bronze or "A," "B," and "C" tiers are important in a marketing plan. The above approaches should be used according to the tier, to which the target company belongs. For example a "C" company is not worth much more than a résumé alone, whereas an "A" company would get something at the lower end of this list!

The following tale of success is worth noting:

A Tale of Success

The story in the box below is a true tale shared by an excited and grateful client:

Carolyn's Tale

The following story is a success tale of differentiating yourself by using tactics that are easy and the ones that involve making your own rules:

Carolyn wanted to get into an entirely new area, after some 25 years as a marketing communications manager, at a Fortune-50 company and after taking an early retirement, forced by its recent cutbacks. She wanted to get into interior decorating, as her new career. With little formal training in this field and no experience other than remodeling her own home, and having it showcased in a national magazine, anyone would have called Carolyn a mirage chaser in a tough economy!

Carolyn's original approach was to apply to major building material chains, as Home Depot, which sell interior decorating products and has sales people on the floor with some decorating taste and expertise. If that is what any average person would do, she decided to do the opposite: go after the top name in the field. A Madison Avenue designer Lynn H. immediately struck Carolyn. The decorating diva—Lynn H.—was giving a lecture at a local university, during one of her whirlwind tours. Carolyn attended the lecture. At the end of her talk, Lynn announced that those looking for internships at her new local studio, should forward their résumés to an email address, which she flashed on the screen at the end of her talk.

From the large crowd that had gathered to hear the master, literally hundreds emailed Lynn their résumés to the address that evening. Many respondents had years of professional experience and impeccable credentials in interior decorating. Carolyn did the reverse: she sent a letter, with intent to serve as an intern, personally addressed to the diva by FedEx, *with* her marketing communications résumé. The hundreds of emails remained unopened as the FedEx letter was delivered to the diva herself and she signed for it the next day. She was about to inaugurate her new studio, in a day or so, locally and wanted someone to help her do that right away. Lynn, of course, did not have the time to weed through the hundreds of résumés and then go through the selection process. The FedEx-ed letter made the impact. Imagine Carolyn's surprise and delight

---

> when she was personally called by the diva that night asking for help with the new project the next day! The following day, Carolyn was offered the internship purely based on her personality, moxy, and enthusiasm, bypassing the many who were far more qualified than she!
> Such is the power of a differentiated response!

Carolyn's letter to Lynn is below:

Hi Dilip,

Thanks so much for all your advice and support.

The idea of a targeted cover memo, sent two-day Fed Ex directly to the principal, worked for me. Everyone else I was competing against "followed the rules" and sent their résumé via e-mail to the office manager. Mine arrived hand delivered later in the week.

It stood out from the beginning! Then I was told it was well written and I included comments the principal had said in her lecture. It demonstrated I took her seriously.

I've attached a copy of the actual letter used. As you said in the class, "give it a try—there's nothing to lose and everything to gain."

Carolyn

Carolyn DeSoto
Benvenue Avenue
Atherton, CA 94025
(000) 555-0000

September 22, 2002

Lynn xxxx
536 Ramona Street
Palo Alto, CA 94301   **By FedEx**

Dear Lynn,

Your presentation, at UCSC Extension yesterday, was spellbinding. I've always been kidded for my affinity for continuity. However, now I've met the "master."

I'm beginning my journey in your field of expertise. In parallel with my successful management career at Hewlett-Packard, I completed the UCSC Interior Design Program and renovated my 1930's home. *Sunset Magazine* photographed my garage conversion to cabana and *Palo Alto Home & Garden Design* is working on my story for publication.

So, if that's about me, how could I help you? Enclosed is my résumé. You'll find that my management and marketing communications background, combined with a designer's eye, can help you and your staff with the many commitments necessary to run a business. I want to help you and your team *and* continue my passion for learning design.

Consider me for your internship program. Or, remember me when you need a hardworking, conscientious, project manager with a design background. And with the upcoming holidays—I'm sure you'll be inundated with requests from clients.

Sincerely,

Carolyn DeSoto

P.S. I'm ready to get it done for you. As you said, "no task is too small." Just call me!

The ensuing Thank you note after Carolyn's first stint at Lynn's boutique, the next day is below:

Hi Lynn,

What an impressive staff you've assembled! They're committed and share a strong work ethic—from Cathy, Joannie and Angela through to Elle, Lilliana and Bob. They're an important asset to your business.

And your gala opening was a success. I chatted with Leslie, Deirdre and Aurora—who all had a good time and were very excited about the cover on "Traditional Home." (Although, I think Leslie's Mom, in New York, may have been more excited). Meeting your confident son, Culin, was a kick, too.

There's no doubt about it, he's going to make it big time!

So, even after meeting the extended "family" and standing "trial by midnight oil," I'm still interested in the internship. When is a good time to discuss it? If I don't hear back this week, I'll give Cathy a call.

Thank you for the opportunity. I look forward to it.

Best regards

Carolyn

Needless to say, Carolyn was offered the internship the following day!

Follow-ups and Actions

Follow-ups for every response are as important, if not more, than the responses and actions themselves. Why? It is easy for a response to get shuffled and lost in an organization. As the market gets tougher, the number of responses and the overall activity, on the job front, increase dramatically inside any organization. As company resources get cut, this becomes increasingly more difficult. Even though you have sent a response that is highly differentiated, you cannot assume that someone has read it and will respond to it. Once again, you need to differentiate yourself by doing follow-ups and making an impact.

How? Just the same way the response was sent in the first place. If the response went by a courier, then calling the person who signed for the delivery is a good starting point. Then, tracking to see to whom the package went next and so on. The person who actually opened the package should be the one with whom you need to follow-up. This person may not be the one to whom the package was originally addressed, based on your best research and guess. Initially leaving a voice mail, and then calling again after a few days works well. The idea is to get this person to invite you for an interview; first telephone and then face-to-face.

If you sent your response on the Web, then the person to follow up with is the one named in the posting. Often such names are not given in a tough job market. Calling the main number and then asking someone in HR or recruiting can work, but this approach is not very fruitful. This is why sending a differentiated response is critical, if the target is a "Gold" or an "A" company for you.

Another approach to follow-up is to use your internal contact or network to present the résumé in person. The electronic submittal can be in addition to this approach. The contact can give the details on how to follow-up and with whom. Here persistence pays and the approach to following-up should be just short of being a pest! One way to manage this is, at any given time, having many activities and targets to follow-up so that you do not fixate on one target.

As we shall see in this section, a bit later, how to manage your pipeline (Managing Your Pipeline), having multiple actions on which to follow-up creates a backlog of activities that need to be checked off daily. This then, becomes a routine activity.

Those who send a few responses and have no marketing plan, zero in on following-up with the obvious names that are announced in the job postings. Some call them nearly every day and keep leaving messages. At this rate of follow-up, your anxiety is tantamount to stalking, which can turn off the recruiter or hiring manager. There is a thin line between persistence and stalking, so it is a good idea to know what that is. If you have a good marketing plan and you are managing a full or near-full pipeline you should not have to resort to "stalking" (see Managing the Pipeline in this Key, and Table-6, following that discussion).

Unconventional Approaches

Unconventional approaches to job search include adopting methods that are not usually embraced by the masses. This is one sure way of differentiating yourself. Unconventional approaches should be used for all opportunities, including posted jobs for which many respond. There are three categories of jobs presented using this approach: posted jobs, unposted jobs, and non-existent jobs.

Unconventional job searches entail doing things in an out-of-the-ordinary way, to get what you want in your job search. This type of search goes well beyond merely ferreting out the jobs that are not posted; it goes to explore how to present a message so that new jobs are created because of what you present. This approach is suitable for your Gold or "A" companies. Once you make your case, then you become the only candidate for that job!

This section will present a variety of ways of doing an unconventional job search and provides examples of letters and other communications, so that you can pursue this as a *part* of your campaign!

Posted jobs

For posted jobs, the competition is fierce, so there will be a cataract of résumés flooding the employer. Using an unconventional approach is even more important here, to stand out from the crowd. The following list provides a summary of how to provide unconventional responses for a posted job:

- Research the company to find out more about why the posted job is now being filled and use that knowledge to fortify your résumé and the cover letter; update the résumé to reflect this. This insight should go beyond what is in the posted description. See the example in Key-3: Sample Cover Letters, particularly, the letters of John Mortons and Catherine Jenkins. See Key-3: Résumé and Researched Letter for a Posted Job.

- Find the name of the hiring manager to whom you send a response—résumé and the cover letter—via a courier.

- During the phone interview, show your knowledge gathered from the company and competitive research you have already done to stand out.

- During the interview, use your research to show that you bring more to the company with your insights than anyone else.

- Talk to the company's customers, suppliers, and channel partners to get nuggets of information, so that you can leverage that information, to show that you know more about the company's dealings with its constituencies than even the hiring team does (see following story)!

- If you have a solution to the problem that the company faces and *acknowledges*, and your research shows what the company is seeking, then take your solution, show it to those whom you meet, and discuss it giving details. Make sure you do not leave anything behind or give copies of your material. Politely refuse or use your best judgment. See example of a letter from Walter Chase to Palm, Inc. in Sample Letters: Unconventional Approaches in this Key.

- Create intrigue around how you can fill a company's need by doing research and showing confident insight:

One candidate who was being interviewed by a high-tech company, for a position of sales trainer, found out that the company Website had endorsements by its customers, who were identified by name and their affiliations. For a sales training to be effective, the ultimate test of its success is the customer experience, and how the customer feels about the company's sales force. So, this candidate decided to call each of those customers whose names appeared on the company Website. This entailed some research to connect the names with the location of each person. He called each of the six customers listed and represented himself as a potential sales trainer looking for ideas to improve customer experience, through improved sales training. Most customers responded with alacrity because they were intrigued by this idea. They had a selfish motive; to have an enhanced experience through the company's sales force. Although the first four raved about the sales force, the last two gave critical information. The candidate was able to leverage this input in the interviews to show that he knew more about what the training focus needed to be than did the hiring manager. As this story circulated among those who interviewed the candidate, the higher-ups quickly realized that no one else could beat this candidate in his initiative, originality, and customer focus.

He was hired within a week from a crowded field of respondents, on a salary much higher than even he expected!

This approach to talking to a company's customers can also be used in developing a letter to get its attention. Some find it difficult to approach customers directly, as this client did, and in some cases, customers may decline to speak specifically about a company without betraying their relationship, when asked directly. One approach that worked, with yet another client, involved contacting customers who appeared on that company's Website. In this instance, the client felt more comfortable representing himself as someone writing an article or presenting a conference paper about a certain business practice in that industry. He probed to explore how one of its suppliers—a company he was interested in pursuing as his target—was faring in this particular area and got insights that otherwise would not have been possible.

Unposted Jobs

Unconventional approaches for the unposted jobs are similar to the ones for the posted jobs with the *addition* of the following:

- Find some compelling way to get the attention of those who have the knowledge of the unposted jobs. Good networking skills are critical here.

- Look for media coverage of the company, find competitive information, read analyst reports, and infer what the company might need.

- Keep in contact with at least a few search firms, especially those who are in the field of your industry and those who know you so that you can get the scoop of the unposted jobs. More than likely, you will have to work with the search firm to get in. What do you care? The employer pays the fees!

- Talk to the customers, suppliers, and channels to learn about the company and how it is trying to move ahead. This search will give clues about possible opportunities.

Non Existing Jobs in Your Dream Company

This category of jobs stem from your own view of how a company should position itself in the current economy, to move ahead of its competition and achieve things that it has not yet achieved. The following list is a summary of what can be done to discover this knowledge:

- Research company's competitors and discover what they are doing, which your prospect company should be doing, and then make a case for it through a letter written so that some one higher up (at least two levels above the hiring manager) gets to see it.

- Talk to those who sell or service the company's products to discover what the company might benefit from to enhance the overall product or customer experience. If you are in product development, sales, marketing, or customer support, your argument on how to do this better can be compelling and an attention getter.

- Research company's finances and read its SEC filings (10-K/10-Q), publicly available. Use this research, to make a case, for why its management may need someone with your skills to beat out its competitors. This can be done at job levels starting from a hands-on design engineer to a senior VP! See examples below.

Sample Letters: Unconventional Approaches

The following sample letters (sent FedEx) show how to do an unconventional search to pursue your dream job! The letters are enclosed with the résumé for posted jobs and are sent *without* any attachments for unposted and non-existing jobs.

Note: throughout this book, there are references to sending responses by a courier (FedEx, for example) so that they stand out. The suggestion here is not that sending a weak message by attention-getting means, as FedEx, makes a difference. No! On the contrary, a couriered message had better be compelling. Otherwise it becomes fodder for ridicule. The idea behind this approach is realizing that the message, package, mailing method, and target addressee are all important in creating a direct and positive response. The message: "I am different in any way you look at me!"

Notes:

Walter Chase
Echo Lane
Saratoga, CA 95444
(000) 555-0000; email@email.com

November 22, 2003

David Davenport   POSTED JOBS "UNCONVENTIONAL APPROACH"
Vice President,
Operations
Palm
300 Dixon Landing Road
Milpitas, CA 94330

Dear Mr. Davenport,

I am pleased to apply for your position of Packaging Engineer, job #2231. My résumé is enclosed.

My research shows that Palm is currently undertaking aggressive initiatives on cost cutting and product yield. To that end, I have done some specific research, about opportunities that exist at Palm, in the areas of product packaging and cost savings. For your current model of the handheld, which is the most used organizer in the market today, as much of 52 percent of the product is considered "rejected" after it enters the channel. This is a high number by any standards. Typical return rate for consumer electronic products is in the low 20s! I also found that nearly 80 percent of these rejects stem from a single cause: the breakage of the liquid crystal display!

I also went and purchased one of your models and took it apart to investigate why such high incidence of breakage and returns can occur. My initial conclusion: the way the liquid crystal is packaged is prone to shock and impact, in the most benign transport environments. By merely inserting a small pad of any of the resilient materials—and I know just the ones right for this application—the breakage incidence can be reduced by half! This will bring down the overall return to a more respectable 25 percent or so. This alone may result in a savings of over $13 million per quarter and almost wipe out the loss you reported in the latest quarter.

I am excited about this possibility and plan to call you in a few days to follow up.

Cordially,

Walt Chase

Enclosure: Résumé

Alan Brown
Smith Lane
Los Gatos, CA 95032.
(000) 555-0000; email@email.com.

September 16, 2002

NON-EXISTENT JOBS

Dr. James Smead,
Research and Technology Center,
BMW,
1990 Page Mill Rd,
Palo Alto, CA 94304

Dear Dr. Smead:

I have read a great deal about the Telematics and Smart Vehicles work at the BMW Research Center in Palo Alto, over the past several years. I believe that your work is paving the way for the convergence of automobiles and "smart" technology.

I am a researcher in consumer electronics and mobile computing, who has been following your work. I believe that, like other technology convergences, moving telematic technologies, from early innovators/adopters, to the user majority, will require their creative application to the market. Based on my past research at IBM and Bosch, I believe that by viewing telematics from a different viewpoint, and thus structuring the platform technologies differently, can allow it to move to the user majority. Doing so, would increase user flexibility and platform openness, reduce implementation costs, and improve the user's experience. Giving telematics the potential to be applied to the whole product range and adopted incrementally.

I would like to explain the ideas behind these concepts with you in person and shall call you in a week or so.

Cordially,
Alan Brown

Brim Brene
James Circle
Saratoga, CA 94302
(000) 555-0000; email@email.com

June 9, 2003

NON-EXISTENT JOBS

Mr. Lew Smithson, Jr.
Executive Vice President, CFO
Genentech, Inc.
1 DNA Way
South San Francisco, CA 94080

Dear Mr. Smithson,

As someone deeply involved with Information Technology and how it supports strategic growth and competitive advantage, I have researched your company. Recent successes with the FDA approval of your new drug, favorably poise Genentech for imminent rapid growth.

I worked at Hewlett-Packard during several years when it was growing at 10–20 percent annually. This level of growth posed challenges to infrastructure providers, especially the IT function. I had a leading role in several IT initiatives driven by this rapid growth. I believe that my knowledge and experience can bring significant value to Genentech.

As a biotech leader, Genentech probably spends about four percent of revenues, or $100 million per year, on IT, much of it on infrastructure updates, and related costs. Rapid growth poses unique challenges to an organization and if these challenges are not managed, it can impede its strategic position. Particularly:

- In periods of growth, IT must respond proactively, so as not to impede growth of the core business. The challenge, of course, is to expand capability and maintain profits. I believe it is possible to reduce ongoing IT expenditures by 10 percent or more—an annual savings of at least $10 million. Much of this will come from carefully reviewing capital acquisitions and then focusing on how to make the existing infrastructure more effective, utilized, and available—most are used only about 10 percent. These savings can not only offset expenses necessary for growth, but also provide for a more productive infrastructure.

- I facilitated management and financial planning processes, as HP's infrastructure was transforming itself from a technology focused to a global services organization with customer experience as the driver, delivery of integrated solutions, and profit/loss/growth targets per service. I can leverage that recent experience into Genentech.

I look forward to speaking further with you about this and shall call you in a week.

Cordially,

Brim Bene

Walter Johnson
Alexander Ave.
Santa Clara, CA 95051
(000) 555-0000; email@email.com

December 4, 2002

NON-EXISTENT JOBS

Mr. Stephen P. Jobs
CEO and Director
Apple Computer
1 Infinite Loop
Cupertino, CA 95014

Dear Mr. Jobs,

As someone steeped in technology in the Valley, I have always admired Apple Computer products. I am deeply grateful for your work in transforming Apple back to its product leadership position, as it was originally under your helm.

Looking ahead, I think that there is an opportunity, in an aspect of your product suite that may interest you. This aspect deals with design for service and the overall customer ownership experience, following the initial buyer excitement, as well as how all this affects the bottom line and long-term loyalty. My research shows that there is a movement afoot at Apple, to change *attitudes* about emergent product reliability, maintainability, and serviceability. My long and hands-on experience in this discipline shows that changing mere attitudes into disciplined *habits* is a long and expensive journey.

I am expressing my interest in exploring Apple's future plans to improve products in these areas of design and how, what I bring in this area can be of value to your company. Would you take a moment to forward this to someone with whom I can explore this further?

If I do not hear back from you within a week, I plan to call you soon thereafter. Thank you for your attention!

Cordially,

Walter Johnson

Within a week of this letter, sent FedEx, Walt got a call from Mr. Job's office, stating that Steve Jobs would like to see his résumé! Walt is a hands-on individual contributor.

Jean Soder: email@email.com

February 22, 2003   NON-EXISTENT JOBS

Mr. D. S. Smith,
Director, Customer Advocacy
CISCO Systems
2323 North First St.
San Jose, CA 94352

Dear Mr. Smith:

I am writing to you, because the role your organization is engaged in intrigues me and I have some proven ideas on how to make your mission more customer focused.

As a customer advocate at HP's Executive Briefing Center, I was leading the charge of ensuring that strategic customers came to the Center, to hear about our new offerings and went away wanting to buy more and keeping loyal relationships. Initially, when I was learning about this process, I discovered that there was a disconnect between what the customers came expecting and what was presented to them. Interestingly, there was no robust process to ascertain this disconnect, until I started a process and took the initiative to approach visiting customers and found a way to get to the core of their issues. This simple process of "structured discovery" entailed researching the customer account history, talking to those who service the account, and then formulating a discovery interview with the customer face-to-face.

This simple dynamic of face-to-face discovery, yielded actionable information that helped HP attend to many inputs in a personal way. The result was immediate change in customer attitude and increased business. Additionally, I made sure that the follow-up with the account teams, was diligent and that the customer experienced an outcome that was positive.

This discovery process that inevitably results in immediate improvement in customer loyalty, appears simple initially, but it is *not* easy! There are many details that can make or break the overall impact of what this process can accomplish, and I have now learned of those elements.

As someone who is in charge of customer experience and advocacy, you would be interested in making such an initiative work at CISCO. The results are worth the effort and they are immediate. I would be interested in exploring this with you, and show some of my work at HP that resulted in my getting a

Customer Advocacy Award. The practice, I initiated, went on to become a company-wide best practice, very quickly.

If I do not hear from you, I plan to call you in a few days.

Cordially,

Jean Soder
(000) 555-0000

Sandy Smith
Glorietta Circle,
Santa Clara, CA 95051
(000) 555-0000; email@email.com

January 28, 2004

NON-EXISTENT JOBS

Sheila Bonet
Human Resources Client Services
Stanford University
Redwood Hall, Rm G-12, MC 4120
243 Panama St.
Stanford, CA 94305-4120

Hello Sheila,

Thank you for your prompt response to my recent query about job #002479. Although this position is no longer open, I would like to express my continued interest in similar positions, which may open up.

Reading from some of your recent job requirements, ITSS appears to need highly effective and energetic matrix managers, with a proven track record, for influencing and working across multiple organizations and serving the needs of diverse user constituencies.

ITSS is probably in the best position to identify and implement high impact change initiatives, across multiple IT organizations, and deliver a differentiated cross-discipline value at the lowest possible cost. However, in a constituency as diverse as Stanford, implementing consistent change across parochialism of individual departments, can sometimes be challenging, particularly when executing in a matrix organization. I have a demonstrated track record of influencing diverse interests to embrace a common cause, develop integrated plans, and execute on established targets. Time and again, in a highly dynamic and rapidly changing environment, I have proactively detected forces of resistance, and then neutralized them effectively to keep the project momentum, creating broad alliances in the process, and always delivering my commitments on schedule!

I am confident that with my extensive experience and proven project management successes in a high-tech environment, I would be an asset to the ITSS team.

If some of your positions are temporarily frozen, due to budgetary con-straints, I am more than happy to discuss creative approaches that can lead to a win-win outcome.

I look forward to exploring this further with you.

Cordially,

Sandy Smith

Sandra Jenkins
Hillview Court,
Los Altos Hills, CA 94022
(000) 555-0000; email@email.com

October 23, 2003

Mr. Hakim Mashouf
Chief Operating Officer
The Fashion Center
22 Union Square
San Francisco, CA 94101

Dear Mr. Mashouf,

I heard, through a mutual acquaintance, that you recently canceled your plans to search for vice president of IT at Fashion Center. Although I understand the reasons for possibly making this decision, I would like to present the following solutions.

My research into your operating strategy, business growth objectives, and potential risk factors makes me reflect on my own management skills and experience in high-tech, suggesting that at this juncture, I could create unparalleled value for you. Additionally, my passion for fashion and retail would be an asset to your franchise. I can create differentiated value for you in the following ways:

- Your executive team is highly knowledgeable and skilled in fashion and retail. I bring a unique balance to this team with my strong and proven technology leadership and experience combined with keen business acumen.

- In order to maintain your edge, in a highly competitive fashion industry, you may need a strategy for:

  o End-to-end (design to store-front) value chain integration.

  o Chosen technology needs to effectively meet the needs of the target non-technical user: interface must be user-friendly.

  o The IT&S solution must enable real-time delivery of quality information to a diverse user profile, ranging from executives to store employees, to enable high-quality decision-making across the value chain.

o   IT investment is 'background' to your business: it must produce the best ROI.

•   You need a leader who has demonstrated success in managing remote teams, has the ability to recruit and retain the needed technical expertise in a "non-technical" company. At the same time, the ability to effectively communicate with top executive team, as well as other users of IT&S, is critical for success.

I am confident that my extensive management experience in high-tech, will be an asset to your company. At a more personal level, I am excited about this opportunity for the following reasons:

In addition to my experience managing technology teams, I have a flare for fashion. I have a good understanding of your customer profile. Your business presents me with the unique opportunity to combine the two.

In looking at your current international business reach, I look forward to discussing potentially extending that reach to other countries as India. I am of Indian origin and see strong potential for business opportunities on both, the supply and consumer side.

Being a Stanford alumna, it was heartwarming for me to learn about your active involvement in education of future graduates and business leaders.

I look forward to exploring this further with you.

Cordially,

Sandra Jenkins

Kris Valaries

Churchill Drive
Milpitas, CA 95035
email@email.com
(000) 555-0000

May 24, 2002

Mr. Naoto Yoshioka
Director of Engineering
Sony Computer Entertainment America
919 E. Hillsdale Blvd.
Foster City, CA 94404-4247

This is from
Hoover's:
took 10 Mins.

Engineer:
Software Engineer

Sony Computer Entertainment America, Inc. has positions available for software engineers in Foster City, CA. Please send résumés to:
Sony Computer Entertainment
Attn: Staffing Ref. SJIA
919 E. Hillsdale Blvd. 2nd Floor

Dear Mr. Yoshioka:

The reason for writing you this note is because there is, perhaps, an opportunity for Sony Computer Entertainment to significantly increase the eye appeal and animation quality to its PlayStation 2 platforms through focused firmware and software engineering.

As a seasoned hands-on software architect and someone familiar with the products that originated at Sony Computer Entertainment, I have the following observations: the PlayStation 2 still continues to enjoy good consumer following; it is still the market leader. My research shows, however, that recent advancements by your competitors, have gradually eroded your market position and that trend seems to be on the rise. Sony's new pricing may be a partial acknowledgement of this.

The recent resurgence of your competitors' products, perhaps, stems from their ability to deliver a superior overall game experience to the players. Your competitors' animation is perceived as more dynamic, smooth, and realistic, their colors more vivid. One way to achieve or exceed that level of rendition and effect is to have an experienced software/systems engineer creatively collaborating with the artists, early in the development. By preserving the basic game script, keeping the integrity of animation, and making the motion more real-to-life and smooth, with vivid colors, players can enjoy a more enhanced and thrilling experience. I have done similar work with creative artists and am confident that such an integrated product enhancement can be realized (with some effort).

I would like to explore these ideas with you more in person and shall call you in a week or so.

Cordially,

Kris Valaries

> Called Fry's
> Electronics:
> 10 Mins for
> research.

> When Chris called Mr. Yoshioka within a few days, he acknowledged the letter and had a conversation about the next steps with him!

Priti Jain
May Avenue
Cupertino, CA 95014
Cell: (000) 555-0000
E-mail: email@email.com

November 20, 2003

NON-EXISTENT JOBS

Mr. Stephen James
Executive Vice President,
SureSoft Inc.
10 Maguire Road, Suite 332
Lexington, MA 02421

Dear Mr. James:

Congratulations on your recent win at United Nations and continuing inroads in the ASP market share, in the mid-to large-size markets!

SureSoft Inc. can further increase its market share, by insuring dominance in new segments as BPO services in finance and accounting and off-shoring. My research also shows that for on-demand services, a space in which your competitors are currently outperforming you, there is an opportunity, where I can help you close that gap, and soon, position you to vault them. With these new services, SureSoft can expand their presence in Europe and APAC rapidly.

As Director of Business Development/Sales of HP's Managed Services, I am in discussion with several ASP providers, on ways to aggressively capture out-sourcing opportunities. I offer:

- Over10 years in strategic global IT management, primarily focused on building and growing start-up businesses in Offshore and Hosting Services market space.

- Expertise in PeopleSoft Hosting Services, Messaging on Demand (Adaptive Network Infrastructure Services), Business Process Outsourcing (BPO), and Web Hosting Services.

- Experience with small, medium, and large-scale customers ranging from $5M to $25M.

- Leader in designing, structuring, and implementing opportunities with end-to-end solutions.

- Expertise in sales, operations, marketing, engineering, R&D, and customer support/service.
- Competitive intelligence to win opportunities against competitors (primarily technical solutions, costing and pricing in application outsourcing business space).
- Strong experience in managing US, Asia-Pacific, and European multicultural opportunities. I speak both Hindi, and German.

I shall call you in a week to discuss this further and follow-up.

Cordially,

Priti Jain

Pam James
Mary Avenue
Cupertino, CA 95014
Cell (000) 555-0000; E-mail: email@email.com

November 22, 2003

Ms. Stephanie Charles
Vice President
Mayfair Mall
39000 Stevens Creek Blvd
Cupertino, CA 95014

Dear Ms. Charles:

As someone who shops at the Mayfair Mall regularly, I am excited about the recent renovations you have done to attract more customers. I think that with your new design, layouts, and the way anchor stores are positioned, your foot traffic should greatly increase and your overall appeal, as a trendy mall, should become a showcase for other malls to follow.

In addition to your current initiatives, to spruce up the physical appeal of the mall, I wonder if you have considered other avenues to reach the community, by sponsoring events that make you more visible in the eyes of those who are within a 10 mile radius of the mall. I have the following ideas:

- Sponsoring specific events that entail student contests at local schools. Awarding winning entrants certificates from merchants who are mall clients will bring students and their parents to the mall, in addition to their regular visits here. There are 23 schools in this area and the student population of about 5,600. If you count parents of students, who come with them, this can substantially increase the flux of customers to the mall. I have worked out details of this program, after talking to my daughter, her classmates (they are all around 13 years of age), and some of their parents and teachers. They thought that this was a workable idea. We can also design this program to make the schools get something out of this, in this era of budget cutbacks.

- There are also 12 playgrounds nearby that hold weekly tournaments and games for kids, ranging in age from nine to 18. Their parents often come to these events. I also have some ideas on how to sponsor events at these playgrounds, on a regular basis, that will tie into increased traffic to the mall. I can show you these ideas in person.

- We have two movie complexes with 12 screens within a block of this mall. I do not see any mall advertising before the main feature. Tying the movie tickets to discounts at mall merchants can be a win-win situation for all, since the movie complex is within walking distance from here. The mall has plenty of parking spaces and the movie theater does not.

I have other ideas on how to promote the mall through community outreach. I would like to meet with you to discuss this in person. I plan to call you in a few days to set up a meeting.

Cordially,

Pam James

Charles Smith
Emerson Street
Los Gatos, CA 94556
(000) 555-0000: email@email.com

January 27, 2003

NON-EXISTENT JOBS

Mr. James Burrows
Executive Vice President
New Ventures
Enterprise Computers, Inc.
Austin, TX,

Dear Mr. Burrows:

Enterprise Computers has made impressive strides in capturing home and small-business markets. As someone who has followed Enterprise, for the past few years, your new initiatives to aggressively pursue Enterprise space, imaging, and printing are equally impressive.

As yet another area ripe for Enterprise to pursue, I wonder if you have considered total/high availability critical computing systems. For the past sixteen years, I have been steeped in this area and have made seminal technology contributions that have advanced the state-of-the art in this area. Particularly in the past seven years, I was a key player in helping HP NonStop penetrate into taking over NASDAQ. I architected the major part of the transaction software and worked on integrating that with its matching engine. There were many challenges, both in technology and applications. Throughout this period, I collaborated closely with the marketing team and customers, helping each achieve an appreciation of possibilities and then making it a reality. Even after the full deployment, I continued to work to support the customer on enhancing performance to a level where customer felt assured, even on the worst trading days.

I am proposing that you, as someone leading strategic initiatives at Enterprise, take a closer look at what you might be able to do, using the existing and emerging technology, and leverage that to penetrate this promising and high-visibility market space.

What I bring to this initiative is my passion, track record of unparalleled success, and an ability to deliver at every level of the project: technology, business, customer hand-holding, and follow-up support, to provide the kind of assurance both Enterprise and its critical computing customers are going to need in such an endeavor.

I would like to discuss this personally with you and explore how this can be moved forward to achieve success. I plan to call you in about a week to follow-up.

Cordially

Charlie Smith

Contingent Engagement

Contingent engagement entails positioning as an immediate value creator or problem solver, for the target employer. There are two possibilities with this approach:

- You have already been interviewed by the employer and turned down.
- You have targeted the company and are now making headway past the first interview.

If you are already interviewed and something has interfered with your being offered the job, find out why. It is always a good idea to follow-up with the hiring manager or the recruiter, to understand why the process did not conclude favorably. Sometimes circumstances force the hiring manager to consider other candidates.

In one case, a client was invited to make a presentation on new approaches for developing and delivering training to a group of managers, to make their overall training more effective and their performance more valuable to the company. As a part of the process, the client was asked to present ideas with examples to a group of HR specialists and line managers, during the third round of interviews. She was feeling more and more certain that she had the job bagged! She went through a great deal of effort preparing the presentation with many ideas she had developed over the years, and after researching the company and its needs. She also had gathered much information about the company, during the earlier round of interviews. She had prepared a compelling presentation for her "final" selection round that, she was sure was going to be a winner.

The final presentation went well and she was sure she had bagged the job. Two weeks went by and she did not hear from the hiring manager, who had championed her in the organization. When she finally connected with the hiring manager, she found out that the job had been offered internally to someone else, who the manager had said was not originally interested ("not qualified for the position"). Organization politics resulted in this person getting the position, although he was not as qualified.

Feeling betrayed by what had happened, the client initially thought she needed to do something to remedy the situation. She then decided to swallow her pride and contacted the hiring manager to explore if he could bring her on board as a consultant or an expert. She knew that he could use her help. The manager agreed, and she ended up working with the new candidate for several months. This candidate soon decided to quit the company; the client was then offered the job, some six months later.

Similar examples are many where you are a shoo-in and something interferes with your getting the offer. In a tough economy, this may even include the position getting cancelled.

When the position gets cancelled after a series of interviews, or just before an offer is being made, a good tactic is to suggest to the hiring manager that the job still needs to be done and that you would be willing to consider creative ways to making that happen.

In another instance, a major university was interviewing for an IT software and support engineer. After three rounds of interviews the field was narrowed from ten candidates to four and the position was put on hold. One client was able to overcome this obstacle with a proposal to the hiring manager. See Carol Lee letter in this Key under Sample letters.

As yet another possibility where you have had interviews and are not sure that the process is going to materialize in an offer, it is a good idea to explore if the hiring manager would consider bringing you as a consultant to see the quality of your work and then decide if there is a match.

Two sample letters that illustrate these situations—contingent employment—follow.

Sample Letters (Contingent Employment)

The following samples illustrate how a contingent employment situation can be handled with a letter, following some action preceding it, as a series of interviews or something leading to a job offer, but the offer does not materialize.

Note: This approach may *not* work if you lost out the opportunity to someone else competitively.

Notes:

Carol Lee
Lake Merrit View
Saratoga, CA 94333
(000) 555-0000; email@email.com

July 23, 2003

CONTINGENT EMPLOYMENT

James Harbrake
Manager, IT Operations
Stanford University
Stanford, CA 94305

Dear Mr. Harbrake:

Thank you for your call yesterday and your explanation why the job opportunity that I was pursuing in your organization, is now put on hold. I was looking forward to concluding the interview process and coming on board quickly, to help you get ready for the flux of events that suddenly start with the Fall Quarter, now just a few weeks away!

During the three rounds of interviews I've had with you, your staff, and higher-level managers, I saw the following challenges that your organization must deal with to make IT infrastructure support the academic and administrative functions:

- Making the student data available to *all* constituencies on the campus, within 24 hours of the enrollment, so that services can be made available to the entire student body quickly, efficiently, and without any errors. The current system and processes take up to a week to do this. I have some ideas that we discussed previously that are very practicable.

- The ability of the IT staff to help different office areas with new applications and special software to make them work more efficiently in administrative tasks. With recent cutbacks of administrative personnel, this is now even more urgent.

- Integrating the myriad procedures for handling student needs so that regardless of where students are pursuing their studies—and now this is global for many students—they are able to have a uniform method by which they can do their administrative chores easily and focus more on their studies. I talked to a few students, just to check this for myself, and there is a crying need for this initiative.

In an era of cutbacks and reorganizations, it is tempting to hold off on critical initiatives and let things continue as they have in the past. My view is that these cutbacks can exacerbate the impact of older IT systems on the entire campus and not just the student body.

I am willing to work with you now, to help you get started on these and other IT initiatives. With the Fall Quarter fast approaching, wouldn't you like to be ready when the students start flooding in? I am willing to work on a contract basis, at a rate that you can afford. Once the budget matters are settled and you see what I can do for you, we can go from there.

I plan to call you in a few days to see what you think.

Cordially,

Carol Lee

Soujil Vasques
(000) 555-0000: email@email.com

November 12, 2003

CONTINGENT EMPLOYMENT

Mr. Tom Cotton
eBay, Inc.
2145 First Street
San Jose, CA 95125

Dear Tom,

It was a pleasure meeting you yesterday. Thank you for giving me the opportunity to introduce my new idea about customer events to eBay.

After our meeting, you expressed interest in the speaker program that I developed at Cisco. In reviewing your eBay Web site and having attended an eBay University seminar in San Jose, four items immediately came to my mind.

- Session Class Offering. Could use a stronger framework.

- Session Content. How do participants know what to attend? At eBay Live! there were 75 classes offered. Some classes had similar-sounding titles. How can you indicate progressive presentations to leverage attendee learning and have attendees using eBay more productively?

- Customer data. What type of data collection devices do you use on-site for customer breakout session entry and why would you need this customer data?

- Session and speaker evaluation processing. I noticed that speakers presented their class more than once. How can speakers access feedback from their presentation on-site and make adjustments or improve the content for their next session?

The thrust of my approach in suggesting improved design for your eBay Live! event is differentiation, segmentation, customer friendly offerings, and actionable outcomes. These actionable outcomes are natural fallout of the design eBay can easily adopt. The benefit to eBay, of course, is dramatically improved customer mind share, loyalty, and increased business volume. I am confident that I can help achieve this with ease!

I have mapped out some details and would like to meet with you to share this. I'll call you early next week to see when you're available. If we agree on this, I would like a short engagement to prove my value to eBay.

Best regards,

Soujil Vasques

♠ Managing the Pipeline

A pipeline, an idea presented initially in Key-4: Target Segmentation, is a metaphor for all campaign activity that is in flux at various stages. Having a level of activity on different fronts is critical to maintaining the job-search project active. Once the pipeline is actively functioning, different targets will be in different stages of maturation. There will be a few that will be close to making an offer. In such cases, it is too easy to just focus on those, at the exclusion of others. If too much time passes, waiting for some offer to materialize, momentum that you have so carefully built and gained on all other targets, slowly wanes. If no offer comes through, jump-starting activities on targets that have now fallen in neglect can be difficult. This can also be downright depressing and many, who get themselves in this state, find it difficult to reenergize their job-search campaign. Do *not* let this happen to you, no matter how close you think you are to getting the final offer!

Job-search is a full-time venture, especially for the jobless! In such cases, job-search activities during a day's course should occupy about the same amount of time as a full-time job! How the different activities are structured and their mix is a matter of where you are in your job search and your appetite for adventure. Table-6: Suggested Activities in Different Phases of Search suggest a possibility.

In most cases the transition between the different phases are not sharp. There is much softness in transition between phases. The table is designed to give some guidance to those who have difficulty budgeting their time in their job-search activities and who do not have a clear understanding of how this process evolves. The phase designation is not based on the time you are into your job search. It is an indication of where you are in the execution of your job-search plan. There are some who have been out of work for nearly a year and are still not fully past the "onset" phase!

Table-6 assumes that you are practicing job-search methodologies in this book and not merely using traditional or familiar approaches alone!

During a tough job market, those who spent 30 or more hours every week on job-search (using methods presented in this book) were found to land within five weeks of such sustained activity. Efforts under this threshold did not result in much action, no matter how long they waited doing this level of activity!

#	Phase	Activity	% Time	Comments
1	Onset	Regrouping	60	This is particularly true if the job search is a result of a sudden layoff. See managing change in Key-1.
2	Onset	Communicate	10	Communicate your changed state to others, especially if this is a job loss.
3	Onset	Plan	25	Plan your finances, routines, and organization during transition. Get family support.
4	Onset	Organize	5	Develop ways to bring structure in your life.
5	Early	Research jobs	25	Research should be done on the Internet and in person networking equally.
6	Early	Network	25	Find whom to network with and expand your network. Go out to see people.
7	Early	Résumé	25	Make résumés in different versions based on markets
8	Early	Marketing Plan	25	Formulate your marketing strategy and make detailed plan for execution. Vet it.
9	Established	Responding to opportunities	40	This includes a mix of approaches: e-responses, informational interviews, POV letters, and unconventional approaches.
10	Established	Networking	25	Be out talking to others, making new contacts, reestablishing old ones.
11	Established	Follow-ups	15	Use a variety of methods based on your original response to an opportunity.
12	Established	New targets	10	Constantly add to your list of targets.
13	Established	Organize/ administration	10	Keep constantly organized and keep your administrative chores to a minimum.
14	Late	Respond to opportunities	25	This is an ongoing effort to ferreting out opportunities and sending an appropriate response.

#	Phase	Activity	% Time	Comments
15	Late	Follow-ups and interviews	30	If at this stage of your campaign, you are not getting interviews you must reexamine your campaign.
16	Late	Networking	20	Continue to expand your circle of contacts,
17	Late	Research new targets	15	Continue to research new targets for responses.
18	Late	All other	10	This includes admin. work but keep all personal work as finances and medical insurance, etc. out of this activity!
19	End	Interviews	40	
20	End	Follow-ups	20	Especially interview follow-ups and thank you notes (with specific messages).
21	End	References/ Research	25	Continue to research the target company to nail the interview and the job!
22	End	Responses	10	Continue to open up new opportunities/respond to new
23	End	Miscellaneous	5	Whatever is remaining to be done

Table 6: Suggested Activities in Different Phases of Search

Organizing Overall Campaign

We have covered much ground in this section, with many novel ways to get a productive job-search campaign underway. Almost all approaches suggested here are practicable and have been presented because they are culled from actual cases through which clients navigated *successfully*. The strategies and tactics presented here are novel, fresh, and attention getting. They also require diligence, perseverance, and confidence to practice and a sense of adventure!

To make the overall campaign work, one has to decide which of the methods work and create one's own mix of different approaches. In a given week, though, one should attempt to pursue a variety of ways suggested here to move the campaign in high gear and not focus on just one or two targets, or the ones you are most familiar with. Making constant adjustments and making sure that one manages a mix of different approaches are critical to quickly landing a job!

The second aspect of this campaign should also focus on constantly pushing the comfort-zone envelope. What does this mean? It simply means that it is very easy to fall into a rut or routine of activities with which one becomes comfortable. The driving metric should be action and results, and not activities and hours spent. Instead of blasting out some 100 résumés and not knowing with whom to follow-up, it is better to send only a few, based on the ability to follow-up and the rest should be based on using other approaches, as sending letters as we discussed in the Key. Constantly pushing one's comfort zone and developing new routines will keep a job-search campaign fresh enough to have a reason to get up in the morning on difficult days!

♠Your Toughest Challenge

A well-run campaign is characterized by many target opportunities in various stages of progress. A typical pipeline for a well-managed campaign, will have in it activities that represent an entire spectrum of progression for different opportunities. One of the toughest challenges, under these circumstances—for a well-managed campaign this is a certainty—is to continue to keep all the balls in the air despite an imminent offer. This was discussed briefly in Managing the Pipeline, and is presented here for emphasis, and in more detail. When one or two targets appear within reach and offers seem certain, it is tempting to put everything else on hold and keep waiting to see what happens. As time ticks, the offers can get delayed and all other activities that were so carefully nurtured can now suffer from neglect and lack of visibility. In such a situation, it is tempting to not waste time on all other activities and just wait for the pending offer(s) to materialize. In a tough job market, some offers can take weeks or even months to materialize. If at the end of that period they do not, then one has to jumpstart all the activities in the pipeline again and then nurture them back to life. This can be discouraging to many. Emotionally this can be disruptive. It is even more tempting to just wait when a verbal offer is made and the formal offer does not come through in a timely manner (one week) or come through at all. This is a BIG mistake!

Avoid it all costs!

An offer is not final until it is presented, negotiated, accepted, and a start date is agreed upon. In a tough economy even after the start date had been agreed upon, candidates were turned away from the plant as the start date coincided with unexpected plant closures. This is rare, unfortunate, and unexpected, but has happened. In one case, a client was made a verbal offer after waiting for a month after the final interview. He was asked to come to the HR department to pick up his offer. As he pulled into the parking lot, his cell phone rang. It was his hiring manager telling him that he did not need to come in as the position was cancelled. The client turned around and drove home in disbelief. During that period (nearly six weeks), he had abandoned all other search efforts, many of which were well along the way, in anticipation of *this* offer.

*Your Marketing Plan

A marketing plan is a comprehensive document that pulls together your key elements of how you navigate through getting your message out to the right targets.

Notes:

Strategic Marketing Plan

Purpose: The purpose of a marketing plan is to provide an articulate view of how one is going to pursue opportunities and targets to get what they are looking for. This can be a job, a consulting engagement, or any other value creation or capture opportunity. This plan is an organic document and should be reviewed frequently—even daily—to ensure that it is meaningful, current, and actionable.

When to do it: A good time to do a marketing plan is after you have completed your résumé. If you are looking for *ad hoc* opportunities and consulting engagements, do your plan after completing the Positioning Statement. You must have clearly defined what you are going to be doing, and after having a good sense of the competitive landscape.

Elements of a Good Marketing Plan:

Value Proposition: One per marketing plan.
Integrating Factor: What makes you create greater value by integrating a diverse portfolio of competencies? It is a synthesis of your Unique Skills *portfolio* written as a sentence or two to show value creation process.
Competitive Landscape: What is the *total* competition and how are they positioned?
Value Space Estimate: What is the overall size of the target market in the geography?
Geography: What is the geography?
Target Companies:
Gold: Need 10 Companies in this list.
Silver: Need 25 Companies in this list.
Bronze: Need 100 Companies in this list.
Penetration Strategies: What strategies will be used to get the attention of the companies in which you're interested? Open jobs, job leads, targeted research with a Point-Of-View (POV) letters are typical attention getters.
Networking Strategies: What specific strategies are you planning on using to reenergize, create, leverage, and expand your networks?
Milestones: What specific measurable milestones are you planning to set up to ensure that your execution is on track? Numbers of letters, contacts, and companies in the pipeline (each type) are good metrics.
Hours: How much time do you plan to spend on your search activities to execute the marketing plan each week?

Revisions: How often are you going to revise the marketing plan to make sure that you accomplish your target objectives with momentum to spare?

Tactical Marketing Plan

Sample

Name:
Address:
Contact:

Position: Senior Software Design Engineer and Team Lead:

Positioning Statement: A highly experienced and hands-on software engineer, well grounded in collaborating with customers and developing product requirements; skilled at organizing teams, both locally and globally, to deliver highly complex product on time and within budget. Highly skilled at off-shoring activities, including parceling out projects, monitoring their progress, and then integrating the final solutions for delivery to final customer. Well-versed with managing product life cycles and working with customers developing technology roadmaps.

Skills:

Customers	Teams	Leading Projects	Product Life	Coaching/Mentoring
Business needs Product requirements Technology-roadmaps Customer solutions Customer support	Organize and lead cross-functional teams Technical lead Mentor teams	Define, plan, and execute complex projects. Develop risk and early warning systems to keep on track. Deliver on time and budget.	Develop life cycles models. Develop how to manage life cycles to maximize revenues and profits and manager customer needs in emerging technology.	Mentor and coach new team members. Coach technical talent. Develop mentoring infrastructure.

Target market with sample companies:
Geographic area: SF Bay area. Types of industries: high-tech, biotech, banking, insurance, consulting firms, contracting firms. Organization size: over 1,000 employees.

High-tech	Biotech	Services	Consulting/ Contracting
Intel (Gold=G) Hewlett-Packard (G) Intuit (Silver=S) Sun Micro (Bronze=B) Cisco (S)	Applied Biotech (G) Becton Dickinson (S) Amgen (S) Genentech (G) Roche (G)	Wells Fargo Bank (G) Farmers Insurance (S) State Farm Ins. (S) Kaiser HMO (S) Hallmark Securities (S)	Deloitte and Touche (G) Accenture (G) Mckinsey (G) Samina Group (B) Handley Group (B)

This table should be expanded until 135 target companies are in the table.

Tool-7

A Sample Plan

Purpose: The purpose of a marketing plan is to provide an articulate view of how one is going to pursue opportunities and targets to get what they are looking for. This can be a job, a consulting engagement, or any other value creation or capture opportunity. This plan is an organic document and should be reviewed frequently—even daily—to ensure that it is meaningful, current, and actionable.

When to do it: A good time to do a marketing plan is after one has completed their résumé. For those looking for *ad hoc* opportunities and consulting engagements a good time to do a plan is after one has completed their positioning statement and have clearly defined what they are going to be doing and after having a good sense of the competitive landscape.

The following entries are filled as a sample plan to illustrate how the plan can be developed.

Value Proposition: A software team lead who can collaborate with customers and translate their needs into profitable products by being responsible for the entire development, delivery, and support functions in a highly competitive environment.

Integrating Factor: Using unparalleled technology knowledge, systems thinking, market savvy, and customer insights, articulate product features quickly and then demonstrate viability through rapid prototyping. Develop a comprehensive plan to organize development, including off-shoring and lead teams to deliver on time and budget. Create an ongoing stream of exciting and profitable products.

Competitive Landscape: There are about 25, 000 unemployed here, a million or so already employed, and overseas resources.

Value Space Estimate: There are 345 companies in the 25-mile radius of my own zip code.

Geography: A radius of 25 miles from my home as a starting point.

Target Companies: (See Table on next page)

    Gold: Need 10 Companies in this list. See Table

    Silver: Need 25 Companies in this list.

    Bronze: Need 100 Companies in this list.

Penetration Strategies: In order of priorities: Networking (unposted jobs), unconventional search, search firms, and finally posted jobs

Networking Strategies: Rebuild existing network (about 250); attend C-Six and ProNet meetings weekly; attend IEEE Chapter meeting monthly. Volunteer at the Senior Center.

Milestones: What specific measurable milestones are you planning to set up to ensure that your execution is on track? Numbers of letters, contacts, and companies in the pipeline (each type) are good metrics. (Make a separate chart.)

Hours: 35–45 per week.

Revisions: Initially once a month; then as needed.

Marketing Plan: Template

Strategic Marketing Plan:
Value Proposition:

Integrating Factor:

Competitive Landscape:

Value Space Estimate:

Geography:

Target Companies: Attach Table
Gold: Need 10 Companies in this list.
Silver: Need 25 Companies in this list.
Bronze: Need 100 Companies in this list.

Penetration Strategies:

Networking Strategies:

Milestones:

Hours:
Revisions:

Notes:

Tactical Marketing Plan:

Name:

Address:

Contact:

Objective:

Positioning Statement:

Skills:

Target Market with Sample companies:
Geographic area:

♠Keeping the Momentum

In a job search, the toughest challenge becomes keeping the campaign running and maintaining its momentum. Building and sustaining campaign momentum of course, depends on how it is organized, executed, and kept energized with fresh ideas. It gets especially hard when things do not go well at certain times. It is easy to get into a slump, accept defeat and retreat. Part of the challenge is to keep your hopes up, despite setbacks and defeats while believing in the vision.

Suggestions for sustaining the momentum are presented for the following three (of 14) categories of job seekers. Some of these suggestions can apply for other categories but these three are prone to suffering the most from losing momentum and presented here for that reason:

➢ Out of work and looking

➢ Working but looking for change

➢ On notice and must find something within the organization to keep employment

Each present unique challenges for those engaged in the transition.

➢ **Out of work and looking:** Re-establishing your cash flow becomes the chief motivator here. For those who are running out of funds, the prospect of having no money can create fear, which can go against a good and productive campaign. This is why early planning is critical when running out of funds is a real threat. The best strategy is to know when to shift from a sprint into a marathon, (Key-2: Switching from a Sprint to a Marathon) and how to quickly regroup and rework the plan and the campaign. Some of these tactics can include doing whatever to sustain some cash flow and prolonging the eventuality of running out of funds before a job is in hand. This may include part-time work, taking a lesser job, or sending a family member to do odd jobs.

Job-search campaign takes time and energy. To manage the job-search campaign takes focused energy and ongoing distractions can be insidious to its energetic flow. So, managing job-search activities using a scheduling calendar to reflect the priority it deserves, is critical for a committed campaign. The watchword of any effective campaign is discipline! If any week ends up being short, in meeting this level of commitment reflected by the schedule on the calendar, then one needs to develop coping strategies to make up for the lost time. Usually keeping track of hours, letters, résumés, and contacts during a well-managed campaign are good metrics to keeping and staying motivated. See Key-4: Keeping track.

➤ **Working but looking for change:** Here the toughest challenge is overcoming the comfort and inertia of the current job! Once the decision to move on is in place, disengaging from the current job and focusing on the next one are critical. Once again, making a weekly commitment chart for activities can help manage the process. It is very typical for those looking for a change outside, to keep draining themselves with the current job and then blaming their situation. Managing the regular workload, especially overtime work, is critical so that energy and time to focus on the job-search campaign are not frittered away!

➤ **On notice; must find inside employment:** The greatest challenge, for those facing this situation, is getting out of denial. This is exacerbated by their having to go back to work every day after getting notified. The best strategy is to adopt an attitude that the grace period given, is for getting ready for a real job-search campaign outside and not relying on the promises or prospects that are lurking. There may be scores of jobs the company has open, but, in tough times, companies go after the best talent to fill the opening. Getting notified of a layoff is as if your fate has already been sealed!

The best strategy is to get ready and follow the guidelines in Key-2: The False Hopes Syndrome. Concurrently explore what is available from the inside, as if it is just another opportunity, as you get ready for a serious outside campaign. This strategy is critical to success. Building and sustaining momentum early are critical immediately upon notification.

*The Momentum Curve

Although each category of jobseekers is faced with ups and downs and surprises and defeats throughout a campaign, how these are perceived and how they affect the ongoing momentum of the campaign and the state of one's mind are relative. In general, though, these ups and downs have a pattern, regardless of the category of jobseekers under which one falls. The graph below is a typical representation of how this may be experienced!

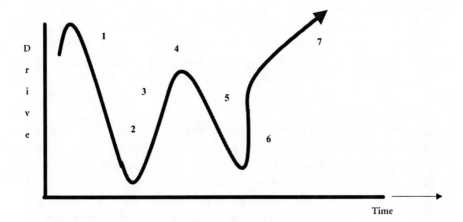

Figure-4: The Momentum Curve

A brief explanation of the Momentum Curve follows:

1. This is the Denial state from the Change Curve (Key-1) discussed in Figure-2: The Change Curve

2. This is the Deal state also from the same curve

3. This is the *first* Develop stage from this curve where job seekers are in the belief that they are running a sprint and not a marathon in a job-parched market

4. As early parts of their campaign begin to bear fruit, job seekers feel like things are working

5. This is where the first wave of defeats begins to form a pattern and job-seekers realize that they are facing the same setbacks in each advance that gave them hope, but they are not able to sustain the action to get the results they were hoping for. They feel stuck at a certain level of their campaign. Their self-esteem takes a pounding and they start having self-doubts.

6. This stage gets them thinking about regrouping and developing alternate strategies. This is where they realize that they now need to run a marathon.

7. This is where sustained momentum of action is seen. Many interviews, advanced discussions, and networks begin to pay off. Eventually there is critical mass and offer(s) start materializing.

This curve, as shown, is a typical and conceptual representation of how campaign momentum can manifest over time. In some cases, there can be multiple dips over time and the level of these dips (depths) can be varied. This graphic is presented to assure those who go through this process and wonder if they are ever going to see the light at the end of the tunnel. What they experience is typical!

As is depicted in the curve, the speed with which each dip appears gets faster. A good sign of hope! If the jobseeker spends time and effort early in the process getting ready, the number of dips can be minimized. This is one reason why having a written statement in Key-1: "My Truth!" can help a despaired jobseeker during their low times. As you start seeing yourself faced with repeated defeats and setbacks, having a touchstone as in an honest "My Truth!" can help you reenergize and regroup, assuring you to stay the course. You may decide to revisit this statement for its relevance to what is happening to you!

Keeping Track

This tool is designed to help you track your weekly activity on the job-search front. During the 2001–2004 job market, deemed the toughest in the past 40 years, anecdotal records indicate that those who spent 30 hours or more each week, in the following activities, landed a job within about five weeks of sustaining such activity.

<u>Notes:</u>

Tool-8: Tracking Log

Week of_____

Job Search Activity	Hours	#
Searching for open opportunities		
Responding with résumés and cover letters (total)		
Identifying possible opportunities in "A" or "Gold" companies		
Researching companies *and* forming a point of view		
Sending POV letters (with or without résumés)		
Networking with current contacts		
Developing new contacts		
Talking to recruiters and hiring managers		
Telephone interviews		
Face-to-face interviews		
Talking to those above hiring managers		
Visiting marketing plans and making adjustments		
Follow-ups with targets already in the pipeline (phone calls, visits)		
Doing something totally different to reenergize job-search campaign		
Total		

♠Seeking Professional Help!

One of the challenges in managing a campaign is to know when to seek help. If there is a good network, mentoring resources, and others who can help during transitions, it is a blessing. However, seeking help from a good professional can be priceless. Why? One reason is that many from within a network find it hard to be objective. Their time is limited, too! They are unlikely to have the professional training required to assess and analyze a situation objectively and use their insights to provide options that can be explored with a professional outlook. Many who feel lost, stuck, or frustrated in their transitions, keep looking from within to bootstrap and continue to fritter away their own valuable resources—time, money, and energy—without realizing that often these resources cannot be replenished. Why? The hardest thing yet to regain is one's will to continue in the face of repeated defeats and not having a clue what is really going on! This is important for generating the right outcome as a campaign marches forward. Without regrouping and jump-starting a campaign in a timely manner, it is possible to get into a funk and slowly despair!

What is the antidote? Seeking qualified professional help can go a long way in jumpstarting a flagging or floundering campaign. Sure, it is not easy to find the right professional and, sure, it costs money to engage one; but the cost side of the equation will be overwhelmed by the benefit one can derive, from the right guidance at the right time. A month saved in landing the right job, through seeking professional help, is hard to equate to its actual cost paid out to a helpful professional. A few hundred dollars spent with the right professional, can yield an outcome that is worth the peace of mind in more ways than one! If good professional advice and mentoring can help you overcome your limiting beliefs and get you past the hurdles that keep you from attaining your dream, it is a worthwhile pursuit. When a main source of cash flow stops and everyone in the household retreats into expense hibernation, it is difficult to contemplate spending money. Separating expenditure that is a leveraged benefit against a sunk cost, is one way to justify this expenditure.

Notes:

Summary Key-4: Marketing the Product—You!

This Key deals with the tactical aspects of sending your message in response to opportunities that you see (posted jobs), uncover (unposted jobs), or identify (non-existent jobs). Strategic marketing is presented in Optimizing Your Targetability in the previous Key.

In order to differentiate, merely sending a résumé response is not as compelling as the one that includes a targeted résumé and a well-crafted cover letter sent to a person who can act on it. There are various sources of this information commonly available but they are not commonly exploited to create differentiation. Tracking down customers (from company Websites), suppliers, and other stakeholders in a company's success, and then creating a discovery around your needs with them, can give invaluable insights that you can leverage in your penetration strategy.

In addition to traditional information gathering through databases and channels, spotting job trends and then using this information to position yourself in a differentiated way, can also add punch to your campaign.

A part of the Key focuses on how to work with third parties such as recruiters, search firms, and outplacement agencies. Understand this material before you start working with third parties, especially when there is money involved. Even with no money, your campaign can be compromised if you do not know what the nature of their interest is in marketing you.

Using an unconventional approach to job search can be done successfully if you know what the employer is looking for. Even if you do not know this, you can do research and surmise this and then position yourself for getting the attention of someone at the higher levels. Examples of such campaigns are shown.

Managing your pipeline comprises keeping on top of activities and chasing your targets. In an effective campaign the following mix of target opportunities is recommended:

Gold or "A" companies =   10
Silver or "B" companies =   25
Bronze or "C" companies =   100

It takes time to build this pipeline. Your planning should include putting a certain number of each type in the pipeline. At any given time, your activity should consist of following up on what is happening with this list of companies, in fleshing out job opportunities. Using unconventional approaches, you do not even need a posted job to be able to develop some action with the Gold or "A" companies. These approaches are discussed in this Key.

Managing your time and how much of it you spend on any particular way in your job search, should be driven by how much action you are able to generate. The following table shows typical breakdown of action—landing jobs:

Networking	64%
Search firms/recruiters	12%
Advertising (Print)	11%
Other (Job fairs, referrals)	9%
Internet	4%

Using the Internet for research and then leveraging that information into job leads through networking, can be a far more effective strategy.

Networking Universe is presented in Figure-3. Review the figure to revisit how you should structure your networking contacts and build your own networking universe.

Using Unconventional Approaches is presented, with specific examples.

Keeping campaign momentum is critical, in the face of repeated setbacks and rejections in a tough job market. There are strategies to keep the momentum despite these setbacks. Specific strategies are spelled out in Keeping the Momentum. Revisit the Momentum Curve, Figure-4, to understand how the momentum changes with time and what you need to do to manage it.

If your job-search campaign is flagging and you are getting down over your ability to make progress, seek professional help. The cost of such help, if properly sought and selected, can far outweigh the benefit, emotionally, financially, and in every other way!

Key-5: Acing the Interview

"The meeting of two personalities is like a contact of two chemicals; if there is any reaction, both are transformed."

—Carl Jung, psychiatrist (1875–1961)

The Interview

In critical human interactions, many look for the chemistry. Going through the interview process is not leaving to chance the chemistry of one's makeup. This Key demystifies how such chemistry can be "created" through careful preparation, targeting, and execution. The presentation here is in the sequence in which events occur after a résumé gets someone's attention. It is aimed at showing how to develop a process, to minimize leaving to chance, the matter of one's "chemistry."

The Telephone Call

Getting that phone call, from sending a response to an opportunity, is the first thing jobseekers yearn for. And yet, it is alarming to see how many are not fully prepared to handle *that* call. This all-important call is a gateway to being invited to a job interview; all subsequent actions depend on how this call is handled. It can be a passkey to the world of landing a job and working at a dream company, even though the initial call may be from a lesser company. How? This is because the first call may lead to a job. Even if that job is not ideal, it opens the door for using that success and leveraging it into a company of your choice. What are some of the common roadblocks to the next step after the first call?

The following list delineates the most common impediments, which can block success:

- Making it difficult for people to reach you
- Taking calls on a cell or cordless phone

- Not having ready access to the material sent in response to the opportunity

- Taking the call when unprepared to provide a best response

*Making it Difficult for People to Reach You

The following checklist is a good reminder to audit telephone habits and make sure that this most critical element, in a successful job search, is not taken for granted because of its familiarity.

1. **Having a single telephone line:** In this world of the Internet, people spend much of their time in cyberspace. Having a single telephone line, on which to do all the activity, including being on-line, can be a problem for those calling you. Many give out their cell phone numbers, as their primary point of contact, on their résumés. It is advisable to give your home phone as the preferred point of contact, with the cell line as an alternate. Cell phones and connections can be unreliable. Not being at a convenient spot can be a problem, too, when such a call comes on the cell phone.

    The best defense against missed or lost calls is to have at least *three* residential lines: one for business and job searching, one for the Internet, and the third one for family and personal calls. If there are teenagers in the house, there may be a need for additional lines depending on one's lifestyle. The line used for job searching must have a warm, personal greeting that is concise and business-like. That line should have a distinctive ringer so that only *authorized* members—preferably only you—of the household answer that line. Additionally, that line should be available at multiple points in the household so that it can be answered conveniently and promptly with an ability to transfer an incoming call to a quiet and well-organized place of choice. At this location a workstation, laptop, or a computer and other resources should be available for easy access. A headset that is integral or connected to this line is helpful for a hands-free conversation. An interview or screening call, taken in a stressful environment, will show that stress to the caller, in addition to the customary nervousness. And, the price paid for this disadvantage, can jeopardize the next step of being invited to the interview! See Key-1: Getting Organized.

2. **Having caller-ID:** Having caller-ID on the business line is a good idea. It provides the ability to identify and decide if the incoming call is worth the distraction.

3. **Greetings and voice mail:** The business line must have a professional greeting that is short, pleasant, and personal to welcome those calling. Do not have a child singing a song as a welcome greeting on a business line! Avoid robotic or canned greetings that come with store-bought machines. Such greetings can convey an impression of laziness to record a personal message. If there are time restrictions on the recording device, they should be part of the greetings: "You have 30 seconds for a message." Doing so will warn callers to be aware of this so that they can manage their message. Not being forewarned of this time limit can result in missed calls. Few hiring managers may bother calling back to re-record a cut-off message, if that mishap was not caused at their end, especially in a tough market.

4. **Not ready for the call:** When a screening or interview call comes, being ready for that call is important, otherwise that call should be rolled over to voice mail. Although this is chancy, proper judgment about taking that call can protect the opportunity. Sometimes when you are not ready to take a call, because of your state of mind or the circumstances in the household, it is best to pass up the call for a possibility of a future reconnection with that caller. It is also a good idea to have a voice mail recording system that allows for screening incoming calls so that it is easy to listen to the caller speaking into the machine and then deciding on taking that call or chancing it. Old-fashioned answering machines allow this feature.

5. **Security screens:** Many install a security screen on their incoming lines, despite the legislated "Do-not-call list," to avoid telemarketers or unwanted callers from intruding their phone space. This feature thwarts random callers by asking them to identify themselves and asking them to wait until someone is willing to take the incoming call. This barrier to calling can be a turnoff, especially if the caller is in a hurry and has other calls to make for the open position. The set up may result in a missed call and the caller may not call back because of the set up. Simpler means of screening incoming calls, as answering machines that allow listening to the callers' messages, can avoid this possibility.

6. **Quality Check:** Imagine being frustrated because of no action on the phone, even after sending hundreds of résumés! When this happens, checking the telephone number on the résumé is a good start to verify if it is correctly listed! Transposing digits is easy and there are about 10 percent, who have mild dyslexia. Few bother to call themselves by *reading* their number, as they know it by memory. Calling oneself by *looking*

up, or asking someone to call from reading what is listed on the résumé is a good practice. This also provides for someone to audit the incoming voice greeting for quality.

7. **Message back:** When responding to someone's call and leaving *them* a message, it is a good idea to be clear. Instead of saying "Hi, Jim this is Dave, and I am returning your call from yesterday. You have my number since you called me, so I'll wait to hear from you." Instead, try "Hi Jim, this is Dave Gifford, three-two-three—five-five-five—zero-zero-one-two (avoid saying *double not* as those from some European and commonwealth countries might say). I am responding to the message you left yesterday about the job for a program manager, your posting # 2342. Thank you for your message and I am looking forward to talking to you. My number, again, is 323-555-0012, the same one you called yesterday. You can also reach my cell at 323-555-1121. Once again, the cell phone is 323-555-1121. Looking forward to hearing from you soon and thank you!" can be much less puzzling to the caller. Speak the numbers S L O W E L Y and C L E A R L Y, as the called party may have trouble writing this fast enough, have a hearing problem, or may be dyslexic themselves.

If in doubt, leave yourself a message and ask someone to hear it!

When answering the incoming call it is a good idea to be situated for an efficient setup (See Key-1: Getting Organized) and having all the materials necessary for a good conversation at your fingertips. A good way to achieve this is the low-tech way of using an old-fashioned three-ring binder, which is discussed in the next section.

The initial call typically comes from someone in HR or recruiting. The caller in this position has the task of connecting with a selected group of candidates to make sure that they are real, and, if their initial screening goes well, to arrange for an interview. So, if the caller sounds unsophisticated, has an accent, or who speaks English in an unpolished way, treating them with disdain or contempt is ill advised as they have the power to decide if the face-to-face interview is the next step in the process. They typically start out calling with a list of names. If a candidate does not treat them well and dismisses them because of their perceived low status, the caller has the power to either take the name off that list, put it at the top of that list, or at the bottom. Respectful and businesslike response to the caller is recommended, regardless of the level at which they are perceived to be functioning. Being polite and thanking them at the end of the call can help being called for an interview.

Taking the Calls

Taking incoming calls is critical. This is such a familiar task that most underestimate the variety of ways it can go wrong, or at least put you at a disadvantage. Let's look closer:

Cell Phones

Cell phones are everywhere now and people routinely carry them and conduct their business on the move. For a job-search, a cell phone should *not* be the primary contact line. Why? For one, it can ring at any time, making it awkward to take the call. Cell phones do not typically have reliable connections and they can drop chunks of messages, when connected. Another factor is that it is unlikely that you have ready access to key information needed to ace the interview if conducted on a cell phone, while on the move.

Cordless Phones

Cordless phones are ubiquitous. In addition to the cell phones, they provide callers and those receiving calls mobility over a range well beyond what was possible with long cords on conventional instruments. Although cordless phones offer the convenience of taking the call in a walk-about mode, they create a disadvantage for an important call such as an interview. Why? It permits the call taker to pace or move about while talking. This can be a distraction. To the calling person this distracted attention may come across negatively. The other disadvantage of a cordless phone is the static noise that can occasionally interfere with the conversation. When the power goes out, too, so does the connection; one can face a suspenseful wait wondering if the caller will then call back!

The other reason for not taking an incoming call for an interview on a cordless phone, is possibly the voice and how it sounds to the calling party. Taking the call standing or pacing on a cordless phone invariably results in a higher pitched voice than when sitting down. A higher pitch can communicate anxiety. The other disadvantage of the cordless, or any phone, where you have to hold the handset, is that, for an extended conversation, it can be stressful. Holding the handset between your cocked head and the shoulder, while talking for any length of time, can be taxing, if you are required to use your hands for taking notes or keyboarding. This can further exacerbate the negative "tone" to the caller.

The best arrangement for taking incoming calls for a telephone interview, is to be comfortably sitting down with easy access to materials. Ability to be focused and to take notes, to be relaxed and sound confident, can only help graduate you to the next step for an interview. Having a headset is a boon to this set up. Keeping a beverage to sip on during long conversations can help a dry mouth and throat, which can only betray nervousness or anxiety to the caller.

Having Ready Access to Material

During an interview call, having ready access to files and correspondence is critical.

There are, of course, a variety of ways of keeping such information, so that there is ready access during exigent times as an incoming interview call, which can come without any notice. With computers obsolescing the old-fashioned paper files, most keep their important files now on their PCs.

For job-search related matters, here's a low-tech alternative that is more effective:

A three-ring binder, big enough to hold important outgoing responses to job openings and other correspondence, is such an alternative. Thumb tabs organize it, alphabetically, with each company response filed under its respective name. Each stack of papers, under a tab, consists of the cover letter, résumé, any company research, notes, and other materials. All generic responses go under an "Other" tab. Why is this a preferred organization? Simply because it affords the most convenient, reliable, and simple arrangement of files for ready access, regardless of what the PC decides to do at a critical time! Yet, another psychological advantage is that having a stack of papers in a binder creates visibility to what is in the "Pipeline," as we discussed in the marketing chapter.

When an incoming call comes on the "Red Phone," answering it promptly and then holding the conversation from the designated place, can give an edge to ace the interview. It does not matter now if the PC were on—the three-ring binder should be right next to the PC! Putting on the headset, opening up the three-ring binder to the tab for the company calling and launching into a professional conversation, with a smile in your tone can begin immediately! With your hands free to take notes, a relaxed, poised, and engaged conversation can now take place without any distractions!

The other advantage of having a three-ring binder for all outgoing job responses is that it is available to be taken wherever it is needed, for studying without the technology paraphernalia. Maintaining the discipline, by constantly organizing the materials, to keep it slim and uncluttered with extraneous information that becomes obsolete, is critical as the outgoing responses mount in a long campaign!

Having the PC as a *back up* for files and folders is a good idea. Here, too, keeping the entire system well organized and managing similar sounding file names, especially for résumés, are critical. This naming problem can result, when in a hurry, in sending as an attachment the wrong files. The best antidote for this confusion is to keep all versions of a résumé separate and carefully naming them, so that they are not confusing during harried moments. Anything that has become out of date or obsolete should be periodically purged, regardless of the size of the hard drive! As we discussed in Key-3, Presenting Yourself, having multiple flavors of your résumé is a good idea. Each flavor can evolve over time as you learn new ways of presenting your message. Each revision must be tracked carefully by labeling your résumé with the version number, which can be located in the bottom right corner with a size eight font. This simple discipline will allow you to correctly respond to a caller, who may have an old version of your résumé, by simply asking them to check the number printed at the bottom right corner during the conversation, and then clicking open that document on your PC screen.

Taking the Call When you are Not Ready

Most interview calls come at home, when that is the primary telephone contact on the résumé.

If the call comes as a surprise, then it is a good idea to find some reason to defer it. It is hard to pass up an opportunity for an interview—phone or other-wise—without wondering if it would come back. This is why this judgment should *not* be made casually. But, if your judgment is that the call should be deferred, find some way to dodge the call and politely ask the caller if you can call them back. Otherwise, taking the call is prudent, especially in a tough job market!

Here are some occasions worthy of avoiding taking an interview call:

- You have fallen asleep and the call wakes you up. Let the voice mail take the call. If you are just waking up from a nap or sleep, you will sound groggy to the caller and disoriented. The caller may think that you are under the influence of a drug or alcohol! Not a good first impression.

- You are harried and are in the middle of something critical. You are dis-tracted. Let the voice mail take the call. If you have the ability to screen the call and you hear the caller talking into the machine, you may have enough time to mentally regroup and then pick up as the caller is hang-ing up, with the message now on the machine. This is a matter of judg-ment.

- You are enjoying your evening cocktails and the call comes. Do not take the call as your gaiety and inebriation can compromise making a good impression.

- You are angry or frustrated about something personal and are not in a best frame of mind. When the call comes let the machine take the call and hope that you are able to reconnect with the person.

- You are driving and are about to enter a tunnel or a bridge. Your cell phone rings and the hiring manager wants to interview you. In addition to a potential safety problem, the connection can be cut off because of where you are headed. Ask to be called back or pull over to the shoulder and hold the conversation, if it is safe to do so.

- The call comes when you have a definite time pressure. If possible hold an initial conversation if the time allows and then explain the situation. There is nothing worse if the caller feels rushed and you feel cheated for giving flighty responses to interview questions.

When you do take the call and have to dodge it, be polite, apologetic, and businesslike in handling it. Make sure that the caller feels welcome for having called, despite your exigency!

No matter how you take the screening call, your mission should always be to parlay that into a face-to-face interview. All your energies and focus should be on this outcome! You should learn how to finesse it in a smooth, businesslike, and easy fashion.

If one of the reasons for the call is to schedule an interview, do not jump at the chance by saying "Of course, I am free all week!" A better approach is to say that you need to consult your calendar, and as you are reading it convey to the caller that you are genuinely a busy person! If you have entered your daily routine on your calendar, you are busy; just leverage that discipline to make yourself more desirable to the caller!

♠ Face-to-Face Interview

A successful phone screening leads to a face-face interview. In a tight market, candidates are screened several times and many of these phone screens can be long conversations. Employers do this to ascertain that there is a good fit, before the in-person interview, to save time and expenses for both sides.

Interviewing face-to-face, after the telephone screening, is the most dreaded event in the job-search process. Why? For one, candidates feel that all their apprehensions and fears will militate against them and gang up to frustrate their efforts to land the job they are after. For another, there is a lot riding on an interview and a rejection can be a crushing blow to the sometimes-fragile self-esteem of the job seeker. All these emotions result in job seekers feeling apprehensive, even fearful about this critical step for which they have waited and prepared for so long! *They* become their worst enemy.

One way to overcome and conquer this feeling is to become fearless during this process. Being ready and prepared is one way. Another is doing some exercises and getting prepared to face this dreaded event. Looking at it as a fun and adventurous opportunity can also help, but to many, this is a stretch! Of course preparing well for an interview helps, too! See Key-1: Managing Your Fear.

Following the guidelines suggested in the preceding paragraphs, the chances of landing an invitation for a face-to-face interview are good. The mission now is to ace the interview and get the offer. The following discussion is a good guideline for a successful interview:

Before the Interview

Before delving into company-specific information, it is a good idea to get a general sense of the state of the industry. Why? Every company belongs to a certain industry and each industry has its "culture." How this culture drives a company's operational needs is a skill that many do not have and even fewer know how to leverage that into a successful interview.

For example, the biotech industry does product development using its own "best practices." These practices differ from those in high-tech, which are highly evolved over the years. Finding a common theme across many companies in biotech and how their practices, as a class, can be transformed to fashion after those used by the high-tech companies can be an additional piece of insight into the interview process. If this insight is forcibly presented during an interview, it may even create a compelling case for someone migrating from high-tech, without the detailed knowledge of the biotech industry!

Yet another example may be taken from IT in *any* industry. The traditional focus of IT has been technology first, how it is integrated into the business operations and its availability, effectiveness, and ease-of-use second. Even less of concern, historically, has been how the human factor interacts with the technology to create meaningful change that serves—or impedes—a business. So, when going in for an interview as a director of IT services, the preparation focus should be how factors, *outside* of technology, can help make any IT initiative successful inside the target company. These factors may include: managing change, leading cross-enterprise integration, socio-technical factors, as how those using technology embrace it and feel comfortable with it. An IT expert is *expected* to know the technology. But very few would have insights on the other aspects mentioned here. Having some articulate and studied views on any or all of such "adjunct" factors can be a great differentiator in an interview. These insights are not limited to "executive" ranks. Individual contributors and other professionals can frame this perspective in their own context as well.

Once the industry landscape is understood, the following step-by-step company-specific homework can help in the interview:

1. Pull your materials together so that you can review all that has happened so far. This includes your notes, your responses from the binder, all your research about the company and the position for which you are being considered.

2. Research the company and its affairs for the past two years for a good understanding of what it does, its current challenges and outlook. There are several excellent research tools available: Hoover's, Reference USA, InSite-2, Dunn and Bradstreet, Lexus Nexus, among others. Many of these tools are online and are available from the local library. Subscription is expensive.

3. Visit the company Website for any endorsements posted from its customers, suppliers, and others who are stakeholders in its success. If they are identified by name and affiliation, make a point of calling them. Your call should be for discovering some insights about the company, so that this discovery can help you position yourself more strongly and in a highly differentiated way during the interview process. See related story in Key-4: Posted Jobs.

4. Find out anything from the Website that you can use to leverage your interview.

5. Look at the financials, using the annual report, either from the Website or from any of the tools mentioned in #2, above. Infer some information and draw some conclusions based on this research. For example, if you are targeting a position in this company as a lead R&D engineer, look at any data about research expenditures during the past two years. If these expenditures are declining, you can suspect that the company is focusing less and less on R&D, which can both be good and bad. The good part is that the company is now more conscious of how it spends its research dollars; and the bad is that you may be expected to deliver a heroic effort. You can use this research to explore more clearly how you will be positioned once you get in and your chances of success. The interviewers will be impressed by your research and insights. They can then provide their own take on this trend. With several interviewers, you have the unique advantage of integrating all inputs and deciding for yourself if there is a common theme and evaluate what is being presented as they are courting you, a definite position of advantage!

6. Look for the track record of the company in the area of your pursuit. If you are in marketing communications, look at the company's recent marketing campaigns and their successes. Talk to customers and those who are affected by them. See if you might do this to create a different impact. Then present this information during the interview and have a discussion on this. The interviewers will be impressed by your impeccable research: a good thing for someone who should be doing the research before putting out a marketing message!

7. Get a résumé updated, again with the latest insights reflecting your research. Pull together your portfolio of materials that you may want to take, to showcase your accomplishments. Make this portfolio a professionally packaged presentation.

8. Line up and prime your references, as you get ready for the interview. Always have about a dozen or so names ready. The reference mix should include: previous bosses, peers, customers, suppliers, and other professionals who have worked with you and who will not betray your confidence by saying something less than stellar about you. Call them one by one and tell them where you are in the process, and what aspects of your past association with them is now important to you during this process.

9. If you have letters of recommendation or references from the past, integrate them in your portfolio (see #7, above). Do not take your past performance reviews!

10. Get out your interview wardrobe. If you are in doubt as to what is appropriate, go and check out the building where you would be interviewed and park outside. Observe who goes in and out of that building and their dress; wearing one cut above what you see; shine your shoes, spruce up your accessories! Thus, if you see most of who come in and out of the building where you will be interviewed, wearing a tie with no jacket (for men), or a skirt and blouse with a jacket (for women), it is safer to wear a business suit. A jacket and tie might work for men, too, as would a smart fashionable attire that is conservative for women. Do not wear business casual. One thing about interview attire is that you can always remove something if you feel overdressed. If you walk in and suddenly feel underdressed, then you feel bare and that conscious feeling can compromise your confidence at a critical time. This can be an edge that you just lost.

11. The idea behind this attire suggestion is, that when you go for the interview, you should feel special but not conscious! Think conservative. An interview is not a place where you want to make a statement about the fashion world. Don't let your interviewer see what you're wearing before they see you! If you are not in a habit of wearing a suit, buy one and wear it to some occasion prior to the interview so that socially, you can get used to the idea of being seen in a suit. Do not wear the suit for the first time at the interview. You may feel self-conscious; also something about the suit may surprise you, and make you feel ill at ease. You may end up compromising an important opportunity on account of your attire.

12. Find out who will interview you. Someone organizes all interview logistics, and then notifies you. That person then calls you with confirmation details about the event. If you do not hear about these details, ask that person who they are and what their role is in the interview. Get the correct spelling and functional title of each person you are going to see on that day. Once you have this information, you have a good sense of what kind of information will be part of the interview. You can then research that information and get ready!

13. Make a dozen copies of your résumé on a premium stock. Organize your materials in a well-presented briefcase with your business card on it and a supply of them inside. Carry a small, unopened bottle of spring water and a dry snack.

14. Now you are ready to head on to the interview!

At the Interview

The following tips will help you to ace the interview:

1. Arrive 30 minutes before the appointed time! Why so early? For one, you want to be at your best for the interview. Coming early allows you to check in and make sure that you are in the correct building. Sometimes, the entire interview set up gets changed at the last minute, and everything gets moved to another building clear across campus. Now you have to rush to find the new building and be on time. Even if this were not the case, coming early can allow you to settle down and get used to the environment and feel relaxed to be ready for the interview.

2. Introduce yourself to the receptionist and smile. Be courteous and pleasant to everyone from now on. Do not demand coffee or any other

favor from this person. Get it yourself. Sign in at the register or login device and wear your security badge. Make sure that the host is in the same building where you arrived or that the location is close to the lobby of the building. This is important to ascertain early. In some places, the behavior you display and the attitude you exhibit towards the receptionist are reported as a part of the interview. Do not assume anything from here on!

3. Strike a pleasant conversation with the person at reception. Make small talk. This can be of help on your way out, especially if you connect with this person.

4. Observe what is in the lobby. Any company literature, periodicals, news, or product literature can be great icebreakers. So, too, can the awards on the walls of this lobby. Be observant of the people coming in and out. Take in how the receptionist talks on the phone to others and how those coming in and out of the building interact with the receptionist. You are now sampling the "culture" of the work place! For you to be compatible (one of the three "Cs" to be discussed later) this could help.

5. Make sure, as you sign in, to tell the receptionist that you are early and not to announce you yet to the person you are seeing for the interview.

6. Relax, breathe deeply, and think happy thoughts. Visualization can also help you feel relaxed at tense times.

7. Bring some of your own reading material. Some lobbies have nothing to read. This way, although you are sitting there pretending to be reading, you can still look businesslike and engaged in something besides gawking at something or someone. Working on your laptop is also a good way to while away these tense minutes. Do not curse or get angry if your system crashes while you are doing this! Do not play portable video games as someone might get the idea that, this is how you while away your time; not a good impression to make!

8. When the appointed time comes, politely ask the receptionist to announce you to the interviewer. If this person is on the phone for a long time or is constantly answering calls, do not cut in or look impatient standing next to the front desk. Do not pace. You should observe, as you are sitting and waiting, the call frequency and the talking habits of this person before you decide when to approach them for announcing yourself to the host. If you cannot get their attention, hand them a note stating that you are now late for your interview and you would

appreciate their helping you as they continue on their phone—personal call or not!

9. Once you are announced, close your magazine, laptop, or whatever else you were engaged in. Sit comfortably and wait for your host to come and get you.

10. When the host arrives, smile, greet, shake hands, and follow them!

The Handshake

Much has been written and said about shaking hands. Some claim that a handshake is a window into personality; much the same way as others who say the way you write is also a hallmark of your personality. Regardless, some tips on good handshake etiquette are in order here.

A handshake is a good way to convey, during the first moments of apprehension and anxiety when meeting someone important, that you are comfortable, confident, loyal, honest, and eager to prove yourself. A weak or reluctant handshake gives the impression that you are tentative, diffident, and simply not interested in your surroundings.

There are various ways and styles of shaking hands and they vary from "The Bone Crusher" to the "Cold Dead Fish," with the "Two-Handed Vote For Me" sandwich somewhere in between. A handshake is a social custom to get to know the other person with a human touch in a warm, friendly, and business-like manner. The Dead-Fish handshake stems from your clammy hands, you are nervous and unable to offer a firm hand, it is also cold from the sweating. This is why coming early and doing some relaxation exercises can help overcome the anxiety prior to meeting someone. If you still cannot suppress the sweaty palms prior to a handshake, keep a handkerchief ready (right trouser pocket for men) and before the host comes to greet you, discreetly wipe your palm so that, at least temporarily, it is dry for the handshake.

The following four-step process is what is recommended for a good handshake: engage, pause, observe, and remember. The first step of engagement has to do with how you engage the other person's hands. Grabbing hands in haste can be looked upon as aggressive. While you clasp the other hand, your shoulders should be squared to the person, eye contact should be maintained, with your palm flat with the webbing between the thumb and index finger fully engaged with the other person's. After pumping the hands a couple of times, the next step is pausing, and it is during this brief time that you make a connection with the person. It is during this pause that the third step also takes place: observing. Here you observe the other person and size the way they connect with you. The fourth step is remembering: this is when you remember if the other person was nervous, tentative, or confident and relaxed.

This entire script can sound intimidating, but is a learned and practiced behavior.

In the Interview

There are three ingredients for a successful interview, or for that matter, any successful interaction with another person: Ethos (*eethas*), Pathos (*paythas*), and Logos (*logas*).

In Greek, ethos means the basic character or essence. In everyday vernacular, it can be equated to personal chemistry. The two other factors also play a part in that dynamic. The second, pathos, means sympathy, or that the two people meeting, harmonize with each other in the way they see their pain. This can be equated in common parlance as compatibility; and finally the third, logos, which means logic or reasoning in everyday use, can be equated to competency or skill that you bring to the position. For a successful interview, all three are critical. This prescription applies to selling something to anyone, or having that person see your point of view. We'll discuss these in more detail on the following page.

It is, therefore, critical to understand this basic dynamic for a successful interview. In the following script, we'll present how to achieve this interview *nirvana* through a tried-and-true method.

Now you have come to the place where the interview is going to take place. During the time you are walking with your host to the interview, you use ice-breakers to connect with the person. If, for example, you saw in the lobby an award—say the Malcolm Baldrige Quality Award—plaque hanging on one of the walls and next to it was a commendation from the CEO stating that your host was instrumental in securing this rare and coveted honor, this is your great chance to show that you read that commendation and to offer your congratulations. Then if you ask what role the person played in securing the award, you are connecting with this person with a rare and compelling means. This is a much more subtle and personal way to access the host's ethos.

Ethos also means "I am like you." In addition to being "like you," if you can get that person *to like you* as well, that further cements the potential desirability. Liking someone goes beyond just ethos. What that person has attained is appreciated and that is important to you! Talking about the weather, the parking, or last night's ball game are mundane and chancy topics because that person may not share your views, and you have now created a discord, right at the outset on a matter that is impersonal!

Yet another way to develop ethos is to observe what is on the desk or the wall as you enter the host's office. The reason is because it is important to that person. Ask questions. Let the person get into the discussion on that item of interest to you. Your commenting on it is an acknowledgment that you share that interest. Once again, ethos!

Figure-5: The Interview Success Trilogy

Sometimes the interview is held in a meeting room or a conference room. In that case, you need to think of some clever way to connect with the person. If anything pops up during your walk with them, use that time to see if you can break the ice and establish ethos.

Once you have arrived at the place for the interview, do not impose by asking for a beverage. If offered, assess if your host is up for it and then decide. Do not take the time to walk down to another building just for a cup of coffee. It is a good idea to carry a small bottle of water in your case, as we presented before. Your throat may be parched, even on a cool day, and your mouth may feel like it has cotton balls. Interviewing in that state definitely puts you in a state of disadvantage!

Individual Interview

The following checklist will help you with the process where it is a 1:1 interview:

1. Once you enter the room where the interview will take place, take charge. When asked, sit comfortably in the designated chair with confidence. Put your briefcase down and not on the table or the desk! Relax. Pull the briefcase in your lap to get things out and place them in front of you. These things may be your notepad, pen or pencil, your organizer or calendar. Do not clutter the desk or table with more than the

essentials. Your résumé should be part of the stack that consists of the writing pad and other material—a *small* stack!

2. Look at your host and smile. Breathe easy. You are naturally anxious. Do not show it by making solicitous comments: "Gee, I am really sorry you are catching cold," if you just saw your host sniffling. He may be allergic to something *you* are wearing and not really catching a cold!

3. Thank your host for taking the time for the interview. Ask politely, how much time is set for the interview, who else might see you, and anything else that is logistically relevant: "Is Tom coming here or I am going to his office?" So that you are clear on the course of the activities planned for your visit.

4. Let this host launch the *formal* part of the interview with the first question—the informal interview began when you first shook hands! Make sure you understand the question. Generally, the first questions are easier. But, do not assume if you do not understand something. The interviewer is nervous, too; use that to your advantage. For example, he may assume that the person who did the phone screening took care of certain preliminaries, as the company's expansion plans, overseas contracts, etc. Politely state the facts and ask for further information. You entire line of response may hinge on this critical information.

5. ♠ There are two things critical to the interview dynamics: the person asking the questions is in charge of the interview; the person doing the talking is doing the selling. You should not automatically assume that your host is in charge of the interview after the first question. They are just in charge of the arrangements for the interview, and that is why they are your host!

6. One way to take charge of the interview without overtly showing that you have now done so, is to first *answer* the question in a leading way. Then ask back a question at the *end* of your response, so that the interviewer has to respond with a thoughtful answer. For example, if the interviewer asks why you see yourself as a good fit for the position, the best response is not to assume what the position is, merely after having read the job posting. A good response is to first advert your response to what is already on your résumé, and state what you have done in the immediate past at the company you left or are leaving. This is all factual. Then, at the end of about a minute or so, pause, and ask the following: "Now that you know what I have done at HP as a product manager, and I also have read the job description for this position, what

354 • The 7 Keys to a Dream Job

is your perspective, and what do you expect the new hire to do to bring value to you?" This is *not* the same as asking what the job is; you should know that, having come this far in the process! But, everyone has a perspective and expectations on how this position will be filled, and what the new hire is expected to deliver.

7. ♠Once the interviewer launches into an answer, take brief notes on what is critical in their response. Watch their body language carefully. Do they betray a discord in stating what is being said, or do they really believe what they're saying? Sometimes hiring managers or other interviewers do not buy into all open positions for political reasons. Your knowledge of this is critical. Once the person stops talking or you see a natural opening into what might be a longer answer (after about 60–90 seconds), interrupt politely and say "That is very interesting, John, because that is exactly what I do well." And, then go on to say, "Let me explain!" Now, go on to those parts of your résumé that have supporting material to what was said, and then build on it. Use the very language and the words that were just used to describe their expectations. Now you cannot lose. If you do not follow this simple script, you are shooting in the dark and you have no clue if you hit the mark.

8. Once you have come to this point, you have probably crossed the tipping point in who holds the control of the interview. Now you can bandy questions and answers back and forth, and you both are having a dialog, not an interrogation. Remember, you have to ask about half the questions—starting early—and do half the talking. This way you are both selling each other, a perfect barter!

9. Throughout this exchange, carefully watch the interviewer's body language. See the following section: ♠ Understanding Body Language, and tips for reading body language.

10. Do not make responses to anything based on your assumptions. Do not infer anything from what you know, especially if it puts the company in a negative light. Let the interviewer suggest, rather than your insinuating something to make a point. This can back fire quickly and is very difficult to get out of!

For example, if you have done some digging about how the company deals with its customers, by actually talking to them, before going into the interview, you can leverage that insight. Do not factually state what they said, if it is negative. If it refers to improvement that you can provide; it may sound self-serving coming from you. Wait for the interviewer to bring it up by your leading them that way. For example, rather than saying "your customers think that your sales people do not have adequate technical understanding of the technology, and often end up providing inadequate or wrong solutions, as a result," ask how the company makes sure that during a sales call there is technical representation, so that the solution is sound. Then, if the response comes in the form of something less than stellar, jump in and say: "I actually talked to some of your customers, and what you suspect is shared by some of them, and I know one way to mitigate that...."

This approach to solving a problem, only when it is presented and owned by the interviewer, is far more appropriate, than merely assuming that the interviewer already knows what you see as a major problem, and that they are looking at you for its solution.

➤ **Never provide a solution to a problem that the interviewer does not even know exists or owns!**

Remember Pathos! Also, as we discussed in Key-1: Career Transition Styles for Different Types, those with NP types may feel compelled to showing their "insights" to impress the interviewer, if the interviewer happens to be an ST, they may be offended!

11. ♠ If you see the interviewer disengaging from the interview, as suggested by their leaning back, showing distracted gestures, or looking at their watch, quickly recognize it, and back peddle what you just said and see if you can recover. It is good to recognize early a potential derailment before it is about to happen than to wait for complete derailment or even a train wreck. (See ♠ Understanding Body Language, in the following section.)

12. One clue on how the interview is going is to check the elapsed time. This is why asking up-front how long the scheduled interview is—item # 3—can be critical. If the interview is going really well, you both lose sense of the time. Good interviews that are really engaging, go well beyond the scheduled time. If you see anything is getting in the way of that, it is your responsibility to make sure that you bring that back on track!

13. Throughout the interview, take notes, if you do not have an answer to any arcane or unexpected question, despite all your preparations, make a note of it, smile, and politely say that you would get back with an answer. In fact, this strategy will help you reconnect with the interviewer

in ways not possible otherwise. Similarly, if you find a natural opening for showing your knowledge on some related topic by having read some relevant material in a journal or publication, state that observation and say that you plan to send that article upon your return. This also gives you one more chance to connect with the interviewer after the interview.

14. If the interview has progressed to a heart-to-heart dialog, then it is safe to assume that you have aced the interview. You are not out of the woods yet. You've got to establish yourself as the only and ideal candidate. The following is one way to achieve *that* goal:

    During the process where you realize that you have now taken control of the interview—without the interviewer knowing it, of course!—asking the following question can give you more insight into how you stand vis-à-vis other candidates. Your mission now is to make you the only candidate by asking: "If you were to bring on board an ideal candidate, what would their performance look like in the first year?"

    The response to this telling question is critical. The interviewer is likely to say something like: "We expect the candidate to do this and that." Once you get a grasp of what that means in terms of what you can do to achieve the same outcome, your immediate but studied response is how you would deliver that performance and how you have already delivered similar performances before. In essence, you have now made it known to the interviewer that you are *that* ideal candidate. When presenting this argument, specific examples will help even further.

    The other advantage this question provides is that now you can leverage this information during the entire interview circuit after this first round. You will not only impress the others with this knowledge and insight, you will plant in their mind, too, that you are *it!*

15. Since this is the first interview, do not bring up any salary or similar information into the discussion if the interviewer does not ask you. If you are asked, politely say that this is your first interview and you would like to explore more by talking to others about this job and then decide how it is scoped. If you show haste in this step, you are likely to come across as too anxious!

16. As the interview is winding down, be mindful of the time and make sure to ask questions so that, not only you get answers to these, but also, more importantly, make the interviewer think of the significance of *your* questions. If you have done thorough research before the inter-

view and know what the hot buttons are, you should be able to pose some trenchant questions that will differentiate you. Often the most obvious questions can stump an interviewer and show that you are not a run-of-the-mill thinker. Also learn to leverage one question in an interview into another one!

17. Throughout the interview maintain eye contact and smile in a relaxed way. Feel empowered by what is happening in front of you; your body language should project this state. You should radiate confidence, control, and calm! The interviewer will be impressed by your aplomb.

18. ♠ As the interview comes to a close and you see things are winding down—you will sense the energy—ask, at an appropriate time, what the next step is. This is a telling question on how well you have done and what the interviewer thinks of you, and how you did. *Never* ask about how the interview went. These questions show insecurity and put the other person in a position of power. The unspoken word says much more here than most realize. If the interviewer says that you should know in a couple of weeks, as there are other candidates, you should quickly pull out your pocket calendar—the plastic variety—and say something like: "Two weeks from today would be November 21, which is a Friday. Why don't I call you on Monday, November 24, if I do not hear from you? What is a good time?" By this exchange, you have ascertained that if you do not get that call on November 21, you are free to call on Monday to follow-up. This also puts you in charge of the follow-up process. In most cases, you will not get that call on the 21st as promised! This exchange also shows that you are good at holding people accountable for actions; a good attribute if you are seeking a program manager, sales, or similar position, where accountability is central to your success!

19. At the end, once again thank the interviewer for their time and express how much you learned from this exchange! Also, express that you are now even more excited about this position than before and would look forward to working for this manager.

20. On the way out make sure you pick up all your trash, put all your papers away in your case, and leave everything behind as you found it when you entered the room. The interviewer will probably escort you to the lobby or to the next spot for the interview.

Interviewing in a Group Setting

This mode of interview has now become more and more common, as resources and time available to process a candidate through a series of interviews become more and more critical. The following rules are worth reading before going to an interview that may be conducted by a group:

1.   Know before hand if you are going to be interviewed in front of a group. Understand how many and who will be in the group. Also, understand what the affiliation of each person is, so that you can anticipate the focus of the questions from each of the interviewers. Ask how long the whole process and the interview itself may take.

2.   Take at least as many copies of your résumé as the number of people in the room and take some additional ones for safety. Also take extra copies of other materials and make sure you keep track of what remains behind and what does not. Do not make more than one copy, of what you consider proprietary or your own intellectual property that anyone can plagiarize. Just having one makes it easy to retrieve and keep track. Mark this document *Proprietary.*

3.   As you enter the room, smile and look at every person by scanning the room. You do not need to shake each person's hand. Just introduce yourself and take a seat, if you are asked to sit down. Say "Thank you!"

4.   In front of a group, you are likely to be even more nervous than with just one person. So, do not hesitate to pull out your bottle of water and place it next to you.

5.   If you are asked a question, listen carefully and then pause before answering it. This shows a studied response, instead of a hasty one, even if you already know the answer. This approach will help you when you do not have a ready answer. Here, you can use the same pause to dig for an answer.

6.   First, look at the person who posed the question. Then scan the other participants, keeping brief eye contact with each one, and then moving on to the next pair of eyes. Smile as you contact each person with your eyes. Watch each expression, as they listen to your response. If you see any apprehension in their expressions, see if you need to rephrase your answer or back peddle your idea.

7.   Using your notepad, draw a diagram of the seating arrangement in the room and write each name as they are introduced. This way you can

refer to people by name, as you look at them in response to a question. This approach will make you look poised and professional.

8. Ignore any person who is engaged in an activity outside paying attention to the interview or to you. Some may talk among themselves, or do some other activities that may be distracting (and rude)!

9. When the interview is over, get up with alacrity, and thank every member as a group and organize your stuff before putting it back in the briefcase and leave the room.

10. Do not ask how you did in front of every one!

11. Do not ask the whole group, as you leave, what the next step is. Save this question to the one who hosted you and see that person on your way out.

♠ Understanding Body Language

During a job interview, your focus is mostly on what is asked and how you *verbally* respond to those queries. Ironically, only 10 percent or less of what we communicate is verbal; the rest is body language and tone. With 90 percent riding on the invisible, the unknown, and the unmanaged, it is no wonder that we are often surprised at the outcome of an otherwise "good" interview. Some pointers below (mostly summarized from what was already presented before):

1. Dress code: always dress up and not down; you should feel special but relaxed.

2. The handshake: relaxed firm, not clammy; smile. Ask to be seated; take charge.

3. Seating erect and confident, 10–15 degrees forward and alert. Men/women knees together. Do not cross legs.

4. Practice some easy icebreakers: observe the office or comment on the lobby.

5. Legs relaxed, but no spreading or bopping up and down of a leg.

6. Breathing with the others, deep and quiet. Smile often. Know nervous habits.

7. Look at the interviewers (in a group interview) without looking through them or staring at just ONE person; this can mean you are ignoring the others.

8. Engage in a *dialog* early; do not surrender to an interrogation. Ask to clarify as needed.

9. Always remember: the one who's talking is doing the selling; make them talk.

10. Speak deliberately, articulate well, and watch the body language response of others.

11. Call on body language. Flicking off imagined lint signals disagreement, as does finger on nose or face, or scratching face.

12. Take manual notes (avoid gadgets) and maintain eye contact, smile, nod, and agree.

13. Do not use *but;* try using *and* instead.

14. Do not engage in an argument, even when you know that the interviewer is wrong.

15. Be prepared to take on invidious or sarcastic comments: respond kindly, with a smile!

16. Stay in charge of the interview, always.

17. Ask not what the job can do for you; state what you can do to/for the job.

18. Don't betray anxiety or desperation by jumping ahead, instead be calm and deliberate.

19. Drop seeds for easy follow-ups later on. Mention articles you've read that support your discussion. Mention articles by name and publication.

20. ♠ Avoid steepling fingers upright (arrogance). An interviewer doing this portends difficulty. If you see an interviewer leaning back, looking away from you, and then steepling (a typical sequence), you are in increasing difficulty over what you might have said. Back peddle early, if you detect this sequence, as the interviewer starts leaning back! (Note: steepling is when you bring your two hands with extended fingers together as a steeple, pointing upwards.)

21. Don't lie, ever, or misrepresent. This is disempowering! Don't volunteer adverse information; we all have it.

22. ♠Throughout the interview, observe interviewer's facial expressions. Expressions on a face are a good indicator of inside emotions. If you observe a reaction to what you said on the interviewer's face, quickly recognize it and regroup. A typical emotion is displayed on a face in less than a second and can last for up to two or three seconds.

23. Focus on your value and not on your shortcomings.

24. Show enthusiasm, excitement, and positive energy. Attitude is more important than intelligence.

25. As you depart, shake hands, create accountability for the next steps; stay in charge.

After the Interview

After the interview you are probably back in the lobby checking out and handing over the badge to the person who greeted you upon arrival and signed you in. Thank that person and tell them that you really enjoyed the experience. Remember the discussion about making friends with this person at the beginning: use this connection to get from the person, anything you might need to close the loop after the interview. If you shook hands with someone during the interview, but failed to record or register the name, this person is likely to give that information. Simply describe the person or say the name in any way that you remember; this person will look up and give you the details you need, so that you get what you came looking for.

Also, get this person's contact information, so when you return and you have something that you need in your follow-up, this is now your inside contact!

Upon your return from the interview, compose your notes into a coherent informational resource. Reflect on the interview; does anything stand out as having gaps or holes that needed a stronger answer? This must all be done in the first 24 hours following the interview.

Compose a thank you note for electronic transmittal. This note should be brief and should make one or two points about what could have been done better. Without an apology, state your afterthoughts so that the interviewer appreciates your diligence in following up with a stronger answer. This further cements your candidacy! Repeat the timeline that you agreed at the end of the interview, so that who calls whom and when are clear from this note.

A sample emailed and mailed thank you note follow. For an important target ("Gold",) send a short thank-you card in the mail instead of a note. The message here is brief and personal.

Thank you note

Dear Jim,   **Via email**

Thank you for your time yesterday, meeting with me, and explaining the initiative to improve customer retention and loyalty at Global Enterprises. I know how valuable your time is and appreciate your spending more time than what we had originally scheduled for our meeting.

After our discussion, I am now even more excited about working with you.

I am summarizing my reflections, since our meeting, to help us move this process along:

- I am impressed that you have started a new initiative to improve customer retention and it is already paying off in less than three months. This is great! Now that we know what works, I would like to share with you my success from similar initiatives.

- Working with sales and customer support, identify customer accounts that are placing undue burden on Global's resources. Using the 80:20 rule I was able to identify which accounts were causing similar disproportionate drain on resources at International Electronics. We used the same rule to identify which accounts were giving us the most revenues and profits. We were then able to identify how to leverage that information in to multiplying that effect.

- Starting a customer loyalty initiative: Provide customers reason to come back to Global and buy more. By creating a tiered incentive plan, I was able to get many customers to shift their business from our competitors to us.

- Customer habits: I did some research on my own in your customers' buying habits. Some of them also buy your products from direct channels and other sources. Have you thought of creating a price incentive model that benefits the customer if they make the sales call a one-stop shop? I have done this in two other companies with great results.

- Not just surveys: I have some ideas on how to go beyond the customer surveys you currently do. Surveys are a good source of sensing the overall mood, but they do not create actionable outcomes. I suggest doing a face-to-face customer discovery. I found this to be a source of actionable input and have developed a simple model.

- Involving the customer: Have you thought of involving the customer during early design phases? You mentioned a disconnect between the customers and product features. This simple process will not only make designs more customer centric, it will also accelerate time-to market. I have some data to show you.

I am excited about the possibilities at Global. I am looking forward to seeing you again!

As we discussed, I plan to call you on November 19, if I do not hear from you on the 17th.

Once again, thank you for your time and thoughts!

Cordially,
Sally Jones

Mailed "Thank You!" Note

A Thank You! Note is sent in the mail in *addition* to the email. This is done for effect and impact! A sample follows:

> Dear Jim,
>
> Thank you for your time yesterday. Spending nearly two hours, when you had only one on your busy calendar, is appreciated. After listening to you, I am now even more excited about the Global opportunity!
>
> Since our interview, I have reflected on many things you said and what we talked about. I have summarized my thoughts in an email I sent you today. I am writing this note to express my special appreciation for sharing with me your most passionate thoughts about customers and how they need to be treated.
>
> I am excited about the possibilities at Global. I am looking forward to your calling me on November 17. I shall call you if you are unable to call me then on the 19th!
>
> Cordially,
> Sally Jones, 11/9/03

Staying in Touch

Despite your best efforts and ways to keep the interviewer accountable, you may feel that you have lost touch. Your call on the promised date does not come, so you call the next day as agreed and the person is not available or gone out of town. You leave a message and even get a hold of the administrator, only to encounter silence and no action. Not knowing what is going on and why no one is calling or responding, can be nerve wracking, especially with a great interview and unspoken signals that told you otherwise.

This is not uncommon, even in the most promising of circumstances. In absence of the expected call, the following course of action is suggested:

1. Find out if the person expected to call you is available. If the person has suddenly gone out of town—a common happenstance—wait till you

have some idea when the person would be back in the office. Wait one or two days *after* that to reinitiate your calling.

2. Send an email to the person, after their return, and state that you plan to call, in a day or so, to reconnect as you had agreed after the interview. This time leave a voice mail.

3. If this does not create any action, just wait for a week or two and call someone else. Your HR recruiter may be a good option. State your circumstances and ask if you can get help on this follow-up. If the person knows what is going on, you will know.

4. After one or two weeks, mail something you discussed in the interview. See item # 19 in the "Understanding Body Language" list. The cover note should state the context and that you plan to call the person in a few days. The idea is not to harass the person with persistent messages. The idea is to give this person a reason to call you or for you to call them.

5. After sending the material, send an email stating what you have sent and mention that you plan to call in a few days. Mailed letters and packages can sit in the boxes for days and weeks, as most important exchanges take place electronically. Sending an email to convey what you have sent is polite and not redundant. Do the same if you faxed the material. Fax numbers can be shared and the material can sit on the machine. In your companion email message, write the fax number where you sent the material so that they can go an retrieve it.

6. Yet another approach to keeping the mind share of the hiring manager is to send some interesting article or publication that supports your point of view during the interview. This is one of the easier ways to get back in the running. Use such an article to get their attention and then follow-up with a message to see if there is any reaction. Do this, however, once or twice, or else move on!

7. Make sure that in all this effort you stay politely non-obtrusive and respectful of the person's space. Often people get busy and distracted by unforeseen or personal events and it makes it hard to keep commitments. Just staying in their mind in a non-obtrusive way is the best method of leveraging your past success. If the person sees you as too anxious, even though they have been remiss, you might not again hear from them.

8. Make sure that you do not obsess on this episode—non-responsive-ness—and keep yourself occupied with other pursuits.

9. When the person eventually gets in touch with you, do not act annoyed or do not sulk! Pleasantly pick up and move forward as if nothing has bothered you about this long silence! For all you know, this person may be testing your patience and see how you behave in a situation quite likely to occur in real life—especially if you are in sales or marketing!

10. If after all these attempts you still do not succeed in connecting with the person, just wait for them to initiate the call.

11. If you have an internal connection in the company, see if you can dis-creetly find out what is going on. Do not contact any one officially as HR or someone in the chain of command. If this fails, too, move on!

Navigating Through the Process

Once you have started the process of connecting with the hiring manager, you are on your way to getting the offer. In tough times, hiring managers have limited time for something that is not their immediate concern: managing their functional areas and departments. As cutbacks continue, fewer and fewer end up doing more and more. This includes the hiring manager. This is why so much time is spent on the telephone interviews and initial screening.

Because of this early screening, there is an opportunity to continue to solid-ify your position in the process and increasingly make you the only candidate left at the end! How? As competition gets more and more intense, fewer and fewer are able to withstand the grueling march of the process. As we discussed in the last section, every step is an opportunity to differentiate yourself and making a mark. As the number of steps increases, so do the chances of making a mistake or doing something inadvertent, which can help eliminate others in a lengthy process. In tough times, the hiring process can take on marathon proportions and only those who can sustain the scrutiny, become worthy front-runners. The following list is aimed at helping you manage this arduous and seemingly endless journey:

1. When something does not happen as expected or planned, think of a way to get back into the race by salvaging what is still within your con-trol. For example, answering a question in an interview, it is possible to have made an oversight. In such a case, it is never too late to correct that answer. How? In the follow-up thank you note, give a thoughtful and memorable answer that is concise and intriguing. No guarantee here, but how you recover from a setback says much about you.

2. Always think of how one of your competitors would deal with the follow-up process. Know what a normal response and expectations are from one of the competing candidates. This means that if two messages do not get you a call back, do not leave a third message or get angry and show it, as most of your competitors would. This simply means that you need to follow another route to get their attention. Most of your competitors are likely to follow the expected route and alienate the hiring manager in the process. This makes you now a stronger contender, too! Send something, as an article in the mail, as discussed in the previous section, and wait to reconnect. In tough times everyone is stretched thin. You are out of a job and are looking for one, and this can make you edgy. Step back, and be rational. Do not compromise all the time and effort you have already invested in the process, by doing something rash or being impetuous.

3. Instead of fretting over the delays and lack of response from just one target, focus on other opportunities. Make sure that other targets in your pipeline are not being ignored while you focus on any one possibility.

4. In uncertain times, even job openings can be precarious. Budgets are suddenly frozen, jobs restructured, projects de-scoped, and managers reassigned. This does not mean that you are not going to succeed in what you started. It just means that higher priority items are interfering with what you are looking for to accomplish. Just be patient and use some of the ideas from the previous section to keep yourself in the running.

5. If you do get a call, perhaps because of reasons described in #4 above, explore if the hiring manager is willing to bring you on board as a consultant or temporary employee until the uncertainty goes away. See Key-4: Sample Letters (Contingent Employment).

6. If you get the subsequent rounds of interviews, always keep the hiring manager in the loop. Do not assume that the hiring manager is fully aware of what is going on. Sometimes HR, or recruiters, will keep the others involved, without the hiring manager's awareness, and it is your duty to keep the hiring manager apprised, just in case. Keep sending those thank you notes with the copy to the hiring manager and the recruiter. Unless it is an important interview, just email thank you notes are sufficient.

7. Use what you learned in the earlier interviews to leverage a better out-
    come from the subsequent ones. For example, the question suggested
    about the "ideal candidate" in the initial interview can be an excellent
    springboard for acing the subsequent interviews.

8. Always stay in charge of what is happening and where you are in the
    process by constantly apprising the hiring manager and the recruiter.
    Often helping them along the way can be your competitive advantage
    and your ticket to the final step of the process.

References

References are usually the final step in the selection process. This being the
case, however, the references should be readied well before the interview
process begins. In fact, as soon as you decide how you want to package your
message, through your résumé, the references should be stroked to see if the
message is consistent with how they can reference you! This also means that
you need to cull your reference list, based on the overall message you present in
your résumé. The résumé is about tomorrow, references are about yesterday, so
there can be a big disconnect between the two. Once you have your marketing
campaign ready and the positions you are seeking are clearly known, you
should begin your dialog with your references. This ensures that your references will not surprise you at the last minute.

One way to ensure proper and supportive references is to write a reference
letter yourself, and send it for a review and signature. This does two things that
will help you in the long run: you will know if the particular reference sees you
the way as you perceive; secondly, if there are any differences in the two perceptions, there is time to correct the record, or drop the reference all together.
This should not be left to chance. Your drafting your own reference letter may
strike some as odd. This is common and a matter of courtesy to the reference,
because this way all they have to do is to edit what you wrote and sign it. Your
script helps them remember you in the context of the job. They may have no
clue, what that is, other than what they generally know about your association
with them. You cannot leave that to chance!

Another effective strategy you can use, once the interview process gets serious, is to have a reference make a call to the hiring manager. They can provide
an input without being asked. On many occasions, this has made enough difference to push the candidate to a front position. The final references can be
done at the proper moment.

It is also proper to carry the reference letters that you have already prepared,
and signed by your star references, in your portfolio so that you can show them

to the interviewers when appropriate. This is also a good way to show that you are prepared with the right ammunition to ace the hiring process.

When references are requested, give a list of names and contact information, so that they are easy to reach for the person calling. Call the references ahead of time, to brief them on what to expect and who might be calling. Also remind them what to emphasize, perhaps once again, so that they are armed with the right and fresh information to make the overall process smooth, swift, and effective. Request, too, that you would appreciate being informed upon completion of the reference check. This is one way you know that the process is underway and that the only remaining step left is the final offer!

Notes:

Summary Key-5: Acing the Interview

This Key deals with the process that begins with a response from the potential employer as to how you presented yourself. Usually this response is a phone call from the interested party. This summary is broken down into each important step of this process.

The phone call:
This everyday routine can be an opportunity killer. If you do not take care of simple matters as making sure your phone number on your transmittals is correct. Details of all suggestions offered for an effective connection and messaging are listed in The Telephone Call. Please use this entire section as a checklist so that you leave *nothing* to chance. Once you get the exploratory call, you must finesse it into getting yourself a face-to-face interview. See how by revisiting this section!

Face-to-face interview:
Protocols for before, at, and during the interview are detailed in Face-to-Face Interview. Study these protocols, internalize them, and make them your habit, even if you need just one interview and one job offer. These protocols—especially the one on body language—can give you the edge you need in this important step.

Staying in touch:
Post-interview jitters make candidates antsy about follow-up. Too many, too soon, too anxious! All these apprehensions make it difficult for job seekers to be effective in this important step. Many lose out because they did not manage this process effectively, despite their stellar interview. Read the details in Staying in Touch.

References:
When the process gets to the point of asking you for references, you can be certain that the employer is serious. Handling this process, from the needs of the employer as well as managing the expectation of the references, is presented in this section.

Key-6: Negotiating the Offer

"In negotiating, the one who speaks first gets the short end of the stick."

—Anonymous

Employment Offer

An offer is a culmination of the campaign, though it is not the culmination of the overall process. An offer is received with a great sense of anticipation and relief. At the same time, it is full of open and unresolved issues. The following process defines how to get the offer and what to do with it, once presented.

Getting the Offer

Once you have navigated through the interviewing process and gone past the reference stage, the only remaining step is being offered the job you are after! Sometimes, it can take several weeks before the final offer comes because the referencing can take time. This is why your ability to persuade your references to call in on their own can accelerate this process. Ask first, so that the right person is called, and, that it is acceptable to do this step your way, and not the way it is traditionally done. As mentioned before, having your references get back to you after each check is a positive way of staying in control, but this is not always possible, especially if you have references at high levels.

There are various ways an offer can be made. The following list is typical in most situations:

- During one of the later interviews by the hiring manager
- Over the phone by the hiring manager
- During one of the interviews by the HR representative in person
- Over the phone by the HR representative after the reference checks

How one deals with what is offered has much to do with *how* it is offered. Of course, you want to get the best offer, and if it is not what you expected, you want to make sure that it is the best that you can get, based on how the entire

371

hiring process has gone to this point. This is why making an end run on an offer is not a good idea; one has to position correctly right from the start, as we discussed before. See Key-3: Promoting Yourself.

Depending on the nature of the job market, company practices, and your own candidacy, the length of the hiring process can vary. But, after a sequence of interviews that ratchet up in their importance, an offer is presented. If the hiring manager is offering the position, the following dialog is useful in protecting your (you are John, in this hypothetical dialog) options to get the best offer possible:

> Hiring manager: "So, John, looks like things have gone well, and you seem to be a good fit for us, what kind of salary are you looking for?"

> John: "Thank you, Sally, I really enjoyed the exploration! Does this mean you are offering me the job?"

> Hiring manager: "Yes, John, I am!"

(Note: If, at this point, you are *not* being offered the job, issue a look, without saying a word, that conveys to the hiring manager "what kind of fool do you think I am?" If you had already given out a number in response to the salary question earlier, even to another person, you can no longer do this. This is the power of learning how to do this right!)

> John: "Thank you, Sally! What position am I being offered?"

(Note: Do not assume that the position being offered is the one for which you were originally considered. This can change as a result of how you presented yourself, and how the company perceived you throughout the process!)

> Sally: "We're offering you the position of Marketing Manager, Consumer Products Group."

(Note: this is the position you were pursuing)

> John: "This is exciting! Thank you, Sally! What is the salary range for this position?"

(Note: the Hiring Manager must know this; she cannot feign ignorance on this point. If she does not know ask her to please look it up!)

> Sally: "Well, John, this position is scoped at $95 K-$135 K with benefits and bonuses."

> John: "Well, Sally, this is within my range of expectations and within the range I made at IBM. As I mentioned to you before, I consider myself a top performer, and I expect to be compensated accordingly! I know that you will not disappoint me here!"

(Note: Neither one knows what this dialog exactly means; however, each person is thinking a different number now. Hopefully, Sally is thinking the higher of the two!)

Sally: "John, we understand that and that is why I am willing to offer you $117K base."

(Note: This number puts you on the right side of the midpoint of the range. At IBM you were at $107, but Sally, hopefully, does not know that!)

John: "That is an interesting number, Sally, may I see that in an offer so that I can look at the whole package and reflect on it before making a decision. When may I pick up the offer?"

(Note: Never betray your emotional reaction to what you just heard (voila')! Be calm, and coolly have the discussion as if you were expecting something like this. If the number is disappointing and is below what you had in mind, and the person wants to know if you would accept that salary before they put it in a written offer, feel out if you can negotiate right there. Read on.)

Sally: "Let me see what I can do here."

John: "If I can pick up the offer tomorrow, I would like to look it over and then get back to you with an answer in a week or so, is that O.K with you, Sally? And, thank you, again!"

By doing what John just did he has put Sally on the spot to rush the offer and have it ready for him in a day or so. If this is not possible, she will probably tell him that the offer would be sent FedEx in a few days.

The thing to remember here is that no matter what the offer is, the numbers have to come from the hiring manager (or someone making the offer). It is better that way, and is in your favor. If you came up with a number, then you cannot negotiate that because it is what you wanted. Also, generally, with the dialog we just showed, the offer comes at a number higher than what you might have secured otherwise!

Not all dialogs go like what is just scripted here. The point of this script, however, is that there is a way to stay in control if you have managed the process thus far. Remember the quote at the head of this Key!

Coming to this point of getting the best offer is not something that should be left to the last minute. You have to have positioned yourself from the start to be considered the tops and everything that you did throughout the process should reflect that level of confidence. You also should defer discussing any numbers till you come to this point.

The following table shows how the total compensation can be looked at as interplay of different elements of the package. Depending on the position and priorities you have at any particular point in your life and your career, focusing on one of these elements can help you navigate through the negotiating process!

Compensation Package

A typical compensation package is shown in a matrix form below:

Compensation	Benefits	Stock
-Salary -Bonus -Sales Commission -Other Incentives	-Insurance -Vacation -Sick Leave -Retirement -Sabbatical -Company Products -Free Refreshments	-Options -ESSPP -Profit Sharing
Development	**Perquisites ("Perks")**	**Relocation**
-Education/Tuition -Training Programs -Management Dev. -Career Counseling	-Company Car -Expense Account -Facilities Access -Company Access (upon termination)	-House-hunting Trip -Moving Costs -Temporary Housing -Low cost Mortgage
Severance Provision	**Employee Services**	**Life Style**
-Outplacement -Severance Package	-Child Care -Onsite Services -Fitness Centers -Valet Service	-Memberships

Table-7: Compensation Matrix

Not all companies offer this comprehensive a package and not all positions in a company qualify for a package this comprehensive.

Win-Win Negotiations

Now that you have the offer, you must consider if you want to take it as it is being presented or if there are areas where you need to negotiate. Regardless of the economic conditions and job market, an offer is considered worth negotiating if you are not happy with some aspects of it. This is why it is best to not react or respond to an oral offer until you have seen the entire offer, including your job title, reporting relationship, and other details in a *written* form.

Once you have carefully reviewed the employment contract, make sure that you can live with it, and identify areas where you need some changes. This does not mean you are going to be able to even negotiate them, it simply means that you are carefully assessing the pros and cons of the offer. Once you have done this, the next step is to write the pros and cons down, perhaps in a columnar format for an easy visual review and then decide where you need to look for opportunities to negotiate. Salary is not the first and the only thing that is worth negotiating, although it is so, for many.

Some underestimate the benefits of parameters that are not on the employment offer. A partial list of items that are not on the table above appears below:

1. **Telecommuting:** If you are living far away and like to work from home a few days, this could be important.

2. **Job sharing:** If you are a working mother, or have some obligations, some companies allow job sharing, so that you work only part of the week, enough to get the medical benefits for you and the family. See Key-2 Job sharing. If you have not already brought this up during your interviews, this is not the time to bring it up for a solution, because for job sharing, you need to have identified and qualified someone before getting to this point. But you can bring it up as a future possibility.

3. **Travel:** Some jobs necessitate travel far beyond what is considered normal. Although this is not negotiable at this late a stage of the process, if you have special needs that are acute—someone ill at home and needs caring for the next six months, pregnancy, among other exigencies.

4. **On-Call Duties:** How you are scheduled for a 24x7 call, when this applies, and how you can structure that assignment based on your own needs and preferences. This is the best time to bring it up.

5. **Overseas Assignments:** How you would be compensated for an overseas assignment, if that is not spelled out and if that is a major part of your job. This can have serious consequences on your taxes, expenses, and living arrangements.

You should discuss these items during the interview process. None of these should be a surprise to you or to the hiring manager when an offer is being made. The reason they are listed here is because, sometimes in the rush and excitement to get the offer accepted, you can forget what factors can have an impact later. Once you have accepted the job, and have started working, it becomes too late to effectively change something that is otherwise much easier, before accepting the terms of employment!

The other reason for this list is that people too often focus on the salary. There are many other factors that can increase their retained wages *and* the quality of the work life, as well as work-life balance, if they look at the entire contract in a thoughtful and studied way.

Once you have decided what part of the package you want to negotiate, pick just *one* from the list that is most important to you. Then list the second most important and so on. This is a good strategy to allow some latitude if the first item of negotiation does not result in a favorable response.

Remember, you should negotiate *only* one major component of the package. Do not stickle over other details after you have exhausted this component and concluded either way. Do not move on to another one thinking that you should now get some consideration because you were shortchanged on the first!

Let us say that you want to explore negotiating a higher base salary—a common negotiating point—then call the *last* person who offered the package and the job, and ask if there is any room to negotiate the package you just received. Do not wait the full period you requested to confirm the offer. If you asked for a week in which to get back with your answer, then you should make this call in the first day or two.

Once you have opened the door for this discussion, you should be ready to work in a businesslike manner: no playing games and no waffling. You should be firm, forthright, and confident. If you are not sure you can marshal this attitude, then consider not getting into this situation. There is nothing worse than entering into negotiating and then cowering down and folding. In negotiating, as the quote at the heading of this Key states: The one who speaks first comes on the short end of the stick. This is why it is best not to bring the salary question first; let the manager raise it. This is further fortified in the examples below. Yet another nugget of wisdom is to hang on to those items you have decided you can surrender, until the end; giving them too early may make you look anxious and like a patsy!

A typical dialog with an HR person—the last person who contacted you about presenting the offer—can go like this:

John: "Hi Nina, this is John. I am calling about the offer you just gave me yesterday. I carefully looked at it, and I am wondering if there is any room to negotiate this offer."

Nina: "Let us see, John, what did you have in mind?"

John: "I was wondering about the base. The range for this position is $95 K-$135 K, right?"

Nina: "Right!"

John: "My salary of $102 K is almost at the low end here, Nina. As I mentioned to you and Jim Smith (the hiring manager), I consider myself a top performer. My references will confirm that, too! In view of this, I am wondering if there is any latitude to move this figure to the right and take it beyond the mid point. This is how I was compensated at my last position. I would like to explore this to see if this can be accommodated, please!"

Nina: "So what number are we looking at here, John?"

John: "Well, Nina, I did not want to throw out a number, but something that reflects my superior performance and my previous seniority would be a good consideration!"

Nina: "John, I'll have to get back to you on this. I need to consult with Jim Smith and my HR manager before I can give you an answer here."

John: "That makes sense. When would you know, Nina? I have committed to confirming my answer back to you by Friday, and that gives us four more days. I am very interested in this position and am looking forward to working with General Electronics and Jim Smith. Actually, I am quite excited about it!"

With this conversation, you have left an option open to the employer to get back to you. If they decide not to make the change then you know you have explored it. If they did give you the increase then take it and do not haggle, even if that number now is still to the left of the one you were *thinking*. If this conversation took place in the way the script is laid out, then more than likely you will get what you went looking for, and perhaps even more!

Nina can come back and say that she is sorry that she could not do anything to change what has already been offered. Your best recourse, then, is to accept what is offered and agree to come on board. This assumes you have no other offers or options. While accepting, you can put a caveat. Remind them that you are a top performer and that General Electronics should watch you perform for six months, and then make an adjustment to your salary commensurate with that performance. Even if this is then changed to the full year, they are now on notice to honor that. When you offer this counter proposal, sometimes, the employer comes back with a response and a number that is pleasantly surprising! This is because not many companies conduct reviews in six months (see "Sally's tale" on the following page).

Yet another creative way to explore getting a higher salary is to carefully look at the entire offer and see if you have not tapped into some aspect of the offer because of how you are situated. Let us say that the employment package offers a relocation allowance. You do not need to claim it because you are already local to the company.

In one particular instance a client was *not* able to negotiate a higher starting salary but was able to split the relocation allowance as the hiring manager said, upon the client making an observation about this allowance, that he would be happy to give him half of the amount of the relocation allowance, as that equaled to the salary increase the client was seeking in his base pay. The manager perhaps thought to himself that the relocation funds came from another budget—probably HR funds—so he was able to swing the deal without any impact on *his* budget!

Do not haggle over benefits and other details, because to HR, these are policy matters, and they are unwilling to make exceptions.

Another area that is a sticking point to some senior employees starting in a new place of employment is their vacation—a mere two weeks every year—as it is for all new employees. This can be approached, not at the HR level, but at the individual manager level. Upon *accepting* the offer, approach your hiring manager in person, and explore if there is any latitude or discretion in the way your start date can be structured. Explain that you had been used to six weeks vacation at the previous employer, and you would appreciate some consideration. One way that can work is to start officially on a certain date and ask the manager to consider your showing up to work at a later date. The manager ignores that period that you are not at work and you treat it as vacation. This "hidden" vacation approach can work only during the first year.

Negotiating: Sally's Tale

This incident shows that anyone can negotiate if they are positioned correctly from the start, even in a seemingly impregnable situation. Having a clear understanding of what is worth negotiating, having a script, and having practiced that script with contingent scenarios, and then having an exit strategy can be of help. Never enter a negotiation without a clear exit strategy.

Sometimes when you are turned down, you still need to stay in control and salvage what is still available without losing face. As it played out in Sally's case, she had an exit strategy that worked well for her, and she did not have to execute her ace card, as at the end she got what she was looking for and then some. Also read Mike's tale that follows, in contrast.

Sally was an administrative assistant who lost her job in the middle of 2001 from a Fortune-10 company. She was single, in her mid 50s, and was discouraged at the prospects of finding anything in the Valley, as the lay-offs mounted. She had pulled together a résumé that was a compilation of her past, and had sent over 250 responses. She abandoned hope when she did not even get one call in return. She was frustrated at the impregnable nature of the hiring process, as she found it impossible to contact anyone where she had sent her résumés.

In November, Sally had reconciled herself to selling her condo in the Valley and moving to a modest locale out of California—perhaps in the Midwest.

Sally, in her last act of resignation, decided to redo her résumé per the suggested template—Résumé Showcase, Key-3—and selectively target companies with a well-researched cover letter. To her surprise, she got calls for interviews, and within five weeks, had two job offers. One was from a mid-sized law firm, and another, from Stanford University, as an adminis-trator for a senior executive. The offer, however, was about $5,000 below her needs.

Sally wanted the Stanford job badly because of the prestige and bene-fits. She was terrified to consider negotiating the offer, as she was sure she would lose it—she had never negotiated in her life and was raised in the belief that you get what you deserve, and not what you negotiate!

With some coaching, Sally marshaled enough courage to initiate nego-tiating the Stanford offer. The following script summarizes the dialog that took place:

Sally: "Hi James (Stanford's HR Rep) this is Sally. Thank you for your offer yesterday. I am calling to explore if there is any way we can negotiate this offer, as I am very interested in accepting the position. I was looking for a base more in line with the value I bring to this position."

James: "Let me go and check. I shall call you tomorrow."

James: "Hi Sally, this is James. As I checked the possibilities I found that there is *no* way to make any upward adjustment to the base. We have many candidates interested in this position, as you can imagine."

Sally: "I am sorry to hear that, James. I'll tell you what, though, since I am so interested in this position, and I am so confident that I can do a great job there, I am willing to join you at the salary you offered. As I have mentioned before, I consider myself a top performer, and my references will attest to that, and you will see that for yourself as well. If I accept what you are offering now, can we have an understanding that three months after I start working there, my salary is adjusted commensurate with what I deliver, and what you observe?"

James: "Let me go and check. I shall call you later today."

James: "This is James again, Sally. I checked with our senior staff and they all said that we review only once a year, regardless of any circumstances. That is our policy. However, if we offered you $10,000 more to your base now, would you still be interested in joining us?"

Sally: "That is an interesting number, James. Let me think it over and call you tomorrow."

The next day Sally accepted the offer!

Negotiations are not as difficult as most believe they are. You just have to take a close look at the entire package and then decide why you want to negotiate certain elements of it. If you are convinced that this is a fair and reasonable thing to do, then you will probably succeed getting what you want and, sometimes, even more! Always wait to start negotiating *after* an offer is made.

Negotiating: Mike's Tale

Mike was a software quality engineer who was laid off and was looking for nearly a year. He finally found a contract-hiring agency that offered a position that would place him at their client's company as a QA lead. The following transpired, resulting in Mike's offer being withdrawn:

Mary: "Looks like we have made our decision and we are going to make you an offer, Mike! We're going to offer $40 per hour as a QA lead and get you started right away at Harris Electronic Arts."

Mike: "Wait a minute, Mary, that is not the number I had in my mind. I was thinking more along the lines of $60 per hour. I have checked the salaries for the region and industries in the geography and looking at what I was making from the last job just a few months back, your number is way below the market."

Mary: "In that case we'll get back to you. I'll talk to my boss and see what he thinks."

The following day Mary sent Mike a terse email stating that as a result of his demands, they had decided to go back to other candidates and search some more. Mike, now desperate, tried repeatedly calling her and sending her emails, pleading that he was willing to come on board for what they originally offered, and suggesting that they observe his performance after he came on board and then decide about the hourly rate.

Mary did not respond to Mike's pleas!

Reloading Mike

The following hypothetical dialog is presented here to show how Mike might have approached the situation differently and perhaps would have landed a different outcome:

Mary: "Looks like we have made our decision and we are going to make you an offer, Mike! We're going to offer $40 per hour as a QA lead and get you started right away at Electronic Arts."

Mike: "Thank you, Mary. May I reflect on this and get back to you in a day or so. This is exciting! EA can wait a day or so, right?"

Mary: "Of course, they can! I am looking forward to hearing from you tomorrow, then, Mike."

Mike: "Thanks, again, Mary for your offer yesterday. I am excited. I just wanted to check with you if there is any room in the number you gave me. Can you please tell me now or do you want to check and get back to me on this?"

Mary: "Did you have a number in mind, Mike?"

Mike: "No, no, Mary. I was just reflecting on my exit salary at General and what I did there for a number of years. That was a higher number by a significant amount and I just did not want to casually dismiss that without at least checking to see if the market now is shifted that much."

Mary: "It actually has, Mike! With all the jobs going to India now, we can get a good QA person for even less. We thought we are offering you top dollar."

Mike: "I understand. I'll tell you what, Mary, I would like to start on this assignment. I would like to show you what I could do for you and EA within the next few months. If I am able to deliver greater value than you expect can we revisit this then?"

Mary: "Maybe, we can. Does it mean that we can count on you to start there next Monday?"

Mike: "Yes, Mary, you can!" And, thank you, again!

With this dialog, Mike sends his acceptance by email to Mary, and mentions their conversation about the last part and sees how things go for the next three months.

Approaching an earnest offer in this spirit would have Mike employed again after being out of work for so long and would have given him an opportunity to "plug in" with the market; a definite plus.

Accepting the Offer

Accepting the offer should be done after considering all aspects of negotiating the final points without stickling over minutia.

This is also the time to shake loose and leverage offers from others, who have gone through their process and are just waiting. In a tough economy, the hiring process is long and often several weeks or months can go by between subsequent interviews. An offer from *any* employer can change that. How? For example, if you have had two rounds of interviews with another company and you feel as though it is dragging its feet, the best tactic is to call and mention that you have a *bona fide* offer from one of the companies you were pursuing. You must also state that by a certain date you have committed to accepting that offer. You do not—and must not—disclose the name of the company or the salary for *any* reason. Requesting to move the process along before that date to get an offer from them because of your continued interest there is appropriate. If this can be done before starting negotiations with the first company, it is even better. This is why getting a longer period to accept any offer is advantageous because of the possibility of multiple offers.

A well-managed job search can result in multiple offers in a short time if the final steps of the process are handled with finesse. Having multiple offers can create problems for some. They find it difficult to manage this important part of making the final choice, without alienating some employer. The challenge here is to *not* do that to the one who is the most desirable. That is why handling the process during this step with great professionalism is critical.

A temptation you may feel when a company is getting close to making an offer is to *assume* that the offer will be forthcoming and leveraging that assumption to get others to make offers. This is lying, and is not recommended! Do not ever lie about an offer, if you do not have one *in* your hand. The person at the other end has an ability to sense this from the tone of your voice, no matter how clever you think you are at disguising it! If an offer is pending or is imminent, stating it forthrightly is appropriate—"I am expecting an offer in the next day or so and just wanted to give you a heads up. Can you do anything to accelerate your process to get me an offer, as I am very interested in working at your company?" This works most of the time if the circumstances are favorable.

Having to decide between multiple offers, even in a tough job market is not that unusual if the overall campaign is handled as laid out in the discussion throughout this book. One word of caution: after concluding negotiations with the original employer, going back and reopening the offer is generally not a good idea. The only exception to this is that after concluding the negotiations with one employer ("B" or "C" company), another offer (an "A" company), looks better. In that case calling the original employer and stating why the offer is being declined in a *diplomatic* manner is the right thing to do. If a counter offer is made, then all factors have to be considered once again, before moving ahead and the disparities between the companies ("A," "B," or "C") reconciled.

Once an offer is acceptable, calling the person who made the offer and orally accepting it is appropriate, including the start date. The signed offer should be in the mail in a day or so confirming this call and then calling to make sure that it *was* received.

Accepting the offer does not mean that you have to honor it! If something happens to change that—another offers comes along *after* confirming the first one—confirming the one you want to accept and then *calling* the contact at the company that made the original offer is appropriate.

The next section shows how to do this with an actual example.

Declining the Offer

Having to decline an offer can happen for a variety of reasons:

- You got a better offer elsewhere
- You changed your mind because you learned something adverse about the company
- You changed your mind because your circumstances changed since your acceptance
- You want to continue to look for a better opportunity
- You simply changed your mind about working and want to retire

Whatever the reason, occasionally you end up in a situation where you have to decline an offer, even after your accepting it or indicating that you would be accepting it. As long as you are honest to yourself, and present that honesty in a message that is not offensive to the company, where you are declining the offer, it is fair game. The reason for taking some trouble to do this is that you want to protect yourself from any future need you may have of this employer, or those who worked with you during this process. You want to stay in good stead with this company that considered you worthy of their trust in addition to protecting your own prospects with those who may leave the company and move on to other opportunities.

The following sample letter (an actual case, with names disguised) shows how this can be done gracefully. But before sending a written response, calling first is recommended!

Victor Smiths
Acorn Way
Alameda, CA 97665
(000) 555-0000: email@email.com

November 21, 2003

James Garragos
Director,
Product Development
General Electronics
2121 Osaka Way,
San Jose, CA 95131

Dear Jim,

Thank you for your ongoing dialog during this difficult time in making my final decision.

As I explained to you over the phone, my personal situation prevents me from joining General Electronics, primarily because of the commute. From where I now reside, it is a five-hour drive for me each day. My wife works, too, and we have three small children. This is an extreme hardship and will be a major factor in negatively impacting my work-life balance.

Originally, when I negotiated your offer, I was not that concerned about the distance, although it was on my mind. Since we concluded our negotiations, I was surprised to get a very attractive offer from Lockheed, which is only 25 minutes from my home. The job is challenging and I am excited about the possibilities. I had not considered this as a viable alternative as I entered your employment negotiations.

I hope that you understand my situation and agree that my choice is based on what is best for us mutually in the long term.

I hope that we get a chance to work together in a future opportunity. I feel that you are an excellent manager and I can learn much from you!

Once, again, thank you for your confidence in offering me the position.

Cordially,

Victor Smiths

Starting Your New Job

Starting a new job is exciting. It is a new chapter in a career journey filled with anticipation and hope. Starting a new job is also an opportunity to create and manage expectations for what is to come. If you have not done this in past jobs, it is time now to start.

The first day on the new job is important in setting and managing expectations. The following checklist will help for the better management of that day with some sense of control. If you do not do this on the first day or soon thereafter, it is difficult to go back and recover:

1. If you have not been successful negotiating the salary you wanted, and, in fact, accepted a lower salary in your new job, the time to bring it up is in your first meeting with the manger. State that you are glad to be part of their team and are looking forward to making the overall team look good to the customers, competitors, and others within the company.

    Mention to the manager that you were unable to get the salary you hoped, but decided to come on board and demonstrate what you said during the process: superior performance. Ask the manager that if you were to demonstrate a superior performance, if he has any discretion in giving you an adjustment to the salary commensurate with that performance at the end of the year. It is unlikely that anyone would respond negatively to this idea.

2. Once this is out of the way, you can have a discussion about your assignment, organization, and other details. Following that meeting, send an email to your manager thanking them for the welcome and that you were glad to be on their team. At the end, mention the agreement you just made about the performance and the salary adjustment at the end of the year. This way if the manager moves on, having this document covers you when the time comes, regardless of who is writing the performance review.

3. Have a discussion about how the assignments will be made and how your performance will be measured. How often you will meet and how the manager would like to receive reports from you or by what means. If there is an intermediate level between you and the manager, ask how that arrangement will work from a reporting standpoint and how he will have access to how you perform. Reiterate that you are not trying to circumvent the command structure, but get clarity about your expectations.

4. If you have anything else on your mind before starting your new job, this is the time to air it so that there are no surprises. It is much easier to get clarity on things that can impede good performance than waiting for an adverse situation to develop.

5. If you have any special needs that are circumstantial, this is the time to bring it up. For example if your expectant wife is concerned about her delivery complications in two months, mentioning this early will create awareness. You may want to explain what the needs may be when the time comes—"I may have to suspend my travel within a month or so until the situation is cleared up"—so that there are no surprises.

6. If you have any special support needs that are situational or acute, mention them at this time so that there are no surprises and that the manager can accommodate them. The manager may also feel more comfortable communicating that to the rest of the team so that you feel welcomed!

There is no magic or mystery here. It is about being forthright, honest, and making sure that yours and your manager's expectations are made clear at the same time. For many, the first few days set the tone for the tenure in that organization; you want to do nothing to compromise it.

Keeping Yourself Employed and Employable

If you have just been re-employed after your first job loss, treat this as a wake-up call. This may be one of many such situations, if you are in the early part of your career. If you were able to transition from a job to another one smoothly, consider yourself fortunate. Your best defense against being out of work is to keep yourself valuable and useful at all times. The following guidelines will help manage this well:

1. Keep looking for opportunities of growth in the company. Compare them to outside jobs as they are posted and evaluate what skill sets can make you get there. Specifically ask for those assignments during your meetings with your manager. Seek these out and make sure that you position yourself well for being assigned those projects. If you keep your eyes and ears open and keep good networks within the organization this should be a natural process for you!

2. If you see anything that can jeopardize your future—an impending merger, acquisition, or a reorganization—make sure that you have some way to get an early warning and that you have someone who can help you find a position that is safer. Once the process starts everyone is

going to jump ship and you are at a disadvantage. No matter how well you think you have done or are doing, do not defer the inevitable. Look out for yourself!

3. Take on high visibility and tough assignments. Once you take these on you'd be surprised how help comes your way and how much easier they are because of the support you get from others. Everyone loves a hero! So, become one!

4. Do not complain and do not explain is the simple mantra to stay out of trouble. When hard times hit those who complain or spend more time explaining why they failed are the first to go!

5. Keep yourself well networked and well liked. No one wants to forget the ones who pitch in or are well connected.

6. Do not forget to credit openly those who helped you by sending thank you notes that are distributed. Everyone likes to be visibly acknowledged for a good job they did.

7. Much of your success at the new job—any job for that matter—will depend less on your knowledge and how smart you are, but more on your attitude to get along with others and your cooperation to get things done, even though you may not always be in agreement with the cause. Remember the adrenaline factor discussed in earlier Key-1: Managing your Chemicals. You do not want those around you to have their adrenaline flowing when you just show up in the room, instead you want their endorphin flowing!

8. Always keep your résumé current, looking to build it up as you grow in your job, so that you are a desirable commodity in rapidly changing markets. Ask for résumé-building assignments. This is why constantly scanning for job opportunities and what skills are in demand will allow you to seek those assignments that are résumé builders and not just résumé fillers!

9. Develop relationships with those whom you want to be your references at the new place of employment. Create special bonds with those by getting to know their family and personal life to the extent it is proper.

10. Go out of the way to become valuable in company events and showcase your skills by speechmaking, acting as an MC or helping out some cause that puts the company or your organization in a good light. Make sure that you get visibility for that volunteer work!

Summary Key-6: Negotiating the Offer

Getting the prospective employer to make an offer is a matter of confidence and will that you display and the professionalism with which you navigate through the hiring process.

Do not raise salary issues before it is presented during the selection process. The only time it should come is when the offer is being made. For details see how to navigate through this dialog in Win-Win Negotiations.

Do not give out a salary number unless it is absolutely necessary any time during your hiring process. Avoid giving numbers. Never lie about your salary (up or down). Always give a range unless someone asks for a number specifically.

Temper your anxiety to get an offer by being relaxed at all stages of the interview process and during the follow-ups. The more you are relaxed about it the more likely that you'll get what you are looking for. The offer may even pleasantly surprise you!

Carefully look at the whole offer in the way it is presented. Look at the table: Compensation Package.

Negotiating the Offer: Most are skittish about negotiating an offer. Don't be! Remember the saying: You do not get what you deserve, you get what you negotiate. But, do not wait till the last minute to present your case for a higher salary. You should position your value and expectations throughout the process that culminated your being brought to the offer table.

Always wait to negotiate until an offer is made in writing or just before it so that you are sure that the offer is being made in earnest and that the potential employer has some commitment to your joining the company. Revisit Win-Win Negotiations, Accepting the Offer, and Declining the Offer, to review how an offer is negotiated, accepted, or declined. Before you enter negotiations, have a walk-away threshold. This figure or criterion gives you your own exit point; if you do not get what you are looking for, you should be prepared to walk away from the offer *with no regrets!*

You have some latitude in how you position the offer you accepted until the time you start your job. Read Starting Your New Job to see why. To keep your employment on solid footing and to keep yourself employable, read Keeping Yourself Employed and Employable.

Key-7: Making it All Work!

"Creativity is not always inventing something new, sometimes it is rearranging the familiar."

—Anonymous

Introduction

So far, we have covered how to shepherd the process of job searching. Throughout the process, there are skills and topics that are important to maintain the differentiation, a critical theme we have hammered in the book. The topics here are organized to round out what has been already presented, to further help you with the finer points of managing an effective campaign.

The following topics are covered in this Key:

- The Age Advantage
    - Age-transparent résumé samples
- Overcoming Cultural Barriers
- Understanding Program Management
- Informational Interviews
- Job Fairs
- Understanding Job Trends
    - Sample Letters
- Contracting
    - Résumé Samples
- Guerilla Job Search
    - Sample Letters
- Job-Search Etiquette

The Age Advantage

As the baby boomer generation gets to the traditional "retirement" age, more and more are discovering that they are not ready to retire yet. Many feel that they still have some salt left in them. To others, it is a matter of economics. Stock-market performance, early in this Millennium, and other factors in their personal lives, have necessitated them to work for another decade or so.

The biggest challenge the baby boomers face is leveraging their age to get a job, without being considered too old for it. But, this issue is not just limited to this age group; it covers those in any group that can be classified as "age conscious." It may sound like a cliché', but this entire section is based on the simple truth: your age is a state of mind!

Why? It is because this is how you see yourself. If you see yourself as old and as someone who cannot carry their own weight, then you have no business looking for work, and getting paid for it. Being employed is about creating value for others, and getting paid for doing so. The following list is presented to disabuse the notion of age in *any* job market. The prescription equally applies to those who think that they are too young for certain jobs, as well as to those, who think that they're too old for the work force:

1. First, do a self-audit and evaluate if you must work. This can be for earning money, engaging yourself, learning, or for whatever reason that compels you to get back into the workforce.

2. Prepare your résumé and take out any reference to items in your chronology that betray your age. Typically these are: graduation year, first job, and other events in your career that have definite age-related significance.

3. Write the Career Objective in your résumé so that your value proposition is unquestionably compelling. Remember, getting a job is about the ability to create value *at any age.*

4. Provide your Experience Summary and Professional Experience so that it does not go back more than 10–12 years. The guideline is: if the chronology going back does not support your value proposition, or does so marginally, stop stating the year of experience before that job. All previous jobs, then, are listed as "1990-Prior." Similarly, if you just graduated, do not list the year of graduation. See Age-transparent résumé samples in this Key.

5. Show your value and experience in the way you present yourself in every message to the prospect employer: letters, calls, appearance, energy, and your ideas.

6. The concern potential employers have around age is that you would stop learning. That you would rest on your laurels and find it hard to relate to the younger colleagues. Show that you have no problem with reporting to managers, who might be much younger than you, and that you are willing and eager to learn, despite your flat learning curve.

7. Yet another concern around age is the perception of expected compensation. Many are used to the notion that salaries go linearly with age and experience. Changing this belief to: salaries go with created value or value delivered, can be a counterweight.

8. During the interview, appearance counts. Remember that you have deleted any chronology going back beyond 10–12 years; the employers are going to be naturally curious about your age. Look vigorous and youthful and wear clothes that show you that way. Your appearance, too, has to match that image. Touch up any gray hair or shave facial hair if that improves your image in the right direction. Some jobs need seasoned and mature employees. Career counselors, coaches, and consultants fall in this category. Even in these professions make sure that you look your part by proper grooming, attire, and attitude.

9. Sometimes, being older can raise concerns about your health and its possible impact on group-rate premiums as well as your ability to have a regular work schedule. Show that you are in vigorous health and are not a medical liability.

10. Show your value-add beyond what you can do in your job by observing the obvious. For example, if you see younger employees, mention how you would mentor them.

11. Do not expect a salary or a title based on seniority in your past job. Your compensation at the new job will be based on the value you create there and the competitive forces that shape the current job market.

12. Always act age appropriate, even after you're on board.

Age-transparent Résumé Samples

Two examples of résumés are attached here. One is for a person who is 23 and another, 63. Read them carefully and see for yourself how age is not the first thing you wonder about after you've read them. Both were able to navigate through a tough job market with their message, as presented here.

DELIVERING **BULLETPROOF** SOFTWARE
A 23-YEAR-OLD FRESH GRADUATE

KARLO MENNIG
Adriana Avenue
Cupertino, CA 95014
Phone: (000) 555-0000: email@email.com

PROFESSIONAL OBJECTIVE:
A position as a **software design engineer** responsible for the design, development, testing, and documentation of technology products, including identifying and defining product features as well as implementing designs to deliver functional products.

EXPERIENCE SUMMARY:
Eight years in a variety of companies and industries, including a Fortune 50 high-tech leader as well as a start-up. Responsibilities include coding solutions, developing product specifications, identifying user requirements, system administration, and delivering industry-defining results while also beating deadlines. Versed in methodology for rapid cycle times.

UNIQUE SKILLS:
- **Identify** user needs and then translate them into product specifications.
- **Develop** and implement efficient algorithms.
- **Communicate** exceptionally well via both written and verbal means.
- **Write bulletproof** code to implement new features or version-one products.
- **Troubleshoot** mission-critical bugs, and then incorporate enhancements.
- **Collaborate** with others as part of a team as well as with internal and external partners.

PROFESSIONAL EXPERIENCE:
Hewlett-Packard Corporation, R&D Software Engineer   2001
- Served as the top Linux expert in the NetServer Division, resulting in a highly focused and forward-looking business outlook for Linux services. Developed plans for new offerings.

- Performed research and collaborated with internal and external partners to change the direction of support for Linux for NetServer platforms.

- Integrated IA-64 Linux operating system pre-releases with NetServer platforms.

- Made recommendations to other groups for utility of Linux and its suitable applications for their projects, resulting in an improved development platform for next-generation products.

Elusive Entertainment, Software Design Engineer (Consultant)   2001–present

- Wrote an optimized 3-D collision detection module for complex object interaction.

- Mentored and supported other engineers, delegate responsibility, and meet deadlines.

- Identified key goals and characteristics of the "Urban Jungle" project.

Minerva Networks, Software Engineer (Internship)   2000

- Developed alpha-blending and text anti-aliasing engines for most successful DVD authoring.

- Used MFC and ActiveX controls to embed video from the company's presentation product into Web pages to drastically expand the customer base for the product.

- Planned and wrote foundation library for spline-based object representation and manipulation for an MPEG-4 authoring tool. Assisted in defining goals and characteristics of the tool.

- Implemented automatic generation of HTML menus, incorporating JavaScript, to remotely control the playback of video server content through set-top boxes.

Compression Technologies, Contract Programmer (Consultant) 1998–present

- Coded a Java port of the Cinepak Pro video compression codec.

- Developed applications to order products online and monitor demo product downloads.

Pinnacle Systems, Software Developer (Internship)   1997

- Developed a windows-based program to run diagnostic tests on video products using C++.
- Defined and implemented an extensible, general plug-in model for the diagnostic tests.

Micro Computer Products, Software Engineer   1996–1997

- Coded "Story Tools," a digital video application that captures, edits, and publishes content.
- Managed source code control system for a project with an approved budget of over $1.2M.
- Administered/maintained many servers and workstations running various operating systems.

Sun Microsystems, Web Programmer (Consultant)   1995–1996

- Identified goals, guidelines, and appropriate tools for the Disneyland project.
- Wrote and tested professional HTML code for the Disneyland Website.

NASA Ames Research Center, Computer Engineer (Consultant)   1994–1995

- Managed NASA's Quest UNIX server and provided support to users of the system.
- Served as a student instructor for Internet classes with over 30 students each.
- Designed HTML and graphics for NASA's K-12 Initiative Web servers.

COMPUTER SKILLS:
Comprehensive knowledge of C, C++, Java, Scheme, Pascal, HTML, and Perl languages; experience with MIPS, OpenGL, and Matlab. Experienced with UNIX (Solaris, SunOS, Linux, SCO), Windows (9X and NT), MacOS. Server/network administration/support Windows/Unix.

EDUCATION:
B.S.E.E. and Computer Science, University of California at Berkeley, Berkeley, CA

PROFESSIONAL DEVELOPMENT:
Coursework and experience in a variety of computer and science-related topics include:

Machine structures	Data structures
Computer networks	Operating systems
Efficient algorithms	Intractable problems
Compilers and languages.	Computer graphics
Database systems	Fractals, chaos, and complexity
User interfaces	Human-computer interaction

Paul Simpson, P.E.
(000) 555-0000
Mill Way, Sunny Valley, CA, 94080
email@email.com

Career Objective
A position in an engineering organization responsible for **overall facilities design of electrical and mechanical systems**, with opportunities for innovation leading to optimal use of scarce energy resources.

Experience Summary
Twelve years at a Hewlett-Packard responsible for engineering design of data centers, videoconference rooms, and manufacturing facilities. Additional experience includes working as Energy Manager for overall utilities management, including cost reductions and incentives. Total utility cost reductions of $15 million were achieved and total incentives of $5 million dollars were obtained from utilities and the California Energy Commission. Implementation of novel designs in energy management have resulted in a bottom-line impact of over $20 million from a combination of cost savings, incentives, and grants over ten years.

Unique Skills

- Champion energy cost reduction programs
- Design electrical power, air-conditioning and ancillary systems for data centers, manufacturing facilities, videoconference rooms, and conference rooms and centers
- Obtain grants and incentives for energy conservation projects for industrial facilities
- Develop business continuity agreements with utilities that permit major facilities to be exempt from rolling blackouts
- Work with manufacturers to develop more efficient energy-efficient products
- Train engineers, facility mangers, contractors, and electricians to design systems

Experience Summary
Hewlett-Packard
Energy Manager for HP Silicon Valley Facilities   1991–2001

Overall responsibilities for energy cost reductions, incentives, and rebates

- Pioneered multi building outside air control using chemical monitoring for cost reduction

- Obtained $1M in grants from the CEC for controls to avoid blackouts

- Obtained $267M in grants from the CEC for building features better than Title 24

- Obtained over $14M in incentives from utilities for saving energy

- Achieved energy costs reductions of $15M in energy conservation, over ten years

- Obtained blackout exemptions for five major HP facilities avoiding worker lost time

- Worked with manufacturers to develop very high efficiency products

- Managed the HP energy team that achieved cost reductions and <u>maintained them</u>

Senior Facilities Design Engineer   1991–Prior

- Overall responsibilities for design of data centers, manufacturing facilities, videoconference rooms, conference centers, and meeting rooms.

- Designed the first HP data center to utilize over 100 watts/SF, permitting larger scale computer development.

- Designed one of the HP's largest data centers, the Mega Room, permitting large-scale system demonstration of compatibility of HP, IBM, and DEC equipment.

- Designed over seventy thousand square feet of data centers.

- Designed over sixty thousand square feet of high tech computer manufacturing facilities including the electrical power distribution, air-conditioning, pneumatic, exhausts, etc.

Paul Simpson, PE   (000) 555-0000   email@email.com   Page 3/4

- Designed and managed the installation of one 1.5 and two 2 megawatt 12 KV to 480 volt transformers and switchboards permitting 100 watt per square foot computer rooms needed for large scale computer development.

- Designed, obtained permits, and installed millions of dollars of development test equipment permitting development and products getting to the market quickly.

- Designed indirect lighting systems for over 200,000 square feet to reduce glare improving worker productivity.

Education
University of Illinois, BS in Mechanical Engineering
San Diego State University, MS in Mechanical Engineering
San Jose State University, BS in Electrical Engineering

Licenses
State of California, Electrical Engineer, E 011446
State of California, Mechanical Engineer, M015419

Professional Organizations

- Past Chairman of the Power Engineering and the Industry Applications Societies of the Institute of Electrical and Electronics Engineers for the Silicon Valley.

- Trained engineers and contractors to perform electrical designs using the National Electrical Code at Intel, IBM, Applied Materials, AMD, Cupertino Electric, ETI, Tandem, Cisco, NASA, Lockheed, Stanford University, Lawrence Livermore, Cal Trans, East Bay Municipal Utility District, SMUD, City of San Jose, Bechtel, and the Naval Post Graduate School for the Institute of Electrical Education (IEEE).

- Educational Chairman of the International Association of Electrical Inspectors.

- Vice Chairman of the Silicon Valley Electrical Inspectors Recommendations Committee.

Paul Simpson, PE   (000) 555-0000   email@email.com   Page 4/4

- Past Chairman of the Business Continuity Committee of Silicon Valley Manufacturing Group.

Overcoming Cultural Barriers

Cultural barriers are perceived or real impediments to successfully navigating through a job search process. They typically stem from the cultural value differences between the jobseeker and those in the selection process. These barriers manifest as unspoken signals that the jobseeker has to intercept and overcome to conquer the job.

Cultural norms are real. They vary from country and culture. However, if you are conducting your search within the US, the cultures of other countries are less of a concern. While in the US, you are bound by the cultural norms practiced here.

First-generation immigrants can be most challenged by the cultural norms and this applies to those on both sides of the process. If you are an immigrant, you do not need to surrender your roots or identity, to integrate into the culture here. You will be better accepted, however, if you show that you are well adjusted to the norms of this society. One way to achieve this, is to make sure that your own lifestyle is not too steeped into your past. Many immigrants often socialize frequently—sometimes exclusively—with those from their own country or region, speaking their native tongue in their normal daily exchange, even at a place of business. Many speak only their own native language at home; and even watch their native movies. As a result, they are unaware of the gross cultural norms of this society, let alone the finer points of social etiquette. Often, they are unable to even follow colloquial English in a conversation. If you feel yourself at a disadvantage because of some of the points listed here, make serious attempts to change your habits and try to create ones that allow you to integrate the cultural norms of *this* country.

The following list summarizes cross-sexual and cross-cultural barriers that can be overcome with some awareness. If you are culturally raised to treat an employer as a provider or a master, then be mindful of the following areas. These considerations apply, even if you were raised here, with the cultural norms of this country, and the interviewer holds other norms:

1. Do not hesitate to ask questions during an interview when the time is right. Do not wait till the end of the interview—you may not have time. Do not confuse being respectful with being deferential or solicitous. The latter is a matter of your attitude adopted towards someone of superior status.

2. Always maintain eye contact with the person interviewing you. Some cultures believe that looking directly at superiors is a sign of disrespect. In the US, not looking at someone, while talking to them is considered a sign of disrespect. If you avoid eye contact, you may come across as

evasive, non-committal, or less than truthful. Do not stare; instead, use a five-to seven-second eye contact with the person, and then look away at something else, as writing notes or making a gesture. Smiling is a great aid when you are confused about how long to look at someone.

3.   In the section on interviewing, we reviewed the concept of Ethos ("I am like you")—we analogized ethos with the personal chemistry. An easy way to strike ethos is to find as much about the decision maker, before the interview, as possible. Dressing in colors that the person favors can be a good ethos builder. Of course, for the interview, you may want to dress a bit more formally, and make a good impression. It is all right to dress a notch above the person who will see you—the main decision maker—and dress for that person. Other signs to watch are speed with which this person talks, gestures, and mannerisms. Of course, you do not want to mimic this person—that can be fatal—you want to make this person feel comfortable in the responses you provide. Observing the way in which speaking language and tone are used can also quickly overcome cultural barriers and even personal barriers, especially if you are able to mirror that usage.

4.   If something is important to the interviewer, you might see that displayed in their office or on their desk. Take it all in, and do not make any disparaging comments, even inadvertently, about any symbols that this person may hold in high regard. Once, a candidate made a humorous comment about a particular image of a goddess that the hiring manager was displaying in her office, just as he finished a long interview session. Her husband, who was of East Indian descent, had given her that image as a symbol of wealth and prosperity. This candidate never heard from the hiring manager again, despite a "great" interview!

5.   Do not suggest any religious, spiritual, or personal preferences unless the discussion comes from the interviewer. Even if the interviewer brings it up, dodge the issue and move on by cleverly switching topics. Such discussions can be minefields and are dangerous grounds. They are illegal, but do not go there on those grounds.

6.   Do not wear any cultural or religious symbols during an interview. Some cultures display elaborate body decorations on their hands, and other parts of their bodies as an omen of good luck. Avoid such superstitious practices. Do not wear ethnic clothing for an interview, no matter how elaborate. You are signaling that you have not integrated in this culture, and may come across as making a statement.

7. If you are invited to go out for a meal with the interviewer, make sure that you practice good etiquette and manners in restaurants. This is not a cultural matter, just social. Do not go out to *eat* but to ace the interview. Read a book on proper table manners, if in doubt.

8. The overriding criterion is value. As long as you are able to clearly articulate your value and show that you are not just an applicant (of many), but also a must-hire candidate, the chances of cultural barriers getting in the way are minimal. Showing compelling value deflects any focus on minor cultural gaps that may be perceived by the interviewer(s). It may also result in minor infractions becoming a non-issue.

9. At times, the hiring manager could also be a first-generation immigrant, with yet-to-be aligned cultural norms. If they exhibit behaviors that are unacceptable to your sensibilities then you have to decide if you want to work for such a person. In such a case, you have to wonder how the company accepted such behavior to begin with, and you have to assess, if you want to be working for such an individual and the company.

10. Do not confuse behaviors stemming from cultural upbringing, from those that are simply rude, boorish, and antisocial!

Understanding Program Management

Program management has become an often-expected skill in today's job market. This is especially true in high-tech and other industries that have time-limited initiatives, in addition to their ongoing functional activities. Everyone who has run a team, as a team leader, can make a claim of having done program management. This discussion is presented here as a summary, to make those who pursue program (or project) management opportunities, aware of different aspects of this term, and how to leverage the past experience for the right opportunity.

Program management is defined as disciplined process for planning, organizing, and leading resources to accomplish a deliverable on time, within budget, and to expected performance standards. Project management is its subset in that, many projects can constitute a program. Program management deals with three main parameters, as we just presented:

- Cost
- Schedule
- Performance

There are three functions within program management that one is expected to fulfill:

- Define
- Plan
- Execute

If your experience in the past assignment does not include these functions, then you have not been a program manager in its full context. Some confuse running marketing programs (rebates, promotions, incentives) as program management. This confusion comes from how the term *programs* is interpreted in these contexts; here it is used more as an *initiative* to promote a product in the channel. Although this *can* be a program from the perspective of our definition above, it is generally not considered a program in a classical sense.

Different organizations have different emphasis on program management. There are three organizational structures in which program management can exist:

- Residing within a functional group. This is called "weak" program management.

- Metrixed program management. Here resources are *assigned* to a program manager from within the functional groups. Once the program is complete, these resources are assigned back their function.
- Program Management Office or PMO: here the program manager controls the resources to execute a program.

Before getting into deep discussion with your interviewer, explore to see what flavor of program management their organization practices. Some organizations expect the Program Manager to lead both the technical and management efforts, while others separate the two. Learn more about program management from www.pmi.org.

♠ Informational Interviews

Informational interviews (preferred term: Introductory meeting) are a means to exploring ideas from the perspectives of those in the "know." Here you're not asking for a job, but positioning yourself for an exploration, which *may* lead you to new and uncharted territory, especially, if you're contemplating a career change or a significant transition.

Once you have an idea of what interests you, visit those places and talk to people doing what you see, perhaps, yourself doing. The purpose is to explore and discover if *that* is the line of activity and environment of which you want to be a part. This process is called informational interviewing. Informational Interviewing can be equated to meeting with influence brokers, including hiring managers. The focus is mainly on building relationships, understanding an industry/organization, developing mutual interest, exploring, and building a high-influence network. *Never* use the word "Job" in this context or mention that you are currently unemployed.

Seeking and getting informational interviews is difficult when the job market is tough.

Informational interviewing is done as a part of an overall marketing campaign and can be used in any one of the following approaches to a job search:

➢ Open posting and responding to them by résumé and cover letters

➢ Reading into an opening, beyond what is stated and positioning yourself

➢ Executing your "A," "B," "C" target marketing plan and exploring some companies and their opportunities through Informational Interviews

➢ Pursuing a change in your positioning

➢ Pursuing a change in your career

➢ Exploring something new

➢ Creating new networking contacts and building on them

➢ Testing your value statement(s) through consulting gigs

Job Fairs

A brief write-up of job fairs was presented in Key-4 as a part of a discussion on working with third parties. This section presents a broader perspective on job fairs with specific tips on how to leverage these events in an overall campaign.

For the corporate recruiters and hiring managers, job fairs offer an opportunity to reach interviewing on an assembly-line model; the highest possible number of prospects in the shortest possible amount of time. For many job seekers, job fairs provide an opportunity to meet with hiring employers and get a feel for the interview process.

However, unless you do your homework, you will end up wasting your time at a job fair or worse, feeling discouraged and overwhelmed. Job fairs are the meat markets of the employment scene, with employers sizing up candidates quickly, based on appearances and first impressions. Job fairs have a set of rules and protocols all their own. But if you understand how to effectively work within the system, by first understanding it, you can easily multiply your productivity and effectiveness.

Usually a large percentage of employers at job fairs are "window shoppers," who are just browsing to see what is available. While this approach may seem apparent, job fairs can get serious if you are prepared and are ready for a meaningful encounter. Yes, even the two- to three-minute greeting, and exchange of sound bites, after waiting for hours in a line, is considered a real interview. Those who come targeted and prepared to impress can be ushered out of the booth in a private setting for a series of interviews. You are being evaluated, whether it is for a few seconds or few hours. You must be at your very best. To productively leverage a job fair you must use a disciplined approach.

Understanding what type of job fair you are attending is crucial to your planning, since each type has distinct differences in approach, setup, and general level of success.

Types of job fairs

There are two main categories of job fairs: private and commercial. Other categories as campus job fairs and community affairs fall somewhere in between, as is briefly discussed below.

Private job fairs: Individual companies seeking candidates for current or future positions host private job fairs. Although these fairs are announced in the public media, there is no commercial presence as advertisers, sponsors, and others promoting their wares, and using the job fair as a theme to promote themselves. Career consultants also hold private job fairs, as do out-placement firms, where they urge their clients to participate, and invite interested employers by showcasing the talent that is currently in their care. Many have their own résumé banks, which the prospect employers see to assess the quality of the job fair. These fairs are open to special invitees only.

Commercial job fairs: Commercial job fairs are events organized by professional organizations with commercial overtones. Employers participate in large numbers, as do sponsors and advertisers to promote their own franchise during these carnival-like events. These fairs are generally announced in the media and anyone is allowed to come. They are now on the decline because of the cyber fares, conducted in virtual space.

Campus-Sponsored Job Fairs: The campus-sponsored job fair is by far the most popular for college students. For many students, this is *the* job fair. Larger campuses will often have several different job fairs, each one geared toward a specific profession. The campus Career Center usually sponsors them. The campus-sponsored job fair is ideal for most college students, since it is convenient, the lines are generally shorter than commercial job fairs, and the employers are predisposed to and familiar with the college. Many employers attend the job fair in advance of their on-campus recruiting activities, while some use this as their only campus visit. Often the more astute employers will bring along recent alum to talk with prospective grads and to showcase their prize. Smaller colleges often combine together to create consortium job fairs.

Community Job Fairs: These are free-for-all job fairs offering everything from Swing Shift Manager at McDonald's to professional and management positions. There are often over 100 employers involved. If you choose to attend, make sure you are very targeted and very direct about the type of jobs and type of employers you are seeking. Identify the employers you want to work for, and target their booth locations, before entering the crowd of people.

Getting ready

Résumé: Yes, you *may* bring one, but it is not required. If you are a new graduate, a trade professional, or someone in a non-exempt category, you must bring your résumé. However, if you are in other professions, where there are a variety of flavors and needs that vary, you are better off exploring those needs first before committing them to a message in your résumé. But, if you do bring one, it had better be an outstanding one, because at the end of the day, it is often difficult for recruiters to sort out the bad from the good. Bring at least two copies of résumés for each employer. This is a good time to use colored résumé paper (colored, yet conservative—light salmon, light green, light blue-green) so if a recruiter finds your résumé appealing and remembers it while in discussion with you, they can quickly sift it out, at the end of the day, from a stack. If you have multiple job objectives, bring multiple résumés.

No cover letters—you are the cover letter to your résumé. If you want to write a cover letter, it is best to send it *after* the job fair interview to capture what was said in a language that will resonate. If you have made a good impression, sending a cover letter and a résumé again as a "Thank you," is an attention-getter. Most job fairs have copying facilities, but then you are stuck with paper stock they have in *their* machines!

Business Card: If you did not bring your résumé, then bring your business card with a clever tagline as suggested in Key-2: A Fresh Graduate. This rule, however, applies to all, and not just the fresh graduates. Sometimes coming without a résumé can help you better present your case after you discover what the real needs are. These needs can be explored in an interview at the job fair, after you present your business card, and stating that you are in the process of finalizing your résumé. After you get a good sense of what they are looking for, complete your résumé, and then send it personally to someone you met at the fair.

Portfolio: Your 9"x12" attractive portfolio that has all your projects to showcase your past, is a good differentiator at a job fair.

Dress: Image is crucial at any job fair—even more important than at a normal interview since decisions are made much more quickly. If you are going to a job fair sponsored by your employer, or your Career Center, do not discount the opportunity. Make sure you wear a conservative or classic business suit (both men and women) for professional positions, so that they focus on you and not on the suit you are wearing. Some individual contributors may want to consider wearing business attire as slacks, jacket, and a tie. If you are looking for a trade job, wearing something well thought-out that is presentable, is appropriate. Some may balk at dressing up, especially if they consider themselves tied to their jobs, without the need to socialize or see customers, as many individual contributors might perceive. In this shifted market many such professionals are routinely required to now meet customers, suppliers, and alliance partners.

Teaming: Attending large job fairs can be intimidating. Some major events draw large pools of employers and as many as 10,000 attendees in tough times. It gets difficult and tiring to stand in long lines, cover all the interests you have on your agenda, and get all the useful information from the event. One way to increase your coverage and leverage your visit, is to team-up with someone you are close to and share the load. Once at the fair, scope out the scene and then split. Reconnect after every few hours to share what is learned, so you can multiply your learning. Remember, no matter whom you are teaming with, they are your competitors.

Interviews

It's important to understand the basic types of interviews that take place at a job fair since your approach should be different with each. As you watch and listen, while waiting in line, you will be able to determine which type of interview is being conducted and modify your approach accordingly. Following are the three basic types:

Screening Interview: This interview usually lasts a few minutes and is usually conducted by employers, whose main interest is gathering résumés and initial impressions, before making decisions as to whether they will move to the next step. Your strategy should be to quickly point them to the key areas, in your résumé, that reflect their needs. You may have overheard these needs, as you stood in line waiting for your turn. Ask for a business card and inquire as to the next step.

Mini-Interview: This interview usually lasts five to ten minutes and is conducted at the employer's booth. Be prepared to give a full introduction of your background and quickly position yourself as someone who is a good fit in relation to that employer's needs. The recruiter will usually want you to elaborate on the information contained in your résumé, so it is crucial that you are prepared to comment on each and every item in it. Often, there will be final questions related to some of the qualitative issues that résumés do not reflect. Make sure all your answers position you as the candidate that meets the employer's needs. Ask for a business card and inquire as to the next step. Also, learn to do something, or say something to make your visit to them memorable. So, when you call them to follow-up-up, you can repeat what you did to jog their memory of you!

Full Interview: The full interview (if there is one being conducted) typically takes place behind a curtain or screen at the employer's booth, or may be in another part of the hall altogether. Most employers use the full interview only as a secondary interview. In other words, you have to be invited to the interview, based on the previous screening interview, or mini-interview. Be prepared for 20 minutes or more, but probably no longer than 30 minutes, since most employers have a tight schedule to keep. Consider this interview the same as you would any full-length interview. Be aware that you may actually be interviewed by technical or line managers. You will be asked a great number of qualitative, open-ended questions, and will be expected to provide elaboration of your answers. Make sure you are prepared for the interview. At the end of the interview, if you are truly interested, let the interviewer know and ask what the next step will be. Assume that they are also interested.

Making them remember you

Most recruiters have very little time to get away from their booth and when they are working, they are stretched to their capacity. So, what can you do to make yourself memorable? Bring them lunch or a beverage. There is a line a mile long, and it is not getting any shorter. If you notice that they are in need of something, you can either ask them if they want you to get it, or just get it for them. They will be eternally grateful, and it may be what sets you apart from the crowd, at the end of the day.

Yet another way to have a recruiter remember you and getting ahead of a mile-long line, is to invite them to lunch. Most are so busy, in pushing the assembly line of jobseekers, that they do not even have time for lunch. You can even bypass the long line, by setting up a lunch reservation nearby, and then going ahead of line, in front of a booth of interest, and whisper in the ears of the recruiter that you have a lunch reservation nearby. This magic works about 25 percent of the time, so, start with the most desired employer and go from there. If you do get the lunchtime, you have a grateful recruiter's undivided attention for at least 30 minutes. Whereas at the booth, after a long line, you are lucky if you get three minutes!

Yet another way to make them remember you is to have a clever tagline on your business card. This was discussed in Key-2 for the category of A Fresh Graduate. For example, saying Joe Smith, *Customer Support* is not as memorable as saying Joe Smith, *Customer Delighter*!

Also, about how you present yourself can be made memorable, too. Say your name is John Coak. As you shake hands with the recruiter say your name and then say "Coak like the popular beverage Coke! If the person is thirsty for a drink, or even otherwise, they are sure to remember that name. So, when calling for a follow-up, introduce yourself again and say, "Remember me? I am John Coak, like the popular beverage!"

Before you leave the job fair, return to the booth of any employer in which you have an interest. Wait for a break in the action, then step up to the recruiter and thank them again for their time. Let them know that you will be in touch and look forward to speaking with them again.

This lasting impression will help the recruiter to remember your name and face when you do make contact again. After all, there will be a stack of one hundred to two hundred résumés for the recruiter to filter through, after the job fair is over. This is a guarantee that you will be remembered.

Following-Up: As with any other part of the job search, you must follow-up! Yet sadly, very few ever do (fewer than five percent). Many feel that if the employer has interest, they have all they need to call you. Wrong! First, call the office number on the business card, of the person you met and leave a personal "thank you." Then send a "thank you" card, by mail or e-mail, to confirm your ongoing interest. What to say? Keep it short and sweet. Make sure you cover the following topics:

"Thanks for taking time to meet with me today…" During this message, repeat something you did during your encounter with them that will make them connect with who you are.

"Here is why I feel I would be an outstanding employee for your company.

I would appreciate the opportunity to speak with you further…."

Do some further research on the company and the open position before you call again the following week, and then call with some additional insights from this research. This initiative will impress the recruiter to push you ahead for an interview with the hiring manager.

Job Fair Tips

1. Before you line up for a booth, check out the entire layout and scope how you want to spend your two hours (most productive time) with an "A," "B," and "C" company list

2. As you wait, network and connect with others. Collect their business cards and contact information

3. If you first go around collecting company literature for information, go to a quiet place. Then organize to see which ones are your top priorities, and then make a plan based on those priorities

4. Get as much information about the company and recruiter as possible. This will allow you to reconnect for a good follow-up

5. Learn to listen and talk about 50-50. Take mental or written notes

6. Do not wander aimlessly through the maze or dawdle. In your movements, show purpose. Someone may be watching you. When your mission is done, quickly exit the area, and go away.

A job fair is a meat market. If you make an impression with your superior appearance and attitude, recruiters will remember you over other candidates more readily. Be mindful of this opportunity.

Contracting

Contracting has now become a major source of job opportunities for many. With more and more employers adopting an "accordion model" for their workforce, the contract industry is booming. Those who provide the contract labor are specialized in the industry of clients they serve by focusing on a particular talent pool. From a list of contract agencies, it is easy to identify which specialty a particular agency is focused on.

When you are contracting, your employer is not where you do the work; rather, it is who puts you there. Your place of work can change from time to time based on the needs of the client organizations that the contracting agency serves. With more and more contracting work, fewer and fewer consultants are being hired.

Contracting résumés are different from those where someone is looking for a full-time employment. Why? The main reason is that those hiring you, are placing you at their clients' sites. Clients can vary from assignment to assignment, and each is different. This is why, contracting agencies are looking for both depth and breadth of skills.

The following résumés show examples of how the same person can restructure their résumé to run their campaign on both fronts:

Résumé Samples

These résumé samples are presented to showcase how a résumé for a full-time job can be *repackaged* and presented for a contracting opportunity.

Job-Search Résumé

Ram Vijay
Terrace Court
San Jose, CA 95131
(000) 555-0000; email@email.com

Career Objective

Technical Project Lead/Senior Software Engineer translating customer needs into product requirements, setting up aggressive teams to deliver those needs, supporting post-release activities, and managing product life-cycle to generate profitable revenue streams.

Experience Summary

Ten years collaborating with highly demanding customers to translate their business needs into highly profitable products; concurrent eight years leading creative and motivated teams delivering on-time software products that delight customers; four years providing ongoing product enhancement and supporting customers get better value from products already delivered.

Unique Skills:

- **Customer Needs:** Collaborate with customers to translate their articulated and unarticulated business needs into unique products that delight them.
- **Leading Teams:** Lead global teams to execute complex projects.
- **Product Development:** Collaborate with teams globally to develop customer-centric products.
- **Product Lifecycle:** Manage overall product lifecycles to provide profitable product life revenues.
- **Product Enhancements:** Work with to enhance products and create ongoing value to end-user.
- **Infrastructure Architectures:** Develop novel architecture for efficiency and high availability.

Ram Vijay   (000) 555-0000   email@email.com

Professional Experience:
Hewlett Packard Company, Cupertino, CA   1999–present
Lead Software Designer

- Expanded the usability of a critical product line—SQL/MX—by making this already successful product ANSI compliant. Led a team of four in development for complaint standards, releasing the final version within schedule Resulting product is expected to provide greater market coverage and revenues.

- Led the development effort for SQL/MX Preprocessor, targeted to make this product ANSI compliant with internationalization support.

- Responsibilities included preparing design specifications, developing, testing, building, and releasing the product. The product was developed in C++ on MS Windows and deployed on Non-Stop Himalaya system.

- Quality Champion for SQL/MX Preprocessor. Gathered and evaluated historical quality data, established base-line quality parameters and software inspection plans to ensure that software process and quality metrics for the project were within planned limits.

iManageSoft, Inc., Cupertino, CA   1995–1999
Some critical projects executed during this consulting period include the following:
Safeway Stores, Inc., Walnut Creek, CA

- Overall responsibility included design, development, testing and roll-out of following systems developed in 'C', Cobol85 and SQL on Nonstop Himalaya systems for their divisions and *warehouses: Warehousing and Distribution system, Supplier Ordering* systems, Migration to Nonstop Himalaya systems and Year 2000 conversion.

Implementation of these systems helped to establish centralized control of the divisions and warehouses with better support capability.

Stanford University, Stanford, CA
Project Manager

- Responsible for "Use Case driven' design for Web-based 'Faculty Recruitment System."

- Involved in pre-sales meetings and preparing the proposal for the project.

- Other responsibilities included analysis preparation of User Requirement Analysis and Design document. Managed the development, testing, and implementation of the system. The system was developed in ASP, VB Script, FrontPage98, and SQL Server 7.0.

Reez.com, Cupertino, CA
Project Manager
Managed a team for development, testing, and implementation of an eCommerce application system for **Reez.com** to handle B2B Real Estate transactions using ASP, Java, VB Script, XML, and SQL Server 7.0.

Covansys, Inc. (formerly CBSI), Cupertino, CA   1991–1995
Project Manager

- Managed the development effort of a team of 6 analysts and developers for "Dispersed Data System" for Cabledata Corp, CA. The application system was developed in "C" and SQL on Nonstop Himalaya system. Responsibilities included analysis, design and co-ordinating development, testing, and implementation of the system.

- Developed and tested "Fixed Income Pricing System" (FIPS) using "C" and Nonstop SQL. The system catered to trade reporting and surveillance of high-yield fixed income bonds for *NASDAQ*, Connecticut.

- Developed, tested and implemented "Parts Distribution System" using Cobol85 and Nonstop SQL for Electronic Data Systems (EDS) team working for their client *John Deere Company*, Michigan.

Novartis Pharmaceuticals (formerly Sandoz), Bombay, India   1990–1991
Project Leader

- Carried out an Information Strategy study of existing systems, leading a team of 3 analysts to ascertain areas of concern and additional computerization needs of various divisions.

Ram Vijay	(000) 555-0000	email@email.com

- Prepared Information Strategy reports to include projected key requirements of various divisions for evaluating third party supply chain software solutions. Assisted in evaluating the hardware and software alternatives proposed by various vendors.

The project went through complete Software Development life cycle and was developed using Cobol and SQL on Tandem Nonstop system.

Education:
B.S in Electronics Engineering, Bombay, India

Professional Development:
Java, EJB, RMI, Servlets, XML, VC++, VB, OOD using UML, UNIX shell scripts,
Leadership and Team building skills, Project Management, Communicating for results.

CONTRACT RÉSUMÉ

RAM VIJAY
\# Terrace Court
San Jose, CA 95131
(000) 555-0000; email@email.com

Position Sought:
Technical Project Lead/Sr. Software Engineer. Contract off-shoring alliance/project management.

Summary of Qualifications:

- Comprehensive software development experience with the last ten years spent working for large corporations in the USA including Fortune 50 companies.
- Over twelve years experience of managing people and projects including technical supervision of entire projects, design, development, implementation and customer liaison.
- Extensive experience in project management, schedules, budgets, technical, communication and customer service skills.
- Proven track record in developing and delivering software solutions to match customer requirements, keeping projects on schedule and within budget that meet or exceed customer expectations.
- Extensive experience outsourcing and off-shoring software development projects and IT initiatives for cost reduction and streamlining.

Professional Experience:
Hewlett Packard Company, Cupertino, CA   1999–Present
Lead Software Designer

- Led the development effort for SQL/MX Preprocessor, targeted to make this product ANSI compliant with Internationalization support.
- Responsibilities included preparing design specifications, developing, testing, building, and releasing the product. The product was developed in C++ on MS Windows and deployed on Non-Stop Himalaya system.
- Quality Champion for SQL/MX Preprocessor. Gathered and evaluated historical quality data, established base-line quality parameters, and software inspection plan to ensure that software process and quality metrics for the project were within planned limits.

iManageSoft, Inc., Cupertino, CA   **1995–1999**
A contract software services provider. Some of the critical projects delivered:
Safeway Stores, Inc., Walnut Creek, CA
Lead Software Designer

- Overall responsibility included design, development, testing and roll-out of following systems developed in "C", Cobol85 and SQL on Nonstop Himalaya systems for their divisions and warehouses: Warehousing and Distribution system, Supplier Ordering system, Migration to Nonstop Himalaya systems and Year 2000 conversion.

- Implementation of these systems helped to establish centralized control of the divisions and warehouses with better support capability.

Stanford University, Stanford, CA
Project Manager

- 'Use Case driven' design for Web-based 'Faculty Recruitment System.'

- Other responsibilities included User Requirement Analysis and Design document. Managed the development, testing, and implementation of the system. The system was developed in ASP, VB Script, FrontPage98 and SQL Server 7.0.

Reez.com, Cupertino, CA
Project Manager

- Managed a team for development, testing, and implementation of an eCommerce application system for Reez.com to handle B2B Real Estate transactions using ASP, Java, VB Script, XML, and SQL Server 7.0.

Covansys, Inc. (formerly CBSI), Cupertino, CA   **1991–1995**
Project Manager

- Managed the development effort of a team of 6 analysts and developers for 'Dispersed Data System' for Cabledata Corp, CA. The application system was developed in 'C' and SQL on Nonstop Himalaya system. Responsibilities included analysis, design and coordinating development, testing, and implementation of the system.

Novartis Pharmaceuticals (formerly Sandoz), Bombay, India   1990–1991
Project Leader

- Carried out an Information Strategy study of the existing systems, leading a team of analysts to ascertain areas of concern/additional computerization needs.

- Prepared Information Strategy report to include projected key requirements of various divisions for evaluating third party supply chain software solutions.

Previous experience:
Tata Consultancy Services, Bombay, India

- Led a team of analysts and designers for analyzing user requirements for External Database Inquiry System to extract data from various systems of Royal Hong Kong Police Force. Prepared User requirement analysis and design.

- Led a team of analysts analyzing user requirements of Non-Trading systems for Hong Kong Stock Exchange. Prepared User Requirement and System design.

- Project Manager: ID user requirement to customize an On-line Retail Banking package for **Bank of Bahrain and Kuwait**, Bombay.

- ID User requirements and System design and Test plan documents. Led a team of 10 to develop, test/install Cobol/SQL on Tandem Nonstop system.

Education:
B.S in Electronics Engineering, Bombay, India

Professional Development:
Java, EJB, RMI, Servlets, XML, VC++, VB, OOD using UML, UNIX shell scripts,
Leadership and Team building skills, Project Management, Communicating for results.

Guerilla Job Search

Guerilla job-search uses methods that employ non-traditional and highly leveraged approaches for pursuing an opportunity. Some of these are covered in the unconventional job search in Key-4: Marketing the Product—You! The following discussion summarizes some additional methods using a guerilla approach.

Guerillas are generalists and not specialists. You are required to become knowledgeable about a broad range of topics to be a successful guerilla. Guerillas think non-linearly but systemically—backwards, strategically connecting the dots in their minds. This thinking involves creating results, which require specific actions. Although this backward thinking is at the heart of any guerilla strategy, their success comes from how they execute this strategy situationally: guerillas are tactical magicians and opportunists! One of the key aspects of guerilla tactics is how to translate emotional responses that result in "we want to hire you!" to a logical train of cause-and-effect tactics in each situation that interests the hiring manager. Going back, a comparison between guerilla tactics for job searching and the unconventional approaches discussed in Key-4, correctly suggests that the latter is a more methodical and brute-force approach, whereas the former is a mental game! Guerilla is a mindset. They must understand psychology. Why?

Every buying decision is based on someone making up their mind about it. So, buying is a mental process. To be able to change someone's mind, marketing plays a key role. The hiring process entails a mind thinking of acquiring a particular talent or object, and then executing that thought. There are two types of marketing:

- Freudian Marketing
- Skinnerian Marketing

Freudian approach deals with changing others' *attitudes* (mind) about things and people, so that they buy what is presented to them. This is an indirect approach to selling. The Skinnerian approach is more direct and is based on the fact that you understand the behavior that results in acting the right way—hiring you! This means saying, showing, or doing something that causes the employer to hire (behavioral) you! This approach to marketing deals with hitting the target in the gut and approaching them viscerally once you have grabbed their attention cerebrally—a more blunt and crude approach but very effective. The Freudian approach is based on appealing to the subconscious, the most powerful part of the person's mind. If you can translate the cerebral thoughts to the visceral actions, you can successfully get that person to act.

Thus, guerilla marketing combines both changing attitudes and behaviors in a quick way. This allows you to eliminate any competition for the same job. One guerilla tactic may involve luring a potential employer to take a closer look at you with some of the methods suggested before, and then getting them to move and consider you as a must-hire candidate. When you sense some hesitation, you lure them by showing no interest in getting hired and suggesting that the employer does not appear ready to buy into the sophisticated approaches you presented. Now, the employer moves in quickly to preempt the next move—taking a chance on losing you, and you get hired immediately. This works more than most give credit for, and yes, it requires some guts and self-confidence. This is a classic guerilla tactic.

The following list is a partial compilation of some guerilla tactics that are effective:

1.   Always carry a business card with an intriguing tag line. Think of creating curiosity in the minds of those reading your card. Instead of saying "Jim Smith, Software Engineer" try "Jim Smith, Software Wiz."

2.   When going to a job fair, instead of taking your résumé, take your business card and explore the needs of the hiring managers. Send your response after you hear what they are looking for.

3.   Remember employers do not pay attention to just any job seeker; they'll listen only to jobseekers that draw their attention. Research a problem that when presented correctly, hits them in the gut. Show that you not only understand their problem, but you know how to solve it! Now, you are the only candidate running for the job!

4.   For the guerilla approach to work, you must have the courage to tell the employers what you want them to do, exactly. Lead them through the hiring process.

5.   Employers do not hire bodies with skills that are in need for a job; they want talent that creates value for them. Show your value and how it matches what the employer is trying to create for his company.

Sample letters are shown here to illustrate how guerilla campaigns can work:

James Brimley
Circuit Place
Cupertino, CA 95014
(000) 555-0000; email@email.com

November 21, 2003,

Mr. Michael Salhlstrom
Vice President
iVidia, Inc.
332 Moffet Field Blvd.
Mountain View, CA 94040

Dear Mr. Salhlstrom,

I was a supply chain manager at Hewlett-Packard for many years. During the past year, iVidia approached me to explore how it could get on the vendor list for the $4 billion annual product line I was handling there. My answer then was that since HP did not actually either design or manufacture the products it sold, the ODMs who designed and made these products should be the ones doing what you wanted us to do for you!

Now that I have left HP as result of its merger with Compaq, I am free to discuss how you can still pursue your original intent to be a supplier of choice for the products that bears HP labels. The ODMs in Taiwan and the Pacific Rim have their own process of qualifying suppliers so that they become part of the overall supply chain. I know this process intimately and can use this knowledge to help you get on the list. I am also fluent in Chinese.

I would like to explore this more fully by meeting with you in person. We can discuss the main idea in about an hour.

I plan to call you and explore your current interest in becoming HP's supplier of choice for their new and established products.

Cordially,

James Brimly

> James met with iVidia executives the following week. They realized that accomplishing what they originally set out to do would entail someone having to work full time with the Taiwanese ODMs, something they did not appreciate before. Within a week of the first meeting, James was offered a comparable job and he had no competition!

Catherine Jenkins
View Court
Los Altos, CA 94022
(000) 555-0000; email@email.com

July 21, 2003

Ms. Megan Eiken
Director, Marketing and Sales
International Meetings and Events
33 Great America Parkway #22
Santa Clara, CA 95054

Dear Megan,

Thank you for meeting with me today and explaining to me what you are looking for to start a new sales territory in the Silicon Valley. Your company's track record is, indeed, impressive! I think that the Silicon Valley is a good point of entry for your expansion plans in this state.

As I research your competitors, how they market and sell in this area, the market itself, and the forces that are shaping the current market, I find the following:

- Your competitors' main selling strategy is based on opportunistic and transactional selling. They look for companies that are holding or planning to hold major meetings and events, respond to their requirements and then give a low bid to win the deal.

- The overall experience the attendees walk away with is marginal at best. Yes, they come to attend the event but what impact did the overall event and the way the logistics was organized leave on the attendees mind? Are they likely to do more business with the client companies as a result of this experience? My view is pessimistic!

- With the current state of the economy, especially in the Silicon Valley, I think that there is a greater opportunity to be had if you approach the client companies with a more strategic view of these events. One approach can entail doing some research with their attendees and participants and then helping the clients design the entire event based on the expectations coming from this research. I have some ideas on this.

Since California is your new frontier for expansion, wouldn't you like to break new ground in the way this entire offering is presented to your clients here and blow the competition out of the water?

With all your staff that already has their CMPs and direct selling experience, many of whom I will be teaming with, I think the critical areas of focus are what I have outlined above: creating a memorable and actionable participant experience, and strategic selling.

I am looking forward to our next meeting to present some of these ideas in more detail.

Cordially,

Catherine

> CJ did not have either of the two job requirements: CMP or sales experience. But by sending an earlier letter to pique their curiosity, she was able to land an interview. This letter was sent subsequent to that interview, where she was told that there were six candidates ahead of her who met *all* the job requirements. Catherine was invited to the next round of interviews based on this letter and was offered the job two weeks later!

Job Search Etiquette

The dictionary defines etiquette as conduct or procedure required by good breeding or prescribed by authority in social or official life. This definition can be used as a guiding principle. It suggests that etiquette is even more important in a job-search situation than in others. This is perhaps because, often, job-seekers do not even realize that their social behaviors make it difficult for employers to be gracious about being considerate. This consideration can range from returning a repeated phone message left on their voice mail, to explaining something that puzzles a potential candidate. Why? Etiquettes are the lubrication that makes things move smoothly. Ignoring them can create unnecessary friction and hurt. Regardless of their starting point, jobseekers need to be aware of the appropriate etiquette. This is because, when in transition, their focus shifts to their own needs, and they become less aware of how they may be coming across to others. Being unaware of this factor can go against their moving forward and getting what they are looking for. It does not matter if you are out of work looking for a job, or if you already have one and are looking for a change. The level of stress is the same; it may just have a different level of urgency!

Practicing the right etiquette will not only get what you want, it will help you position yourself in a differentiated way, in the eyes of the employers. The converse is that if you are clumsy in the etiquette department, you may not only lose an opportunity that is yours to claim, you may permanently alienate the potential employer beyond the immediate context! If you are a talented person, otherwise fully qualified to claim an opportunity, you will always wonder what went sour in your landing the job you so wanted and were so fit for! Ironically, etiquette demands that those who see your boorish behavior in the process, keep mum about it!

In a limited space it is impossible to provide a complete guide to job-search etiquette. The flavor of the tips provided here can be used to understand the basic behavioral principles that you can leverage in similar situations. When in doubt, think of the other person, not yourself!

The etiquette varies from situation to situation in the job-search process. However, within a certain situation, a particular etiquette can be considered a norm. The following discussion is presented for many of the steps typical in the job search process:

Responding to Posted Jobs

Posted jobs can be either published in the print media or on the job boards. Jobs posted on company bulletin boards and Websites have the same etiquette considerations:

1. Respond to a posting only if you are a strong candidate. Marginal match of your skill to the competencies posted on the open position is a disservice to the process, even if the résumé is sent electronically. In the era of the Internet, where it costs nothing to post your résumé and takes a few seconds to respond to a position, it is all the more important that you follow this discipline. Merely flooding a Website with yet another marginal résumé, is a good way to ensure that you are making the process difficult to others, who may be more qualified than you.

2. Sending an overnight courier package to get attention is a good idea. It takes some effort to find the name of the hiring manager or recipient where you want to send such a response. However, before sending your response in such an impactful way, make sure that your message has enough clout to warrant this special delivery. As more and more find out that sending a FedEx—or other courier—package in the hands of a decision maker can get an audience, the more and more vigilant the recipients are going to become. If this mode of sending a response is just to hector the recipient with the same trite message, that might as well have been sent by email, the impact of the FedEx approach diminishes quickly for all those who rely on it. Ergo, use an appropriate method of sending your message to create an impact commensurate with your message. Do not use a sledgehammer to kill a fly!

3. Do not send a response to a posted opening to everyone in sight. Send it to the recipient named in the posting, unless you have a compelling case for sending it to someone higher up for an impact and action that the response deserves. Use your judgment.

4. Do not call immediately to verify receipt of what you sent. Remember the more common the approach to sending what is asked, the less your "right" to follow-up. You should not even bother to follow-up, where you sent a conventional email response to a job posting, in a tough market, where there are potentially a large number of respondents.

5. Even if the target employer is nearby, do not go personally to hand the résumé to someone there. You may be able to leave it, in the in-basket, at the lobby at best. Unless your response has something compelling, do not waste someone's time by having them come down to the lobby, just so that they have your résumé!

6. Comply with all the *requirements* of the posted position, when sending your response in a familiar way—email. Employers do not like it when respondents do not comply with clearly spelled out requirements. If

you want to use some of the approaches suggested in this book, as guerilla tactics or unconventional methods, use appropriate means of transmittal and connecting with the decision maker.

7. Do not send your response in a format, color, or package that may appear to the recipient as off-the-wall, or presented just to get their attention. The message must have the same attention-getting power. Remember the saying: the medium is the message.

Following-up

After sending the response to an opportunity, following up depends on how you responded and what the original opportunity was. If you responded to a job with a résumé and cover letter, in a routine way to a generic address, you have no recourse to any specific follow up. This is why sending such responses put you at a disadvantage. The following list summarizes etiquettes for following up on what you already sent:

1. If you know the name of the person to whom the response was sent, leave a message with details, so that the person can easily track your response without having to research it further. For example, if you are David Smith—or have a similarly common name—don't just say, "Sally this Dave Smith and I am calling about the résumé I sent about a month ago. Could you please call me and tell me what the status of that job is?" A more actionable message might be, "Hi Sally this is David Smith. About a month back, I sent my résumé, in connection with your posting for a shipping clerk, job # 22342. I would really appreciate your calling me at 123-555-2212 and leaving me a message about the status of that job. Once again, that number is 123-555-2212 and thank you!" Preferably this telephone number should be the same that you used on the résumé. Do not expect to hear if your original response was a routine one, and do not keep calling, if you did not hear back the first time.

2. If you are calling to follow-up on a courier package you sent in response to a job opening, do not assume that the package is with the addressee. Look at the delivery signature commonly available for courier deliveries, and start with that person. Then sequentially trace the package and see where it might be in the chain. Then call that person. Sometimes, a package is redirected after it is opened.

3. Once you connect with the person who has your package, gently explore whether they had a chance to read it. Give them a reason to open the package, by saying something intriguing and suggest that you talk later. Be brief and diplomatic and assess where you need to begin

so that the person is obliged to open it and take the next steps—your original intent behind sending such a message.

4. If the person with whom you connected asks you to call back, or suggests that they would call you back at a certain time, give some additional time to reconnect if they fail to call you, so that you do not look overly anxious.

5. If you are navigating through a battery of administrators, to get to someone higher up in an organization, treat them with courtesy and respect. They may decide to "disconnect" you if, they see you as a pest.

6. Always be thankful for any information you get and any courtesy you are accorded, no matter who that person is at the other end where you are trying to get in.

7. There is a thin line between being persistence and being a pest. After two rounds of reminders, find some alternate approach to getting the attention to be called back.

Networking

Networking etiquettes are flouted most frequently with unwitting consequences! How? It is perhaps because people are not even aware of the simple slipups that can cascade into a full-blown avoidance by the person at the other end of the network; amity can turn into enmity with a simple oversight, especially if you are looking to the other person to do you a favor! The following tips are a good starting point to adopt proper "netiquettes":

1. Your successful networking is based on giving more than you take. Always keep track of what is coming your way from your network and make sure that you maintain the balance with the network owing you. Not the other way around! For example if you get two leads from your network in a week, give three or more back to the same network. Always manage to give in kind.

2. If you want to contact someone, based on a tip you got from within your network, make sure that you tell the person, how you came about their name. Always reveal the source of the referral when making new contacts.

3. Make sure you keep the boundaries of your expectations, with each person, within your network. Do not push these boundaries. Your desperation, in getting what you want, does not constitute an emergency on the part of the person who is trying to help you! This is why it is a good idea to make networking a habit in times, good and bad.

4. If your source gives you the name of a hiring manager, do not assume that you can directly contact that manager. Some companies have strict rules about keeping the hiring managers away from the flux of inquiries and persistent calls from interested candidates. Ask the person if it would be appropriate for you to contact the manager or if they are able to present your response to that manager. All things being equal, you should prefer the former. It lets you keep track of what is going on, and you eliminate a third person from getting in the way of your future interactions with that manager. If this were to materialize your way, always keep your contact appraised of what is going on by sending a courtesy copy of your exchanges with the manager.

5. In addition to saying "thank you," every time you get help, *call* once in a while just to thank that person and for no other reason! Also send a thank you note in the mail. Many consider receiving this special gesture, much more meaningful than just receiving a "thank you" email.

6. Make sure that you keep the boundaries of when and where to call your network contact, to get what you are looking for. The only contacts you should consider calling at home and off hours, are the Nuclear Contacts of the Networking Hierarchy, Figure 3, Key-4: Networking.

7. If you are using the Internet as a channel of communication within your networking group, do not use emails to solicit petitions, send spam, and other messages of commercial import or the ones that promote your personal agenda.

8. Do not assume that those within your networking group share your religious, political, or social beliefs. If you foist them on the group, it may retaliate by alienation!

9. Do not assume that if you subscribe to an email group, such as a Yahoo! Group, that your message posted on such a board will be read and heeded by all who receive it. Many routinely ignore such group messages. If you want someone's attention, then send at least a personal message to each one!

10. Keep your email messages brief and with a subject line carefully phrased to pique curiosity and get action!

eMails

Over time, emails have become the preferred means of communication, even in job search. Initially emails were considered an informal and a more intimate means of communication. As a result, those using them were relaxed about their use; usage, spelling, and other oversights were considered excusable. Now that emails have become ubiquitous and lifeblood of all business communications, more attention needs to be paid to such messages.

The list of suggestions below for emailing is not just limited to job search domain; following this etiquette will enhance your social savvy as well:

1. When composing *important* emails, use a good word processing application and compose the message as if writing a letter. This discipline will force your having to write with care. Using the more sophisticated features of the word-processing applications, as grammar and spell check will formalize the message. This approach also provides a retrievable record of the file that can be stored on the hard drive under a suitably named folder, as *Important emails*. Do not compose an important message in an email itself for these reasons. Once the message is satisfactory, cut and paste the message in the outgoing email window and put the final touches on the entire message, including the Subject line.

2. Every email should be spell-checked to ensure no obvious spelling problems. Messages composed within an email application allow for a limited ability to check for errors in a composed message. Reading a spell-checked message can further assure a more correct outgoing message. Spell-check programs do not differentiate between words that sound similar but have different spellings such as "to" and "too."

3. To prevent an accidental transmittal of an incomplete or unvetted message, especially for critical emails, insert the recipient address *after* you have completed writing the entire message. Your sending a blind copy (bcc) of the outgoing email to yourself will further ensure how the transmitted message actually looks.

4. Some email browsers allow retrieving messages, if the retrieval is done before the recipient opens your message. Avoid this practice for critical emails. Using the above tips will prevent many errors and inadvertent oversights that prompt these retrievals. The reason for avoiding email retrievals is that the recipient is notified that you are retrieving your message. For important emails, this may not be to your best advantage.

5. If you are not sure if a certain message is appropriate or that it may be misconstrued, wait before sending it and then read it again. If possible, ask someone else to read it to be sure.

6. It is a good idea to avoid attachments to emails because of the computer viruses. If the message in the body of the email was composed using a word processor application, as in #1, a recommended practice is

to copy and paste this message, in the email body, in preference to attaching that file to the email. If you are sending a résumé, make sure that the recipient will accept it as an attachment.

A safer bet is to compose the body of the message and below the message pasting the electronic version of the résumé, in addition to attaching the file in its original version to the same email message. This leader message could be your cover letter. Mentioning this fact in the body of the email, or even in the Subject line of the email, prevents any confusion as to what the attachment is. This approach gives the recipient an option to deal with the attachment, the way they prefer, and you have a better chance of your résumé getting read.

7. Choose the email Subject carefully. Most people get dozens of emails. It is estimated that hiring managers typically get over 250 messages every day (including voice mails). For your email to get noticed, it must have a compelling Subject line to get the reader's attention, as they scan their inbox for important messages. So, instead of choosing the Subject as *Dave's Résumé*, using *A Must-Interview Candidate* may create enough intrigue to the hiring manager to take a look at your email. One fresh graduate from Stanford had his résumé opened by a recruiter because she felt that the Subject line *Fresh meat from Stanford* was curious and creative.

8. Do not rely on the screen name (also known as User ID or email address) to identify you to the reader. You must have a complete identifier in the Signature block so that the reader does not have to guess who the sender is. This common courtesy should be extended to *all* emails, not just to those for hiring managers or recruiters.

Many screen names are cryptic and do not mean much to others. Having a complete signature block as a template created for all outgoing emails is a good practice. This block should have your fill name, telephone contact information, and any other detail that you consider relevant. It is also a good idea to have your email address as a part of this template. Why? Often, emails are forwarded, and in some browsers, the originating email header is dropped. In such cases, the person to whom the email was forwarded, does not have the originating address, other than that of the person who forwarded the message. In such cases you miss the opportunity to hear back directly from this person. Some have a pithy quote as a part of their signature block. If you do have such a quote, it is a good idea to make sure that it is memorable, appropriate, and is refreshed every month or so.

9. It is a good idea to choose your screen name carefully without making a statement. Avoid sending negative messages (unhappy@yahoo.com, jobless@hotmail.com) through your screen name; also avoid making a statement, political, social, or otherwise (Democrat@aol.com, antiwar@sbcglobal.net, atheist@Webtv.net), even if you feel strongly about how it ought to be. In the stages of making a first impression, your identification should not make an impact; your message should. How you choose to identify yourself may prevent your message from ever getting through, no matter how compelling.

10. Because of the casual nature of the medium, many respond to emails with minimal forethought (writing like they think). Responding to a message that is negative, insinuating, or downright angry, can start a cycle of angry exchanges. Do not send angry emails. Do not say anything in an email, you would not on a TV interview or a public address system.

11. It is good idea to maintain the original Subject header in responding to someone's email. This allows for an easy contextual connection for the sender, when receiving your message. It is also a good idea to include the original message, above or below your text in the body of the email. Often, many keep the same Subject header for emails long after the original context becomes irrelevant. For example, someone looking for an email address from an old message may locate the old message and use a "Reply to" to create a new message, now with a completely different subject matter, without changing what pops up in the email window with the old Subject heading. Avoid this practice. It shows laziness.

12. Avoid sending email messages with large files. Some graphic files, even in the body of an email, can easily hold megabits of data, which can clog mailboxes and create problems loading the messages, especially with a slow Internet connection.

13. Use "Reply All" button carefully and sparingly. Make sure that your response does need to go to all those whose names appear in the original message.

14. When you can use a more personal means of communication, as a telephone call, a handwritten note, or a face-to-face meeting consider it. It makes you stand out. Remember, too, that many employees do not check their mail slots regularly, since such messages are becoming rare.

So, if you do send a message by mail, mention that in an email to alert the person to look for it. Doing so, also will make you stand out.

15. When an email message requires you to do some research before responding, and the response will be delayed beyond a day or two because of this, *acknowledge* the message immediately and mention when you might be getting back with the *response* and state the reason briefly. Once you make this commitment, make sure you meet or beat the scheduled response date.

16. When you are on vacation, make sure your auto response is turned on, notifying the email senders of your unavailability. It is a good idea to give an avenue for connecting for urgent matters.

17. It is difficult to know whether an organization has a dominant email or voice mail culture. The best defense against this quandary, when sending a message, is to do both: whenever possible, leave a voice mail after sending an email to a person, using the same Subject header as the one in the email. Also be *very brief* in the voice mail message. This simple expedient will create a memory jog for the recipient when looking at a barrage of unopened emails.

18. If you have not received a response from someone to whom you had sent an email, do not assume that they have received it or seen it. I once received an angry message from a jobseeker. I had presented a seminar to a group, to which he belonged, and had volunteered to help with their résumés. He had sent me his résumé, attached to an email, which was lost in a sea of other emails. There was no mention of a résumé in the body of the message. The subject header was: Nice meeting you! He had a cryptic screen name to boot, which made it even more difficult to identify who he was. To prevent such mishaps, always make it easy for the email recipient to know what they are getting, and how to get at it quickly. Clearly stating what you expect from them at the top of the message also helps.

19. It is common to have multiple email boxes. If you send an email from one mailbox, make sure that when the response is received to that box, your system will accept it. Many email addresses that are available for free, limit the size of the incoming messages. Even mentioning the email box to which you want response sent in the body of the message, will not prevent a mishap, because most respondent just hit the "Reply" button in response to an incoming message.

Telephone Calls

Telephone calls are the mainstay of networking communication. And yet, few follow the etiquettes to make this a pleasant experience! The following etiquettes are a summary of some of the key telephone etiquettes:

Incoming calls:

1. Have a businesslike greeting on your voice mail. Identify yourself and your telephone number in the greeting.

2. With the caller ID, a standard feature now, do not install security screens on incoming calls. These filters can be barriers to callers trying to reach you, including your potential employers. Use voice screening instead, available on recording machines.

3. Have a separate line for all your Internet activity. An Internet connection on a line can block it for hours and frustrate those who are trying to reach you, including your potential employers.

4. If a call comes at a time when it is inconvenient for you to take it, explain why and ask if you can call them back at a time that is best for them.

5. If you are angry, upset, or feel that you are not in balance, let the machine take the incoming call.

6. Do not betray your emotions or state of mind to the caller. Telephone calls are notoriously sensitive to the way your tone comes across to the other party. Be very aware of this and manage your emotional state for all calls, incoming and outgoing!

Outgoing calls:

Make outgoing calls at a time that does not impose on the called party. Typically these times are on a weekday: 9 AM to 10 PM (9 PM is preferred) for calls made to a home, and during regular business hours for all business calls; weekends 10 AM to 6 PM for all home calls. Avoid dinner or lunch hours even for home calling. The only exceptions may be those within your Nuclear Contact list (See Figure-3, Networking Universe, Key-4).

1. If you are calling someone on their cell phone, ask if they can talk, or politely ask where they are so that if they are driving, you may want to ask them for a more convenient time for that call. With the one-number system now in place, it is difficult to ascertain if the person you are calling is on the cell phone or wired phone. Always ask, after identifying yourself and stating your reason for the call, if they can talk. Do not

assume that they can, even if you are returning their call *within* minutes of receiving their message.

2. When the called person answers your call, immediately identify yourself fully—and not by merely saying, "Hi this is Dave"—so that you can engage in a conversation without the called person having to wonder "which Dave is this?" and losing time in engaging with you right away. Also, do not assume that even though you are calling someone in response to their message, that they will immediately recognize who you are, and why they should be talking to you.

3. If you called someone and the line gets disconnected, no matter what the reason, *you* reinitiate the call. The called person waits for the phone to ring again for a few minutes, otherwise they will go about their business.

4. Do not discuss sensitive, gossipy, personally offensive, or insinuating information on the phone. If you want to give some adverse feedback to the person, ask them to meet you, and do it in person. Likewise, do not leave messages of similar nature on someone's voicemail.

5. Keep your calls brief and to the point.

Interviews

Interview etiquettes range from how you appear for the interview, to what to do with your briefcase when you are ready to sit down prior to the interview, to how you leave the lobby on your way out. The following is a suggested listing of etiquette that govern these behaviors:

1. Be on time for the interview. In fact, the guideline is to arrive at least 30 minutes prior to the interview and get settled. The details are in Key-5: At the Interview.

2. Dress appropriately for the interview: dress up and not down. You can always remove one or more pieces of your clothing or accessories and carry with you, if you suddenly feel that you're overdressed.

3. Dress conservatively. If you need help, visit a clothing store that specializes in business attire and seek advice of floor personnel. Do not plan to make a statement with your clothes; you may not get past it. Do not let your clothes enter the door before you do.

4. Introduce yourself to the receptionist and state why you are there, whom you are going to see and when. Mention that you are early and not to announce you quite yet. Make friends with this person by holding

a casual conversation. Do not demand a beverage or any other service from this person. They have job to do—typically, answering phone calls and greeting visitors.

5. Do not make any adverse comments about the parking facilities, temperature in the room, coffee (too strong!) or any thing else to the receptionist (Lobby Ambassador). You really do not know how this person is connected. In one instance, a candidate made an off-the-cuff, disparaging comment about who might be running the company, at which he was interviewing, not realizing that the receptionist was the CEO's daughter, doing a summer internship.

6. When your time comes for you to be announced to the host or the interviewer, do not assume that the receptionist would remember this, since you mentioned it when you checked in. A variety of duties in which they are engaged can easily distract them from your needs. If that person is on the phone for a while, wait patiently even though your time to be calling your contact is nigh, and you cannot get this person's attention. If appropriate, hand the person a note politely and unobtrusively.

7. If you spill something in the lobby, as you wait for your time, clean up, even if the receptionist does not see the spill. Often, these people and others who causally come in contact with you are asked to report their impressions of you for critical hires.

8. When the interviewer or their representative comes to greet you, be cordial even if they have kept you waiting. Do not suggest their lateness by looking at your wristwatch. Smile and shake hands. Let them lead you to the place where the interview is going to take place. Practice some icebreakers with this person on the way to the interview.

9. At the place of the interview, ask to be seated and then sit down comfortably where you can put your briefcase or other interview paraphernalia. Place it down on the floor and not on the desk or table in front of you.

10. Do not interrupt the interviewer. Do not argue even if you know that the interviewer is wrong.

11. Take notes on a notepad and not on a laptop or a handheld device close to your face!

12. Do not ask any questions about the company's woes to the interviewer, the answers to which may put that person in a compromising light. You

are also likely to compromise your chances of getting in. Once a client, while being interviewed by a company's CEO asked him about the SEC investigation that was announced in the media the morning of her interview. After several rounds of successful interviews, she was a shoo-in. This question put off the CEO and the process died in its tracks.

13. When the interview is over, get up, organize your belongings, and quickly get ready to leave the area with the person escorting you out. Do not stretch their patience as you carefully organize your many belongings, if they became disheveled during the interview. Organize them later, on your own.

14. Shake hands, and thank the person for their time and ask what the next steps are and a timeline. Do not get overly obsessive about timelines, or accountability in the follow-up process. Do this somewhat naturally by practicing it before the interview.

15. On the way out thank the receptionist for taking good care of you and ask the person their name.

Thank-you! Notes

Thank you notes following an interview are critical to making them remember you. They can also be used to recover from something that might have gone wrong during the interview. Mailed thank you notes are more formal and memorable than emails. Do both for interviews that matter. Samples of thank you email and notes are shown in Key-5.

References

Etiquettes where references are concerned vary, depending on the level of the reference. Although they all deserve to be treated with consideration and courtesy, those who offer to give you high-level reference need to be treated with special care and you should let them know that!

The following etiquette guide may help you finesse your references well:

1. Identify your references early in the process. Let them know that you are planning to include them in the reference process. Remind them about the aspect of your reference you expect them to provide.

2. Some companies have a policy of not providing a reference. Many managers, however, are willing to provide a personal reference. This is why asking early in the process can help you position your references so that there are no surprises.

3. Occasionally, some will agree to give you a written reference. If this happens while you are in the job associated with this person, it is that much more convenient. In any case, if the person agrees to a written reference, write the reference letter yourself and pass it by the person. This way you can decide what is appropriate from that reference in the context of your needs. Do not assume that this person will reference you the way you need it. Usually, it is much easier for anyone to merely edit a letter and sign it than having the need to draft it first. Use this advantage to modulate the message the way you want it written—within some constraints.

4. Carry these letters of reference in your interview portfolio and when the time comes for the reference discussion, show the person asking the question. Sometimes this may obviate the need to calling your reference, and hasten the process to your advantage.

5. When the potential employer asks for them, call your references, even though you had put them on notice earlier. The reason is that for final referencing, you may need to remind them again, and it also gives you a chance to prepare them to respond in line with what the needs are to bolster your case. Request the reference to highlight that aspect of the discussion that you think is relevant.

6. If appropriate, request that they call you upon being contacted by the potential employer. This is a courtesy to you and this helps you confirm that the process is underway. Do not expect this courtesy from all references. Do not keep calling your references to check if they have heard from your potential employer.

7. Once you know that the process is complete, either through the offer, or rejection, or any other means, promptly call each of the references or send a note (email is acceptable) of thanks. If you get the job, going the extra distance—a thank you! card, flowers, or a gift, as appropriate, can protect the references for your future needs.

8. During the process, check with the person to whom you gave the list, to see if there are any problems contacting the references on that list. It is appropriate for the references to call that person preemptively as well, if you so chose.

9. It is not appropriate to call and ask the potential employer what the references said about you, especially if you are turned down for the job.

10. If you are turned down, it a good idea to ask for a debrief from the company. This, again, is a courtesy that the company is extending to you. If the debrief mentions any items related to a reference that surprise you, do not probe for details, unless they are volunteered as a part of the debriefing.

11. After you confirm that the process is completed, call all your references and inform them that the process is complete. Tell them the outcome, if you already know it, and thank them for their support. Some of them may not have been called and they should know that they are now off the hook. You must promptly communicate with all your references and thank them, even if you did *not* get the job.

12. If you were turned down after reference checking, do not assume that it was because of what the references might have said. Do not hector references to tell you what they might have said in their conversations. You must protect your references for future needs.

Negotiating Offers

Much of the process during this step is outlined in the section on negotiations. The following is a summary of etiquettes during this step:

1. Do not assume that you can negotiate what is being offered. Ask.

2. Always go back to the last person who made the offer and not necessarily your hiring manager.

3. Do not assume, that just because you are in negotiations, that you will get what you are seeking. The offer can be withdrawn if the employer so decides.

4. Tread lightly. You should decide before entering into negotiations the down side. You should be willing to walk away if the negotiations collapse.

5. After you have been turned down, and your offer is withdrawn, do not go back begging for the same or lesser job for lower pay!

6. Decide on which items you want to negotiate, lay them out as you enter the discussions and then stop after the process is completed. If the outcome is not favorable, do not plan to move on to other items of the offer.

7. Above all, be pleasant, flexible, and courteous throughout the process. Always remind them that you are excited about the job.

Acknowledging Help

During your job search, many provide help, even unbeknownst to you or some even unexpectedly and pleasantly! Keep a list of all those who have helped you, going all the way back to the original lead that got you the first interview. The following etiquette lists what you can do after the process is completed:

1. Depending upon the significance of the help you received from a person, thank them appropriately. Those who provided help above and beyond acknowledge it commensurately: a gift, lunch, or a thank you card can be some suggestions in this department.

2. Acknowledge your gratitude in a timely way. The times following a job offer can be hectic. Within the first month of your being offered the job is a good time.

3. Be *specific* about acknowledging the help that got you the job. Merely stating a vacant "Thanks for your help" is not as impactful and proper as saying "John, your lead and the insight you gave me about what the company was looking for, and what I could present them during my interviews, was instrumental in my landing this job. Thank you very much!" is far more appropriate. The person who went out of their way to help you likes to know that you acknowledged correctly what that person did to help you in the process. Do not skip this detail, because you feel that the person already should know. It is not what they know, it is how you acknowledge it that makes for proper etiquette!

4. Do not forget to thank all those with whom you came in contact, during the interview process at the company where you would be working. They are now your colleagues and associates. Even the person in the lobby who greeted you on the first interview is worth sending a thank you to! If you do that, it would be much easier to make them your friends, once you start working there.

Starting your New Job

Starting a new job can be exciting, especially if you are coming out of being jobless. The following etiquette is suggested at this step of the process of your transition:

1. On the first day, show up on time. Dress a bit more formally than you would normally at that company. You may be taken around and introduced to others that day; your photo might be taken. If you are senior

staff (director and above), you might even be introduced to important clients and dignitaries.

2. During the initial stages of employment be patient with all the administrative work that has to be done properly. Do not show your impatience with those who are trying to get this done. Let them do their job.

3. Express to your manager that you are glad to be on board and that you are looking forward to teaming with this person.

4. Many companies have initiation traditions that can be as benign as going out to lunches or bars at the end of the day. Accommodate these rituals, even if they seem odd, and enjoy them.

5. If you have some habits that define how you do your job, be open to seeing how things are done at your new place.

6. Do not criticize something just because it looks odd or different to you. Wait to offer your opinion. Go with the flow, at least initially.

7. Do not to gossip and talk behind someone's back. Understand the power structure in the new place before you decide which camp you want to belong to. This can portend your future there!

8. One week after you have started in your new job, visit all the job boards and Websites, where you had originally posted your résumé and delete it!

During the Holidays

Holidays are a great time to be showing appreciation to others and showing it in a memorable way. It is also a good time to reconnect or otherwise show that you care about the relationships. Recruiters, references, counselors, and network contacts are among those who need to be shown gratitude in a fit way. This ranges from sending holiday cards to special gift baskets and mementos with notes that express your gratitude for what they have done and what they might do for you. Use the following guidelines:

1. Make a list and segment it by how much each person in a category has done to advance your cause and present them with something appropriate. If you expect that you may need someone's help in the near future, put them on the list as well.

2. Send a personal note or greetings with a specific message of gratitude and not a generic one. The more specific you craft a message and the more specifically you acknowledge the person, the more impact the note carries.

3. If you are on a budget, as those out-of-work might be, create your own gifts as baskets of goodies or a work of art that is presentable. Wrap it nicely and present it elegantly so that it looks thoughtful and expensive.

4. If you do not receive an acknowledgement, do not call to find out if they received your gift. Send a subsequent note and mention that you hope that they received the gift you had sent them. A note or email wishing them a Happy New Year is a good opportunity to do this. If they still do not acknowledge, move on.

5. If convenient and appropriate, take those who have done things for you to lunch during the holiday period. This is yet another way to make them remember you.

6. Where possible, hand-carry your gift, present it in person, and show your gratitude.

Summary Key-7: Making it All Work!

This Key rounds out the information needed for a successful job search and has a variety of topics, which can give you an edge in the job-search campaign. Each is summarized below.

The Age Advantage: This topic deals with how to overcome perceptions and barriers around your age and leverage these to get what you are looking for. Age can cut both ways—too young or too old. Examples of two résumés, one a 23-year old fresh graduate and, another, a 63-year old out-of-work engineer, are presented as cases in point.

Overcoming Cultural Barriers: Cultural barriers stem from your upbringing, prejudices, preferences, and ignorance. They can vitiate your otherwise effective campaign to land a job. Review the 10 tips provided in this section.

Understanding Program Management: Before you go pursuing a program management position it is important to understand what it means and how different flavors of program management can mean different things to different employers.

Informational Interviews: This section covers informational interviews as a tool to get insights into a job or career of interest. It shows when you can set up an informational interview and succeed using that to leverage it into a job search.

Job Fairs: This section covers the whats and the hows of job fairs including tips on how to leverage a job fair to maximize your involvement in one.

Contracting: With more and more employers outsourcing their routine activities and hiring contract labor force to develop a flexible cost model for their enterprise, contracting has become a growing industry. Pursuing a full-time job can sometimes interfere with a contracting opportunity. This section presents some tips and two sample résumés for both a job-search campaign and a contracting campaign.

Guerilla Job Search: This section deals with how to manage the non-traditional and highly leveraged approaches to a job search. It presents two mindsets of a buyer, which entail two marketing avenues: Freudian and Skinnerian. How a guerilla campaign integrates these two to create an effective outcome is discussed with sample letters.

Job Search Etiquette: This section deals with how one needs to behave to keep their social and professional interactions with others in good order to successfully complete their job search and keep good ongoing relationships with those with whom they come in contact. Etiquette protocols in 12 situational categories are described to help those navigate through the minefield for smooth interactions with others. This is for your own success and not so much to benefit others! Following proper etiquette will create differentiation that is easy, and is a habit that goes well beyond the job search. It is a life skill.

Epilogue

"Change before you have to."

—Jack Welch, Chairman (1981–2001), General Electric

Introduction

This book is written for those facing a career transition. It is also for those who need to manage life's transitions, triggered by job-related episodes. Regardless of the nature of their transition, the process is not just about survival, but also about success. What better place to start the discussion of success than to begin where it all started, from the one who defined the very concept of survival: Charles Darwin?

Revisiting Darwin

Although Darwin maintained that the fit species survives and flourishes, few understand the meaning of what this profound statement really implies. In simple terms, it means that those who can *adapt* survive. To take this concept in today's context, those who anticipate change and can reinvent themselves *before* the change comes, have the best chance of surviving.

Ongoing globalization, outsourcing, mergers, and industry consolidations have created tsunami-like economic forces, which have knocked many, who were otherwise sailing placidly, out of the water. Such forces, too, are not temporary. They will morph with time and will continue to challenge the unwary and the unprepared. Continued off-shoring and outsourcing, and ongoing shifts in the models of full-time employment, as we know them, will whipsaw broad spectrums of the workforce unabated.

What lies ahead now is even more uncertain, challenging, and chaotic. Times, good and bad, are cyclical. To change the current tide of events, everyone affected by them, especially in the way their jobs have emerged, must individually and collectively transform their mindsets, and invent a new set of rules and redefine how they look at value creation and compensation.

447

What endures is what survives the passage of time. In the emergent job scene, it is the change that is constant now, and not its aftermath! But, even then, everyone needs a formula for survival. But, what *is* it?

The following seven-point survival guide can be of help. It is hoped that regardless of what state you are in, and regardless of the times, you can start adopting this guide in your own everyday living.

1. **Sense Change:** Being alert to the first signs of change is key. Find ways to look for *patterns* and develop a *systemic* view of what is happening around you. To acquire a systemic view requires transcending the simple cause-and-effect perspective. In a systemic view, one learns to adopt a view based on *interrelationships* within a complex environment, sometimes counter to conventional wisdom. It is the counterintuitive view that reveals the hidden opportunities.

    Those who dismiss each onslaught of change or signal, as just another discrete incident, can never overcome those who can detect the *patterns* of change, and then take decisive action. It is the sudden change that is easy to react to and marshal enough action for, so that one can move past it. But more insidious is the slow and imperceptible change, the early detection of which can give an edge to those who can sense it.

    Mere sensing of change is not enough; one must learn to manage it. Accelerating transition through the change process is critical. No one can avoid the change transition, but anyone can manage how to navigate through it effectively as discussed in Key-1, in The Change Curve.

    Also, it is difficult to prepare for adversity when things are going well. Most tend to do more of what is causing them success, hoping that their momentum will be their ally. In times of rapid and chaotic change, this momentum can be an adversary. A leader is one who can transform that momentum into agility when the going is still good, and not let it translate into inertia. Most, on the other hand, wait for something to go wrong, before they think that change is required. And, then, it is often too late! The biggest enemy of assured success is past success. There is no teacher like failure. Surprise is not a preamble to failure; it is the result of it. That does not mean that you have to wait to fail to reinvent yourself. Anticipating failure is also a way to avoid it and finding ways to reinvent yourself before you *have* to!

2. **Discover Opportunities:** Change often brings losses as it brings opportunities simultaneously. This is even true of what is happening in the current job market. Yes, there have been massive job losses in the US,

Europe, and the developed economies due to off-shoring and other factors. There have been brand new jobs too, during the same period, just for the asking! The best part is that these "hidden jobs" are "up" the value chain, closer to the customer; hence, they are worth more to the companies prescient enough to fill them. Many examples of such hidden opportunities that even companies did not recognize, is how this book came to life. Examples of these successes are presented throughout this book. Every change spawns opportunities. Those who can claim first can trump everyone else!

3. **Manage Fear:** In uncertain times it is normal to fear what is next, and develop apprehension around the unknown. Fear is healthy. It makes us cautious and allows us to plan for contingencies, rather than making us reckless. Being brave does not imply being fearless; it implies being decisive in the presence of fear and knowing how to manage that fear. This is what leaders do! Courage is required only in the presence of fear; if you are not scared you are not leading, especially your own destiny! This topic is addressed more fully in Key-1: Getting with the Program. Developing familiarity with it is critical to success in any endeavor, not just career management.

4. **Reinvent Constantly:** If change is a constant, reinvention is its handmaiden. Constantly asking what creates value today and what will create value tomorrow and the day after are good beacons for one to signpost their reinvention agenda. Transforming everyday skills into a portfolio of transportable gifts is not as hard as most think. Articulating Unique Skills in the résumé section of this book—Key-3: Presenting Yourself—is one way to do this. This concept must be expanded to our everyday thinking of how we create *ongoing* value and in our defining and *consciously* owning our own genius.

5. **Court Progressive Minds:** In times good and bad, surrounding yourself with progressive and open minds is critical. It is easy to find those who share your predicament and woes and find comfort in commiserating. Skeptics and cynics are plenty, but finding responsible optimists, who can map out a future from the jungle of chaos to energize even the most despaired and paralyzed minds, is key to the future. It is easy to find those who can spout off ten ways why certain approaches would not work, but finding just one who can galvanize those that they touch with an inspiring message, are worth celebrating because they mobilize you to win.

Playing to win has to do with having an abiding faith in one's potential and trusting the universe for help in difficult times. It is often said that we, as humans, often operate at about five percent of our own potential. Much of the limitation to the full use of our faculties comes from our own limiting beliefs, otherwise known as our judgment. By extending or suspending our judgment, even a little bit, so that we can tap an additional five percent in our judgment, we can easily double our operating powers and creativity! Finding ways to tap deep within our own reservoir of talent, spirit, and power can provide us the impetus we need to creatively find ways to identify opportunities and to overcome challenges.

On the career front, this book shows many avenues of how to claim even non-existent jobs to keep a career on track. In life's journey, then, this practice needs to be expanded to every endeavor we undertake.

In tough times, it is easy to despair and surrender to whatever comes and accept it as inevitable. Those who despair give up hope and abandon their dreams. The universe puts you on this plane with a purpose, and if you believe in its power to help you, while focusing on your dream, you will achieve it.

6. **Display Self Respect:** When times are tough and nothing is going right, it is easy to feel beaten down and lose self worth! But, if you take what is happening in stride, you will realize that this is just a phase that one needs to deal with until better times come. They always do; not just by waiting, but by taking positive action. There is no reason to surrender self-esteem in condescension just because times are bad. Remember what Eleanor Roosevelt said: "*No one makes you feel inferior without your consent.*"

7. **Forge Core Values:** As much as we have exhorted about change and embracing the new, there is only one legacy: your core values. Take time to define what you stand for. On the life's anvil, hammer out your core beliefs. Tough times are golden opportunities to define what you stand for and what your core values are. Being authentic in everything they do is a core value for many leaders. This is why in Key-1 "My Truth!" one tool is provided to help those in transition so that their job-search campaign can be authentic. Reflecting on what has happened and what you want to have happen are key to forging your core values. The acid test comes when the going gets tough and you have to make choices

that dictate your survival. When all else evaporates what still remains of substance are your core values and true relationships!

These are scary times. These are also exciting times because they present to us an uncertain world. It is the uncertainty that provides abundance of opportunities for those who see themselves as leaders of their own destiny. Leadership requires confidence, courage, speed, creativity, simplicity, a sense of ordinariness, and a deep faith in oneself. All of these qualities will be tested in times of crisis. The thought I would like to leave you with is this: if you cannot dare yourself in the present times to do what you have never done before, no one will!

Notes:

Summary: Epilogue

This end chapter focuses on how to look at change and how to make it your ally and not your enemy. A seven-point prescription is presented on Darwin's dictum, as it applies to the current and future job market. The message in the end is that change is constant and one must develop strategies to stay ahead of the change. During uncertain times, one must exploit opportunities by first finding them and then daring oneself to conquer them to come on top!

The following is the summary prescription:

1. Sense Change

2. Discover Opportunities

3. Manage Fear

4. Reinvent Constantly

5. Court Progressive Minds

6. Display Self-Respect

7. Forge Core Values

Bibliography

"Our life is like a ten-speed bike. Most of us have gears we never use."

—Charles Schultz, Cartoonist (1922–2000)

Key-1: Getting with the Program

Adrienne, Carol. *The Purpose of Your Life: Finding Your Place In The World Using Synchronicity, Intuition, and Uncommon Sense.* Harper Collins, 1999.

Black, Joe D., L. Tyler Nelson. *The Leadership of Change: A Workshop for Leaders and Managers,* 1991.

Briggs, Isabel Myers, with Peter B. Myers. *Gifts Differing: Understanding Personality Type.* Consulting Psychologists Press, Inc., Reprint Edition, 1995.

Bronson, Po. *What Should I do with My Life? The True Story of People Who Answered the Ultimate Question.* Random House, 2003.

Buckingham, Marcus, Curt Coffman. *First, Break All the Rules: What the Worlds Greatest Managers Do Differently.* Simon & Schuster Adult Publishing Group, 1999.

Carnegie, Dale, Dorothy Carnegie (Editor), Arthur R. Pell, (Editor). *How to Win Friends and Influence People.* Simon & Schuster Adult Publishing Group, Revised Edition, 1982.

Covey, Steven R. *The 7 Habits of Highly Effective people: Powerful Lessons in Personal Change.* Simon & Schuster Adult Publishing Group.1990.

Embree, Marlowe. *Type Reporter* No. 79, 12/00. Chapel Road, Fairfax Station, VA 22039; 703-764-5370.

Goldman, Daniel. *Emotional Intelligence: Why it can matter more than IQ.* Bantam Books, Inc., 1997.

Johnson, Spencer. *Who Moved My Cheese? An Amazing Way to Deal With Change in Your Work and Your Life.* Simon & Schuster Adult Publishing Group, 1999.

Laney, Marti Olsen Laney. *The Introvert Advantage: How to Thrive in an Extraverted World.* Workman Publishing, 2002.

Osborne, Carol. *The Art of Resilience: 100 Paths to Wisdom and Strength in an Uncertain World.* Crown Publishing Group, 1997.

Ray, Michael, Rochelle Myers. *Creativity in Business.* Double Day & Company, Incorporated, a division of Bantam Doubleday, 1981.

Susan J. Jeffers. *Feel the Fear And Do It Anyway* Fawcett Book Group, 1996.

Tieger, Paul D., Barbara Barron-Tieger, Deborah Baker, (editor). *Do what You Are: Discover the Perfect Career for You Through the Secrets of Personality Type.* Little Brown & Company, 2001.

Key-2: Starting at the Start

Anthony, Mitch. *The New Retirementality: Planning Your Life and Living Your Dreams At Any Age You Want.* Dearborn Trade, 2001.

Beer, Michael, Bart Spector, et al. *Managing Human Assets: The Groundbreaking Harvard Business School Program.* Free Press, 1985.

Block, Peter. *Flawless Consulting: A Guide to Getting Your Expertise Used.* John Wiley & Sons, Incorporated, 1999.

Bolles, Richard. *What Color is Your Parachute? A Practical Manual for Job-Hunters and Career Changers.* Ten Speed Press, 2004.

Bridges, William P. *Transitions, Making Sense of Life's Changes: Strategies for coping with difficult, painful, and confusing times in your life.* Addison Wesley, 1980.

Dalton Gene W., Paul H. Thompson. *Novations: Strategies for Career Management.* Addison Welsley School, 1985.

Deming, W. Edwards. *Out of the Crisis.* MIT Press, Reprint, 2000.

Gurney, Darrell W., *CPC: Headhunters Revealed.* Hunter Arts Publishing, 2000.

Huff, Priscilla Y. *101 Best Small Businesses for Women.* Prima Publishing, 1997.

Keup, Erwin J. *Franchising Bible: How to Buy a Franchise or Franchise your Own Business.* Enterprise Press, 2004.

Morel, Pierre, *Games Companies Play: The Job Hunter's Guide to Playing Smart and Winning Big in the High-Stakes Hiring Game.* Ten Speed Press, 2002.

Otterbourg, Robert K. *Switching Careers: Career Changers Tell How—and Why—they Did It. Learn How You Can, Too!* Kiplinger Books, 2001.

Porter, L. W. and Edward E. Lawler. *Attitudes and Performance*. Richard D. Irwin, 1968.

Thomas, David R., Michael Said, et al. *Franchising for Dummies*. John Wiley & Sons, Incorporated, 1999.

Key-3: Presenting Yourself

Adrienne, Carol. *The Purpose of Your Life: Finding Your Place In The World Using Synchronicity, Intuition, and Uncommon Sense*. Harper Collins, 1999.

Bolles, Richard. *What Color is Your Parachute? A Practical Manual for Job-Hunters and Career Changers*. Ten Speed Press, 2004.

Buckingham, Marcus, Curt Coffman: *First, Break All The Rules: What the Worlds Greatest Managers Do Differently*. Simon & Schuster Adult Publishing Group,1999.

Covey, Steven R. *The 7 Habits of Highly Effective people: Powerful Lessons in Personal Change* Simon & Schuster Adult Publishing Group, 1990.

D'Alessandro, David F. Michelle *Owens: Career Warfare: 10 Rules for Building Successful Personal Brand and Fighting to Keep it*. McGraw Hill Companies, 2004.

Damp, Dennis V, Salvatore Concaild (Illustrator). *The Book of U.S. Government Jobs, 8th Edition, Where They Are, What's Available, and How to Get One*. Brookhaven Press, LLC, 2002.

Goldman, Daniel. Emotional Intelligence: *Why it can matter more than IQ*. Bantam Books, Inc. 1997.

Hamilton, Leslie, Robert Tragert. *100 Best non Profits to Work For*. Thompson Learning, 2000.

Krannich, Ron L., Caryl Ray Krannich, et. al. *Job Hunting Guide transitioning from College to Career*. Impact Publishing, VA, 2003.

Segal, Nina, Erich Kocher. *International Jobs and where They Are and How to Get Them*. Perseus Publishing, 2003.

Whitcomb, Susan Britton, Pat Kendall. *EResumes: Everything You Need to Know About Using Electronic Resumes to Tap into Today's Hot Job Market*. McGraw Hill Companies, 2001.

Trautman, Kathryn Kraemer, Barbara Guerra (Ed.). *Ten Steps to a Federal Job! Navigating the Federal job System, writing Federal Resumes, KSAs and Cover Letters with a Mission*. The Resume Place, 2002.

Key-4: Marketing the Product—You!

Adrienne, Carol. *The Purpose of Your Life: Finding Your Place In The World Using Synchronicity, Intuition, and Uncommon Sense.* Harper Collins, 1999.

Bolles, Richard. *What Color is Your Parachute? A Practical Manual for Job-Hunters and Career Changers.* Ten Speed Press, 2004.

Crispin, Gary, Mark Mehler. *CareerXRoads 2003: The Directory to Job, Resume, and Career Management sites on the Web.* MMC Group, 2002.

Damp, Dennis V, Salvatore Conciald (Illustrator): *The Book of U.S. Government Jobs, 8th Edition, Where They Are, What's Available, and How to Get One.* Brookhaven Press, LLC, 2002.

D'Alessandro, David F., Michelle Owens: Career Warfare: *10 Rules for Building Successful Personal Brand and Fighting to Keep it.* McGraw Hill Companies, 2004.

Lucht, John: *Rites of Passage at $100,000 to $1 Million+: Your Insider's Lifetime Guide to Executive Job Changing and Faster Career Progress in the 21st Century.* Henry Holt & Company, Incorporated, 2000.

Krannich, Ron L., Caryl Ray Krannich, et al. *Job Hunting Guide transitioning from College to Career.* Impact Publishing, VA, 2003

Leslie, Hamilton, Robert Tragert. *100 Best non-Profits to Work For.* Thompson Learning, 2000.

Montag, William E.; *CareerJournal.com Resume Guide for $100,000 Plus Executive Jobs* John Wiley & Sons, Incorporated, 2002.

Riley, Margaret Riley Dikel, Francis E. Roehm. *Guide to Internet Job Searching.* McGraw Hill, Company, 2002.

Segal, Nina, Erich Kocher. *International Jobs and where They Are and How to Get Them.* Perseus Publishing, August 2003.

Key-5: Acing the Interview

Adams, Bob: *Everything Job Interview Book.* Adams Media Corporation, 2001.

Adrienne, Carol: *The Purpose of Your Life: Finding Your Place In The World Using Synchronicity, Intuition, and Uncommon Sense.* Harper Collins, 1999.

Bolles, Richard. *What Color is Your Parachute? A Practical Manual for Job-Hunters and Career Changers.* Ten Speed Press, 2004.

Conniff, Richard: *Reading Faces*. Smithsonian, Volume 32, Number 10, January 2004, pp 44-50.

D'Alessandro, David F., Michelle Ownes. *Career Warfare: 10 Rules for Building Successful Personal Brand and Fighting to Keep it*. McGraw Hill Companies, 2004.

Medley, Anthony K. *Sweaty Palms: The Neglected Art of Being Interviewed*. Ten Speed Press, 1991.

Porot, Daniel. *The Pie Method for Career Success: A unique Way to Find Your Ideal Job*. JIST Works, Inc., Indianapolis, IN, 1996.

Ryan, Robin. *60 Seconds & You're Hired!* Penguin Books, 2000.

Veruki, Peter, Peter Venki. *The 250 Job Interview Questions You'll Most Likely be Asked and the Answers That Will Get You Hired*. Adams Media Corporation, 1999.

Key-6: Negotiating the Offer

Bolles, Richard: *What Color is Your Parachute? A Practical Manual for Job-Hunters and Career Changers*. Ten Speed Press, 2004.

Chapman, Jack: *Negotiating Your Salary: How To Make $100,000 a Minute*. Ten Speed Press, 2001.

D'Alessandro, David F., Michelle Ownes. *Career Warfare: 10 Rules for Building Successful Personal Brand and Fighting to Keep it*. McGraw Hill Companies, 2004.

Jeffers, Susan J. *Feel the Fear And Do IT Anyway*. Fawcett Book Group, 1996.

Krennich, Ronald, Caryl Krannich. *Dynamite Salary Negotiations: Know What You're Worth and Get IT*. Impact Publications, VA, 2000.

Laney, Marti Olsen Laney: *The Introvert Advantage: How to Thrive in an Extraverted World*. Workman Publishing; 2002.

Porot, Daniel, Saniel Porot with Frances Bolles Haynes. *101 Salary Secrets: Negotiate Like a Pro*. Ten Speed Press, 2001.

Ray, Michael and Rochelle Myers: *Creativity in Business*: Doubleday, A Division of Bantam Doubleday Dell Publishing Group, New York, 1989.

Key-7: Making it All Work

Anthony, Robert, Leslie Pearlman Breither. *Essentials of Accounting and Post Test Booklet*. Prentice Hall, 2002.

Argenti, Paul A. *The Fast Forward MBA Pocket Reference*. Wiley, John & Sons, Inc., 2002.

Blanchard, Ken, et al: *Whale Done: The Power of Positive Relationship*. The Free Press; 2003.

Brad Minor. *The Compleat Gentleman: The Modern Man's Guide to Chivalry*. Spence Publishing Company, 2004.

Brown, David W. *Organization Smarts: Portable Skills for Those Who Want to Get Ahead*. AMACOM, 2003.

Erickson, Jean, Erickson Walker: *Age Advantage: Making the Most of Your Mid-Life Career Transition*. Berkeley trade, 2000.

Griffin, Gerry, Cirian Parker. *Games Companies Play: An Insider's Guide to Surviving and Winning in Office Politics*. Capstone Publishing Company, 2003.

Kezsbom, Deborah S., et al. *The New Dynamic Project management: Winning Through the Competitive Advantage Vol.-1*. John Wiley & Sons, Incorporated, 2000.

Kolmel, Ranier, Ranier Kolmel (Editor): *Babel: The Cultural and Linguistic Barrier between Nations*. Aberdeen University Press, 1990.

Levnison, Jay Conrad. *Guerilla Marketing: Secrets for Making big Profits form your Small Business*. Haughton Mifflin Co.,1998.

Post, Peggy, Peter Post: *The Etiquette Advantage in Business*. Harper Collins Publishing, 1999.

Ruskin, Arnold, W. Eugene Estes. *What Every Engineer Should Know about Project Management*. Marcel Decker, 1994.

Satterfield, Mark: *VGM's Complete Guide to Career Etiquette: From Job Search to Career Advancement*. NTC Publishing Group, 1995.

Wysocki, Robert K., Robert Beck, David B. Crane. *Effective Project Management*. John Wiley & Sons, Incorporated, 2000.

Epilogue

Darwin, Charles R. *The Autobiography of Charles Darwin:* Edited by Nora Barlow. Harcourt, 1958. Also in paperback from Norton.

Ray, Michael and Rochelle Myers: *Creativity in Business*: Doubleday, A Division of Bantam Doubleday Dell Publishing Group, New York, 1989.

Index

"The secret to success is to plod on and keep the passion fresh."

—Anonymous

This comprehensive listing has been cross-indexed to help reader quickly find topics, and is reconciled *manually* for accuracy.

"Even you can make God laugh by telling what you are going to do tomorrow"

—Virginia Arnold (1924–2003)

0-595-31017-6

Printed in the United States
123582LV00001B/131/A